Developments in American Politics 4

If you have any comments or suggestions regarding the
above or other possible *Developments* titles, please write to
Steven Kennedy, Publishing Director, Palgrave,
Houndmills, Basingstoke RG21 6XS, UK, or e-mail
s.kennedy@palgrave.com

Developments in American Politics 4

Edited by

Gillian Peele

Christopher J. Bailey

Bruce Cain

and

B. Guy Peters

palgrave

This new book is designed as a direct replacement for *Developments in American Politics 3* (1998).

Published in 2002 by
PALGRAVE
Houndmills, Basingstoke, Hampshire RG21 6XS and
175 Fifth Avenue, New York, N.Y. 10010
Companies and representatives throughout the world

PALGRAVE is the new global academic imprint of
St. Martin's Press LLC Scholarly and Reference Division and
Palgrave Publishers Ltd (formerly Macmillan Press Ltd).

ISBN 0–333–94874–2 hardback
ISBN 0–333–94873–4 paperback

This book is printed on paper suitable for recycling and made from fully managed and sustained forest sources.

10 9 8 7 6 5 4 3 2 1
11 10 09 08 07 06 05 04 03 02

Printed and bound in Great Britain by
Creative Print & Design (Wales) Ebbw Vale

Contents

List of Tables, Figures and Maps

Tables

Figures

Preface

The dramatic events of the 2000 election and the first year of the presidency of George W. Bush make this a particularly exciting time to write about developments in American politics. As with its three predecessors, our intention in this volume has been to provide a systematic account of key changes in US governance and of the most salient issues and debates in its politics.

As in its predecessors, all the chapters in *Developments in American Politics 4* are entirely new and have been specially written by a new team of contributors from a wide range of universities and research institutes on both sides of the Atlantic. Each has worked to a common remit to analyze recent developments – both empirical and theoretical – in their respective fields and to assess the impact of the Bush administration in the context of the Clinton legacy.

Our contributors on this occasion have had the further challenge of addressing the profound implications for the conduct of US politics and indeed for American life generally of the attacks on New York and Washington in September 2001 and the ensuing international crisis and war on terrorism. This challenge has necessitated substantial changes throughout and in some cases major rewriting of chapters between the first and the final drafts and we give special thanks to our contributors for all the extra work this has involved.

We have made a few changes in format compared with the previous volumes, dispensing with the division into parts and the rigid demarcation between shorter issue chapters and the rest. In terms of substance *Developments in American Politics 4* also has more focus on political culture and the nature and quality of American democracy as well as a wider coverage of policy areas than in previous editions. The central objective is unchanged, however, and we hope that all students and other serious observers of American politics will find it a useful state-of-the-art assessment of US politics under George W.Bush.

The editors would like to thank our publisher, Steven Kennedy, for the help and encouragement he has given to this volume. We also thank our anonymous referee who at an early stage in the project provided very valuable help and advice. The editors acknowledge with gratitude the intellectual support given by our respective colleagues at Oxford University, the University of Keele, the Institute of Governmental Studies at the University of California at Berkeley and at the University of Pittsburgh. We also wish to thank friends on both sides of the Atlantic who do so much to make travel and research on American topics possible. In particular on this occasion we thank Christine Whittaker and André Navez who gave hospitality and support following the attacks of September 2001. We are also grateful to the library, secretarial and support staff in our respective institutions and especially to Vanessa Windsor, Glynis Beckett, Dianne Rollinson and Roberta Staples at Lady Margaret Hall and to Liz Wiener at the Institute of Governmental Studies in Berkeley. We also thank the many grant-giving bodies who have supported our research and especially to the Mellon Trust which provides support for American studies at Oxford. A number of friends and graduate students helped in the final stages of assembling the book: Kevin A.Sabet, Catherine Needham, Meg Mullin, Jonathan Treadway, Stuart Valentine and Elizabeth McLeish.

Finally we record with sadness the sudden deatth (aged 46) of Steve Reilly, one of the contributors to our last volume. His lively presence at gatherings of British Americanists will be much missed.

Gillian Peele
Christopher J. Bailey
Bruce Cain
B. Guy Peters

Notes on the Contributors

Christopher J. Bailey is Professor of American Politics at Keele University.

Bruce Cain is Robson Professor of Government and Director of the Institute of the Governmental Studies, University of California at Berkeley.

Elisabeth Gerber is Professor of Political Science at the University of Michigan.

Alan Grant is Lecturer in Politics at Oxford Brookes University.

Tim Hames is Associate Editor of *The Times* (London).

Susan B. Hansen is Professor of Political Science at the University of Pittsburgh.

Jonathan Herbert is Lecturer in American Studies at Keele University.

Stephen Linder is Associate Professor of Management and Policy Sciences, School of Public Health, University of Texas.

Dean McSweeney is Principle Lecturer in Politics at the University of the West of England.

Gillian Peele is Fellow and Tutor in Politics at Lady Margaret Hall, Oxford.

B. Guy Peters is Maurice Falk Professor of American Government at the University of Pittsburgh.

Pauline Vaillancourt Rosenau is Professor of Management and Policy Sciences, School of Public Health, University of Texas.

Fiona Ross is Lecturer in Social Policy at the University of Bristol.

Virginia Sapiro is Sophinisba P Breckinridge Professor of Politics at the University of Wisconsin, Madison.

Eric Schickler is Professor of Political Science at the University of California at Berkeley.

Robert Singh is Lecturer in Politics at Birkbeck College, London University.

David Williams is Lecturer in International Relations at the University of Oxford.

Stephen Welch is Lecturer in Politics at the University of Durham.

Tinsley E. Yarbrough is Distinguished Research Professor of Political Science at East Carolina University.

List of Abbreviations and Acronyms

AARP	American Association of Retired Persons
ABA	American Bar Association
ABC	American Broadcasting Corporation
ABM	Anti Ballistic Missile (Treaty)
ACLU	American Civil Liberties Union
ACU	American Conservative Union
AFDC	Aid to Families with Dependent Children
AFL-CIO	American Federation of Labor/Congress of Industrial Organizations
ALEC	American Legislative Exchange Council
AMA	American Medical Association
APA	Administrative Procedures Act
CBO	Congressional Budget Office
CDF	Children's Defense Fund
CEA	Council of Economic Advisors
CEO	Chief Executive Officer
CHIP	Childrens Health Insurance Programme
CIA	Central Intelligence Agency
CNN	Cable News Network
CPI	Consumer Price Index
CQWR	Congressional Quarterly Weekly Report
CRS	Congressional Research Service
DJIA	Dow Jones Industrial Average
DLC	Democratic Leadership Council
DNC	Democratic National Committee
EITC	Earned Income Tax Credit
EMILY's List	Early Money is Like Yeast
EOP	Executive Office of the President
EPA	Environmental Protection Agency
EPB	Economic Policy Board
EPC	Economic Policy Council
ERISA	Employee Retirement Income Security Act
FBI	Federal Bureau of Investigation
FEC	Federal Election Commission
FECA	Federal Election Campaign Act
FEMA	Federal Emergency Management Agency
FOMC	Federal Open Market Committee

FY	Fiscal Year
GAO	General Accounting Office
GDP	Gross Domestic Product
GOP	Grand Old Party (the Republican Party)
GPRA	Government Performance and Results Act
HMOs	Health Maintenance Organizations
IMF	International Monetary Fund
IRS	Internal Revenue Service
MBA	Master in Business Administration
MFN	Most Favoured Nation Status
NAACP	National Association for the Advancement of Colored People
NAFTA	North American Free Trade Agreement
NARAL	National Abortion and Reproductive Rights Action League
NATO	North Atlantic Treaty Organization
NCSL	National Conference of State Legislatures
NEC	National Economic Council
NGA	National Governors' Association
NMD	National Missile Defense
NPR	National Performance Review
NRA	National Rifle Association
OMB	Office of Management and Budget
OSHA	Occupational Safety and Health Administration
PAC	Political Action Committee
PBO	Performance Based Organization
PG&E	Pacific Gas and Electric
POSs	Point-of-Service Organizations
PPOs	Preferred Provider Organizations
PRWORA	Personal Responsibility and Work Opportunity Reconciliation Act
RDI	Real Disposable Income
RNC	Republican National Committee
S&P500	Standard & Poor's 500
SCHIP	State Child Health Insurance Program
SSI	Supplemental Security Income
TANF	Temporary Assistance for Needy Families
UDAGs	Urban Development Assistance Grants
UN	United Nations
USAID	US Agency for International Development
VRA	Voting Rights Act
WHO	World Health Organization
WTO	World Trade Organization

List of State Abbreviations

AK	Alaska	MT	Montana
AL	Alabama	NC	North Carolina
AR	Arkansas	ND	North Dakota
AZ	Arizona (also Ariz.)	NE	Nebraska
CA	California (also Ca.)	NH	New Hampshire
CO	Colorado (also Colo.)	NJ	New Jersey
CT	Connecticut (also Conn.)	NM	New Mexico (also NMex.)
DC	District of Columbia	NV	Nevada
DE	Delaware	NY	New York
FL	Florida (also Flo.)	OH	Ohio
GA	Georgia	OK	Oklahoma
HI	Hawaii	OR	Oregon (also Ore.)
IA	Iowa	PA	Pennsylvania
ID	Idaho	RI	Rhode Island
IL	Illinois (also Ill.)	SC	South Carolina
IN	Indiana	SD	South Dakota
KS	Kansas	TN	Tennessee
KY	Kentucky	TX	Texas (also Tex.)
LA	Louisiana	UT	Utah
MA	Massachusetts (also (Mass.)	VA	Virginia
MD	Maryland	VT	Vermont
ME	Maine	WA	Washington (also Wash.)
MI	Michigan	WI	Wisconsin
MN	Minnesota (also Minn.)	WV	West Virginia
MO	Missouri (also Mo.)	WY	Wyoming
MS	Mississippi (also Miss.)		

Seattle

WASHINGTON

Portland

OREGON   IDAHO

                Boise

MONTANA   NORTH
                DAKOTA
● Billings   Farg

                SOUTH
                DAKOTA
                        Sioux Fal

Salt ●   WYOMING
Lake   Cheyenne   NEBRASKA
City
Sacramento ● Reno   Linc
San   NEVADA
Francisco ● Oakland   UTAH   Denver ●
                                     COLORADO
      San José
                                     Colorado Springs   KANSAS
CALIFORNIA
                                                        Wichita

Los Angeles   ARIZONA   Albuquerque ●   Oklaho
                                               City
San Diego   ● Phoenix   OKLAHC
                NEW MEXICO
                Tucson ●
                                               Fort Worth

                                               TEXAS

0   200 Miles   Austin ●

Chapter 1

Introduction: The United States in the Twenty-First Century

GILLIAN PEELE, CHRISTOPHER J. BAILEY, BRUCE CAIN
AND B. GUY PETERS

The inauguration of a new president in the United States is customarily seen as a decisive turnig point in the country's politics. Presidential rhetoric and public expectation combine to produce an expectation of new policies along with the new incumbent in the White House. Whatever the realities of the American political situation at the time or the more general problems with the workings of its political institutions, the transition from one president to another will emphasize the ability of the American democracy to overcome its defects and hold out the promise of a renewal of the government's compact with the people.

A tarnished victory

The urge to emphasize a break with the past and the prospects for a better tomorrow were particularly strong in 2001. Not merely was the new president the first to take office in the new century, but there was an inevitable desire to draw a line under the Clinton presidency which, for all its successes in the economic field, had been associated in the minds of many people with sleaze and sexual scandal. Although Clinton had survived the attempt to impeach him (and indeed had retained high levels of personal popularity and job approval ratings), there was a feeling that the office of the presidency had been subtly undermined by his behavior and that a nation already cynical about its government had been given further cause to distrust politicians. There was a strong sense that the presidency and American government as a whole needed to have their legitimacy restored.

It was thus ironic that the inauguration of George W. Bush as the 43rd President of the USA in January 2001, far from uniting the American people and restoring faith in the country's political institutions, had the effect of casting further doubt on the legitimacy of the political system. The unusual closeness of the presidential contest (which saw his opponent

– Vice-President Al Gore – winning a majority of the popular vote, though not of the crucial electoral college) would by itself have placed a question mark over the legitimacy of the Bush victory. Much more damaging, however, to a smooth transition from the Clinton presidency to a Bush presidency were the prolonged and complicated challenges and counter-challenges to the election returns in Florida, the state whose 25 electoral college votes gave Bush his 271–267 victory. As a result of these challenges not only was the identity of the winner itself in doubt for five weeks after polling day but a very public searchlight was shone on the highly politicized nature of America's courts as well as on the extent to which the electoral process was itself subject to manipulation. Indeed the Supreme Court's final 5–4 resolution of the legal controversies surrounding the presidential election which handed the White House to Bush was seen by many commentators as "the most controversial judicial decision in several decades" and perhaps likely to rank in the fullness of time as among the most controversial in the Court's history (Sunstein and Epstein, 2001). Some groups, such as African-Americans, felt especially disadvantaged by the way the electoral system had operated in the 2000 presidential election as Jesse Jackson (among other black leaders) alleged that the election in Florida revealed a historically familiar pattern of irregularities and intimidation calculated to disadvantage racial minorities. There was inevitably also a more general concern that George W. Bush would enter the presidency without the advantage of a mandate as a result of such a tarnished electoral process. Presidential leadership, already made more difficult by developments in the 1990s, would accordingly, many observers thought, be more constrained.

Somewhat surprisingly perhaps, despite the rancor of the election process itself, what remained of the transition period and the early days of the Bush presidency passed in a fairly low-key manner. Yet the first eight months or so of Bush's period of office did indeed raise questions about whether George W. Bush had the political experience or personal skills necessary to meet the challenges of providing political direction for the complex American polity where fragmentation and pluralism have frequently frustrated presidential aspirations.

The process of forming an administration and the clarification of a policy agenda occurred slowly as the new incumbent of the White House struggled to deal with a Congress which was initially narrowly in Republican hands but which in May 2001 became a source of opposition as the defection of one Republican Senator (James Jeffords, R-Vt) threw control of that chamber to the Democrats. What had appeared to be unified government became divided again.

The administration George W. Bush formed in 2001 was overwhelmingly white, male and over 50 years in age. This was in marked contrast to his predecessor's administrations which Clinton had tried hard to make reflective of the United States's increasing ethnic diversity and of the rapid career progress made by women. It was also a government that appeared to value previous experience in government. At first sight this was surprising since George W. Bush had adopted the familiar tactic of campaigning against the Washington establishment and presenting himself as an outsider, who would have no truck with the vested interests and establishment mentality that were allegedly dominating the capital. In fact George W. Bush's key appointments not merely drew on people with previous experience in federal, state or local government, but specifically on people who had served in his father's administration between 1989 and 1993; so much so that critics used the word 'retread' to describe many of the cabinet nominations. One survey of the top 300 posts in George W. Bush's administration found that fully 43 percent had served in the elder Bush's administration, and most notably that 86 percent of those in the top echelons of the State Department had been drawn from the earlier administration's policy-making elite (Barnes, 2001). The same survey noted that 43 percent of the younger Bush's top appointees had served in the elder Bush's government, and at the State Department 81 percent of top officials had served there.

Such appointments did much to reassure those who feared that the new president lacked expertise, especially in the field of foreign policy. Discontinuity is a major problem in the American system. All incoming presidents – unless they have been vice-president in the previous administration – lack detailed familiarity with the governmental system they are about to head and need to familiarize themselves quickly with a range of policy and administrative issues. The tendency to reward friends and campaign loyalists with key administration posts often compounds this systemic weakness. Bush's use of expertise in his senior appointments went some way to compensating both for this perennial problem and for his own relative lack of experience. Of course Bush did want some close friends and supporters inside the administration; but he has apparently concentrated these appointments in the White House in his personal staff.

That said, some aspects of the composition of the Bush administration were in a number of respects surprising to observers. Bush had campaigned on a programme of "compassionate conservatism" and this appeal, together with the narrowness of his electoral base, suggested that he should try to position his administration toward the middle of the political spectrum and self-consciously reach out to non-Republicans. In fact, for all its emphasis on expertise, his administration soon took on a distinctly right-wing character. Although he appointed one Democrat (Norman Mineta) to his administration (as Secretary of Transportation), the effect of this attempt at bipartisanship was negated by the appointment of many ideological conservatives. Perhaps the most inflammatory appointment in ideological terms was the nomination of John Ashcroft, an ultra conservative with a long record of hostility to abortion rights, as Attorney General; but there were several similarly conservative appointments. Richard Cheney's position as Vice-President meant that there was a prominent and knowledgeable conservative at the heart of the administration and one whose congressional and administrative experience by comparison with the new president's meant that he was bound to exercise substantial influence.

The external circumstances in which the Bush administration found itself were not as favorable as those which President Clinton had enjoyed for most of his presidency. The economy in particular had, by the middle of 2001, apparently taken a sharp downturn threatening not merely American prosperity but world recession. And its early policy moves in the field of foreign policy generated worldwide criticism. The new administration's ideological leaning toward a more narrowly self-interested stance was starkly underlined with the abandonment of the Kyoto Accord on climate change and the renewed commitment to building a defensive missile system (NMD). Both moves generated harsh criticisms from allies abroad and a good deal of domestic opposition.

The combination of a conservative tilt to the administration and uncertainty about his own political agenda did little to buttress Bush's uncertain mandate. By early September 2001 his personal approval ratings stood at 51 percent and Democrats were confidently predicting both a single-term presidency for George W. Bush and a very good chance of Democratic Congressional gains in the 2002 midterm elections.

Terrorism and war

The situation was transformed when on September 11 a series of horrific terrorist attacks occurred on two American cities, New York and Washington. The scale of the attacks and the coordinated nature of the conspiracy created a new political situation. An unprecedented attack on American soil ended any preference within the new administration for a more isolationist foreign policy. The United States was put on a war footing, its president catapulted into the role of unifying symbol of a grieving nation and Commander in Chief of a country engaged in a war against terrorism. A wide-ranging coalition was put together to invade Afghanistan (where the Taleban, who were quickly identified as the source of terrorist attack, were based) and military attacks began a month later. At the same time a range of measures were brought forward to cope with the threat of repeated terrorist attacks at home. Observers noted that

George W. Bush's presidency had been redefined by the events, a comment that was clearly true both in the sense that they created a new political agenda and a new political mood. Bush developed a new public stature and oratorical style (most notably in his September 20 2001 address to Congress) thereby dispelling some of the initial mockery which his convoluted and innovative use of language had generated. The atmosphere in Washington, which had been intensely partisan for the first eight months of 2001, was replaced temporarily at least by a bipartisan determination to deal with the threat of terrorism, including a second wave of biological warfare which spread anthrax spores through the mail. Public opinion, although often divided over the proper way to handle international challenges, registered overwhelming approval of the way the administration was handling this crisis. George W. Bush's popularity shot up from 51 percent to an astonishing 90 percent (the highest figure ever recorded by the Gallup Poll) and his overall approval ratings rose to 87 percent , with 60 percent "strongly approving" of the job he was doing (Gallup, 2001).

Although it is too early to be certain of the political impact in the long term of these events three possible scenarios suggest themselves. In the first, Bush's handling of the crisis rewards the Republicans at the mid term elections of 2002. In the second scenario, memory of the crisis would be overtaken by more routine domestic concerns once the crisis is past. This pattern is, of course, the one experienced by George W. Bush's father in the aftermath of the Gulf War as the popularity brought by victory evaporated in the face of recession and enabled Clinton (an unexpected Democratic challenger) to win the presidency in 1992. George W. Bush is reputedly acutely aware of that unhappy family precedent and the capacity of even the highest popularity ratings to disintegrate. Both of these scenarios assume that the United States is in fact able to achieve its war objectives. There is, however, a third and more gloomy scenario in which American action against terrorism fails to yield decisive victory so that the United States and her allies became bogged down in a worldwide conflict against an amorphous enemy. Were this scenario to occur, few predictions could safely be made about the ability of the incumbent president to maintain his political popularity.

All of these scenarios also have the effect of transforming Democratic thinking about the next race for the White House. While Al Gore had disappointed Democrats in 2000 by his failure to run a stronger campaign, the new emphasis on foreign and security policy and on experience in government would probably strengthen his candidacy, if he decides to run again, in 2004, by comparison with other contenders such as Democrats Richard Gephardt (D-Mo.), John Kerry (D-Mass.) or Joseph Lieberman (D-Conn.).

The war into which the United States was plunged in September 2001 was a salutary reminder of how quickly the American political scene can change and of how swiftly assessments of American policies and institutions may need revision. That said, however, it is also important to bear in mind the extent to which even the most dramatic of contemporary events take place against the background of institutional, policy and political constraints and continuities which shape the response to them. Indeed it is often impossible to understand the way in which the United States responds to contemporary policy challenges, even ones as extreme as that produced by the terrorist attacks, without an appreciation of the political and institutional context in which issues are framed and decisions taken. Thus, although this book is inevitably affected by the war against terrorism which the United States and its allies were engaged in as it was being written, the primary focus of much of it is on the longer term trends in the operation of America's governing institutions and its politics.

Four themes stand out in any attempt to interpret the character of American politics at this early stage of the Bush era. The first is the extent to which the political landscape of the United States consists of a country that is closely divided in terms of partisanship, values and political attitude. Forging consensus in this "49 percent nation" – to use Barone's phrase – has thus become difficult (Barone, 2001a).

Linked to this theme is a second theme; the dynamic change which has transformed the composition of the American people, and which emerges dramatically from the 2000 census and from other assessments of America's population. The United States has always been a diverse society and a magnet for immigrants from across the world. The last quarter of the twentieth century witnessed a radical shift in America's demography. Partly as a response to the Hart-Cellar Immigration Act of 1965 and subsequent amendments to immigration legislation, the United States experienced a massive influx of newcomers comparable in number to that of the first quarter of the twentieth century. But whereas the immigrants of the early twentieth century were almost exclusively of European origin, the immigrants of the century's last quarter were mainly from outside Europe: most notably from Mexico, Latin America and Asia. Their presence added to the pluralism of American society and raised the question of whether these "new Americans" would be as easily assimilated into the mainstream of American life as previous generations of immigrants (Barone, 2001b). In addition the scale and diversity of this new element of the American population presented in stark form a challenge to the cultural identity of the United States. This challenge was especially visible at the state level where in some states – notably California – ethnic minorities became the majority.

Third, there were concerns that in a number of ways the institutional arrangements of the United States had ceased to work efficiently and that as a result the processes of government had become more difficult. The pluralism of the United States is one factor which some cited as a contributory cause of America's governmental difficulties (Bok, 2001). Political scientists now regularly draw a distinction between "government" and "governance" to point up the difference between hierarchical and clearly demarcated, structures of political authority ("government") and the broader process of coordinating decisions which involves a multiplicity of actors and agencies ("governance"). Perhaps in this sense the United States has always had governance rather than government; but the processes of policy-making and coordination appeared more problematic in the 1990s even within the context of a system of governance which has always been highly fragmented. Efforts to cope with these dilemmas of governance constitute a third theme marking contemporary American politics.

Finally, anyone looking at the contemporary United States has to confront the paradox of a country where, although there is widespread support for the constitutional framework, there appears to be widespread dissatisfaction with the way it is working in practice. Although it is important not to exaggerate the significance of this alienation, equally it is necessary to address both the causes of the discontent and the suggested remedies, some of which have already produced important innovations in American political life (Bok, 1996; Ladd and Bowman, 1998; Bok 2001). In the remainder of this chapter we explore these themes in more detail, linking them to the chapters which follow, but highlighting as well the extent to which they shape the political culture and political dynamics of the contemporary United States.

A closely divided people

Beneath the close presidential election of 2000 there was the fact of a closely divided polity. Bush's 47.9 percent of the popular vote was slightly less than Al Gore's 48.4 percent but the results at the congressional level showed similar closeness. Moreover, this division followed similarly close results in 1996 and 1998. Thus for three sets of presidential and congressional elections neither the Democrat nor the Republican Party has been able to muster 50 percent of the vote. As one respected political commentator put it, the United States had not had "such stasis in successive election results since the 1880's, which was also the last decade when a president was elected despite trailing in the popular vote and when the Senate was equally divided between the two major parties" (Barone, 2001).

The last quarter of the twentieth century witnessed recurrent speculation about realignment. Frequently this speculation (whether by journalists or academics) took the form of predicting the emergence of a new majority party (usually the Republicans) to replace the Democratic majority coalition put in place during the New Deal period of the 1930s. Sometimes there seemed room for a new third party to emerge, though observers could rarely agree on what would unite it. Often there was speculation about the death of parties whose functions seemed either to have become completely redundant or were easily performed by other political actors: interest groups, political consultants and the media. Yet parties have survived and in many respects seem in the early years of the twenty-first century to be stronger than ever, not least because of their ability to exploit campaign finance laws. One of the features of the 2000 elections was the extent to which the money-raising war between the parties had escalated and the full party campaign coffers led to new records in campaign spending (Stone, 2000). What appears to have emerged from the electoral cauldron of the 1990s is a finely balanced party system in which partisan attachments endure and there has been a return to straight ticket voting. Virginia Sapiro, Dean McSweeney and Alan Grant in their respective chapters (Chapters 2, 3, and 18) explore the significance for the American polity of the country's close electoral politics and the survival of an intensely competitive party system where money plays such an important role.

One significant consequence of such a closely divided polity is the likely continuation of divided government. The constitutional framework deliberately separates powers, but for much of American history the party system and other linkages operated to modify that separation in practice. In the last 40 years, however, many of the linkages between institutions appear to have weakened and, more tangibly, divided party control of government has become the norm rather than the exception. Thus a President may expect to face a Congress with at least one chamber in the hands of the opposing party, putting enormous constraints on his ability to provide leadership and direction and forcing the adoption of a very different governing strategy from that open to a president in a situation of unified party control. President Clinton had faced that scenario in the period 1995–2001 after Republicans took control of both chambers of Congress in the 1994 midterm elections. Yet, as Jonathan Herbert shows in Chapter 5, Clinton managed to play the apparently unfavorable political situation after 1995 to his advantage, modifying Republican inspired legislation and exploiting the various tools available, such as the veto, executive orders and his public appeal, to outface the Congressional leadership. Whether George W. Bush can learn from those tactics or whether they were specific to Clinton is a vital question in the wider debate about how far the American presidency has retained its effectiveness and influence.

A second consequence of the electoral closeness in normal circumstances is heightened party competitiveness and partisanship at the federal level, and a concomitant decline in either party's willingness to cross party lines or develop a bipartisan approach to problems. The management of congressional parties in both the House and Senate in such circumstances becomes additionally demanding. Eric Schickler in Chapter 6 looks at the changes in the operation of Congress in the contemporary United States, and specifically at the legacy of the Republican "revolution" that was initiated in the aftermath of their 1994 midterm victories and produced the intensely personal and partisan (but short-lived) leadership of Newt Gingrich.

While ostensibly more remote from the electoral arena, the Supreme Court is indirectly affected by the close electoral divisions of the United States and in an odd way appears to mirror it. As Tinsley Yarbrough shows in Chapter 7, there is little cohesion in the current Court's jurisprudence and many of its decisions are not merely split narrowly but further fragmented over the proper way to approach major constitutional questions. Increasingly, however (and this was certainly true in 2000) one of the most eagerly watched issues in a new presidency is the character of its judicial appointments because of the extent to which the courts have a policy impact in a number of areas, including those to do with personal liberties and minority rights.

Increasing social diversity

The narrow partisan split that was so apparent in the 2000 elections itself reflected important demographic and behavioral trends within American society. The multiple divisions of race, region, gender and the increasingly important marker of religion, as well as of income, culture and lifestyle which have always marked American politics, have profound implications not simply for the balance within the party system but also for the public philosophy and the character of the political agenda. But as the early results of the 2000 census and other population surveys underlined America had changed radically even since 1990. One aspect of that change was the country's growth in size: the decade between 1990 and 2000 registered the largest increase in overall population of any inter-census period.

Race and ethnicity

Awareness that America's ethnic diversity had become more varied as the new century began was parallelled by a mixed assessment of the prospects for the various groups within the population. African-Americans (who, by 2000, constituted 12.8 percent of the population) had made significant gains in the Clinton years. On many criteria such as poverty, unemployment and educational attainment they had achieved their best ever scores, closing to some extent – but not entirely – the gap with white Americans. Yet much of this improvement had come as a result of economic growth rather than governmental intervention. Indeed it was noticeable that the Clinton years saw growing public skepticism about race-conscious remedies for black inequality, a skepticism which was reflected in closer judicial scrutiny of affirmative action at all levels of the political system. At the same time the rebalancing of the federal system and the greater policy autonomy of state and local governments (especially in the area of welfare policy) created a new environment in which the federal government, for much of the post-1945 period a major protector of African-American interests would play a reduced role. At the same time surveys and examinations such as that produced by the *New York Times* in 2000 pointed up the continuing dilemma of race in society. The immediate question for African-Americans at the opening of Bush era was, therefore, how far the gains which they had made would survive an economic downturn.

Politically, black Americans had remained strongly Democratic and had increased their voter registration in 2000. Disappointment at the failure to return Gore to the White House led to speculation towards the end of 2001 that the Reverend Al Sharpton, the controversial New York black politician, might be considering a campaign for the 2004 nomination, especially if, as was anticipated, African-Americans found themselves disproportionately affected by Bush's policies.

By comparison with the African-American population, the United States Latino (or Hispanic) and Asian minorities were at once newer and more heterogeneous. By 2000 the Latino population amounted to 11.8 percent of the total but it was made up of immigrants from central and southern America, the Caribbean and Mexico. The Asian population was also diverse, its 4.1 percent of the population coming from a range of countries including China, India, the Philippines and Vietnam. Both of these populations were fast growing and young populations, thus setting up a new dynamic within American society. The presence of a substantial Latino minority within the United States had long before transformed the understanding of racial and ethnic divisions from a two-dimensional one (based on black versus white) to a multi-dimensional one. Population growth within the Latino community in particular created new tensions as Latinos were projected to overtake African-Americans as a percentage of the population, perhaps by as early as 2010. Certainly by 2050 the Latino minority was estimated to have grown to 24.3 percent of the whole, by comparison with a projected figure for African-Americans of 14.7 percent.

Religion and gender

Religion has always been an important force in American life, injecting a distinctive moralism into its public discourse and political culture. The way religion affects politics has changed, however, since the 1970s. Much attention has correctly been paid to the impact of the organized conservative Christians within the Republican Party and in the wider polity (Peele, 1984; Hoover, 2001). What became very apparent in the 2000 elections was the extent to which religious adherence and denominational attachment correlated with voting behaviour, with conservative Christian and fundamentalist groups opting overwhelmingly for Bush and the Republican ticket (Barone, 2001). At the same time Bush made a very deliberate effort to reach out to Roman Catholic voters.

The United States was by 2001 also beginning to be aware of the presence in its population of significant numbers of adherents of religions outside the Judeao-Christian tradition (Eck, 2001). Even before the events of September 11 turned a new and not always accurate spotlight on Islam, the political role of American Muslims had become increasingly acknowledged. For the first time both Democrat and Republican conventions opened with an Islamic prayer and the Republican Party Convention apparently contained 100 Islamic adherents (Khan 2000). Although there is doubt about the precise numbers of Muslims overall in the United States, which could be as high as 5 million, there is no doubt it is becoming significant; and some Islamic groups claimed that Islamic political participation in 2000 had benefitted George Bush's candidacy.

Gender also remained an important issue within the US both at the level of voter preference and at the level of wider issues relating to equality and discrimination, themes which are addressed in a number of chapters but especially in Susan Hansen's exploration of the inter-relationship of issues of religion and morality.

Cultural divisions and the public philosophy

These divisions of ethnicity, gender and religion fed into (but did not neatly correlate with) divisions about the proper role of government in the United States and other complex questions about culture, morality, identity and lifestyle, the so-called "culture wars" which had become such a marked feature of American life in the late twentieth century. These not surprisingly created an agenda of highly charged social issues which were difficult to resolve through the normal political channels, not least because they involved absolutes rather than negotiable issues and because they touched on the balance between majority and minority rights. The abortion question (and related issues such as the ethics of stem-cell research) was perhaps the most obvious example of such an issue but there were also profound differences over such issues as same-sex marriage, drugs and assisted suicide as well as over social policy, crime and the death penalty. For some areas a solution of sorts was found in state authority; in others policy was shaped not so much by the normal institutions of representative government as by the forces of direct democracy.

Governance

Even without the complexities of divided institutions and increasing pluralism there were in the last decades of the twentieth century a number of challenges to governmental organization and policy-making. In the US as in many other polities, the 1980s and 1990s had witnessed a resurgence of belief in the power of market forces as a way of bringing additional efficiency into government. This interest in private sector disciplines was one factor driving new approaches to bureaucracy and public management which, as Guy Peters shows, have affected American thinking about how to staff, organize and structure governmental agencies.

Part of the interest in importing private sector techniques and philosophies into government stemmed, of course, from the perception which became widespread in the United States after the heady days of the 1960s that government, especially at the federal level, was inherently inefficient both in terms of its use of resources and in its ability to address policy problems. One response to that perceived failure at the federal level was to devolve more responsibilities back to the states, a process which is examined in Gillian Peele's chapter on federalism (Chapter 9). Another response was to try to cut back on the responsibilities of the federal government by involving the voluntary sector, an approach which Bush has tried to utilize with his so-called "faith-based initiative". There have also been repeated attempts to remove what are seen as unnecessary or burdensome regulations on business and the voluntary sector through deregulation.

Policy-making in the United States is thus fragmented and incremental and, as Chapters 10–14 on specific aspects of policy by Christopher Bailey, Robert Singh, Fiona Ross, Stephen Linder, Pauline Rosenau and David Williams show, involve multiple actors and present unusual problems of coordination. Take, for example, law enforcement and national security. The necessity for an official with oversight for internal security in the aftermath of the September terrorist attacks was underlined when it became apparent that not merely was responsibility for airport security hopelessly fragmented but that there were over 40 different agencies with some role in law enforcement related to the incidents. The performance of the Federal Bureau of Investigation (FBI) and the Central Intelligence

Agency (CIA) came in for critical appraisal after September 11 and the Attorney General announced his intention to reform the role of the Justice Department to cope with terrorism. One by-product of the terrorist attacks was indeed a certain public support for strengthening the role of government in order to deal with the threat even if it meant weakening some traditional civil liberties.

American public policy-making more generally presents us with something of paradox, however. On the one hand the political system seems marked by stronger sectional interests and partisanship than ever before; on the other hand the public preference – at least as registered in the polls – seems to be centrist in orientation, the product of compromise rather than convergence .

Alienation and its remedies

The final theme which runs through the book relates to the quality of American democracy itself and the related issues of the legitimacy and efficient functioning of its political institutions. A variety of evidence has proved the existence of a widespread malaise in the American body politic, an alienation from politics and the political system. Most frequently cited is the evidence of opinion polls which show dissatisfaction with – even contempt for – Congress and other governing institutions. The decline in electoral turnout is also taken as a sign of apathy and alientation, and has proved especially worrying when evidence has shown that nonparticipation in the political process (even at the most basic level of voting) has been disprotionately a feature of minority ethnic groups and the poor. Behind this alienation and apathy some authors have detected a much deeper change in American social patterns – a decline in civil participation and public trust and these factors together constitute a worrying decline in America's social capital (Putnam, 2000).

Not everyone accepts this gloomy analysis of American political culture. Even among those who see some truth in it there are differences of emphasis and different weight accorded to the causes of the malaise. But some features of the contemporary American system are constantly and repeatedly mentioned, notably the role of money and vested interests in American politics, and the apparent failures of policy-makers to cope with endemic problems in the society and to be responsive to its citizens.

Contemporary America is witnessing a variety of pressures to open up the system and make it more responsive to the popular will. The movement to impose term limits on political office holders has become a major symbol of a renewed progressive surge. Term limits now circumscribe a number of political positions, including many governors, state legislators and mayors. One reform of the Republican Congress elected in 1995 was to impose term limits on committee chairs, thereby weakening their independence. In some respects the imposition of term limits is a draconian solution to the perceived evils of incumbency and lack of responsiveness. Term limits undermine expertise and professionalism and create new uncertainties in the careers of politicians without any proven benefits. Their spread, however, as a mechanism for holding politicians accountable suggests they are likely to become a permanent feature of the American system.

The criticism of American government's ability to respond to its citizens has led in many (but not all) states to a growth in the use of mechanisms of direct democracy. These are explored in Elisabeth Gerber's chapter (Chapter 15). Such mechanisms, as she shows, have advantages but many disadavantages also, not least the extent to which referendums may be manipulated by well-organized pressure groups. Criticism of the role of money and vested interests in politics has led to a search for ways to control it through campaign finance laws which, as Alan Grant shows, are difficult to pass and likely to have unanticipated results. Dissatisfaction with established politics has also produced new social movements, some of which (as Stephen Welch shows in Chapter 4) operate in a very different manner and on different assumptions from older interest groups.

These developments raise important questions about the fundamental character of American democracy and its relation to the rapidly changing social forces of the country. In the last chapter of the book Bruce Cain examines the tensions which have always been present in American democracy but which are now in many ways exacerbated by recent social and political trends and by the advent of new technologies which make alternative forms of democratic participation possible. On this view the American system should be seen not as a settled entity but one which is still very much in evolution, developing new and often conflicting responses to changing circumstances.

Chapter 2

Electoral Politics: The 2000 Elections and Beyond

VIRGINIA SAPIRO

The riveting closeness of the 2000 election severely tested the mechanisms of American government and politics, its culture and norms of democracy, and the people's patience with and faith in their system of governance. This closeness stripped off the smooth veneer of politics as usual, revealing aspects of American politics that are not often visible. Most of all, it tested the electoral system, and for many people, called into question its validity as an adequate measure of "the people's will". The 2000 election provoked re-examinations of the electoral system and related governing mechanisms, much as we might recheck and recalibrate other instruments when increments matter and the mechanism appears faulty. This chapter therefore departs from the usual practice of general election analysis, in which the election results dominate center stage. In the political spectacle that was the 2000 election, the nature of the American electoral process, and how it played out during the course of the electoral season, fully shared the limelight. We therefore devote more attention to the election process than usual. After outlining the story of the 2000 election process, the chapter analyzes the results, then focuses on a series of problems of American politics raised by different elements of the election, especially its effectiveness as an aid to understanding what is meant by "the will of the people".

The Nomination Process and the Campaign

Pundits accurately predicted the major party candidates a year in advance. Vice-President Al Gore, a former Senator and son of a Senator, first tried for the presidency in 1988 and was widely regarded as the Democratic heir-apparent to President Clinton. Former Senator Bill Bradley challenged him for the nomination but never won a primary, and withdrew from the race in March 2000 after his defeats on "Super Tuesday", a single day hosting many important primaries.

Governor George W. Bush of Texas, a wealthy businessman and son of the forty-first president, had well-stocked campaign coffers before the electoral season officially opened. Nevertheless, he faced five opponents representing somewhat different dimensions of the Republican Party (see Chapter 3). Senator John McCain of Arizona, a former prisoner of war and co-author of a major campaign finance reform bill, won three early primaries largely by appealing to voters outside the Republican core. Despite the initial shock which these defeats caused, Bush soon recovered, swept the early March Super Tuesday primaries, and McCain, the only viable opponent, immediately discontinued his campaign. The Democratic and Republican nominating processes were over almost five months before the national nominating conventions took place in the late summer.

After the nomination process, the only remaining drama was the choice of the vice-presidential candidates, and both selections offered an interesting balance to the presidential ticket. Gore selected Senator Joseph Lieberman, the first Jewish member of a presidential ticket in American history (and an Orthodox Jew at that), and the first Democrat to criticize Clinton openly during the Senate postimpeachment hearings. Lieberman defined himself as a moral crusader despite his generally liberal political views, thus serving as a potential amulet for warding off attacks associating Gore with Clinton's moral failures and, for that matter, Gore's own lapses in fundraising practices.

Bush, in contrast, selected Richard Cheney, an oil executive and former Representative from Wyoming, and most importantly, a former member of both the Ford and Bush administrations. Cheney was widely interpreted as an antidote to the charges that Bush was inexperienced on many policy issues, especially foreign and defense matters.

Both candidates campaigned on a limited menu of contrasting issues, differing most clearly over tax policy, health care, education, social security, and abortion. Bush's main theme was "compassionate conservatism," which meant "not leaving a single child behind," bringing faith and morals back to Washington, and "trusting" the people by cutting taxes to return money to them, allowing them to invest for their retirement rather than depending on social security. Gore, in contrast, repeatedly charged that the Republican platform would merely benefit the "wealthiest one per cent" and presented himself as a defender of the common person. He promised to put social security funds away "in a lockbox" for protection and to pursue government programs that would help all the people but especially the most vulnerable. Gore also emphasized his long history of environmental activism.

Despite the repeated discussion of these key issues, the 2000 campaigns continued the trend of emphasizing the candidates' differences of personality and character rather than policy. Bush presented himself as an ordinary man who could be trusted to understand what average Americans cared about, including their disgust with the Clinton administration's ethics. At the same time, Bush did not hide his own "youthful indiscretions." Gore could not compete on the character issue and his disappointing performance in the televised debates failed to compensate for this apparent remoteness.

Two prominent, but ultimately unsuccessful, "third party" candidates emerged in 2000. To Bush's right was Patrick Buchanan, former Republican candidate, who fought for and won the nomination of the embattled Reform Party, founded by Ross Perot. To Gore's left was Ralph Nader, the longtime consumer rights advocate, who was the candidate of the Green Party.

Both candidates could have been seriously threatening to the major party candidates. By pulling on the right and left, they could have made the Republican and Democratic candidates pause before making the characteristic strategic moves to the center. Bush balanced his platform of "compassionate conservatism" with some straightforward appeals to the right. Buchanan's Reform Party experienced a divisive nominating convention and had little impact on the campaign.

Gore, whose career had been nurtured by the centrist Democratic Leadership Council (DLC), found he had to jeopardize his "third way" centrist approach to counter Nader's appeal to some key Democratic constituencies. Nader attacked Gore relentlessly on environmental issues, claiming that there was little difference between the Democrats and Republicans. The attacks were so pointedly aimed at Gore that Bush supporters used the Nader attacks as television spots for their own purposes. In the final weeks of the campaign, Gore and his allies in environmental organizations, women's groups, unions, and abortion rights groups were forced to spend valuable time and resources campaigning in areas that should have been safe for Gore.

The polls were very close and conflicting throughout the final weeks. Both campaigns therefore stepped up their appeals for donations to intensify their efforts in key states. There was a growing possibility that either house of Congress – especially the Senate – could change hands. The fact that the Democratic vice presidential candidate was also running for re-election to the Senate heightened this uncertainty.

The endgame

The election night television reporting offered one of the oddest spectacles in the history of American political journalism. The networks began to announce their predictions for each state as soon as possible after that state's polls closed. Attention focused on the key swing states. By 8 pm (EST) they were announcing that Gore had won Florida, thus opening a probable path to electoral victory. At about 10 pm, the networks retracted their declarations, placing Florida back in the "too close to call" column. At 2.15 am the networks declared Bush the winner. Gore phoned Bush at 2.30 am to concede the election, then phoned him again an hour later, while he was on his way to make his concession speech, to retract his concession. At 4.15 am the networks retracted their declarations as well. As the next day dawned, the electoral vote count was stalled: whoever won Florida would win the presidency, but Florida's verdict remained undecided for another 34 days. Because the country did not know whether Lieberman would become Vice-President or would sit in the Senate seat to which he had been re-elected, the Senate results were also unknown.

A series of irregularities and inaccuracies led to contention over which ballots in Florida could be counted, how they should be counted, and which agencies and persons had decision-making power in cases of conflict. Had the race been less close either in Florida's popular vote or in the national electoral vote these problems would still have existed; but the long postelection endgame would not have happened. Indeed, some similar problems were encountered in other places, for example, in Atlanta and Chicago; but because their resolution would not change the results, they did not become a national issue (Mintz and Keating, 2000).

The basic elements of contention were as shown below.

1 Many voters found the specific form of ballot confusing; and there was significant evidence that voters in the heavily African-American and Jewish (and therefore Democratic) precincts of south Florida either voted by mistake for two candidates for president, or voted for the right-wing Reform Party (and former Republican) candidate, Patrick Buchanan.
2 Many voters, especially African-Americans, claimed that when they asked for assistance they were rebuffed; many African-Americans said they were barred from getting to the polls or voting in the first place.
3 Evidence from the punch card ballots suggested that in many cases the punches did not go completely through the counting machine, and thus were not counted by the scanners.
4 Many absentee ballots were flawed by technical problems.
5 Some Republican Party workers "helped" by correcting some of those flaws but, in so doing, engaged in illegal ballot tampering.

As a result of the variety of issues involved, especially in the context of a federal system, many different actors became involved in the arguments including the Secretary of State of Florida (whose job it was to certify the state count), state courts at all levels, federal courts including the Supreme Court, the Florida State legislature; and ultimately, the US Congress. These agencies have overlapping jurisdictions, discretion in decision-making and, of course, they were facing a unique confluence of circumstances with extremely high stakes. Moreover, they had only loose – and conflicting – guidance in precedent. The two candidates tried every legal and political means, often simultaneously, to advance their cause. The legal and political processes themselves became objects of contention. All of the legal maneuvering took place with a backdrop of daily demonstrations packed with activists brought in from other states.

The resolution on December 12 resulted from a Supreme Court decision which essentially called a halt to reconsideration of the Florida ballots (see Chapter 7). The Court decision split along ideological lines. On the same day the Republican-dominated Florida House of Representatives voted to choose a slate of pro-Bush delegates to the Electoral College. On January 6 2001, Vice-President Al Gore, in his final act as President of the Senate, presided over a joint session of Congress fulfilling its constitutional duty to certify the tally of the electoral votes, awarding his opponent the presidency.

The results

Bush won the presidency with a bare majority of electoral college votes and a minority of the popular vote. Al Gore won 48.4 percent of the popular vote and George Bush won 47.9 percent. The two closest contenders, Ralph Nader and Patrick Buchanan, won 2.7 percent and 0.42 percent of the vote, respectively.

The popular vote was close, but not as close as the Garfield–Hancock election of 1880, the Cleveland–Blaine election of 1884, and the Kennedy–Nixon election of 1960; the Nixon–Humphrey election of 1968 was not far behind. Bush received 50.5 percent of the electoral votes, with 271 votes to Gore's 266 (one Democratic delegate from Washington, DC abstained because of the lack of issues regarding governance of the city). That the popular vote winner did not win in the Electoral College heightened the sense of a "close call" even though this had happened before, in the Tilden–Hayes election of 1876 and the Cleveland–Hayes election of 1888.

How can we explain the electoral results? Three perspectives offer clues: micro-level analysis, focusing on the characteristics and attitudes of the voters to explain their voting behavior; macro-level analysis, considering the state of the economy and the country as a whole; and campaign effects, probing the impact of the actions of the candidates and campaigns. Of course, all three explanations overlap and each tells a piece of the story.

Voting behavior

The 2000 election may have been unusual, but the underlying dynamics of voter behavior were completely ordinary by contemporary standards. Partisanship, as usual, was a crucial factor. Although the percentage of Americans who describe themselves as Democrats or Republicans declined in the second half of the twentieth century, relatively few people – generally between 10 percent and 15 percent since the late 1960s – define themselves as pure independents who lack a sense of closeness to any party. Among those who have any partisanship, party identification is still a powerful determinant of their voting behavior (Bartels, 2000). This was certainly the case in 2000. Few Democrats voted for Bush, and even fewer Republicans voted for Gore. Most of the interesting questions to be raised about why people voted for one or the other candidate concern the substantial minority of "independents."

The electorate is very divided along a number of demographic lines associated with particular patterns of political behavior and, while 2000 may have differed in degree from other recent elections, the voting behavior of different demographic groups followed customary patterns. In America, class and income are not straightforwardly related to the vote, although in 2000 (as in most elections) they were correlated with partisan support. The poorest and most economically vulnerable voters tend to vote Democratic and the wealthy form a crucial part of the Republican constituency. But working-class people, especially men, are often attracted to Republican anti-government messages; and many professionals, especially women, find Democratic policies more appealing.

The vast majority of African-Americans have been Democratic since the 1940s, and 90 percent voted for Gore. Hispanic and Asian-American voters also leaned toward Gore. Religion played a role, too. Roman Catholics have long been part of the Democratic camp, except in the two Reagan elections, but they only voted marginally more for Gore than for Bush. Jews as usual voted overwhelmingly Democratic and white Protestants voted Republican, as they usually do.

In the 1970s differences between men's and women's partisanship began to open up as groups of white men who had been part of the Democratic coalition began to move away from that party. From 1980, American elections have regularly been marked by gender differences and these have sometimes been substantial. Despite Bush's appeals to "compassionate conservatism," intended in part to appeal to women, the "gender gap" reappeared massively in 2000. The difference was so large that if we counted only women's votes, Al Gore would have won the Electoral College with 368 votes, while if we counted only men's votes, George Bush would have won with 437 votes.

Political geography played a crucial role in determining the election. There has been a growing North/South divide since the 1950s, especially because white Southerners moved the South from the Democratic to the Republican column. In 2000, region still made a difference, with the Democrats' strength resting mostly in the North plus the crucial state of California. But a more finely grained map shows that the regional differences mask an even sharper differentiation between voters in urban centers versus the rest of the country. A map of electoral outcomes by county shows that the Democrats were the winners along the metropolitan areas of the East and West coasts, the Great Lakes and down the Mississippi River. This little-noted divide is probably the most important of all.

Turnout which had reached the worrying low of 49 percent in 1996, witnessed a slight recovery: about 51 percent of Americans voted, representing an additional 9.5 million voters more than in 1996 (Center for Voting and Democracy 2000; Putnam, 2000).

The economy

Many observers expected Gore and the Democrats to win because the Clinton administration had presided over a strengthening economy. On this analysis, Gore should have reaped the benefits of "retrospective voting." As later analysis showed, however, the economy weakened throughout the course of the campaign. Most importantly, as Larry Bartels and John Zaller (2001) demonstrate, while most analysts tended to take gross domestic product (GDP) per capita as their important measure of economic success, real disposable income (RDI) per capita has been a much better predictor of electoral outcomes; and per capita RDI was falling in the year before the election. On Bartels and Zaller's analysis the 2000 presidential vote conformed to their macro-level model developed from recent elections.

Campaign effects

Most journalists and most campaign operatives tend to analyze election results as though they were exclusively the result of their campaign strategies. Good campaigns can certainly help, and bad campaigns hurt, especially at the crucial margins in terms of both mobilizing people to vote, and in convincing people that it is their party that will do what the people want. But, as suggested earlier, the major campaign effects will be on those who are less attached to the major parties, or exactly those who are actually less likely to be actively paying attention. Although polls showed that more of the public probably agreed with a wider range of Gore's issue stands than with Bush's, apparently Bush's "compassion conservatism" and his emphasis on trusting the people to handle their own money served as the better mobilizers of swing voters. In addition, Bush won the personality race, especially among men. Experts within the Democratic Party will still be arguing for years over whether Gore's association with Clinton, or his decision to hold Clinton at arm's length during the campaign, had a negative effect on his popularity.

In talking about the ability of campaigns to mobilize voters, it must be remembered that interest groups play a crucial role as campaign operatives. Given the structure of campaign finance, interest groups fund many aspects of the campaign, including advertisements. Interest groups use a variety of means to mobilize their own constituents. Among those groups most visibly active in 2000 were the environmentalists, women's groups, African-American organizations and labor unions on the Democratic side, and the National Rifle Association (NRA) , anti-abortion groups, and the Christian right on the Republican side. Although many of these groups hardly needed to convince their people about which candidate they should prefer, they played a crucial role in getting people to the polls through phone calls and offering transport.

What can we conclude about the 2000 election in terms of explanations of the actual vote and results? The underlying dynamics were entirely ordinary, a good example of current trends. This is also true of the vote at other levels, including for members of Congress and state-level races. No single model can ever fully capture the complexity an election but they are especially difficult to construct for an election as close as this one (Bartels and Zaller, 2001).

Congress

Although much of the media's attention in 2000 focused on the race for the White House, the Congressional races were also interesting. After decades of jokes about dead people voting in Chicago – a reference to that city's infamous era of corruption – a dead man actually ran for Senate and won. In Missouri, Democratic Governor Mel Carnahan challenged incumbent Senator John Ashcroft. Carnahan died in a plane crash the day before the St Louis presidential debate. The new Governor announced he would appoint Carnahan's widow, Jean, if Carnahan won, and Ashcroft declined to challenge this plan, even though he could have made the case that the Democratic candidate could be said not to be qualified to run for Senate by the US Constitution because, being dead, he was not actually an inhabitant of the state. Carnahan won; and the defeated Ashcroft became Bush's

Attorney General. In another high-profile race, First Lady Hillary Clinton ran for Senate in New York and handily defeated Republican Rick Lazio.

The congressional races provided many close calls. According to constitutional design, all House seats and one-third of the Senate seats were subject to election, and after the Republican majority in both houses had been reduced in 1998, Democrats were expected to make gains in 2000. A few races were so close that they took days to certify the winner. As usual, incumbents tended to regain their seats, although the majority of Congressional races were more speedily decided. Of those who sought re-election, 98 percent of House members and 79 percent of Senators won re-election, a proportion roughly comparable to that of the previous two decades. Nevertheless, 2000 also saw some of the most expensive Senate races in history, including the $60 million dollars of his own money that successful Democratic New Jersey candidate, John Corzine, spent and a similar amount spent by Hillary Clinton and her opponent in the New York race.

The crucial electoral closeness was reflected in the overall partisan breakdown of the two houses of Congress. The Democrats picked up one seat in the House, leaving it split among 221 Republicans, 212 Democrats, and 2 independents. The Republicans lost 4 Senate seats to the Democrats, leaving it in a 50-50 tie. Vice-President Cheney constitutionally became President of the Senate and was thus given the tie-breaking vote, which conferred on the Republicans the right to continue in the "majority" complete with the right to chair all of the committees. This position was changed when Senator Jeffords (R-Vt) defected and threw the Senate back to the Democrats.

State races

Election 2000 saw 11 state governor races, resulting in a partisan shift in only one state, toward the Democratic Party. The state legislative races were especially important in 2000 because the resulting legislatures would be responsible for drawing the boundaries of the new congressional districts in each state in which the decennial census of 2000 will require reapportionment. Following the elections, 17 states (a decrease of three) ended up in Democratic control, 17 in Republican control, and 15 (an increase of three) ended up split between the two chambers.

In some states the American system allows for a direct statement of the public will through referendums (see also Chapter 15). Each election presents an assortment of these exercises in direct democracy. In 2000, among others, the people of Alaska and Colorado voted against legalizing marijuana, Californians and Michigan citizens voted against creating a school voucher program, Colorado citizens supported background checks for people attempting to buy guns at gun shows, those in Maine rejected a measure prohibiting discrimination against homosexuals, and people in Nebraska and Nevada voted to prohibit same-sex marriages.

Election 2000 and the American political system

The closeness of the 2000 election underlined many unusual features of the American political system. Some of these features were institutional, such as federalism, overlapping institutional powers, the prominence of courts in the American state, electoral law. Others were the product of contemporary trends in technology, mass communication, and the broader political culture. The 2000 election is thus interesting as a lens through which we can gain special insight into some critical problems of American politics and governance at the beginning of a new century. The remainder of this chapter will outline briefly some of the most important of these features in order to introduce some of the debates which will probably attract the attention of scholars and citizens, as well as policy-makers, for a long time to come.

Central to all these problems is this key point: elections are instruments for measuring the popular will. They can be organized in a myriad of ways, each of which emphasizes a somewhat different balance of values and norms. Yet no matter how these instruments are designed, they can only be vague approximations of popular will, even if that will were actually a specific, well-defined object amenable to precise measurement; and, of course, it is not.

The nominations process: competition or showtime?

How should democracies organize choosing the final set of candidates the electorate will consider at election time? A nomination process must balance many goals. Modern democratic norms require using a plausibly democratic process. But democracy engenders public contention; and significant public contention in the nominations process can compromise the ability to win the widest possible support within and outside their party. It can also limit the ability to develop a clear, principled program.

This winnowing stage of the electoral process was confined to a political elite in early American history; but it was later broadened and democratized through the early period of party caucuses to the widespread use of primaries in the twentieth century. The proliferation of the primary system allowed the national nominating conventions of the early twentieth century to host important and sometimes rancorous disputes on occasion, but the day of the multiple ballot nominations process quickly receded into the past.

The dawning of the television era in the 1960s brought more changes in the nomination process. Because each primary was now more in the *national* public eye, caucuses and primaries which occurred early in the electoral cycle gained disproportionate influence in the nominations process. Campaign finance became more important as attracting the resources necessary to run a mass media-based primary campaign increasingly dominated candidates' attention. Weakness in the early primaries could lead to diminishing funding, which hastened some candidates' demise and a rapid conclusion to the nomination process.

In the 1980s, therefore, state party organizations jockeyed to position their primaries earlier in order to enhance their influence. With the development of increasingly crowded Super Tuesdays – a March date on which many states held primaries – the entire system became "frontloaded," creating a greater probability that the candidates could be selected long before most states had their say, and a political eternity before the nominating conventions of August. The 2000 election is a good example of the new situation.

When front-loading occurs, neither the later primaries and caucuses nor the national nominating conventions have any serious role in measuring the popular will. Bush and Gore had ample time to consolidate their control within their parties, rendering their nominating conventions little more than carefully crafted backdrops for launching their general election campaigns. In an era in which there is much concern about the decline in participation (see Chapter 4), turning some of the most notable occasions for political engagement into empty shells of civic ritual cannot be good for democracy. Some people propose that there should be a "national primary" (so that all states would ballot on the same day rather than having staggered primaries as at present). Such a change would allegedly give each state an equal role in the candidate selection process. A national primary would, however, have serious disadvantages, probably eliminating the last vestiges of intimacy created by a system where candidates must spend time campaigning across the states and developing specific appeals for the votes of particular constituencies.

Polling, public opinion, and democratic practice

During the 2000 elections, public opinion analysts were much in the news. When the pre-election pollsters kept saying the elections were "too close to call" (with some notable exceptions, such as Gallup, which had Bush way ahead in the popular vote) pollsters became the object of derision. In retrospect, the polls' unstable, close, and conflicting results suggest surprisingly high competence given the fast turnaround methods most pollsters use and the growing tendency of people to refuse to respond to polls. Popular opinion on the major candidates *was* very close and probably shifting, and shallow.

Polls are now a ubiquitous and permanent part of politics and governance especially during elections; high quality public opinion polling is potentially one of the most precise means we have for measuring "the people's will." But contemporary uses of polling presents many problems that require thought because of their implications for democratic politics. Consider the following diverse examples drawn from current practices of, respectively, politicians, the mass media, and campaigns.

Advocates of democracy seek ways to increase the attention leaders pay to the will of the public. Regular elections serve as the chief accountability mechanism. But *politicians* know that polls offer a powerful means to know what the public is thinking. Bill Clinton, however, was widely criticized for running his presidency by opinion polls and focus groups. (see Chapter 5). What is the proper balance between being attentive to the public will and leading? How should politicians use polls, if at all?

The *mass media* use polls for information-gathering, but their critics complain that the results are used primarily as the content in horse-race journalism, merely reporting on who is winning rather than discussing the issues, and as the basis for simplistic generalizations about public opinion. Most journalists lack training in understanding polls, and news broadcasts often treat sample survey results and "person-in-the-street" interviews with the same credibility as measures of public opinion. In these cases, the messenger *is* the problem.

Campaign organizations and parties use polling both to gather information and to influence potential voters. While academic and nonpartisan research organizations use scholarly research on survey methodology to construct instruments that can capture public opinion accurately, partisan organizations use the same knowledge to construct polls that can influence public opinion either by rigging them to obtain results that are beneficial for their candidates or by designing "push polls" that directly affect respondents' opinions. ("How would you feel about Candidate Jones if you knew that he had murdered his mother, then vowed to raise taxes 80 percent to pay for the funeral?") The massive increase in polling, the lack of public education about surveys, and many citizens' suspicion of telephone polls make them reluctant to respond. Thus even the best surveys are rendered less accurate, and more counterproductive to democracy.

Campaign finance

American electoral campaigns have become massively expensive. Why? First, television-based campaigns are expensive. Television is the primary medium of electoral communication, and American networks are private corporations that sell their air time on a competitive market basis to electoral campaigns and McDonalds alike (see Chapter 18). Second, since the 1970s, a highly professional campaign industry has emerged. Long ago candidates only had to be able to afford tankards of beer to obtain votes; now they pay not the publican but the pollster, mass mail expert, web designer, speech writer, graphic artist, strategist, advance team, airline, production crew, and network, among others.

Thus, the essential functions of campaigns include *both* vote seeking and money raising. From mid-October to the end of November, 2000, the Democratic National Committee (DNC) reported raising $28 million dollars in contributions and the Republican National Committee (RNC) reported raising $37 million. Some individuals contributed as much as $400,000, with larger sums coming from organizational donors: witness, for example, the American Federation of State, County, and Municipal Employees' donation of $1.27 million (Schmidt, 2000). It is no wonder that campaign finance reform was prominent among the most discussed issues through the 1990s and into the 2000 campaign. Some of John McCain's early support came from advocates of campaign finance reform, and reform was also strongly endorsed by Bill Bradley.

Much as the idea of campaign finance has widespread support amongst the public and politicians, it is difficult to put into effect and faces objections on free speech grounds as well as from politicians who fear the impact on their ability to campaign. Controlling donations – which is how most reform proposals work – without changing the structural costs of campaigns limits all but the most wealthy candidates' ability to campaign and interact with the public.

Voter choice

Does the American electoral system provide a meaningful range of choice? We have seen that choice *within* the two major parties in 2000 was eliminated quickly. As for alternative parties, early twentieth-century reforms made it more difficult for "third parties" to gain a national foothold. The Green Party (Nader) received a lot of press, and the Reform Party (Buchanan) had qualified for federal funding on the basis of its previous electoral support; but both were excluded from the presidential debates.

As electoral scholars have long pointed out, typical campaign dynamics often further obscure degrees of choice *across* parties. Candidates tend to drive toward each other during the campaign to maximize their votes. This was Clinton's strategy in 1992 and George W. Bush's in 2000. Interparty differences tend to be further obscured by the nature of television advertising and journalism. Thirty-second television ads form the core of electoral campaigning. The nightly news rarely offers more than a couple of minutes on the campaign, and that is usually devoted to its horse-race aspects. One result, as we saw in 2000, is increasing emphasis on character and personality as the key "issues" of electoral politics.

Many factors, then, tend to narrow and obscure choice, thus arguably diminishing elections as expressions of popular will in guiding governance. What options are there for expanding choice? Given the structure of the electoral system, the candidates' drive for victory, and the short attention span most citizens have for politics, the answer is not clear.

The mass media and republican citizenship in the twenty-first century

The performance of the mass media in 2000 evidenced all of the problems for which they are often criticized, and more: "pack" journalism, emphasis on the horse-race, a tendency not to push difficult questions, an emphasis on entertainment rather than information. In fact, these problems grew in 2000. While in 1992 Bill Clinton made news by playing the saxophone on a late night entertainment show, in 2000 both candidates appeared multiple times on television entertainment shows. Some reports suggested that a large minority of Americans received their main news about the campaigns from the opening monologues of the late night shows.

Network news is not superficial because the journalists or network executives wish to withhold information from the American public. Depth in political journalism does not sell widely in the mass public, and commercial networks must sell their programming, news included. In fact there *is* substantial information easily available to most citizens who want it, even on television, but it is not on commercial networks. Moreover, the 2000 election revealed the full bloom of the Internet as a widely accessible medium for election information. This medium did not exist in 1992, and was in an early experimental phase in 1996.

By the time of the 2000 election the majority of American households had access to the Internet. Virtually all the major print newspapers, magazines, television and radio stations offered websites with campaign coverage, as did the various "webzines", such as *Salon*, *Slate*, and a host of others. Partisan and nonpartisan groups as well as the campaigns themselves, the political parties, and government agencies such as the Federal

Election Commission (FEC) posted websites through which one could gather information, participate in conversations, or donate money.

Optimists argue that the Internet will create a communications environment for elections that will enhance democracy. But as the 2000 election shows, there is great inequality in the motivation to participate, even among those who have the equipment for access. Does the vast richness of the information sources available to the interested mean that inequalities in knowledge and engagement will grow ever greater?

Calling the race: public education or business?

The election night follies, revolving reporting and predicting results for each state, especially in Florida, provided both suspense and entertainment (and some news) for the television audience, but it raised serious issues about the contemporary role of the "Fourth Estate." Above all, they highlight the conflicts in mission and incentives among the various participants – reporters, network executives, and social scientist experts working behind the scenes – whose joint work produces the news of the results. They bring to the fore the tensions between the journalistic and business functions of news production. Tensions often exist between the academics hired by networks to analyze incoming data to predict the outcomes (and whose main concern is getting it right) and the network executives, who are afraid of being outstripped by other networks. These conflicts of interest were manifest to an unusually strong – and public – degree in 2000.

At each point during election night when the networks determined they had to make a prediction about the Florida vote, at least some of the social science teams were arguing there was insufficient evidence to do so (Shepard, 2000). Soon after the elections were concluded, Congress began inquiries into what happened, and industry participants and observers set to work analyzing the problems. It is unlikely, however, that any reform could entirely eliminate the tension between the business of informing the public and the media's commercial interest in an election (see also Chapter 17).

Elections as measurement instruments

A lot of thought goes into designing accurate measurement instruments whether they be binoculars, speedometers, or stopwatches. The 2000 election raised the question of what value the United States placed on accuracy in the design of its machinery for measuring election outcomes. The choice of election machinery is constitutionally reserved to the states with certain exceptions created by constitutional or federal law. But election technology has changed over history and there is a wide variety of election machinery across different state and even local jurisdictions. Both the design of elections (such as who can vote, under what circumstances, in what manner), and the amount of variation in design across different jurisdictions, have occasionally become the subject of intense political debate. These debates are sometimes rancorous because issues about election machinery usually involve tradeoffs between competing values.

Calibrating inclusiveness

Among the most important historical changes in the design of election processes have been those defining electoral inclusiveness. Electoral inclusiveness may be effected in two ways: (1) altering eligibility requirements for voting, such as those based on age, race, sex, residency, property, or literacy; and (2) altering procedures that facilitate or inhibit voting. Among the most important reasons for procedural change has been ensuring that the right people (however that is defined) are voting, only the right people are voting, and that they are voting only once, which are all important conditions for determining that elections are tapping the will of the people accurately. But procedures designed to allow *only* qualified people to vote also tend to inhibit some qualified people from voting. Practices intended to elicit wider participation may provoke errors in the other direction.

Consider the different ways these dilemmas played out during the 2000 nomination season. *Primary election eligibility* rules had critical effects in the Republican primaries. In some states the only requirement for voting in one party's primary is that a voter should not simultaneously vote in another party's primary for that office. John McCain's successful challenge was based on his ability to garner support from voters with relatively little investment in the Republican Party. Indeed, an unusually large number of Democrats appear to have weighed into the Republican primaries strategically to help the Democrats, especially in Michigan, which McCain won.

The *administrative procedures for holding elections* have substantive implications, and remain objects of political contention. Legislative efforts made throughout the 1980s to encourage registration and voting met with persistent resistance by Republicans in Congress and President Bush, who knew that the people most likely to be brought into the electorate would be members of the Democratic Party's natural base. The National Voter Registration Act of 1993 (the "Motor Voter" Act), signed by President Clinton, required states to make at least three procedures for voter registration available, including assistance for the disabled. Citizens became able to register to vote while they registered for automobile licenses or welfare benefits.

The legislation took effect for the 1996 election, and formed the basis of a campaign by the National Association for the Advancement of Colored People (NAACP) in 2000 to intensify African-American voter registration. Administration of "motor voter" procedures broke down or was sabotaged in many places, most specifically in south Florida, where many African-Americans in particular faced registration difficulties. Investigations and lawsuits followed the election by groups suspecting that Republican officials had systematically organized to inhibit black voting because the vast majority of African-Americans vote Democratic.

Absentee voting has been a regular part of American election procedure since World War I, when overseas military personnel and other citizens with a valid occupational reason for being away could vote by mail. At least 18 states have very liberal absentee voting procedures. In 1997, however, Florida enacted exacting new absentee ballot procedures following widespread fraud in the 1997 Miami mayoral campaign. Thousands of ballots distributed in the 2000 election violated some of the new technical procedures. The Democratic Party unsuccessfully attempted to nullify these ballots, because the ballots were bound to benefit the Republican Party.

In contrast, states other than Florida expanded *options for voting other than in person*. Oregon completely replaced traditional balloting with postal balloting. Thirteen states allowed "early voting," in which citizens could cast ballots from 17 to 21 days before Election Day (L. Wayne, 2000). Meanwhile, January 2000 saw the release of a task force report on Internet voting (California Internet Voting Task Force, 2000), and localized experiments in on-line voting took place around the country. Each of these new means of voting presents possibilities for increasing the accuracy of the election "instrument," but also introduces sources of potential error and new opportunities for corruption and sabotage.

"Mere technicalities?": let the chads fall where they may

Americans vote by machine, punchcard, optically scanned ballot, and direct entry electronic means. Each ballot mode has many variations. All measurement instruments contain "natural" sources of error that can emerge even if the human beings using them do everything perfectly (which they rarely do). Designers of measurement instruments, including voting mechanisms, aim for the *smallest* margin of error possible to get the job done in an appropriate manner. They also aim to eliminate *systematic sources* of error. If error is systematic it will benefit one side or another; if, alternatively, error is random, it is unlikely the error will benefit any side in particular. In a very close election, even under the best of circumstances, both the margin of error and the extent to which it is systematic will be important.

Instrument technicalities became so significant in 2000 that the 20-year-old patent application for the Vote-O-Matic machines used in Florida to count punch card ballots became crucial evidence in the Gore camp's efforts to win a court-ordered manual recount (Barstow and Filkins, 2000). Numerous journalists, academics, and commissions became engaged in studying America's voting systems, and the FEC was charged by Congress to do a full investigation with an eye toward reform. These calls for reform must be tempered by the estimates that retooling the system – which involves about 180,000 precincts around the country – would cost $9 billion (Miller and Anderson, 2000). Regardless of what reforms are implemented in the coming decades, there will always be a margin of error, the errors are unlikely to be equally distributed on all sides and, when the results are very close, there will again be no such thing as a "mere" technicality.

The rules of the game: fair and impartial?

The American electoral system contains many laws and administrative rules designed to resolve conflicts, ambiguities, and indecision points. Some of these are well known. The Constitution provides that, in case of a tie, the presidential election is decided by the House of Representatives. But many are less known, and many vary from state to state. State legislatures generally have the final power to select delegates to the Electoral College if the matter is not resolved by the election. State officials, such as the Attorney General or Secretary of State, have the discretion to certify state ballots to make sure the rules have been followed correctly. Some states, like Texas and Florida, have rules that automatically require recounts of ballots if the first count falls within a particular margin. And there are always courts to deliberate conflict based on state, federal, or constitutional law, or the relationship among them.

Ultimately, rules cannot account for all possible occasions in processes as complicated and essentially conflictual as elections. At some point, unanticipated situations arise, and conditions can be covered by overlapping jurisdictions and inconsistent norms and rules. As the 2000 election endgame showed, the importance of the task and the stakes involved mean there are virtually no purely nonpolitical administrative or technical matters at stake to resolve crucial political questions such as this. In 2000, all the technical matters were transformed into political problems.

Each side believed the other was violating "the rules of the game" and called on evidence from law, history, and public opinion in their own defense. Indeed, in the heat of a close battle, people tend to judge the justice of rules by how they feel about the outcome they would create. The *Los Angeles Times* polls asked national sample of adults in mid-December, just after Bush was declared the winner, "Which statement comes closer to the way you feel: 'It is better for the country to know quickly who the president will be after an election without challenges to the vote,' or 'It is better for the country to take every possible measure to reach a complete count of all ballots even if it means a delay in finding out who won?'" About 69 percent of the respondents thought accuracy was more important, but this result masks the real nature of the division over this "principled" distinction: 91 percent of Democrats thought all ballots should be counted, compared with 60 percent of Independents and 41 percent of Republicans. When the same poll asked whether punch card votes counted by a machine or by hand would yield a more fair and accurate result, 34 percent of Democrats, 62 percent of Independents, and 73 percent of Republicans trusted the machines more. Basic principles and perceptions are shaped by the specific context in which people are thinking about general rules.

Aggregating the votes

The US uses an Electoral College for presidential elections. Each state has a number of electoral votes equal to the number of people in its Congressional delegation, including members of the House of Representatives and the Senate. The winner of a state's popular vote receives all of that state's electoral votes. Real delegates are selected to the Electoral College, which casts its vote in January, but they almost always vote as they have been instructed by their state's popular vote. In the vast majority of cases, the winner in the Electoral College has been the winner of the national popular vote. But the margin of victory in the Electoral College is rarely similar to the margin in the popular vote. The Electoral College vote tends to exaggerate the victory of the winner, sometimes massively. (see Chapter 19). However, any serious effort to eliminate the Electoral College is likely to highlight the conflicts of interest between the ethnically, racially, and culturally diverse populations of the cities who have reason to favor an active government , versus those who live – and in many cases have fled – further from the urban centers. These differences certainly underlay the divisions in the 2000 presidential vote itself.

Conclusion

Each national election is a product of the history that went before. Each one, in turn, helps to shape the political future. This is certainly true of the 2000 election. Its closeness, ambiguities, and procedural uncertainties will leave a legacy in American history. Although it was marked by an unusual set of events, it would be a mistake to think that the underlying dynamics of the event of 2000 were anything out of the ordinary. As we have seen, both the results and the "special" problems are easily understandable in the context of underlying principles and problems of American politics. The 2000 election highlighted some perennial issues of democratic governance, and they underlined the extent to which the role of elections as instruments for measuring the democratic will inevitably makes electoral procedures and election machinery on occasion the subject of political debate and turmoil.

Chapter 3

Political Parties

DEAN MCSWEENEY

At the beginning of the twenty-first century political parties show signs of vitality that belie the gloomy assessments of their role made by academics, journalists, and politicians since the 1970s. American parties have long exhibited distinctive features compared to their counterparts in other democracies and, in some ways, they have been distinctively weak. Because they lack formal membership and possess little control over candidate selection or internal policy unity, American parties have become attenuated as organizations and seemed to serve few electoral or governmental functions. For long periods there was a politically unhealthy absence of electoral competition as one party was so dominant. In the last third of the twentieth century parties appeared to be receding in effectiveness even from that modest range of functions they had performed, such as running election campaigns. Here their role appeared to be displaced by candidate organizations, political consultants, television advertising and political action committees. Even control over the presidential nomination, a rare survival of candidate selection by party, was lost under the onslaught of primaries adopted by most states.

However, there is now a vigor to parties' performance of some functions: they are sources of vast amounts of campaign finance; there is an unprecedented degree of integration between national, state and local party organizations in election campaigns; and there is serious competition between the two major parties to control elected branches of the federal government.

Legal regulation

A distinctive feature of American parties, and a source of their weakness, is the extent to which they been regulated by law. A distrust of parties, expressed by some of the Founding Fathers, has regularly appeared in American political rhetoric. Parties have been distrusted for being divisive and corrupt, enemies rather than instruments of the public interest. Laws were adopted to impose a discipline the parties lacked. In law the parties were not treated as private bodies entitled to control their own affairs;

rather they were like public utilities, privately owned but legally disciplined to serve the public (Epstein, 1986).

Since the early 1970s there has been a trend to deregulate parties. Using protections afforded by First Amendment rights to freedom of speech and association, a succession of Supreme Court decisions has enlarged the private sphere for parties in which they can make their own choices about the running of their organizations. Decisions in 1996 and 2000 continued that trend. In 1996 in *Colorado Republican Federal Campaign Committee* v. *FEC*, the Court allowed parties to make independent expenditures to aid their candidates in federal elections. In overturning a provision of the Federal Election Campaign Act, parties acquired a right to assist their candidates that had been denied to them but afforded to political action committees. Under the First Amendment parties were deemed to be able to spend unlimited money in exercising their rights to freedom of speech. Parties remain capped in the total of contributions they can make directly to candidates; but the right to make unlimited general expenditures removes a ceiling on an indirect form of financial aid. From the 1996 campaign onwards parties have capitalized on their new opportunity to aid candidates, spending $11.5 million in independent expenditure in congressional elections that year, close to double what they donated to candidates (see also Chapter 18).

Parties' rights to regulate who votes in their primaries were extended when the Court overruled a blanket primary (imposed by state law) in *California Democratic Party* v. *Jones* in 2000 (see also Chapters 7 and 19). Open to all registered voters, candidates from all parties competed in the blanket primary, the top two qualifying to contest the general election. The Court held that the blanket primary infringed the parties' First Amendment rights to freedom of association. Parties were entitled to control their nomination processes and define who was eligible to compete in them. Although legal regulation at the state level has sometimes hamstrung parties, it has also protected the two major parties against competition, and a 1997 Court decision continued that tradition. In *Timmons* v. *Twin Cities* the Court upheld a Minnesota law preventing two parties from nominating the same candidate. Anti-fusion laws such as Minnesota's prevent minor parties from exercising an indirect yet potentially pivotal impact on election outcomes by allying with a major party candidate. By barring fusion, *Timmons* deprives minor parties of a source of influence attained with even modest shares of the vote.

The two-party duopoly

Election laws and decisions like *Timmons* have helped the Democrats and Republicans sustain their dominance of elections and government since

1860. Conspicuous in the contemporary period, unlike much of the past, is the fine electoral balance between major parties. The 2000 presidential election was decided by a few hundred votes in the state of Florida. The Senate election yielded a 50–50 tie between the parties, though this was later replaced by marginal Democratic control after one Republican Senator defected. In the 435-member House of Representatives, the Republicans secured a majority of just nine seats. Each party currently controls both legislative chambers in 17 states. Only the 27–21 Republican edge amongst governors (there are two independents) shows one party with a clear advantage.

The fine balance between the parties reflects the disappearance of the Democratic majority that had survived at many subpresidential levels of government for 60 years into the early 1990s. The Democratic advantage had withered in presidential elections after 1964. In Congress and in many states their electoral resilience held until the election of 1994, which elected the first Republican Congress in 40 years. A Republican-controlled House is now in its seventh year, their most enduring Republican majority since the 1920s. Crucial in the Republican revival has been electoral change in the South. For over a century until 1994 Democrats accounted for a majority of southern representatives, senators and governors, whereas Republican majorities became the norm at the end of the twentieth century.

Southern Republicans have benefitted from the strengthening of the relationship between ideology and voting behavior. The increased willingness of conservatives to vote Republican yielded substantial returns in the most conservative region of the country. In House elections Republicans benefitted from the reapportionment in 1990 creating seats with majorities of minority group voters. As minorities were concentrated in particular seats their electoral presence shrank elsewhere, increasing the number of districts with overwhelmingly white electorates where the potential for Republican success is greatest. Having won seats, Republicans were able to capitalize on the advantages of incumbency to retain them. Fifteen of the twenty southern Republicans representatives first elected in 1994 were re-elected to a fourth term in 2000.

The third party challenge

Though two-party dominance persists, third parties are now a common presence in elections. The 2000 presidential elections were the third in succession in which neither of the major parties attained 50 per cent of the popular vote. Although the strongest third party in 2000 accounted for a modest 3.2 per cent of the vote, in 1992 Perot's third party challenge had yielded 19 percent of the vote. Sometimes third party interventions can have a decisive effect on the election outcome. The Greens' candidate in 2000 (Ralph Nader) deflected support disproportionately from the Democratic candidate, Al Gore. Polls of Nader voters showed that in the absence of their candidate they would have voted 50–20 for Gore over Bush with the remainder abstaining. In the absence of Nader, Gore would probably have carried Florida, sufficient to win the presidency. The threat from Nader had also exacted a cost for the Democrats during the campaign. Gore was forced to concentrate campaign resources into otherwise securely Democratic states such as Wisconsin, Minnesota, and Iowa, diverting them from marginal states where the major party candidates were in close competition. Gore won most of the close states but fell one short of winning the presidency.

Earlier in the election year polls showed a much larger potential Green vote than materialized on election day. In some states Nader threatened to win a share of the vote in double figures, helping to realize the Greens' objective of winning over 5 per cent of the national vote to qualify for federal funding for the election in 2004. The shrinkage of the Green vote in the final weeks of the campaign reflects the success of the Gore campaign in rallying Democrats to remain loyal to the party. But to achieve this effect required not only a diversion of resources from marginal states but also a radicalization of Gore's positions. He projected himself as a populist, combating vested interests such as oil and tobacco on behalf of the people. Such an image may have repelled some voters into supporting Bush, offsetting those attracted from Nader.

The 2000 election probably sounded the death knell of the Reform Party. Founded by the millionaire presidential candidate Ross Perot, Reform had demonstrated a potential to compete against the major parties. The party attracted national attention when its candidate, flamboyant 20-stone former wrestler Jesse Ventura, won the Minnesota governorship in 1998. In competing for the presidency in 2000 Reform could afford an expensive campaign beyond most minor parties. Perot earned the party $13.4 million in federal funds for the next election when he won over 5 per cent of the vote in 1996, but the prize of federal funds generated a contest for the Reform nomination that wrecked the party. Supporters of Pat Buchanan who contested the Republican nomination in 1992 and 1996, sought to take over the Reform Party in order to use its federal funds to promote his pugnacious mix of nationalism and traditional morality. Social liberals (backed by Ventura) sought to resist the threatened Buchanan takeover. The outcome was a fiasco. Supporters and opponents of Buchanan held rival national conventions. Both factions claimed title to the federal funds, which the Federal Election Commission resolved in Buchanan's favour. Thirteen million dollars was insufficient to surmount the wreckage of the party and the media neglect of the campaign. Having won under 1 per cent of the vote, whatever survives of a Reform Party will be ineligible for federal funding in 2004.

Below the presidential level third parties have become more common in elections. More minor parties have been competing in elections, and in more contests major party candidates face minor party or independent opposition. In no election year between 1968 and 1988 did minor or independent candidates ever contest a majority of House seats. In 2000 competition from these sources appeared in 74 per cent of districts. Two independents won, both incumbents (one originally elected as a Democrat).

Party conflict

Embittered, adversarial relations between the two major parties marked the end of the twentieth century. This contrasts with most of the postwar period when moderate conflict was the norm, and bargaining and compromise across party lines were recurrent features of government. From the 1980s, confrontations between the parties broke out in a succession of controversies, including the failed nomination of Robert Bork to the Supreme Court in 1987, the enforced resignation of House Speaker Jim Wright in 1989, the government shutdown in the winter of 1995–96, the impeachment of President Clinton in 1998 and the disputed presidential election of 2000. In each of these conflicts the parties were untypically neatly arrayed in opposition to another. Charges of malpractice, corruption, irresponsibility, and crude partisanship were exchanged.

The process of resolving the controversy over disputed ballots in Florida was contaminated by partisanship as each side advocated procedures likely to assure its own victory and disadvantage its opponents. Party elites and activists faithfully aligned behind their respective campaigns' conception of a fair vote count. Objective judgement and respect for existing law and precedent were distorted through a partisan lens. The actions of all the officials involved in resolving the dispute were seen as motivated by party allegiance. Republicans imputed partisan motivations to county canvassing boards and the Florida Supreme Court. Democrats' accusations of bias were directed at the Florida Secretary of State, the state legislature and the US Supreme Court (see also Chapter 7).

Antagonisms between the parties have their roots in ideological differences, rival moralities, and the domineering methods of the majority party in Congress. Parties are now more ideologically distinct than ever before. The broad coalitions that once characterized American parties have narrowed into more compact ideological identities. Republicans tend toward the conservative end of the spectrum, Democrats toward the liberal end. These differences are expressed through all major policy areas from the economy to the environment, defense to social welfare, law and order to foreign policy. These policy differences also intrude into decisions over personnel and procedure. Both contribute to advancing a governing agenda whilst aggravating partisanship.

Conflicting values underpin differences between the parties. On socio-cultural issues such as abortion, prayer in schools, and the death penalty, Republicans believe in traditional values that uphold the family, and individual discipline. A common morality is deemed necessary to sustain social stability and is therefore a legitimate area for government intervention. Democrats regard morality as a private concern. In this conception, choice, self-expression, and tolerance forge a diverse, harmonious society. These rival systems of values, often expressed as moral absolutes, preclude compromise. Where policy is concerned with allocating shares of benefits and burdens it is possible to negotiate distributional outcomes that command broad acceptance. Where absolutes are in contention no middle ground exists. The party polarization on these issues expresses and intensifies hostilities, as opponents are perceived as defending Wrong against Right. In any system of government such fierce antagonisms hinder constructive policy-making. They are particularly destructive in the USA where bargaining and exchanges of favors have provided informal routes around the obstacle course of the separation of powers and checks and balances.

The parties' use of congressional procedures has aggravated hostilities. The majority has sought to dominate and the minority to disrupt. During their long period of control of the House, Democrats capitalized on the party's increased ideological cohesion to employ procedure to impose control. When power in the House changed hands in 1995, the parties switched roles. Exclusively Republican task forces displaced committees as the key stage in the formulation of some bills before they reached the floor. Democrats adopted denunciation to undermine the majority's appeal. In the Senate a similar deterioration in interparty relations occurred. The scope for majority dominance is much smaller but the procedural protections for minorities are much greater. The filibuster was once used as a last resort by a faction to frustrate majority will; now its use is commonplace and partisan. Thus the recent past – at least until the advent of the war against terrorism imposed a more bipartisan approach – has seen increased partisanship and conflict in Congress despite the common urge by both parties to seek the middle ground electorally.

Party differences

Both parties made efforts to capture the political center ground in the 2000 presidential election. Bush did not emphasize socio-cultural themes. The Republican National Convention exuded diversity and tolerance, featuring blacks, women, Hispanics, and a gay member of Congress amongst the speakers. The Democratic platform spoke glowingly of the fiscal discipline of the Clinton presidency, and embraced a tax cut. As his running mate, Gore selected Joseph Lieberman, the chair of the Democratic Leadership Council which has pressed the party to focus on the concerns of Middle America.

However, many of the policy differences between the parties in the recent past remained in evidence. The Democrats' tax cut was targeted to help middle-class families; Republicans promised a reduction for all taxpayers to stimulate the economy. The Democrats called for increased funding for public schools, whereas the Republicans argued for education vouchers to assist parents in paying for private schools. For Social Security, Democrats proposed preserving the existing system; Republicans called for taxpayers to be allowed to invest part of their contributions in private savings schemes. Democrats promised to include more people in Medicaid. Republicans proposed tax reductions to increase access to private health insurance. Democrats called for civil rights protection for gays, while Republicans opposed civil rights on the basis of sexual orientation (Dao, 2000).

Delegates attending the national conventions of the two parties differed in ideology, policy preferences, and socio-economic and demographic characteristics. Ideologically they were opposites of one another. A third of Democrats identified themselves as liberals compared to 1 per cent of their Republican counterparts. Only 4 per cent of Democrats but more than half of the Republicans regarded themselves as conservatives. These broad ideological differences are sharply delineated on specific issues (see Table 3.1). The socio-economic and demographic characteristics of the delegates are indicative of differences in interests represented by the parties and the sympathies they evoke. Over a quarter of Republicans were born-again Christians, more than double their share amongst Democrats. Jews were 2 per cent of the Republicans but 8 per cent of Democrats. Thirty-one per cent of Democrats were black, Hispanic or Asian compared to 11 per cent of Republicans.

New Democrats

Before becoming president Clinton had been active in efforts to forge a more centrist party following three successive presidential election defeats

Table 3.1   *Issue differences between party activists and the public, 2000*

	percent in favour		
	Dem. delegates	Voters	Rep. delegates
Government programmes to help minorities to get ahead to overcome past discrimination	83	51	29
Abortion available to those who want it	71	36	14
Allow individuals to invest part of their Social Security taxes	23	53	80
Trade restrictions to protect domestic industries	50	57	27
Tax-financed education vouchers	10	47	71
A Medicare premium to cover prescription drugs for the elderly	58	37	34
Gun manufactures required to put child safety locks on handguns	94	84	48

Source: New York Times/CBS News Poll, *New York Times*, August 14 2000.

in 1980, 1984, and 1988. He was a founding member in 1990 of the DLC that aimed to reposition the party to appeal to Middle America. New Democrats were the early exponents of the redefinition of liberal-left parties into the Third Way, an alternative to both statist liberalism and free market conservatism which was echoed by Tony Blair and New Labour policies in Britain. New Democratic ideas were championed as appropriate to the needs of an information age, economic globalization and a predominantly middle-class society. For New Democrats the values of opportunity, responsibility, and community supplanted the liberals' attachment to equality, rights and government intervention.

Clinton's 1992 campaign embraced New Democrat themes such as welfare reform and toughness on crime whilst he kept his distance from traditional liberal constituencies like unions and minorities. His victory, if achieved with only a minority of the vote, appeared to confirm the DLC approach to restoring the party's electoral fortunes. Governing as a New Democrat offered the opportunity to redefine the party and rally it around him with durable effect. Inevitably his presidency did not consistently adhere to a single doctrine; and some prominent New Democrat ideas advanced by Clinton divided Democrats in Congress. Free trade encountered opposition for its threat to jobs and the environment. Welfare reform was condemned for its harshness and the abandonment of guaranteed aid to the poor. In the end the welfare reforms which occurred under Clinton were more the result of a need to modify Republican initiatives than of any clash between competing Democratic approaches; but Clinton and the New Democrats were more comfortable with the compromise than were many others in the Democratic Party. Assistance to parents by allowing unpaid leave from work to perform family responsibilities and the requirements for a V-chip to exclude access to violent material on television were less controversial and commanded broad support, but they are not the defining themes of a presidency or a party programme.

Without Clinton in the White House there is less potential for New Democrats to set the agenda for the party. There is a substantial New Democrat presence in Congress, numbering 19 senators and 72 representatives who are members of the New Democratic Coalition caucus, but the House leadership, in particular, is less keen on some of their ideas, such as free trade. Although Gore had been active in the DLC, the organization's director (Al From) faulted the campaign he ran. He criticized Gore for running as a populist rather than a New Democrat. From maintains that Gore's attacks on big business were an anachronistic form of class warfare, unsuitable in a middle class society. Threatening to tame business implied the bigger, more expensive government that damaged the Democrats' electoral prospects before the 1990s (From, 2001). The persuasiveness of that argument will bear upon how the party – and Gore in particular if he runs – present themselves in 2004.

Compassionate conservatives

Attempts are underway to redefine conservatism in the Republican Party. During his campaign for the presidency, George W. Bush advanced the idea of compassionate conservatism. Compassionate conservatives (Comcons) exhibit a concern for the disadvantaged that the free market fails to help. Comcons conceive of conservatism as caring, inclusive and positive about government. According to one of its leading proponents, Marvin Olasky, compassionate conservatism requires a new triangular relationship between government, charities and churches ('faith-based organizations'). The task of government is to facilitate charitable giving by these community organizations by monitoring their performance and assisting with government funds (Olasky, 2000). A White House Office of

Faith Based and Community Initiatives was created early in the Bush presidency, although its first head, John DiIulio, left after only a few months in the post. Bush also argues for government to enable individuals and families to improve themselves. The Republican platform, *Renewing America's Purpose: Together*, called for publicly funded education vouchers to enable parents to choose private schools for their children. A portion of Social Security payroll taxes are to be made available to taxpayers to finance private individual retirement accounts which pay higher rates of interest than the government scheme. Low-income families are promised tax relief and assistance in home buying through tax credits or federal rental assistance schemes.

Bush's ideas signal a new conservative accommodation with government. Whereas Reaganite conservatives wanted to curb government, Bush proposes using it to enable citizens to assist themselves. Government performs different, rather than fewer or cheaper functions. Previous conservative attempts to curb government have been frustrated in practice. Welfare reform, for example, has curbed spending on benefits, but other expenditures have risen to transform the welfare system into an escalator into paid employment. Costs of job training and childcare for beneficiaries have grown.

The attraction of this reformulation of conservatism has been enhanced by the development of a budget surplus. In the 1980s and much of the 1990s the conservative attack on government drew sustenance from a belief that deficits hampered economic growth. The onset of government surpluses has removed one of government's destructive effects. Bush's first budget, promising tax cuts and an increased rate of public spending, was favorably received by congressional Republicans, suggesting that his party finds an expansive role for government more acceptable than in the heyday of Reagan or of Gingrich's radical *Contract With America* (see also Chapter 6).

On socio-cultural issues, Bush offers no revision of conservative thinking. Under his governorship Texas was the most prolific user of the death penalty in the USA. Neither does he appear to share the qualms about miscarriages of justice expressed by conservative writers such as George Will and William Buckley, or Governor George Ryan of Illinois. Bush opposes abortion, and the platform reiterated its recent predecessors in calling for a constitutional amendment to protect the unborn child. It also proposed legislation to clarify the Fourteenth Amendment's right to life provision to include the fetus. One of Bush's earliest actions as president was to remove abortion from foreign aid medical schemes. The platform's opposition to gun control and gay rights are also standard conservative stances.

Interest group allies

Each party is integrated into issue networks of supportive interest groups. Groups are integrated with the party through common activists, campaign activity, and funding. The Democratic network involves trade unions, environmental, women's, pro-choice, and civil rights groups. The Christian right, gun owners and small business contribute to the Republican network. These networks reflect the interests and ideological outlooks shared by parties and groups. The interests and membership overlaps help define the distinctive socio-economic and demographic profile of the parties' activists and electoral supporters.

Many of the parties' activists are members of supportive groups. In 1996 Green, Jackson and Clayton found that only 7 per cent of Democratic national convention delegates and 16 per cent of Republicans had no group affiliations. Large minorities in each party were affiliated to more than one group (Green, Jackson and Clayton, 1999). As the idea of a party issue network suggests, groups connected with one party have little overlap with the other. Nearly a third of Democratic delegates in 2000 were union members (compared to 4 per cent of Republicans). Close to one in five Republicans were members of the NRA, an organization of which 85 per cent of Democratic delegates disapproved.

Group election activity for their preferred party includes rating candidates, distributing literature, operating phone banks, mounting get-out-the-vote efforts on election day and contributing funds to the party and its candidates. In the 2000 elections the American Federation of Labor/Congress of Industrial Organizations (AFL-CIO) aimed to contact 22 percent of its members to encourage support for Democratic candidates. Unions were particularly heavy users of direct mail, sending large quantities and, for some candidates, several different items. Telephone banks to contact millions of voters were used by groups such as the AFL-CIO, Christian Coalition, the National Abortion and Reproductive Rights Action League (NARAL) and the NRA. Christian Coalition and EMILY's List (Early Money is Like Yeast) were amongst the groups using e-mail and the Internet. Groups including NARAL and Friends of the Earth seconded their staff to assist candidate organizations.

Group ratings of elected officials to guide their supporters at the polls demonstrate clear preferences for one party. The American Conservative Union (ACU) awards the title Best and Brightest to members of Congress with perfect voting records on issues important to the group. Members beyond the pale, failing to cast a single vote in the preferred direction, are dubbed the Worst and Dimmest. For the 106th Congress, 44 of the 45 Best and Brightest members were Republicans, while the solitary Democrat ran as an independent in the 2000 elections. The eleven Worst and

Dimmest were all Democrats. Based on voting on environmental issues, the League of Conservation Voters identifies a Dirty Dozen prior to each congressional election. In 2000, eleven were Republicans.

In addition to funding these 'ground war' activities, groups support their preferred candidates and party by several forms of expenditure: media advertising, mounting independent campaigns (funded by hard money) and soft money spending on issue advocacy. Political action committees make hard money donations to candidates and party committees (see Table 3.2). Interest groups make soft money donations to parties. Groups spend on communicating with members, and mobilize supporters to make individual contributions of hard and soft money. Tracking all these sources is impossible with data compiled under existing law but, of those traceable forms of aid to the Democrats, the AFL-CIO was worth $45 million and EMILY's List $20 million in the 2000 election to Congress. Republicans were assisted in various ways worth at least $25 million from the NRA and $15 million from the US Chamber of Commerce (Magleby, 2001).

Election campaigns

From the 1980s parties became important sources of services to candidate-centered campaigns. National and state parties located niches in campaigning that could not be adequately filled by candidate organizations, political consultancies, interest groups, and political action committees. Parties supply expertise in training candidates and campaign managers, and seconding their staff to work for candidates. They provide information in forms such as voter identification and polling data. Parties also provide a linkage function. They act as intermediaries in linking candidates to sympathetic political action committees, and political consultancies with successful records.

In the later 1990s parties added a new role as sources of vast amounts of campaign finance. A post-reform campaign era of campaign finance began in 1996 with the large-scale national party funding its most prominent feature (Herrnson and Dwyre, 1999). The new era emerged as the constraints on parties imposed by the original FECA legislation were pared away (see also Chapter 18). A 1979 amendment legalized soft money. Party spending on issue advocacy in federal elections was permitted by the 1986 Supreme Court ruling in *FEC* v. *Massachusetts Citizens for Life*. The trend culminated in the *1996 Colorado Republican Federal Campaign Committee* v. *FEC* case referred to above, allowing party independent expenditures. In aggregate these reforms freed parties to spend independently large quantities of money to assist their candidates.

Table 3.2   *Political action committee (PAC) contributions to party candidates, 1999–2000*

Type of PAC	Contribution	percent Party Share Dem.	Rep.
Women's	780,044	86	14
Environment	546,422	93	7
Gun Rights	1,969,126	14	86
Pro-Life	431,580	7	93
Pro-Choice	1,163,216	75	25
Unions	52,784,281	91	9

Sources: Center for Responsive Politics Ideological/Single-Issue PAC Contributions to Federal Candidates, 1999–2000; Labor PAC Contributions to Federal Candidates, 1999–2000, http://www.opensecrets.org

All forms of spending by national party committees totalled a massive $1,129,398,530 in 1999–2000, three times what was spent four years earlier. Hard money spending of over $659 million accounted for close to three-fifths of the total. As in the past, Republicans were the superior fundraisers. But in soft money, total Democratic spending achieved parity with Republicans, and in congressional campaigns exceeded them. The principal uses of party money were similar to those adopted by candidates, employing television and radio advertising, direct mail and telephone banks, but the content of these communications was qualitatively different from that of candidates. Party communications were overwhelmingly negative, whereas candidate communications were more positive. Parties and candidates appear to have established a division of labor in which candidates can benefit from negative campaigns whilst escaping responsibility for their use. Party spending appeared to work. Effective targeting of their soft money spending by the Democrats has been credited with helping to gain four Senate seats (Magleby, 2001).

Integration of national, state and local parties mark the postreform era in mounting campaigns. National party organizations dominate the raising of money but much of the spending is conducted by state and local organizations. Decisions made at national level allocate resources between and within states. The heavy investment in Florida by both parties reflects the state's national electoral significance. Florida was electorally marginal and potentially pivotal in deciding the outcome of the presidential election. It was also the site of an open seat in the Senate, one of a handful of swing states where control of the chamber could be won or lost. Money is spent at state level but national parties control its use. Spending is concentrated on media campaigns with the national party organizations exerting control to the point of writing the scripts for television adverts (Blumberg, Binning and Green, 1999).

Parties, like candidates, have utilized the internet as a campaign medium. Compared to television, advertising through the web is inexpensive and holds the possibility of reaching the substantial majority of the public who go on-line. Promotion through the web reaches a qualitatively different audience from that of older forms of mass media. Much of the campaign advertising through television, radio and newspapers reaches inadvertent audiences who come upon election promotions by accident. In contrast, discovering websites is more likely to be intentional. The likely audience is the already committed or inquiring voter. Both were catered for by many national and state party sites in 2000. The committed voter was invited to become active in the campaign by using interactive sections to receive e-mail communications, donate money or volunteer for campaign activity. For the inquiring voter (or journalist) there were quantities of information unavailable in other mass media formats. These included issue positions, party platforms, candidate speeches, and calendars of campaign events. Some sites contained audiovisuals such as video clips of candidate speeches. Hyperlinks to the candidates' websites provided an electronic version of the party as intermediary.

Party activists

Party campaign activity is a mix of modern and traditional forms. The former are capital-intensive forms such as television advertising and direct mail, while the latter are intensive activities such as canvassing voters, distributing posters and signs and getting out the vote on election day. These traditional formats are still widely used by local parties, indicating a supply of party activists to perform them (Frendreis and Gitelson, 1999).

Many current party activists are middle-class professionals motivated by issues and causes. They resemble interest group activists and, as the discussion of national convention delegates showed, many party activists are also involved with groups. One recent characterization of party is that it is a network of issue-based participatory activists (Shafer, 1998). Activists not only work for the party, they also help mold it. By participating in primaries, donating money and contacting officials, they shape the party's image, selection of candidates for election and the positions they adopt in office.

Participation in primaries to select election candidates is low, exaggerating the impact of activists who do become involved. In congressional primaries liberals are dominant in the Democrat electorates and conservatives are dominant amongst Republican voters. The winners of primaries tend to be closer to the ideological end of the spectrum than the typical primary voter, particularly in seats where the party is electorally dominant (Powell and Niemi, 2000). Candidates lacking an appeal to activists may struggle to mount viable campaigns (unless they can compensate by spending large amounts of their own money).

The line-up and outcome of the 2000 presidential nominations demonstrates the activist bias in each party. Three Republican candidates, Steve Forbes, Gary Bauer, and Alan Keyes, centered their campaigns on a moral agenda appealing to secular socio-issue conservatives and the Christian right. Though not focusing on socio-issue themes, Bush's stances were consistently conservative in this policy area. When locked in a close contest in South Carolina, Bush made a well-publicized trip to speak at the fundamentalist Bob Jones University, a formerly segregated institution which still barred interracial dating at the time of his visit. John McCain, who emerged as the principal challenger to Bush, embraced conservative positions on all issues except the most salient, campaign reform, a cause which commands public support but little amongst Republican activists. He was a promising candidate for the general election but an improbable Republican nominee.

On the Democratic side the sole challenger to Gore was former Senator Bill Bradley. The two had served together in the Senate, often voting together. But in challenging for the nomination, Bradley aimed to run to the left of Gore, concentrating on liberal issues like child poverty and government provision in health care. But his problem in defeating Gore was his inability to monopolize liberal support. Gore, for example, was backed by liberal unions such as the teachers' National Education Association (NEA). Bradley's performances in early contests, winning a third of the vote in Iowa and 46 per cent in New Hampshire, were eminently credible except when set against press expectations that he could win.

Another source of activist influence is communication with elected officials. Only a minority of voters contact elected officials but their activism is a signal that they are likely to vote in elections, heightening the impact of their views to officials concerned for re-election. A recent likely example of the influence of activists is the Republican persistence in pursuing the impeachment of President Clinton to its conclusion in a Senate vote where failure appeared inevitable. Not only was Clinton's removal unlikely but also its pursuit was electorally unrewarding. Pollsters found most of the public opposed impeachment. The 1998 midterm election delivered an electoral rebuff to the Republicans when the president's party made a midterm gain in the House for only the second time since the Civil War, yet the impeachment process continued.

Conviction politics at the grassroots contributed to congressional Republican solidarity behind impeachment. Republican activists were untypical of the country at large but a force that could not be ignored by the party's members of Congress. When moderate Republican Representative Amo Houghton (R-NY) publicly temporized over whether to vote for the articles of impeachment, he received several hundred critical letters and a threat from a fundamentalist preacher to enter the forth-coming primary if he failed to vote to remove the president. Houghton, and several other previously undecided moderates, duly came into line with the rest of their party. Following the House vote, polls showed two-thirds of voters wanted Clinton to complete his term. Amongst strong Republicans, where the party's activists are concentrated, 75 per cent wanted Clinton to resign. Amongst the Christian Right, there was outrage at Clinton. A Christian Coalition survey found that 84 per cent of evangelicals were more likely to vote because of the scandal. According to the organization's director Randy Tate, "You don't want to stand between an evangelical and the voting booth" (Gerson, 1998).

Responsible parties?

This chapter has identified some sharp divergences between contemporary parties and those of much of the past. The parties of the past were loose confederations of state and local organizations, internally diverse, staffed by pragmatic activists intent on winning elections. Now, in contrast, national directives exert some control over state and local party units in elections; there are marked ideological differences between the two parties' activists; and there are substantial policy differences between the parties' programmes. These characteristics approximate some of the features of responsible parties, championed as instruments of democracy, providing the electorate with clear choices in elections and accountability in government (Committee on Political Parties, 1950).

However, there remain substantial gaps between the contemporary parties and the responsible party model. Distinctive ideological tendencies amongst activists and elected officials do not result in unity around priorities or specific policies. Republicans, for example, differ over the relative importance and electoral rewards of economics over socio-cultural concerns. Within economics, tax cutters compete with budget balancers and proponents of sound money. For all but the most committed ideologue in government, electoral considerations trump principle. Republican conservative legislators' opposition to government usually stops before it damages their constituencies. They pursue pork barrel projects along with other members (Bickers and Stein, 2000).

Election campaigns continue to be shaped to constituency demands, limiting the cohesive effects of national directives. Candidate organizations are dominant in campaign strategy and management. The party campaign is secondary, and does not control the candidate organization. The record, personal qualities and policy stances of the individual candidates dominate the campaigns presented to the electorate, fostering independence in office. The success of candidates who have switched parties but retained their seats – for example, Senators Richard Shelby (R-Alabama) and Ben Nighthorse Campbell (R-Col.) and Representatives Bob Stump (R-Ariz.) and Billy Tauzin (R-La) – demonstrates that electoral security derives from personal rather than partisan assets.

Pragmatism is still the hallmark of party election activities. Services are provided to candidates who can win rather than toe the party line. Party campaign spending is targeted at winnable seats and there is no test of loyalty; neither is issue conformity a condition of assistance. Certain winners and sure losers are largely left to their own devices, obviating any obligation to the party in government amongst the former.

Party programmes are too infrequent to be informative guides for officeholders. National party platforms are usually confined to presidential elections. These manifestos reflect the preferences of the nominee more than the party. It is unlikely that, in the absence of George W. Bush as party nominee, the Republican platform in 2000 would have contained ideas of compassionate conservatism, for example. Congressional party platforms appeared in 1994 and 1996 but have been absent from the two most recent elections.

Conclusions

The vigor parties have shown in adapting to a changing electoral environment is likely to be tested in the near future if campaign finance laws are reformed. It is a test they are likely to pass given their history of ingenuity in adapting to previous changes. A ban on soft money would eliminate the most controversial form of party funding, but only a minority of the totals they raise. Parties are likely to upgrade their already effective hard money-raising activities, and the interests seeking to influence government are likely to respond. Republicans are better placed to adjust because they already raise considerably more in hard money than their opponents. Democrats still lag in generating donations from a mass base of modest-sized contributions. Rancor between the parties is likely to recur. Accumulated past grievances, and the electoral competitiveness of the parties militate against any durable truce. Bipartisanship induced by the dead heat in the presidential election and the need for cooperation in the closely divided Senate was fleeting. The horrors of the attack on the World Trade Center did evoke displays of unity between the congressional parties, but the substance of unity tended to be concentrated in the policies directly related to the crisis. Disputes over more mundane issues like tax cuts quickly surfaced. Policy differences and the pressures of electoral competition are likely to supersede the temporary unity of a national trauma.

Chapter 4

Pressure Groups, Social Movements and Participation

STEPHEN WELCH

Political participation has always been a key issue in American political discourse. James Madison expressed in the famous No. 10 of *The Federalist* anxiety about pressure from "factions" on the new government. As an answer, he produced the novel argument that the very diversity of interests in a large republic would offer some protection against undue pressure (Madison, Hamilton and Jay, 1987). A similar view was expressed by Alexis de Tocqueville in his study of the America of the 1830s (Tocqueville, 1966). For him, the quantity of associational political activity in the United States was both a distinguishing feature and a necessary support of its democratic system.

The meaning of these views is still debated by historians (Schudson, 1998; Wills 1999). Nevertheless, they have set the agenda for all subsequent discussion of the politics of pressure and participation. Some commentators have repeatedly asked whether social diversity is increasing beyond the capacity of the system to absorb it, and whether pressure itself is becoming excessive, leading to governmental inefficiency or, worse, "gridlock." Conversely, others have asked whether the crucial support of popular participation in communal as well as electoral politics remains healthy.

This chapter examines various issues concerning participation and the American political culture. It will look in particular at developments in recent years which seem to be paradoxical. Since the civil rights movement of the 1950s and 1960s, American politics has been struck by waves of new demands for participation and recognition by previously marginalized groups (Freeman and Johnson, 1999). Alongside this, there has been an intensification of the pressure on politicians from organized groups both old and new, which have invented and quickly disseminated innovative techniques of influence. Both the diversity and the pressure envisaged by Madison have increased beyond anything he could have imagined.

Yet against this dual background of expanding and intensifying pressure there has been an anxious debate about a *decline* in American political

53

participation. Levels of electoral turnout, of voluntary group membership and of social interaction itself are all sources of concern for protagonists in this debate, who refer to these and related trends as a decline in "social capital."

The chapter begins with a look at the structural, cultural and social contexts in which these trends have unfolded. It then focuses on the three trends themselves: the expansion of the range of political issues which are pressed on the government, the intensification of the mechanisms of pressure, and the decline in social capital. Finally, it considers whether the apparent contradiction between expansion and intensification on the one hand, and declining participation on the other, can be resolved.

The Structural, Cultural and Social Contexts

When talking about the context of current developments, it is important to guard against the mistake of seeing the present as the only time of dynamic change, and everything prior to it as a static background. The "context" is, after all, nothing less than the sum total of developments and trends up to now. We should expect some "more of the same" (Schlozman and Tierney, 1983); but we should also expect some novel departures and remember that history too contains this mixture of continuity and radical change.

The structural context

By the "structural context" I mean the legacy of institutional sites and mechanisms for pressure and participation. "Federalism" and the "separation of powers" are the conventional descriptions of what makes the political system of the United States distinctive among liberal democracies; their effect is to multiply the number of "access points" for citizens into the political process. An important mechanism for such access is the electoral process. Many of the institutions of American government are exposed to it: many more decision-makers than is the case in most liberal democracies (sheriffs, judges, school board members) are subject to scrutiny and possible rejection by voters. But voting is not the only mechanism for pressure and participation: it is also the case that the larger the number of sites at which decisions are made, the larger the number of points at which political influence outside the electoral process, ("lobbying" in its various forms) can be brought to bear. This can include pressure designed to *resist*, as well as promote, changes in policy (Dahl, 1967).

The basic federal structure established by the Constitution was of course only the starting point for the development of political institutions. These, however, did not develop on their own. Pressures for participation them-selves brought about, in numerous distinct phases, the ramification and multiplication of political institutions (Morone, 1998). Morone highlights an irony in this series of developments as participatory pressure, expressing what he calls the "democratic wish," has often been premised on a deep distrust of established political institutions and their occupants. Its net result, however, has been to create more of them.

The dynamic relationship between participatory pressure and institutional development may be seen at several points in the nineteenth century, perhaps most poignantly in the development of urban "machine politics" in the latter half of the century. While regarded by posterity (and by critics in the period immediately following the "Progressive Era") as a sink of corruption, with its vote-rigging and vote-buying, nepotism and political profiteering, machine politics nevertheless played an important role in incorporating a rapidly increasing number of immigrants into poli-tics. It also delivered a level of electoral turnout that has not subsequently been equaled.

In the twentieth century, Progressive reforms such as the party primary and the initiative and referendum offered new channels of partici-pation, just as they closed down those offered by the urban machine (see Chapter 15). The New Deal of the 1930s enacted new federal pro-grammes, entailing a massive centralization of government; but at the same time it opened up opportunities for the organization of workers that had been denied (with considerable force and violence) up until then. And in the 1960s, as America's welfare provision was expanded through the Great Society programmes, the federal government tried to mobilize bene-ficiaries by creating new local channels of participation – Community Action Agencies – and by sponsoring national organizations around new benefits such as health insurance for the elderly (Walker, 1991; Morone, 1998).

The 1960s also saw a new use of the legal system by pressure groups. This development required a change in the language of politics toward claims based on "rights" ; but once this change had been accomplished, use of the technique of pressing claims on behalf of disadvantaged groups through the courts, including the Supreme Court, grew dramatically. Thus the Supreme Court heard 106 discrimination cases in the period 1946–64 by comparison with only 33 heard in the period 1850–1945 . In short, the opportunities for political pressure and participation, while they have not expanded smoothly and have indeed sometimes contracted along some dimensions, are distinctively large in the United States and are still growing.

Political culture

Political culture is especially prone to being regarded as a fixed background; indeed, political scientists have often seen it as retarding change (Eckstein, 1988). However, the example of the expansion of "rights discourse" as pressure groups developed a litigation strategy shows that political culture can change quite rapidly: as one author puts it, "culture moves" (Rochon, 1998).

Tocqueville's *Democracy in America* pioneered the observation of what was later described as a "participatory political culture." The first substantial empirical study of political culture using the method of the attitude survey, *The Civic Culture*, described the American case in terms of a balance of participatory and deferential attitudes, with a marked tilt toward participation (Almond and Verba, 1989). Morone's tracing of the ebb and flow of the "democratic wish" through American political history also confirms the centrality of both the practice and the ideal of participation.

However, the very fact that pro-democratic and participatory arguments have played a fluctuating role in American political history reveals that they have not been entirely consensual. Indeed, American political historians have since the 1970s drawn attention to the existence of two founding ideologies of the United States, "liberalism" and "classical republicanism" (not to be confused with ideology of the modern Republican Party), which have justified conflicting ways of conducting political debate (Appleby, 1992). The "liberal" strand originally emphasized the value of freedom from government interference, while the "republican" strand stressed the value of political involvement. Occasions in which these values seem to be in harmony are politically potent – perhaps the Revolution itself is the best example –but rare.

More often politics in the United States, as elsewhere, is conflictual, pitching freedom from government against involvement in it. For example, in the mid-1990s a series of television commercials featuring the fictional couple "Harry and Louise" effectively marshaled concerns about freedom from government and restrictions on choice against President Clinton's health plan. Fears about governmental encroachment are illustrated too by the perennial strength of the "gun lobby," a phenomenon which hardly exists in most European countries. A participatory impulse is certainly not the only longstanding feature of the cultural context: it is rivalled by an impulse toward *escape* from government.

The cultural history of American political participation has also had a distinctly religious cast. Two significant twentieth-century examples are the temperance movement that gave rise to Prohibition in the 1920s, which drew support from longstanding tendencies within evangelical

Protestantism, and the civil rights movement of the 1950s and 1960s (Kazin, 1998). One major component of the civil rights movement was Martin Luther King's Southern Christian Leadership Conference, which drew much of its support from Baptist churches with their social networks and organizational resources (Morris, 1984).

Social diversity

All nations are in part constructed through immigration, but the United States is to a far greater extent than most a nation of immigrants. Initially the product of colonization, resulting in displacement of the indigenous population, the United States has experienced massive waves of immigration, even though it has sometimes met sufficient political opposition to attenuate it for a while. The process continues today, with about 9 percent of the population in 1996 born outside the United States (Morone, 1998). This degree of demographic change has inevitably created both problems and opportunities for political participation.

In the late nineteenth and early twentieth centuries, ethnic solidarity, networks of mutual assistance, and indeed cultural links combined with the political opportunities created by mass party politics and the spoils system to create the urban political machine. Religious identities too were much to the fore in this pattern of participation, as first Catholicism, and later Judaism, were markers of significant social disadvantage and discrimination for waves of immigrants from southern and eastern Europe (Hunter, 1991). The abolition of machine politics did not of course abolish the diverse political interests to which it had given expression, and neither has the flow of new immigrants, from new areas and with new interests, abated. Politics in many localities continues to be strongly colored by ethnic difference, despite the myth of the Americanizing melting pot (Glazer and Moynihan, 1970); and ethnic issues affect a number of policy areas, including the politics of crime and policing (see Chapter 11).

Class conflict has not historically provided a base for political mobilization in the United States, a fact which has frequently puzzled observers (Sombart, 1906). The absence of class divisions has sometimes been seen as producing a politics of consensus (Hartz, 1955). However, such interpretations may be a bit too simple, not least because they neglect other forms of political conflict. Moreover, class politics has been not so much absent as channeled through patterns of ethnic politics. This happened, it has been argued, because of the substantial progress that had been made in the institutionalization of political participation through the urban machines prior to large-scale industrialization (Shefter, 1986). Existing patterns of urban politics, resting on the social structure of dense neighborhood ethnic networks, thus limited the development of trade unions, as well as of any distinctive workers' party in America.

The context of participation in the United States – whether one considers the structural, cultural, and social dimensions – has not, therefore, been static. It has unfolded alongside participatory politics itself, creating new channels and new styles of mobilization and organization, for a people whose increasing diversity has often been a source of conflict and thus of democratic energy.

Expanding issues

Identity politics and social movements

The diversity envisaged by Madison was a sectional (that is, geographical) diversity, and a diversity of economic interests. He could not foresee the huge increase in ethnic and religious diversity which nineteenth-century immigration brought. One aspect of ethnic diversity was, however, quite apparent to the Founders: the presence of a population of black slaves in the south. Slaves were referred to in the Constitution, in Article 2, only for the purpose of apportioning electoral representation: each was to be counted as three-fifths of a person; it was not until the 1960s that the descendants of this section of the population were granted fully effective formal political rights, when the federal government enacted civil and voting rights legislation such as the 1965 Voting Rights Act.

This achievement, of course, owed less to the federal government than to the civil rights movement, which can claim to be one of the most significant social movements in American history. The movement began with the Montgomery bus boycott of 1956. It expanded via a range of unorthodox methods of protest such as "sit-ins" (first used during the workers' unrest of the 1930s) to encompass mass demonstrations and various other non-violent provocations (McAdam, 1999). The civil rights movement marks a crucial point in the history of American political participation, and not only because it rectified the longstanding anomaly of black exclusion from the American political system. It did two other things: it established the principle of recognition for excluded groups, and it popularized a repertoire of methods for the pursuit of such demands (A. C. Morris, 1999).

A wide variety of groups have subsequently emulated both the aims and the methods of the civil rights movement. These groups include women's groups, gay and lesbian groups, and groups for people with disabilities. They have had a variety of goals, ranging from the demand for recognition (often involving intense political debate over labels) to demands for various special financial benefits from government and even (in the case of the women's movement) a constitutional amendment. (The women's movement's Equal Rights Amendment was ultimately unsuccessful, reflecting in part the impact of an anti-feminist backlash.) It is these groups' character as "movements" which has attracted the most attention from academic commentators, although this feature has been remarkably difficult to tie down analytically.

In Europe, a contrast could be drawn between the class politics supposedly characteristic of most of the twentieth century and a "new politics" of "new social movements" that began to emerge in the 1960s. Much effort has therefore been devoted by political commentators to explaining what is "new" about these movements (Offe, 1985), but in America this contrast has been harder to draw because of the historically lower visibility of class politics (Plotke, 1995).

Several observers have suggested that what gives a distinctive spin to many of the new demands that have entered the political agenda since about 1980 is their "postmodern" character (Trend, 1997). For many groups, it is no longer sufficient to gain recognition from the authorities in the form of institutionalized consultation with the government. Such recognition would still allow the authorities to impose *their* methods of negotiation, and *their* classification of reality, on the groups in question. Groups have been increasingly concerned not to relinquish control of the power to define themselves and their issues to political or expert authorities, and that is why struggles over labels have been so visible.

The postmodern tendency in intellectual life, which places in question the foundations of knowledge and thus of political legitimacy, has both drawn upon such forms of participation and significantly influenced them. "Queer politics" illustrates these features well. Its adoption of a derogatory and somewhat shocking label as self-description testifies to resistance to dominant evaluations (including those resulting from previous mobilizations by gays and lesbians); and it makes numerous connections with "queer theory" in academia. Within this framework, the organization ACT-UP, which campaigns on AIDS issues, not only practices tactics of disruption, embarrassment and disrespect, but it also seeks to question and undermine the authority of medical as well as political authorities (for example, by campaigning for "fast-track" authorizations for new drug therapies: Aronowitz, 1995).

Anti-globalization protests have been another recent cause for activist celebration (Gill, 2000). While they do not represent marginalized identities in the way that gay activists do, they too have a postmodern character, in that they seek to question a dominant and authoritative discourse that represents the economic costs of intensified global competition as natural and inevitable (Lynch, 1998). They also display a feature which has suggested new lines of development for activism: their heavy use of the Internet. Much of the planning and advertising of anti-globalization protest, contributing to its international character, has been conducted via this new medium (Scott and Street, 2000).

The World Wide Web is the Internet's most visible component, though newsgroups, e-mail and on-line chat can also be used for recruitment and planning purposes. Its great advantage is its cost-effectiveness as a method of publicity. Cheap web design software, usable on any desktop computer, along with cheap rental of space on a commercial web server, registration of a domain name and use of a search engine registration service (total cost a few hundred dollars per year), enable organizers to set up a site which could receive hundreds of thousands of hits per month (Hill and Hughes, 1998). The web drastically lowers the cost of publicity for any form of political participation. Furthermore, it is a largely unregulated medium, allowing free rein in self-definition and self-expression.

Doubt can be raised about the significance of both of these new features of participation, however. Postmodern protest which questions the foundations of knowledge is undoubtedly distinctive in the extent to which it involves a radical section of the academic community (Harris, 1995). But it should be recalled that "Black Power," a later phase of the civil rights movement, undertook the shocking reversal of identity now practiced in queer politics before the "postmodern condition" was fully diagnosed. It has always been necessary for excluded groups first to attract attention. This must mean a constant quest for novelty – by challenging and even affronting the prevailing common sense – which itself (paradoxical though it sounds) becomes conventional.

As for the distinctive contribution of the Internet, Hill and Hughes explain its likely impact in terms of the example of cable television. The capacity of cable television to "narrowcast" was also touted as significant for participatory politics (see also Chapter 17). But cable ended up providing only an increased range of choice. Political activists did, to be sure, make use of it, but they soon had to take their place in the competition for viewers alongside a myriad of niche-oriented lifestyle channels as well as entertainment and news channels owned by the corporate giants of the media industry.

Culture wars

The use of these "new social movements" to illustrate the theoretical arguments of academic postmodernism, as well as "post-Marxist" or nonclass radicalism, has produced a certain bias in analysis. This is the tendency to regard these examples as "progressive" and therefore to disregard similar examples which are not thought to be progressive. But the resulting celebratory tone from writers with generally liberal or left-wing sympathies is misplaced, especially in the American context.

What is distinctive in the United States is the extent to which the new issues that have entered the political agenda since the civil rights movement have been contested. An example is the anti-abortion or "right to life" movement. This movement, or "countermovement" as some analysts prefer to call it, emerged as a reaction to the Supreme Court's *Roe* v. *Wade* decision of 1973, which struck down state prohibitions of abortion (see also Chapter 16). While claiming to model its tactics on those of the civil rights movement, the group Operation Rescue (formed in 1987), whose main initial strategy was to blockade abortion clinics, nevertheless became actively involved in violent confrontations (Johnson, 1999).

In general, right-to-life campaigners have used a variety of strategies, but these include the most extreme: displaying aborted fetuses to crowds of opposing protesters, bomb and arson attacks on clinics in which abortions are performed, and assaults on clinic staff, including murder. Tactics such as these are no less intended to shock and affront than are the tactics of groups such as ACT-UP. Neither are the participants any more inclined than their radical counterparts on the left to be persuaded by the arguments of scientists and other authorities about such issues as the status of the unborn or the benefits of embryological research.

Yet to call these reactionary groups "postmodern" would be absurd. Far from denying the foundations of knowledge and political authority they assert strongly that such a foundation exists. For many of them, this foundation can be summarized in one word: scripture. It is the controversial thesis of James Davison Hunter that a "culture war" between religious orthodoxy and (religious and secular) progressivism now dominates American political discourse and participatory practice (Hunter, 1991). The "progressive" side of this dichotomy is perhaps not very well defined by Hunter, but he does document clearly a convergence among Protestant, Catholic, Eastern Orthodox and Jewish "fundamentalists" whose political positions stem directly from the Old Testament.

This convergence is especially striking in view of the long history of conflict between religious denominations in the United States (which, as we have seen, has been interwoven with ethnic politics). The convergence is also novel in overcoming the traditional distance between churches and politics (Guth *et al.*, 1995). The scene since the 1960s has been quite different: Jewish, Catholic, and Protestant campaigners openly recognize their common interests and outlook, form numerous collaborative campaigning organizations, and can be frequently heard on radio talk shows and national political platforms (including those of the Republican Party). The values such groups are expressing are not new, but their unity and degree of political engagement are.

Judged in terms of the range of issues which now feature on the political agenda, political participation in the United States can seem like nothing short of a cacophony. Disadvantaged groups clamor not only for policy benefits but also for recognition, and in their own terms (often disagreeing volubly with more moderate groups with similar policy goals). They express and seek acceptance of a dizzying variety of lifestyles. Other groups react to the direct threat to their values represented by changes in the role of women in the family and the liberalization of attitudes to sexual behaviour as well as by the increased acceptance of abortion and embryological research. These conservative groups themselves feel marginalized by what they see as a drift towards secularism. Shock tactics, up to and including violence, are utilized on all sides. As Hunter observes, prospects for compromise, let alone reconciliation, between groups on either side of these various cultural struggles seem remote indeed.

Intensifying pressure

Social movements and pressure groups

As noted in the previous section, analysts have tried to understand some of the trends in American political participation since the 1950s by using the idea of "social movements." Implicit in this idea is the suggestion that "conventional" political channels of influence, such as the electoral channel, are bypassed. Social movements, are, however, not the only form outside the realm of party politics which participation can take: we also have to consider the role of interest or pressure groups. Just as the distinction between social movements and pressure groups operates along the dimension of unconventional versus conventional modes of influence, so a similar distinction has usually been made, within the overall category of pressure groups, between "outsider" and "insider" groups, where the insider groups have direct personal contacts with government representatives, and may indeed be sponsored by the government. So there is, in the accepted analytical framework, a set of three categories – social movements, outsider pressure groups and insider pressure groups – which can supposedly be distinguished in terms of their ideological and policy affinity with the government, and therefore in their visibility, extremism and operating style.

Recent developments suggest that this traditional framework is no longer very helpful, at least for the American context. It assumes that we can clearly map differences between tactics and strategies and type of interest, cause or group. Yet the previous section hinted at a general tendency for participation: tactics that work to be copied. If this is true, then we would expect tactics to spread out across the range of groups, making it harder to make categorical distinctions among them. This, I argue, is exactly what is happening.

The generalization of tactics

There is, of course, no doubt that tactics themselves can be differentiated. No one would confuse these two examples of political influence: a conversation with the President over a game of horseshoes about the interests of bass anglers (Loomis and Cigler, 1998), and an anti-globalization demonstration outside a meeting of the G8 group of advanced industrial nations that disrupts the start of a round of trade talks (Halliday, 2000). There is, however, a wide range of modes of participation between these extremes, and these modes are not only harder to classify, but also are increasingly found in *ad hoc* combinations (McAdam, Tarrow and Tilly, 1996; Burstein, 1998).

Sometimes, at least initially, groups have no alternative but to "get noticed" by relevant political authorities, which may involve doing something unconventional or outrageous. But getting noticed itself has a number of different forms, especially in the dispersed political system of the United States. It requires very different actions to get noticed by the Supreme Court, by a Senator, by an official in a federal regulatory agency, and by a local school board. Moreover, between political action and governmental attention lie the news media. A group first has to be noticed by them, in order to have much prospect of being noticed by anybody else. This is likely to require actions that are "newsworthy" according to the particular criteria of the media, but also making contact with media personnel, developing relationships with them, in general becoming media-savvy and media-connected. There is thus a pressure toward a degree of integration with the corporate apparatuses of the news even for the most marginalized or extreme groups.

Another factor which causes a generalization of tactics is the need of organized groups to attract funding. This usually involves some adoption of conventional fundraising methods. Most important for groups which originated as or within social movements is funding via mass membership: that is, by subscriptions. One technique that has been widely copied is that of direct-mail solicitation. The use of computerized direct mail in political campaigning, pioneered by conservative Richard Viguerie in the 1960s, was a development which ranks in importance alongside the innovations of the civil rights movement. Not all groups have the resources to embark on direct mail campaigns, and some maintain principled objections to it, but stark differences in the fortunes and visibility of groups flow from these choices. For example, Greenpeace achieved a peak membership of

1.2 million in 1991, but membership fell to 400,000 by 1997 after the organization reduced its unusually large expenditure on direct mail (Johnson, 1998).

Some groups, or factions within them, resist such pressures, seeing them as cooptation or "sell-out" (Piven and Cloward, 1979). Disagreement on this score has on many occasions caused groups and movements to splinter. The Weathermen, for example, was a short-lived anarchist organization which was the residue of the 1960s group, Students for a Democratic Society. Its source of funding was the unreliable one of bank robbery (Zwerman, Steinhoff and della Porta, 2000). The environmental movement has repeatedly splintered in this way, as Earth First! separated from Friends of the Earth, leaving groups arrayed across a colour spectrum from "deep" to "light green."

Between the extremes of cooptation and radical purism, however, is the less dramatic and more common option of simply extending the repertoire of participation to include more subtle, conventional, or discreet insider techniques *in combination with* tactics designed to retain public and media, and therefore political, visibility. Such combinations of techniques and tactics are typical of contemporary political participation, and not only in the United States (Jordan and Maloney, 1997).

Groups, then, which start out as outsiders, using the unconventional tactics of social movements, face many incentives to extend their tactical repertoire from the "outside in." But a corresponding trend of repertoires extending from the "inside out" has also become apparent. Traditional practitioners of the most "insider" modes of participation, such as corporations, have been moving into more visible and public forms of participation too. This poses potential difficulties analogous to those of the excluded group which seeks to extend its repertoire "inwards," because of the possibility that less discreet forms of pressure may threaten established relationships. Nevertheless a major development in political participation in the United States has been the growth of corporate pressure groups (Plotke, 1992).

Business corporations and their collective organizations have been at the forefront of the most recent developments in the techniques of mobilization. An example of such techniques is the "patch-thru," whereby a potential supporter is telephoned, informed about an issue, and invited to press a number to be connected directly to the office of the relevant legislator in order to register an opinion (Goldstein, 1999). Techniques like this simply extend the existing expertise and resources of corporations in telephone marketing to a political use, just as the technique of direct-mail solicitation was originally borrowed from mail-order marketing.

From the perspective of elected officials, a significant development of the last decade or so has been the erosion of the division between policy-oriented and election-oriented influence. As Goldstein (1999) documents, referring to the case of the Clinton health plan, groups are increasingly targeting their persuasive efforts on decision-makers who are most vulnerable electorally (those who are facing an imminent election, or who have slender majorities). In this way, groups can make most effective use of the techniques of constituency mobilization which they have increasingly adopted, alongside their existing techniques of consulting and advising, direct lobbying, and advertising. Corporations, for instance, increasingly expect employees to support their political interests, by writing letters or helping to publicize issues; but they also increasingly understand, or hire consultants who understand, how best to target such efforts. For the participant groups, this represents the most efficient use of campaigning resources. For Congressional members it represents an intensified threat to political survival, and a strong inducement to support or – as in the case of health care reform – to oppose legislation.

From these examples it is apparent that, while contrasts can still be drawn between different parts of the tactical repertoire, it is no longer tenable to use these contrasts as grounds for differentiating either types of people who use them, or types of issues which demand them. Large parts of the repertoire are shared by widely different groups and interests. Moreover, this sharing cannot fail to increase, as specialized providers of services continue to develop, just as, in earlier decades, specialist lobbying firms and legal practices developed to service political influence. Providers of telephone marketing, direct mail, advertising and public relations constantly increase their capacity to offer specialized and tailored services in politics as elsewhere, and innovations in one sector of the "participation business" will be rapidly diffused to other sectors through the process of market competition.

Overload and hyperpolitics

An environment in which the number of organized groups and the range of issues they are pressing on to the political agenda, as well as their capacity to do so, is increasing, is a difficult one for politicians and other decision-makers. The idea of overload of the American and other political systems under increasing demand from the population was first floated in the 1970s (Crozier, Huntington and Watanuki, 1975). The crisis predicted then did not materialize. However, not only has the agenda continued to expand, but the pressure stemming from the established agenda has also intensified.

It is true that protest has to some extent been tamed, partly by the development of a style of policing that gives greater priority to first amendment rights to free speech, and the elaboration of "public forum law" which specifies how far and in what places such protection is to be given (McCarthy and McPhail, 1998). It of course remains possible for both demonstrators and the police to exceed the terms of this "settlement," as happened in the anti-globalization protests in Seattle in 1999. But irrespective of this perhaps temporary diminution in public protest, pressure on the individual decision-maker has intensified.

A further aspect of intensification is what has been termed "hyperpolitics": the spread of politicization (and therefore its accompanying mobilization) to an ever widening range of points along the decision-making process (Cigler and Loomis, 1998). Rich and Weaver (1998) have documented the accelerated growth in American politics over the last 30 years of the number of "think tanks," especially those with an identifiable conservative or liberal ideology. The effect of this has been the "politicization of expertise", in contrast to an earlier phase in which think tanks were regarded as producers of neutral policy guidance. A further consequence, it is suggested, is to "devalue" the "think tank currency": expert knowledge.

Thus the aim of radical postmodern critics of official knowledge and expertise, to deconstruct it, is ironically being realized by processes within the Washington establishment itself. It is a case of "*de facto* postmodernism," in which all stages of the decision, from the gathering of information to the assignment of committee jurisdictions, are intensely politicized, and in which this politicization exposes the deciders to highly focused and instantaneous (if not indeed pre-emptive) electoral pressure.

Declining social capital

The preceding sections have looked at the factors which have led to the expansion and intensification of the politics of pressure. Social movements and pressure groups have proliferated, generating two tendencies: the *expansion* of pressure involves the entry into politics of a range of new issues and new ways of drawing attention to them; while the *intensification* of pressure involves a sharing of the tactics and techniques of influence and greater sophistication in their efficient targeting.

Can we conclude from all this that political participation is increasing? Surely, as far as politics is concerned, the associational tendency noticed by Tocqueville must by now be reaching fever pitch, yet there emerged during the 1990s a perspective which runs quite contrary to this, and which is thus hard to square with the expansion and intensification of pressure which I have been charting. It suggests that political participation in the United States is in the process of a sharp decline from a high point in the 1940s and 1950s. In this section I will look at this perspective, the "social capital" approach, and its rivals.

Two optimistic perspectives

What many analysts saw as the "advent" of social movements in the 1960s prompted, as already noted, the view that a fundamental change in politics was underway. Even though the transformation to a "new politics" of "new social movements" seemed more striking in Europe, because of the greater salience of class politics there, it has been held to be an American process too (Clark and Hoffman-Martinot, 1998). Two interpretations and explanations of the social preconditions of this process have been widely accepted.

The thesis of "cognitive mobilization" states that "new politics" arises through the mechanisms of increased education and increased flow of information (Dalton, 1996). Rising levels of education give people greater confidence to challenge the authorities, and make them less reliant on political "cues" from these authorities, or from their parents, neighborhood or class. At the same time, the spread of the electronic media, especially television, makes political information more widely available, and exposes people to a range of alternative and critical views. As a result, "more citizens now have the political resources and skills necessary to deal with the complexities of politics and make their own political decisions" (Dalton, 1996).

Another perspective is provided by the thesis of "postmaterial values." The suggestion here is that the expansion of the political agenda stems from an underlying change in political goals. These are said to have shifted, as new generations replace old, from the supposedly materialistic and redistributive goals of class politics to new "postmaterial" goals concerning "belonging, self-expression, and quality of life" . Ronald Inglehart, the principal author of this theory, claims that steadily rising levels of material wealth provide people with "formative security" in their youth, which in adulthood enables them to turn attention to postmaterial issues. Examples are the environment, or issues surrounding self-expression in sexual behavior and lifestyle choice.

This view, while it differs as to the causes of change, is compatible in its implications with the cognitive mobilization thesis. Indeed the two taken together suggest that a new range of issues has entered politics (as "postmaterial" generations mature) just as citizens' capacities and confidence to press these issues on the government has been increasing. More effective pressure, across a broader front, is the expectation. In contrast to fears about governmental overload, Dalton and Inglehart take the view that such trends are progressive, and that government's adaptation to them will be both possible and beneficial. Support for this optimistic view has come from a recent set of studies entitled *Critical Citizens*, whose main claim is that while there is an increased propensity for citizens of Western countries to question and criticize government, this propensity is found predominantly among those citizens who are most supportive of the basic values of democracy (Norris, 1999).

The social capital perspective

Such arguments have rested largely on generalizations across liberal-democratic systems. A quite different perspective, which focuses on the American case, has been developed since the mid-1990s by Robert Putnam and others, using the concept of "social capital." This is a rather broad concept which has been given a number of different definitions, but in Putnam's usage it refers to "connections among individuals – social networks and the norms of reciprocity and trustworthiness that arise from them" (Putnam, 2000). The emphasis on "connections among individuals" explicitly evokes comparison with the "associational life" that Tocqueville noticed with approval as a peculiarity of America in the 1830s.

Putnam's findings as to the vitality of that associational life run in the opposite direction to what we would expect from the cognitive mobilization and postmaterialism theses, and on the face of it this seems difficult to reconcile with the expansion and intensification of political pressure that has been traced in this chapter. Putnam finds declines in participation almost everywhere he looks. By the late 1990s, he reports, in summary:

- electoral turnout is down by one quarter on its most recent peak of 63 per cent in 1960;
- levels of political knowledge have remained static despite considerable increases in levels of university education;
- while community groups and pressure groups have increased in number, average membership is now 10 per cent of its level in 1962, and more than half of recorded groups have no individual membership at all;
- church attendance is down 10–12 per cent since 1975, and involvement in church activities other than worship is down 25–50 per cent;
- trade unions have experienced a 35 per cent drop in membership since 1980, and now cover only 14 per cent of the labour force; only half of the decline is accounted for by the decline of union-intensive industries;
- informal social interaction, as measured by time diary studies, and active involvement in team sports, are both much reduced.

It is easy to see where these findings contradict the optimistic expectations of the cognitive mobilization thesis: neither levels of political knowledge nor overall levels of participation have increased in parallel with rapid rises in education levels. Where increases are apparent, for instance in the number of organized groups, Putnam makes the further argument that the nature of membership of such groups undercuts the idea that this represents increased participation. Membership is often "checkbook" membership, solicited through direct mail campaigns. And this does not represent the significant commitment that the postmaterialism thesis would lead us to expect. Groups face annual "churn rates" in their membership of typically 30 per cent (P. E. Johnson, 1998), necessitating continual efforts at replacement of members. Increasingly, national membership organizations lack local chapters, so that members are tied, if to anything, to "common symbols, common leaders, and perhaps common ideals, but not to each other" (Putnam, 2000).

Putnam suggests that such groups, relying on checkbook participation and resting on a foundation not of the grassroots but of "Astroturf," should be seen as a distinct form of association. They are not the "secondary associations" of the Tocquevillian tradition (so called because they surround the "primary association" of the family) but "tertiary associations." Tertiary associations, unlike their precursors, neither draw on, nor create, social capital. They do not mediate structurally between the individual and the state, or provide any practice in social or political cooperation. They are thoroughly compatible with the society of sedentary isolated individuals which Putnam seems to fear America is becoming.

If Putnam's findings contradict the theses of cognitive mobilization and postmaterialism, what is their relationship with the more general pattern of expanding and intensifying political pressure outlined in earlier sections of this chapter? It should first be noticed that Putnam's book is not in the main about *political* participation: it devotes only two chapters out of twenty-four to the direct political implications of declining social capital. For the most part, the political consequences are left for the reader to infer.

In one of these chapters, Putnam speaks of associations (not tertiary ones of course) as "schools for democracy": incubators of skills of negotiation and persuasion, and norms of tolerance. Yet he also notes that groups of like-minded people do not necessarily provide these benefits: there can be "bad" social capital as well as good, as when extremists band together and simply reinforce one another's views. In this connection his finding that in faith-based political participation, as well as in participation more generally, it is the moderately committed who have been disproportionately dropping out is significant. This has left more committed and hence perhaps extreme participants to themselves. Thus a moderating influence on political participation has been eroding.

Putnam has more to say about the *causes* of the decline of social capital. His exhaustive survey produces conclusions which again direct attention away from politics. He attributes half of the decline to generational replacement, and about a quarter to the deleterious effects of television viewing. The first of these is of course an incomplete explanation, and insofar as it conveys the blame on to the second (when we ask what is different about younger generations that makes their emergence into adulthood such a depleter of social capital), Putnam's arguments about television are unconvincing. Uslaner (1999) finds that a fuller statistical analysis eliminates most of the explanatory potential of this factor. His own statistics, however, lead to the suggestion that more team sport, not less television viewing, is the answer to declining social capital. Neither of these simple and reductive suggestions seems to get close to capturing the *political* significance of the trends Putnam has identified.

Another tack would be to try to explain not the decline of social capital since 1960, but the *high* level it displayed between 1940 and 1960. Putnam does venture a suggestion on this: "World War II occasioned a massive outpouring of patriotism and collective solidarity. At war's end those energies were redirected into community life . . . By the late 1950s, however, this burst of community involvement began to tail off." Consistent with this suggestion, Putnam has asked in the wake of terrorist attacks on the United States whether these benefits can be recaptured:

> Since Sept. 11, we Americans have surprised ourselves in our solidarity. Roughly a quarter of all Americans, and more than a third of all New Yorkers, report giving blood in the aftermath of the attacks. Financial donations for the victims and their rescuers have reached almost $1 billion. Attendance at places of worship has increased.

He urges the government to support such stirrings of social capital. But this view, while it is a commendable attempt to find a silver lining in a particularly ominous cloud, like Putnam's explanation of the decline seems to place the problem of social capital outside the realm of politics.

It may be worth asking whether, far from contradicting the trends of expanded and intensified pressure, the trend of declining social capital (at least in its political aspects) may in fact be closely related to them. This is indeed already hinted at by Putnam's discussion of the erosion of the moderate middle of political participation, which recalls the "culture wars" between the orthodox and the progressive depicted by Hunter. As extreme forms of participation beget a reaction from their cultural opponents, they may at the same time drive out and alienate the less committed. In this way, expansion of the agenda can readily coincide with the decline of political social capital.

Something similar can be said about the intensification of pressure brought about by the generalization of tactics and competition to target pressure most efficiently. The intensive politics of pressure that results might itself be one of the things that is driving participants away, especially when it intrudes in the form of the unwanted "cold call" at dinner time, or the not-very-optional invitation by the citizen's employer to join in a letter-writing drive to a legislator. Thus the explanation for trends in political participation may lie not in extra-political factors like television viewership or involvement in team sports (or the cure for it in foreign wars), but in processes inherent in the recent development of political participation itself.

Conclusion

The arguments of Madison and Tocqueville about the politics of pressure and participation continue to resonate. Expanding and intensifying pressure from a broadening of the agenda and a sharing of tactics and techniques of influence raises concerns about the stridency of political discourse and the decision-making capacity of political institutions. In turn, the nature of popular political participation is intensely debated. The most influential recent view, though it has not gone unchallenged (Schudson, 1998), is that a decline in the quality and quantity of political participation has been underway for several decades.

However, the social capital thesis, despite appearances, is not incompatible with the trends of expansion and intensification of the politics of pressure. Taking a more specifically political rather than broadly sociological view of social capital suggests the possibility that the decline in certain forms of political participation may indeed be a reaction to the expansion and intensification of political pressure: to the apparent nonnegotiability of "culture wars", and to the entrapment of decision-makers in Washington "hyperpolitics". With such a view of the politics of pressure and participation we can begin to address the contemporary puzzle of expansion, intensification *and* decline.

Chapter 5

The Presidency

JONATHAN HERBERT

The presidency George W. Bush inherited in January 2001 is an institution struggling to maintain influence in an increasingly difficult environment. To achieve leadership in its separated system of government, an American president must confront a re-assertive Congress characterized by increasing partisanship; he must decide how to manage substantial interest group pressure; he must deal with an increasingly intrusive media that prefers to focus on sensational stories; and he must attempt to inspire a largely uninterested public. Yet the presidency has, under Clinton's and the younger Bush's stewardships, also demonstrated notable resilience to attack and continuing status as an institution from which leadership can be achieved.

The decline of the presidency?

Academic discussion of the presidency, has focused on a long-term decline in presidential power since the 'Imperial Presidency' period of the 1960s (Schlesinger, 1974). The 1970s were marked by extensive discussion of a diminished, or "no win" presidency (Heclo and Salamon, 1981; Light, 1991). After the twin disasters of Vietnam and Watergate, the presidency found itself in disrepute, and Congress was quick to re-assert its power through such measures as the 1972 Case Act, the War Powers Resolution of 1973 and the 1976 National Emergencies Act, all of which reduced presidential discretionary powers in foreign policy. Further reforms reduced presidential power to reorganize the executive branch and to control the spending practices of executive departments and agencies. Legislators also made Congress better equipped to resist presidential initiatives. Funds were allocated to run a Congressional Budget Office (CBO), providing legislators with expert advice in budget planning. The Congressional Research Service (CRS) was augmented and funds allocated to increase the size of legislators' staffs. More crucially, Congress launched a series of internal reforms that dispersed legislative power among a greater number of legislators than in preceding decades. The power of congressional elder statesmen was weakened and subcommittees were given substantial independent powers. To persuade Congress to pass his chosen bills, the president thereafter had to earn the support of more than a key group of influential committee chairmen; rather, he had to garner support from numerous subcommittee chairmen. Consequently, presidents found it harder to persuade Congress to convert proposed bills into law.

Broader factors also undermined presidential power during the 1970s. The decline of parties reduced the influence of a tool that had proved useful to presidents. As party identification declined in the electorate, presidents lost the ability to call upon that identification as a means of rallying support in elections. Furthermore, the same rallying cry was undermined as a means to win congressional support. The rise of television and changes in campaign finance laws allowed legislators to become increasingly independent of their parties during election campaigns. Hence, once elected, legislators had less reason to feel indebted to their party, and had less reason to listen to the pleading of the party's nominal leader, the president. The parties' decline was mirrored by the rise of interest groups. These groups multiplied rapidly over the 1970s, providing opportunities for the expression of a range of special concerns. Parties' behavior had been moderated by the demands of practical politics: and parties reconciled different viewpoints and pursued popular appeal to win elections. Specialist interest groups faced no such restraint, exposing presidents to a new range of pressures. Presidents of the 1970s faced a system in which power was more fragmented, and therefore more difficult to influence, than ever before.

Many expected the presidency to suffer even further in the 1980s. Briefly, Ronald Reagan's triumph in passing his 1981 Economic Recovery Act confounded these predictions: the Reagan transition was cited as evidence of the presidency's rehabilitation. Yet, as the USA enters a new century, scholars regard the office as weaker still. In retrospect, Reagan's success appears a mere anomaly in the decline of presidential power. The 1990s brought numerous assaults upon the power of the institution and its occupant.

Traditionally, presidential scholars regarded the office as far more powerful in foreign policy than domestic policy, leading to suggestions that there were "two presidencies": one in each policy field (Wildavsky, 1975). Presidential pre-eminence in foreign policy was thought, at least in part, to be rooted in the unusual circumstances of the Cold War. The presence of a clearly identifiable and powerful adversary in the international system generated deference to the president. The Chief Executive was not only a national figurehead, but also was regarded as the only participant in the fragmented political system whose position allowed him to implement a coherent policy to address a crisis. Hence, legislators were willing to defer to presidential leadership. However, the Soviet Union's collapse removed the enemy, and although China and various rogue states, such as Iraq and North Korea, are seen to pose threats, none of the associated tensions matched the intensity of the Cold War. Consequently, congressional deference to the president in foreign policy has lessened. Globalization has also weakened this deference. As the Cold War ended, the development of communications and transport technology allowed the acceleration of the trend toward a global economy. Economic changes rendered the well-being of the US economy even more dependent on economic activity across the world. Trade issues assumed a new prominence, giving domestic economic interests reason to demand involvement in the foreign policy-making process. Thus, when Clinton advocated the North American Free Trade Agreement (NAFTA) in 1993, he found himself resisting the demands of the labour unions, long-term Democratic sympathizers, who feared that manufacturing jobs would be lost as a result. Clinton's inability to maintain the fast-track authority long associated with the presidency was a significant blow. Until 1994, Congress had delegated negotiation of some trade pacts to the president, but refused to renew the authority for Clinton. Legislators have less reason to defer to presidential leadership in foreign policy due to both the end of the Cold War and globalization.

The presidency faced more fundamental problems in dealing with Congress during the 1990s. Many, including the media, some legislators, and the public, look to the president to lead Congress, hoping that he will steer a chosen agenda of policies through the legislative branch. Given the separated nature of the American system, and hence the president's limited formal power over Congress, fulfilling these expectations would be no small feat. The rise of the filibuster in the Senate has made this task harder, and more fundamental problems have developed due to the hardening of partisanship during the 1990s (see Chapter 6).

Traditionally the filibuster was used sparingly but in the 1990s it became a standard weapon in the minority party's armoury. Clinton's economic stimulus package of 1993 had to be withdrawn in the face of threatened Republican filibuster. Presidents advocating new agendas now face the Senate minority's increased power to block reforms, and accordingly must address the concerns of that minority.

The problem of increased partisanship is even more significant. Greater partisanship complicates presidential attempts to build coalitions behind bills. Majorities are usually won by working with one party's legislators as a base and trying to chip enough opposition party moderates away from the colleagues. With heightened partisanship, more legislators are likely to stay loyal to their parties' ideologically rooted positions, leaving fewer moderates to woo and making coalition-building harder.

The partisanship problem was compounded by the contrast between a polarized Congress and a centrist president. Clinton ran as a centrist to win in 1992 and 1996 but then faced challenges to his New Democrat policies from his own Democratic party base. The electorate's preferences – for example, on the budget and on crime – forced Clinton to look to the centre ground while the demands of coalition-building required that he maintain a party base (Quirk and Hinchliffe, 1996).

Augmented partisanship and changes in Senate practice further reduced presidents' ability to use an "insider" strategy of negotiation and bargaining to build congressional coalitions. However, presidents may also adopt the "outsider" strategy of "going public" to pressure legislators into supporting bills. Here, the president exploits legislators' desire to be re-elected. The president attempts to generate public popularity for both himself and his policies. Presidents calculate that their popularity will make legislators reluctant to oppose presidential policies since legislators will not want to alienate constituencies needed for re-election. Hence, the legislator is pressured into supporting the president's bill (Kernell, 1997).

During the last decade, the president's ability to go public has been reduced. The option of an outsider strategy became available due to the development of the mass media. Franklin Roosevelt could deliver his famous fireside chats and expect a high percentage of the nation to hear his words. Kennedy could televise his first press conference knowing that the television companies would jump to cover the event. Over the 1990s, the structure of the mass media changed sharply. (see Chapter 17). The rise of specialized news networks, local programming and the Internet have given consumers far more control over the type of material they view. Network news services have had to respond to the developing competition. Rather than news being provided as a public service, bulletins must compete for higher viewing figures. Arguably, this competition has led to a more sensation-oriented approach to mainstream news, and these changes have presented presidents with three types of problem. First, rallying support from the public depends on being able to communicate with that public, but some sections of the public have become very hard to reach as the "narrowcasting" of specialist networks isolates viewers from main-stream news coverage. Less than 50 percent of the US population now rely upon the major networks for their news coverage, so presidents face a tougher challenge in communicating with the population (Neustadt, 2001) Second, these new media outlets pose a logistical challenge. The president depends upon favorable coverage of his message by the media, and there-fore he must maintain good relations with journalists. Given a vastly increased number of journalists, many of whom now have specialist inter-ests, and the 24-hour nature of the services, the presidency must now provide a constant flow of stories to satisfy journalists' needs. The third problem develops from this constant coverage. Presidents may be overex-posed. Presidents' public appearances were once exceptional, which allowed presidents to expect public attention for these rare events. Hence, the White House could choose the priorities to emphasize. Now, constant presidential coverage makes it very difficult for the White House to emphasize priorities amid the "background noise" of everyday presidential coverage. The Clinton team failed to establish new tools to transmit clear priorities. Most networks even refused to give Clinton free time for a televised nationwide address during 1995. Instead, networks have more scope to choose the stories they wish to cover, meaning that presidential priorities may be submerged by journalists' preferences.

Hence, just as insider strategies have become more difficult, changes in the media industry have weakened presidents' ability to pursue an outsider strategy. Public expectations of presidential leadership remain high, but the presidency's capacity to make the system respond to those expectations has been substantially diminished (Raichur and Waterman, 1993; Neustadt, 2001).

Clinton and the defensive presidency

While these damaging institutional changes have occurred, the presidency has also remained a highly personalized institution shaped by the conduct of the incumbent. Indeed, some analysts comment that the institution has never been more personalized than during Clinton's term (S. J. Wayne, 1999). Thus Clinton is alleged to have contributed to the institution's decline.

Most obviously, Clinton was dogged by scandal. He burst on to the national scene in 1992 accompanied by accusations of draft-dodging, pot-smoking and philandering. Travelgate, Whitewater and the Lewinsky scandal, among others, followed. After nine years' incessant scrutiny of his personal morality, Clinton left office issuing controversial last-minute pardons, notably to Marc Rich, former husband of a major contributor to the Clinton Library project. Strongly backed by the Republican Party, many observers accused Clinton of bringing his office into disrepute.

Yet, the scandals' long-term impact upon the presidency seems limited. Despite following Andrew Johnson to become only the second president impeached, Clinton's personal popularity remained high. Indeed these ratings may well have saved him, as legislators proved reluctant to dismiss a well-liked president. Furthermore, public respect for the presidency as an institution quickly recovered once the impeachment process was complete (Simmons, 2001a). Ironically, the impeachment may have rendered the office more resilient in the face of congressional attack. Clinton's survival, combined with the public perception that the conflict was on partisan, rather than moral, grounds, did much to discredit the Republicans who pursued the case. In the subsequent midterm elections, Democrats performed unexpectedly well. Most remarkably, polling suggested a surprising precedent: the public proved willing to separate judgements about Clinton's personal morality from assessments of his effectiveness as president. They saw the president as personally flawed, but rather good at his job, and were content to let him continue in office. Such evidence may give pause for thought to those who would launch similar investigations in future.

Clinton's personal behavior may not have damaged the office irreparably, but his tactics as president have suggested major changes in the way the office is pursued. The congressional elections of 1994 delivered Clinton a crushing blow. He faced a Republican Congress that was unsympathetic to his policy priorities, and many regarded Clinton as a lame duck awaiting an inevitable Republican triumph in 1996. Instead, Clinton won re-election in 1996, kept office despite the impeachment process and retired with a popularity rating of 67 percent (Gallup, 2001). His successful strategy in resisting the assertive Congress after 1994 suggests that the presidency remains an influential office, even under adverse conditions.

A prime feature of Clinton's presidency has been his "campaigning to govern." This term embodies the idea that presidents use insider strategies far less than before, but instead frequently resort to going public in the search for influence over other participants in the political system. Clinton repeatedly applied his talent for dealing with the public. His average of 550 speeches and appearances a year was exceptional (Bettelheim, 2001). He also employed new approaches to sell his message. For example, his use of the town hall meeting format was transferred straight from the campaign to his presidency. However, Clinton's campaigning to govern amounted to more than increased public exposure. Again paralleling campaign tactics, the president maintained an unusually vigilant eye on public opinion. He spent unprecedented resources on polling and focus groups (Jones, 1996; D. Morris, 1999; Gergen, 2000). He also highlighted the interaction between politics and policy, hosting weekly White House meetings to discuss different subjects.

Some, including many on the right of the political spectrum, interpreted these actions as a betrayal of the presidential office. They regarded Clinton as a charlatan who, trading on his personable nature, targeted personal popularity and re-election above political principle. Rather than taking risks by attempting to educate the public on his policy preferences, Clinton followed public opinion slavishly. On this view, Clinton selected policies as a campaigning tool, creating an agenda to maximize his chances of re-election.

Others argue that Clinton used this strategy of "cutting with the grain" precisely because the institutional changes of the 1990s, described earlier, left him little alternative (Rockman, 2000). Facing a separated system in which Congress held all the strong cards, increased partisanship and a changing media, the president was forced to campaign to govern, because he had no hope of finding political influence elsewhere. Clinton was reduced to identifying problems, explaining the issues, offering solutions that were popular, and then grabbing whatever credit might be available once the legislature had taken action. As one authority has noted "the president has been shorn of any power to lead and thus has been reduced to acting as a, 'designator and certifier'" (Jones, cited by Bettelheim, 2001)

These interpretations overlook Clinton's notable achievements between 1995 and 2001. Clinton's presidency did not mark the demise of presidential policy leadership. On the contrary, the Clinton years serve to demonstrate the formidable power of the presidency as an instrument of obstruction, when placed in the right hands. Despite a relatively united Republican Party in Congress, Clinton proved capable of undermining both the initiatives and leaders of his opponents. By combining a delicately calibrated veto strategy, a concerted public campaign, and extensive use of executive orders, Clinton not only blocked many Republican reforms, but emerged from the conflict with substantial victories.

As Clinton contemplated the wreckage after the electoral storm of 1994, the veto appeared one of the few powers he had left as chief executive. Normally merely a tool applied by presidents to block legislation they dislike, Clinton's use of the veto proved crucial to his recovery. The key moment proved to be the budget battle of 1995–96. The Republicans proposed substantial cuts in funding for a range of programmes and agencies. Clinton, who was expected to sign the appropriations bills or lose popularity for vetoing them, spotted a chink in the Republican armour. A number of the cuts could be presented to the public in a manner that would discredit the Republicans. For instance, Medicare reforms could be presented as an assault upon federal support for the elderly. Cuts in the Environmental Protection Agency (EPA) budget were easy to portray as threatening the environment. Clinton succeeded in depicting himself as the centrist resisting the risky budget cuts of the strident, radical Republicans. Vitally, he won the battle of public opinion. Republican Party ratings dropped sharply during the battle, and much of their momentum was lost. The 1996 elections did not generate further Republican gains, and Dole's campaign for the presidency rarely threatened the incumbent. Clinton's victory left a permanent mark on the GOP psyche: he had persuaded his opposition that they could not afford another budget showdown.

This victory allowed Clinton phenomenal influence in the budget process, despite being a president of the minority party. Within reason, as long as he chose battlegrounds where he could make the Republicans look dangerously radical, Clinton knew he could veto their appropriations bills without having his bluff called. Over his second term, Clinton chose a series of popular positions, such as his desire to establish a new health-care initiative to protect children (see Chapters 12 and 13). Republicans were forced to adopt his proposals. The 2000 budget process demonstrated this strategy in action. Clinton vetoed five of Congress's 13 spending bills, knowing he would trigger a potential showdown. He demanded increased spending on his priorities of hiring more teachers and community police, funding for the United Nations (UN) and resources for the purchase of environmentally sensitive land. Congress, "held hostage" by the experience of 1995–96, accepted the changes (Allred, 2001). After his public relations victory of 1995–96, Clinton succeeded in turning the veto into a creative tool to achieve additional spending for his priorities.

While innovative in his use of the veto, Clinton also resorted to a more traditional tool of presidents facing an opposition Congress: executive action. Clinton issued a plethora of executive orders and new regulations, building up to a particular peak during his final months in office. During his last year, Clinton issued orders to make federal programmes more accessible to non-English speakers, create new national monuments, and protect areas without road links from economic development. New regulations on workplace safety were also established and time limits were imposed on insurers to prevent excessive delays in decision-making on medical claims. Clinton employed executive action to make public statements of his policy positions without having to confront the legislative process, and thus won his issues public attention. Furthermore, he presented Republicans with an unpleasant challenge: either to accept the president's actions or to endure the long and politically risky process of legislating against his popular positions.

Despite the apparent decline of the presidency, the final years of Clinton's term suggest that the institution is far from irrelevant yet. Given a well-placed opposition, Clinton still managed to use the tools available to him as president to execute a defensive strategy protecting his own position and blocking many Republican initiatives. The victory was not comprehensive. The Democrats were forced to make concessions in response to many significant Republican objectives on the way, notably welfare reform and a quicker schedule to balance the budget. Yet, by careful application of a veto strategy and victory in the public relations battle, Clinton was able both to assert some control over the public agenda, and even to make substantial progress in winning extra federal dollars for his policy objectives.

However, Clinton's successes were achieved as a president in adverse circumstances. His primary achievement was to use his position to resist his opposition's reforms, rather than to advance his own ideas.

His experience tells us little about the ability of a president to initiate change. As Bush took office, observers emphasized that the presidency had been fundamentally weakened and that Bush would be denied the opportunity to lead. Optimists, including Bush himself, noted that the office remained highly individual, allowing a new occupant to reinvent the presidency.

Prospects for presidential leadership under Bush

A presidency's success is not merely the function of the office's power and the abilities of the incumbent. Charles O. Jones reminds us that presidents are created unequal: each faces a set of historical and institutional circumstances peculiar to his time. Jones considers criteria including the size of election victory, the congressional strength of the president's party, the new president's experience of Washington, and the degree of contrast between the newcomer and his predecessor (Jones, 1994). One might add that the public will be focused on a number of specific policy problems. There may be disagreement over the methods the federal government should apply to address policy problems (Skowronek, 1993). Each of these factors will influence a president's ability to exert policy leadership, quite apart from his own talents. Hence, to analyse George W. Bush's opportunities for leadership, his strategic conditions must be considered (Kernell, 1997). In Bush's case, it appears that some presidents are more unequal than others.

A decisive win in the 2000 election would have created the impression that Bush had a public mandate for both himself and his policies, thus improving his opportunity to lead. Unfortunately for the new president, he faced the perception that he was not even the popular choice for the office (see Chapter 2). Bush's legitimacy was called into question from the beginning, a fact underlined by the protesters who greeted his inaugural parade with banners reading "Hail to the Thief." Certainly he appeared to enter the presidency with little political capital.

Decisive victories for the GOP in Congress would also have assisted Bush. Ideally, voters encouraged by the Bush campaign would have selected increased majorities for Bush's party in both chambers. Even better, those elected would have shared Bush's ideological preferences. Bush, with a substantial number of natural allies, many of them indebted to him for his campaigning, would then have been in a good position to lead a highly sympathetic Congress. Instead, Republicans lost seats in the House in 2000 and soon lost their fragile control of the Senate as a result of Jeffords's defection. Even if Bush managed to maintain the support of his entire party on any one vote, he would still need to win ten defections from the Democrats to overcome a Senate filibuster. Bush was in no position to assume command over Congress.

Public agreement on the priorities facing America might also have aided Bush, as long as those priorities correlated with the new president's concerns. Ideally, a president has laid the policy groundwork during the campaign, identifying problems and popularizing his chosen policy responses to those problems. Such a campaign, backed by a victory, would legitimize the president's agenda. The 2000 campaign did not serve this purpose. Both presidential candidates struggled to capture the public's imagination. Bush's policy agenda was dominated by his promise of a $1.3 trillion tax cut, but polling figures indicate that this idea failed to ignite widespread enthusiasm (Simmons, 2001b). Instead, Bush's victory was earned through the personality he projected and his pledges to pursue a different style of government, a pledge which resonated well with a public disillusioned by the partisan wrangling of the preceding decade. Bush's themes of bipartisanship and "compassionate conservatism" presented the candidate as a moderate. Neither theme, though, involved a great deal of policy substance. As 2000 ended, there was no national crisis to address, and the public remained greatly divided over national priorities. Bush faced the difficult challenge of persuading public and legislators alike that they should be excited by his programme.

Finally, Bush was confronted with an unusually short transition. Legal cases contesting the election prevented Bush from claiming the presidency until 13 December 2000 so that his transition period was sliced in half. The transition provides crucial preparatory time for a new president. Not only must he recover from the strains of campaigning, but he must appoint a new administration, organize a White House staff, write an inaugural speech, develop public stature and image, dismantle a campaign team, establish new relationships with potential allies in Washington and decide legislative and budgetary priorities (Pfiffner, 1996; Jones 1998) Although Bush was able to make some decisions before Gore conceded, many tasks were impossible before the result was made definitive. The Republicans were denied access to transition resources, and potential appointees were hard to approach when offers of administration jobs were still conditional.

Bush's strategic circumstances appeared poor. The specific historical circumstances surrounding his rise to power appeared to reinforce, rather than compensate for, the weakened state of the institution. However, Republicans could cite three reasons for optimism.

First, Bush became the first president since the 1960s to enter office enjoying "surplus politics." The federal budget deficit had so dominated the political topography of the 1990s that the period has been labeled one of "deficit politics" (Jones, 1994). The deficit, $300 billion at its 1992 peak, had sharply restrained discussions of new spending programmes. In contrast, Bush took office amid projections of handsome surpluses, suggesting potential for significant new programmes or tax cuts. Concerns over the economy's health, and therefore the surplus's, qualified the enthusiasm but Bush was presented with the unusual opportunity of holding federal dollars to spend.

Second, Bush was understandably buoyed by his status as the first Republican president to enjoy unified government since 1952. Although academic discussion of the impacts of unified and divided government continues, Bush was undoubtedly happier to see his party controlling both houses of Congress than giving power to the Democrats. In the Senate, control had only been achieved through an unprecedented power-sharing agreement, but the Republicans – initially at least – still held the crucial ability to schedule business, thus deciding which issues would receive attention and in what order.

Third, Bush may have felt that he would not be exposed to all of the pressures Clinton endured. Leadership is different for Republicans. While Clinton was beholden to a wide range of Democratic constituencies, the Republican base consists of fewer interests. This narrow base makes it easier for the party to maintain focus on a few priorities and budgetary discipline. Furthermore, the Republicans have a long-established tendency to look to the executive branch for leadership. As head of a "monarchy driven party" Bush could expect a better response to his leadership than Clinton had experienced (Bettelheim, 2001).

Overall, however, the prognosis for a Bush presidency was unfavorable. Using Jones's criteria of assessment, the dismal election result, Bush's limited Washington experience, the tight Congressional numbers, and the vitality of the agenda all tilted against Bush's ability to lead. Surplus politics, unified government and Republican unity did not outweigh the diminished state of the office. Indeed one observer thought Bush was "in the weakest position of anyone elected to the presidency in modern times" (Broder, 2000).

Bush's strategic options

During the transition, Bush and his team had to craft a response to these largely adverse circumstances. A strategy was required to maximize achievement of the president's objectives within the awkward context he faced. A series of fundamental and interlinked decisions had to be made about presidential strategy: the president had to decide how he would approach Congress; he had to choose principles and targets to underpin his dealings with the public; and he needed to select a policy agenda, assessing both that agenda's size and its ambition.

Jones claims that combinations of strategic conditions often lead to specific presidential tactics. Presidents facing similar conditions will employ similar strategies and Jones identifies five distinct strategies each associated with a particular set of conditions. These strategies are assertive, compensatory, custodial, guardian or restorative (Jones, 1994). Applying Jones's model suggested that for Bush to adopt an assertive strategy, promoting radical policy proposals from the start, would have been ill-advised. Journalists agreed. *Congressional Quarterly Weekly Report* (CQWR) predicted that Bush would step back from his more ambitious election promises, as "an excessively bold agenda or assertive style could quickly result in gridlock" (Bettelheim, 2001).

Instead, Bush was expected to follow a compensatory strategy. He would be forced to "devise supplementary means for authenticating his leadership" (Jones, 1994). Lacking adequate resources, he required new sources of power in the system before he could advance his policies. The primary target of most compensatory strategies is public support: high poll ratings can command legislators' respect, thus underpinning presidential legitimacy. To achieve this popularity, the president must build his personal image carefully. He must show himself to be an effective leader quickly, and therefore he must achieve noteworthy legislative successes early in his term. Often, these successes will come at the expense of presidential discretion in choosing preferred policies. The president must be willing to choose items that Congress has already discussed thoroughly and is therefore more ready to pass. Facilitating the passage of pre-prepared measures is more likely to garner victories than attempting to force bold innovations upon unprepared legislators. The president must also be willing to sacrifice policy principles to the greater goal of achieving passage: readiness to compromise is key. Of course, the legislation must be popular with the public. Again, the president should be expected to subordinate his own policy priorities, instead tracing public sentiment and responding through action on issues of most public concern and in ways the public will find sympathetic. However, the victorious candidate should endeavor to extend successful campaign themes into his presidency. This extension will help legitimize the president's leadership, as he will be seen to be fulfilling the pledges that earned him victory (Pfiffner, 1996). Therefore, presidents following a compensatory strategy must address a difficult tension: at one level, the president must be seen to drive his own campaign ideas forward, as these won the election; but at a second level, those ideas did not do enough to win favorable strategic circumstances, so the new president must resort to more popular policies. Big ideas, such as Bush's pledge of substantial tax cuts, are replaced with smaller but passable measures to symbolize the president's policy values. Hence, observers expected Bush to choose some minor tax cuts to symbolize his tax-cutting credentials, such as phasing out the estate tax and eliminating the tax code's disadvantages for married couples. Each reform had been thoroughly discussed by the previous Congress.

Given Bush's advocacy of a moderate, "compassionate conservatism" during the campaign, his extensive discussion of bipartisan compromise, and the awkward strategic conditions he faced, Bush seemed likely to follow a moderate, compensatory strategy.

Bush's strategy

Bush's rhetorical style suggested a type of moderation. Clinton was extremely articulate and, in comparison, Bush's gaffe-prone style made him potentially vulnerable. However, while Bush lacks Clinton's eloquence, his relaxed, folksy style won plaudits, giving him an "everyman appeal" that echoes, without matching, Reagan's rhetorical ability to communicate with the public (Bettelheim, 2001). This genial style proved important initially as, it proved hard for political opponents to portray Bush as a dangerous radical. Some commentators even regarded Bush's style as a calculated and disingenuous ruse, labeling him "a New England aristocrat posing as a West Texas wildcatter" (Hodgson, 2000). Nevertheless, Bush's informal on-screen persona has helped him appear moderate. He has, again in contrast to Clinton, focused on the message he wants to deliver at public events. Clinton was articulate, but ill-disciplined, often roaming 'off-message' and thus distracting from the points he wanted to make. Bush says little off the record, demonstrating focus that may help him to employ the bully pulpit effectively.

Two early policy selections also suggested that Bush was following a compensatory strategy. In announcing an education reform programme and a programme to encourage faith-based initiatives, Bush attempted to extend his theme of "compassionate conservatism" into his presidency. In each case, Bush addressed traditional compassionate issues, but offered relatively conservative reform proposals. In education policy especially, Bush showed an almost immediate willingness to compromise his initial proposals to achieve bipartisan support, quickly softening his language on school vouchers, for example. These reforms were an important part of Bush's message that his approach involved more than just rhetoric.

Bush also emphasized bipartisanship. His campaign had focused on his desire to be seen as "a uniter, not a divider," and this theme was revisited in many forms during the transition period. In his speech claiming the presidency on December 13, Bush spent a surprisingly long period congratulating Gore on his campaign, a speech Bush chose to give from the Texas House of Representatives, which he identified as the scene of many bipartisan achievements during his time as Governor. In his cabinet appointments, Bush selected Democrat Norman Mineta as Transportation Secretary, thus becoming the first Republican to nominate a Democrat to sit in the cabinet since Nixon.

Dealings with Congress, however, provided the real test of bipartisanship. He quickly embarked upon an intensive liaison program, communicating with many legislators from each party. Alongside many other efforts, he met with the Democratic congressional leaderships and attended the congressional Democrats mid-February retreat in a notable attempt to make a positive impression. Bush employed an intensely personal brand of liaison: he brought the same genial and relaxed style to his liaison meetings as to his public addresses. Calling on his experience as Governor, Bush seems to have believed that his charm could ease Washington's tensions. Early reviews of Bush's performances were largely positive.

However, a bipartisan style of liaison does not necessarily equal bipartisanship. Bush had a fundamental decision to make in designing his bipartisan vision. Would he attempt to match his moderate rhetoric with an attempt to build unusual forms of congressional coalition? Traditional presidential coalition building is based on support from the president's party and ideological base. Presidents start by allying themselves with those that share their views and party label; then they try to build majorities by winning "cross-pressured" legislators. These legislators share either their ideology or party label with the president, but not both. Presidents hope to amass enough cross-pressured votes so that, when added to the party base, a majority is created to pass a bill (Bond and Fleisher, 1990). Bush's rhetoric of bipartisanship implied a different approach. The new president's words suggested that he would attempt to become a pragmatic unifier, building the congressional middle ground. Coalition-building might start with a nonpartisan coalition in the ideological centre, and then Bush would attempt to build support by winning defectors from either party base. Bush seemed likely to attack the centrist president's dilemma head-on. In sharp contrast to the partisanship of the preceding decade, he would occupy the middle ground, thus attracting the public support he needed to command future deference from legislators. The president-elect's moderate rhetoric, his enthusiastic consultation with both parties and the perceived need for a compensatory strategy all suggested this direction for a Bush presidency.

For all the predictions, Bush did not adopt a compensatory strategy as president. Instead, he defied the analyses of journalists and academics alike, and took up an approach much more closely related to Jones' description of an aggressive strategy. He chose a broad-ranging and sizable agenda, including some distinctly conservative policies. Bush pursued much of this agenda with fervor, and showed limited willingness to compromise on key issues. He appeared not to feel the restraints predicted by Jones's model. Instead, he proceeded as though blessed with an unequivocal mandate for a conservative agenda.

Between January 23 and February 13, Bush unveiled not only programmes on education and faith-based initiatives, but also tax and defence reforms. This programme was not the narrow programme of a compensatory president struggling for influence. While Bush did focus on a limited group of priorities, he showed little sign of limiting his agenda. The proposed tax cut alone, of $1.6 trillion over 10 years, was a major initiative. Neither did Bush seem willing to compromise on his ideology. His tax cut, reducing the future federal revenues, was unambiguously conservative. He also revived the traditional Republican support for a strong military. Bush endorsed the development of a missile defence system to intercept nuclear weapons entering US airspace (see Chapter 14). Bush's early appointments were also ideologically clear. The nomination of former Republican Senator John Ashcroft as Attorney General drew particular attention. While serving as a member of the Senate Judiciary Committee, Ashcroft had developed a reputation as a conservative ideologue keen to attack judicial liberalism, and this sent a strong message about the character of Bush's preferred judicial nominations (see Chapter 7). Mineta's appointment to a peripheral executive department paled into insignificance. Bush's early stances on the environment also marked him as a conservative. His decision to withdraw from the Kyoto agreement demonstrated a lack of sympathy to the environmental cause. Furthermore, Bush found himself pressured to respond to a developing power crisis in California. His initial reluctance to intervene, leaving the crisis to the markets to resolve, was again conservative. Media coverage began to associate Bush with the concerns of the conservative business community. Few of these actions suggested a willingness to compromise with the moderates.

Finally, in congressional strategy, Bush made little substantive attempt to build a centrist, bipartisan coalition. Bipartisan rhetoric abounded, but the new President employed traditional means of coalition-building. The tax cut was advanced as Bush's first priority. To pass it, Bush's team planned to win the support of the Republican Party base, and chose which conservative Democrats to woo. In the Senate, twelve Democrats eventually defected to join all of the Republicans in supporting the bill. Bush offered concessions to win these Democrats' support, and the support of a few wavering Republicans, but largely stuck to his conservative ground. Allied to stances on the environment, energy and defense, Bush appeared to be taking a clear conservative line. Indeed, he repeatedly proclaimed his belief that he had a mandate to pursue his conservative policies. Representative Tom DeLay, a notoriously rigid House conservative, noted with satisfaction, "I don't hear that talk about a centrist agenda from the administration. I hear about the administration reaching out in a bipartisan way to achieve the goals we [the conservatives] want" (Foerstel, 2001a).

The Bush team decided to confront their unfavorable strategic circumstances aggressively and directly. There were some compensatory elements to their strategy but largely the new administration pusued a bold conservative agenda. This brave approach was rooted in Bush's unusual view of political capital. Claiming that he had learnt from his father's inactivity a decade earlier, Bush argued the need to move "as quickly as you can in order to spend whatever capital you have as quickly as possible" (Harris and Balz, 2001). He believed this approach would bring its own rewards, suggesting: "You spend capital on what you campaigned on . . . and you earn capital by doing that" (Harris and Balz, 2001). Bush believed that fulfilling his pledges would win him the stature to maintain influence.

Bush's organization and style

Bush has employed a style of presidency that differs from his predecessor. The image of Clinton's presidency was defined by the rather anarchic patterns of his early years in office. Clinton, deeply embroiled in policy detail, engaged in many issue debates concurrently. Clinton's White House rarely focused on one issue at a time, often appearing disorganized and squandering opportunities to focus presidential resources.

During the campaign, Bush promised that he would use his business school experience to deliver a corporate style of governance. Bush claimed to see himself as a Chief Executive Officer (CEO) for the federal government. This preference for a CEO role carried a number of implications as to Bush's style of decision-making. A CEO could be expected to show less engagement with policy detail, and more reliance on his officers. Furthermore, a CEO would likely focus on a small number of key issues (see Chapter 8).

Bush has attempted to deliver the focus implied by the CEO model. In a conscious maneuver, Bush, and his White House, have targeted one policy area at a time to mobilize all the resources of the presidency behind one proposal. The first focus was tax cuts. Bush took an active interest in the issue, particularly the congressional tactics. He reputedly shows a great interest in political strategy, sometimes at the expense of policy specifics. Other issues were displaced. The White House, as a whole, has engaged with the policy agenda only selectively. In this sense, Bush has narrowed the focus of the presidency in a way not seen since Reagan.

Selective engagement might be expected to influence the nature of the president's interaction with his cabinet officers. In the modern era, cabinet members have rarely had a great deal of power within administrations; but under Clinton they had sunk to a new low. Clinton's budgetary disputes with the Republicans demanded centralized control over budgetary decisions, and hence he established greater White House control over cabinet members' ability to negotiate with legislators. Despite the CEO model and "selective engagement," cabinet ministers have not found their prerogatives entirely restored under Bush who has overruled his cabinet officers repeatedly, often at the cost of public embarrassment. Secretary of State Colin Powell found his position on North Korean relations publicly repudiated by his president. Christine Todd Whitman, a cabinet member and head of the Environmental Protection Agency, suffered similar embarrassments. Bush retains the right to make his own decisions.

However, Bush is, like all his recent predecessors, greatly dependent upon his White House. Appointing a staff is a challenge for a Washington newcomer: he must have loyalists around him that he can trust. Such trust normally develops through working with the successful candidate for many years (Pfiffner, 1996). Bush had such a team. Communications consultant Karen Hughes and political strategist Karl Rove have been working with Bush for a decade, and both have been appointed to senior roles in the Bush White House. The trap for the newcomer president, though, is that these loyalists are very unlikely to have substantial Washington experience. The new president may find himself unfamiliar with the political system, and ill-equipped to mobilize it. Both Jimmy Carter and Clinton suffered this experience on their arrival within the Beltway. Bush's solution was to appoint advisers with Capitol experience. A series of Washington "insiders" joined Bush's staff. For instance, Andrew Card, Secretary of Transportation under Bush's father, became chief of staff. More unusually, Bush turned to his vice-president for substantial help. Vice-presidents have traditionally been marginal figures in administrations; in contrast, Dick Cheney maintained a high profile throughout the disputed Florida counting process, and then achieved even higher status as the president's primary representative in congressional liaison. He continues to play a central role in the Bush presidency, meeting regularly in private with the president and reviewing the president's daily schedule to decide which meetings he wishes to attend. No recent vice-president has held such a broad-ranging brief.

Bush gathered a small team synthesizing long-term associates and Washington insiders in an attempt to govern effectively. Tellingly, he did not reject the inter-weaving of politics and policy employed by Clinton. Bush is interested in political strategy. Hughes and Rove, neither of whom is a policy specialist, appear very prominent amongst his advisers. Each week, a regular staff meeting reviews polling data and considers the interaction of policy and politics. Again, the style is reminiscent of the Reagan

Presidency and the Legislative Strategy Group at that presidency's heart. No president believes he can afford to overlook the relationship between his policies, his congressional tactics, and the polls. Each president will 'campaign to govern' to a greater or lesser extent if he wishes to make good use of the office.

Results of the aggressive, selective strategy

Bush's strategy had mixed results. Selective engagement proved problematic, as many participants in the political system resisted Bush's priorities. A series of incidents distracted focus from the presidency's plans and the administration struggled to control the agenda, reflecting the increasingly awkward conditions presidents face in dealing with the media.

First, Bush faced the competing presence of Gore. For five weeks after the election, the media focused on developments on Florida, and Bush had little opportunity to advance policy priorities. Second, Bush had to compete with the coverage given to Clinton's last-minute pardons. In a break with tradition, the departing president left office anything but quietly. Then Bush faced his first foreign policy crisis as the crew of a US surveillance aircraft were held in China. As Bush negotiated the aircrew's safe return, an energy crisis in California attracted news coverage. Even the arrest of Bush's daughter Jenna (for underage drinking) distracted from the administration's efforts. Each incident limited Bush's capacity to focus public attention on his tax cuts. Bush received less coverage than Clinton had eight years earlier. Network television carried 41 percent fewer stories featuring Bush than they had on Clinton in the equivalent period (Sanger and Lacey, 2001). Bush's approval ratings stubbornly refused to climb significantly, touching a high of 63 percent in March, but also dropping as low as 53 percent that month. The public remained skeptical about Bush's emphasis on tax cuts and Bush lost control of his image. The president's advocacy of tax cuts, combined with his energy, defense, and environmental policies, overwhelmed his attempts to appear moderate. Instead, Bush became more widely perceived as a conservative. Bush's "Going Public" reaped limited results.

In contrast, Bush won early success with Congress. Given the president's weak position and lukewarm public sentiment, persuading Congress to pass a $1.3 trillion cut was a remarkable achievement. Yet Republican celebrations were muted. The bill's success in the Senate was achieved amid rumors that James Jeffords (R-Vt) was about to leave the Republican Party. Claiming to feel out of place as a moderate in a conservative party, Jeffords announced that he was becoming an independent on May 24 2001.

The defection was a significant blow to the Bush administration. First, Jeffords' action legitimized the increasing Democratic criticism of Bush as too conservative. Second, the media honeymoon was over: a spate of stories criticizing Bush followed. Third, and most importantly, Jeffords's decision threw control of the Senate to the Democrats. Bush no longer enjoyed the advantages of unified government. The Democrats would now have majority representation on the standing committees, and would be able to select the chairmen of those committees and their subcommittees. The Democratic leadership would control much of the schedule for the Senate floor. Democrats would choose who would represent the Senate in conference committees. While the number of Republican votes on the floor had barely changed, the ability of Bush's allies to push any Republican legislation as far as the floor was substantially diminished. The demise of unified Republican government was particularly painful as, beforehand, Democrats had lacked a platform from which to advance their policy priorities. With Senate control, the Democrats could choose issues to discomfort Republicans, laying the groundwork for the congressional campaigns of 2002. The Democratic leadership swiftly availed itself of this opportunity. Within a fortnight of Jeffords' switch, Senate debate and media coverage focused on the so-called "patients' bill of rights," legislation to tighten regulation of the health insurance industry (see Chapter 13). Bush quickly threatened to veto the Democrats' preferred bill. The Democratic Senate had quickly promoted a potential wedge issue which could be used to portray Bush as overly conservative and sympathetic to the concerns of business.

Jeffords's alienation was a product of a fundamental tension for the Bush strategy, which, in turn, reveals a serious limitation of the modern presidency. The Bush team realized that to win tax cuts they would have to focus all of the presidency's resources behind one bill (the office's inherent weakness demanded this concentration). However, this focus also limited the administration's ability to control its image. During the crucial period in which first impressions of the new presidency were formed, Bush became labeled as a conservative keen to support business interests. The single-minded focus on tax cuts prevented the president from advocating other polices that might have tempered this developing image. Moderate measures, such as education and support for faith-based initiatives, all waited in the queue of preferred Bush legislation. However, these could not be discussed as they threatened to dilute the president's tax cut campaign. The structural weakness of the presidency undermined Bush's ability to manage his image and his preferred policy agenda simultaneously.

A second phase of the Bush presidency?

Jeffords's defection appeared to mark the end of the first phase of the Bush presidency. The administration now confronted significantly more difficult conditions. Democratic control of the Senate threatened revived partisan conflict. Democrats seemed unlikely to offer Bush and the Republicans partisan triumphs: it appeared that Bush would be forced to reconsider his interpretation of "bipartisanship."

The new president struggled over subsequent months, and Senate Democrats were not his only problem. In particular, the president struggled to retain the support of moderate Republicans in the House of Representatives. The new administration's campaign finance bill was dropped from the congressional agenda to avoid an embarrassing defeat, and the president's programme to support faith-based initiatives received little congressional attention. The threat of congressional action forced the Federal Energy Agency to introduce limited energy price controls for California, despite Bush's open opposition. Bush's education bill passed both chambers, but without the school vouchers provision he had advocated. A House decision to enforce Clinton's regulations on arsenic levels in water persuaded the administration to stop trying to overturn other Clinton regulations. As the August recess loomed, however, there were a pair of Bush triumphs. Bush managed to avert an embarrassing defeat over the patients' rights bill, and surprisingly he won support for oil exploration in the Arctic National Wildlife Refuge. Overall, however, Bush was struggling. The *Washington Post* commented, "Bush should have no illusions about the difficulties he will face when he returns [after the recess; he] must compete against a determined opposition with its own agenda." (Balz, 2001).

While moderate House Republicans and Senate Democrats proved problematic, Bush also confronted broader institutional and economic threats. As presidencies develop, most suffer from trends that undermine presidential influence in the political system. Bush's public approval ratings were expected to decline as his term progressed. Also, the party occupying the White House usually suffers losses in midterm congressional elections. The Republican majority in the House, already wafer-thin, seemed fated. Bush would then have faced a victorious Democratic Party controlling both Houses of Congress. Only his veto, and the lessons in the use of the obstructive presidency provided by Clinton, would have protected him. Furthermore, the economy proved an increasing source of concern: a long-predicted recession loomed and the hard-won tax cuts had not averted the threat (see Chapter 10) Unemployment rates began to climb, consumer spending fell and economic growth rates dropped. Prospects for the Bush administration looked bleak.

Responding to terrorism

Bush's governing context was radically transformed by the September 11 2001 terrorist attacks which swiftly restored foreign policy to the top of the political agenda. Bush had made a dubious start in foreign policy and was perceived to be ignorant on the subject, an impression largely generated by his inability to name various world leaders during a radio interview. Early press reports suggested that the National Security Adviser, Condoleezza Rice, was providing a series of seminars to educate Bush on foreign policy issues.

Furthermore, many regarded the new administration's advocacy of unilateralism with suspicion. Bush quickly demonstrated a remarkable ability to upset allies and foes alike by directing US policy along an independent path. The new administration's rejection of the Kyoto treaty caused consternation abroad. Choosing the missile defense system as the main focus for defense policy amounted to a pledge to contravene the Anti-Ballistic Missile Treaty. The opponents of the new weapons system feared international destablization and a new arms race, possibly with China. Russia was vocal in her objection.

Observers of foreign policy-making often judge a president's effectiveness by his ability to create a united foreign policy team. Bush appeared to fail on this count too. He appointed a team of vast experience. Powell, as Secretary of State, had served under Bush's father. Rice was widely regarded as a pre-eminent foreign policy authority. Donald Rumsfeld, given unusual influence in foreign policy-making as a Secretary of Defense, had a range of Washington experience. With Vice-President Cheney involved in the policy process, and Bush's father in the background, *The Economist*'s description of "one of the most impressive foreign policy teams in living memory" (*The Economist*, September 22, 2001), seemed appropriate. However, early press coverage of the administration focused upon alleged tensions between Powell's internationalist leanings and the harder-line Rumsfeld's preference for unilateral action.

Hence, when the terrorist attacks occurred, many observers were nervous of Bush's ability to respond effectively. *The Economist*'s label for Bush as "a clumsy-tongued neophyte whose main contribution to foreign policy . . . was to invent ingenious ways of irritating his allies," did little to inspire confidence (*The Economist*, September 22,2001). In the first hours following the attacks, Bush's manner, and his evacuation to Nebraska on security grounds, only reinforced these worries.

However, the events of September 11, in the short-term at least, allowed Bush to demonstrate greater competence. The terrorist attacks restored national security as the key principle underpinning foreign policy-making.

The administration's response to the threat of further attack, labeled "Operation Enduring Freedom," was manifold. Domestically, Bush revealed a new rhetorical style and launched reforms to combat terrorism. Abroad, to support US military action, Bush crafted a coalition of nations from some very unlikely bedfellows.

The administration offered a series of policies in response to the terrorist attacks. Anti-terrorism and aviation security bills were presented to Congress, and measures were imposed to attack the finances of terrorist groups. On October 8, Bush issued an executive order establishing a new White House Office of Homeland Security with responsibility for coordinating executive branch operations designed to resist terrorist activities. Former Governor of Pennsylvania Tom Ridge was appointed as Director of the new unit, and given cabinet-level status. Bush also asked Congress for a joint resolution to permit him to "use all necessary and appropriate force" against terrorism. The Senate passed it unanimously and only one Representative voted against the measure.

Bush's rhetorical performance also changed. Immediately after the attacks, much of his language was combative: the leader of the al-Quaeeda terrorist network, Osama bin Laden, was, in Bush's words, "wanted: dead or alive." The president spoke of a "crusade" and, "whipping terrorists." However, Bush's addresses also reflected more emotion, providing echoes of Clinton's ability to feel the nation's pain. Furthermore, Bush projected a new determination. Press reviews were complimentary, and public reaction was overwhelmingly positive. Perhaps experiencing the "rally around the flag effect" usually associated with foreign policy crises, Bush won approval ratings of 86 percent following the attacks, among the highest ever recorded (Mueller, 1973; Gallup, 2001).

Bush also declared a new focus for US foreign policy. For over a decade, politicians and policy-makers had searched for a new rationale to underpin foreign policy choices. Bush offered such a rationale in his identification of terrorism as the main security threat to the USA, stating that, "Our war on terror . . . will not end until every terrorist group of global reach has been found, stopped and defeated" (Bush, 2001). As a principle for organizing defence priorities, budgetary planning and international diplomacy, Bush appeared to be articulating his own foreign policy "doctrine" to match those of Monroe, Truman or Reagan.

In the short term, many of Bush's actions suggested that this doctrine would guide policy at the expense of other priorities. The administration built an unprecedented coalition to support action against terrorism, and a new multilateralism replaced the Bush team's early unilateralism. Support from Pakistan required to simplify action against al-Quaeeda training camps in Afghanistan was earned through a policy reversal. Pakistan had acquired near pariah status in the international community due to human rights abuses and the holding of illegal nuclear tests in 1998, but Bush quickly moved to lift sanctions. Iran, outspoken in its resistance to American influence for 20 years, was shown a new tolerance in the changed climate. Bush leapt back into the Israeli–Palestinian peace process after September 11, despite his previously declared intent to step back from involvement. Leaders in both Israel and the Palestinian authority experienced severe diplomatic pressure from a USA keen to secure a genuine ceasefire. In each case, the Bush administration adopted new positions to generate support for the action in Afghanistan. Secretary of State Powell even suggested that a new benchmark for judging allies had been established. Each nation presented with American requests for help against terrorism would be judged according to its response.

On October 7, after nearly a month of diplomacy, planning and military build-up, the first US air strikes were launched against Afghanistan. Pakistan, India, Iran, Russia and China all demonstrated a minimum tolerance of the strikes. After an uncertain start, Bush had demonstrated a new competence in response to a wholly unexpected challenge. In constructing the diverse coalition, the Bush team achieved a substantial diplomatic feat. Bush also showed substantially more ability to fulfill the demands of the public presidency. Furthermore, he appeared capable of managing diverse views within his foreign policy team: the administration pursued concerted action, despite press reports of continuing differences between Powell and Rumsfeld. This combination of successes suggested Bush to be a president capable of implementing his chosen foreign policy.

Even as military action was prepared, though, Bush had to confront the further challenge of the US economy. The events of September 11 had serious economic repercussions. The aviation industry faced crisis, which in turn was expected to affect other areas of the economy. Consumer confidence fell sharply after the attacks. The Federal Reserve attempted to increase liquidity in the financial markets by cutting short-term interest rates and using open market operations, but the economy still seemed likely to fall into a full-scale recession.

On October 5, the administration revealed a proposal for up to $75 billion further stimulus of the economy. While providing $15 billion to support the unemployed, the lion's share of the stimulus was to be delivered in the form of tax cuts. At a time of national crisis, the Bush administration had already seen the power of bipartisanship in action. Congress had been decisive in its support for Bush's resolution on military action. Initial spending packages worth $45 billion, to provide emergency support for areas damaged by the attack and to rescue struggling airlines, had passed with similar despatch. On Capitol Hill, the foreign policy crisis appeared to generate a deference to presidential leadership. The White House led on all fronts, suggesting that a popular president might steer a stimulus package through Congress with ease.

However, the partisan tensions remained. Even bills proposed in direct response to the terrorist attacks were not immune. The aviation security bill floundered on the question of whether the federal government should take over airport security operations, while the anti-terrorist bill stumbled over rules governing the ability of law enforcement agencies to share grand jury and wiretap information with intelligence agencies. Partisanship seemed likely to stalk the progress of the stimulus package. Congressional Republicans were concerned by Bush's omission of changes to capital gains and corporate income tax rates. Democrats protested that tax cuts would assist richer Americans, doing little either to assist the unemployed or to increase consumption in support of the ailing economy. Hopes that a spirit of bipartisanship could be translated from foreign policy to an economic stimulus package seemed optimistic.

Conclusion: Bush's reputation in the balance

Presidential scholars largely agree that the institution they study has been weakened over the last three decades. However, the experiences of Clinton and Bush suggest that the presidency remains a force for change in the political system under the right conditions. Clinton's mastery of political tactics, and perhaps even good luck, allowed him to use the limited tools of the office to steer federal funds towards his preferred projects while blocking selected Republican initiatives. Bush managed to win substantial tax cuts, despite apparently adverse conditions. The tragedies of September 11 demonstrated that, under extreme conditions, much of the political system is willing to defer to presidential leadership, if only temporarily. While presidential power is a long way from its peak of the 1960s, given an appropriate confluence of historical circumstance and strategic skills the office remains influential.

Whether Bush will be able to exploit this potential in the long term remains to be seen. After only seven months in office, he was confronted with twin perils of a national security disaster and economic recession. He showed an ability to cajole other participants in the political system, both domestic and international, that surprised detractors and delighted supporters. At the time of writing, however, the reputation of the Bush presidency hangs in the balance. While Bush has done much already to suggest that he can win acceptance for his policy choices, the underlying factors that have weakened the office seem likely to re-assert themselves as the shock of extreme circumstances fades. Furthermore, given the seriousness of the policy problems he confronts, assessments of Bush's overall performance are more likely to depend on his ability to make policy choices that address his nation's problems effectively. The reputation of Bush's presidency will be defined by his success, or otherwise, in responding to the challenges of terrorism and recession.

Chapter 6

Congress

ERIC SCHICKLER

The American Congress has never had the strict party discipline and highly-centralized party leadership that has long characterized the British Parliament and many other legislatures. Indeed, prior to the 1990s, most observers believed that individual members were largely independent of their parties (perhaps too independent) and that committees were the main power centers in Congress. But party voting and party leadership strength grew considerably in the 1980s and 1990s, while committees lost influence. The dramatic Republican takeover of Congress in 1995 furthered this transformation and initially seemed to herald a new era of vigorous party government.

This chapter considers recent developments in Congress, with a focus on the lasting legacy of the Republican "Revolution" and an analysis of the main contours of contemporary congressional politics. Party voting and centralized party leadership have receded from their apex in 1995–96, as divisions within each party have taken on increasing salience. Nonetheless, Capitol Hill remains fiercely partisan. Because both the House and the Senate are closely divided, both Democratic and Republican responses to policy issues are primarily shaped by the race for majority status. This has made for an increasingly bitter and treacherous legislative environment.

What is left of the Republican "Revolution" of 1995?

After 40 years in the minority, Republicans swept to control of the House of Representatives in the 1994 elections. The new Republican majority, which included 73 freshmen, proclaimed that their election provided a mandate for their "Contract with America," a party manifesto that its candidates had pledged to support. US congressional elections are usually fought out on a district-by-district basis, with each candidate tailoring his or her own proposals to local sentiment, but the Contract was different. Never before had a party's congressional candidates so publicly promised to support a specific program. The Contract called for dramatic cuts in the size of government and in taxes; it also pledged to reform welfare programs for the poor, toughen penalties on crime, and uphold "family values."

The Republican election victory catapulted Newt Gingrich (R-Ga), the party's whip in the preceding Congress and one of the lead authors of the Contract, to newfound prominence. Gingrich was selected as Speaker of the House by the new Republican majority. As Speaker, he would be the leader of his party and the presiding officer of the House. But Gingrich sought to move beyond these traditional roles, making the Speaker the driving force behind national policy innovation.

To help push the Contract through the Congress, the Republicans adopted an array of reforms intended to transform the legislative process. Perhaps most importantly, Speaker Gingrich seized a more active role in committee assignments and in selecting committee chairmen. In the past, committee chairmanships were largely governed by the seniority system, in which the majority party member with the longest tenure on a committee would be its chairman. This system had limited the parties' ability to control committee politics, which often were dominated by cooperative relationships between senior members of both parties. But Gingrich bypassed the seniority system in appointing more junior conservative loyalists to lead key committees, including the Appropriations Committee, which handles the spending bills considered by Congress. These appointments sent the clear message that this would be an activist, assertive leadership. Gingrich also circumvented committees by appointing special party task forces to frame legislation for the floor. New rules setting a six-year term limit on both committee and subcommittee chairs further eroded committee leaders' power.

At the same time, the 1995 reforms strengthened full committee chairs' power *vis-à-vis* subcommittee chairs. In a major departure from the Democrats' practice of empowering subcommittee leaders, the Republicans allowed committee chairs to appoint subcommittee chairs and to hire all majority party committee staff, including those assigned to subcommittees. The Republicans also streamlined the committee system by abolishing three standing committees with primarily Democratic constituencies – the District of Columbia, Post Office and Civil Service, and the Merchant Marine and Fisheries Committees – and by reducing the number of subcommittees. In addition, the Republicans abolished Legislative Service Organizations, which had provided resources for member activism independent of their parties. In sum, the reforms strengthened party leaders, made committee chairs more dependent on party leaders for their positions, and made subcommittee chairs, in turn, more dependent on committee chairs for their authority.

Six years after the Republican Revolution, the changes wrought by Gingrich and his colleagues have left a decidedly mixed legacy. First, the aggressive, centralized party leadership that Gingrich promoted is only partly intact: many Republicans blamed Gingrich's poor public image when the party lost seats in the 1996 and 1998 congressional elections. Gingrich also struggled with the need to reconcile moderate Republicans' interest in compromising with the Clinton White House to pass centrist legislation, with many conservatives' insistence on a sharply ideological agenda. Conservatives repeatedly advocated policies that moderate Republicans believed would hurt their electoral prospects at home. By late 1998, Gingrich's leadership was being attacked from both the center and the right, and the 1998 election results led to his withdrawal as a candidate for reelection as Speaker and resignation from the House.

The Clinton impeachment fiasco illustrates the Republicans' dilemma. The Republicans' focus on Clinton's affair with Monica Lewinsky is widely credited with causing the party's unusually poor performance in the 1998 midterm election, which was the first midterm election since 1934 where the president's party gained seats in the House of Representatives. Yet even after the election, conservative Republicans continued to pursue impeachment and the House ultimately passed the impeachment articles on a near party-line vote. This Republican "victory" demonstrates how the majority party can structure House rules to get its way: it is likely that a floor majority favored the milder course of censure instead of impeachment; but Republican leaders used the rules to block a direct floor vote on censure (see Aldrich and Rohde, 1999). The impeachment case suggests both the strength of congressional parties and the dangers posed to individual members by party pressure to buck constituent opinion. The problem, put simply, is that the sort of party image that is attractive to safe seat conservatives is not likely to help moderate Republicans from swing districts. Congressman Jim Rogan's (R-Ca) defeat in 2000 was attributed in part to his role as one of the thirteen House Republican impeachment prosecutors.

The Hastert Speakership

After Gingrich's resignation in the wake of the 1998 midterms, House Republicans selected Appropriations Committee Chair Bob Livingston (R-La) to succeed Gingrich as Speaker. Before the opening day of the 106th Congress, however, revelations of an extramarital affair prompted Livingston to resign. The Republicans then nominated Denny Hastert of Illinois to take over the job as Speaker and party leader in January 1999. Hastert's approach to party leadership is more typical of past Speakers than Gingrich's. Whereas Gingrich took on an aggressively public role, at times even portraying himself as a Prime Minister with more influence over policy than President Clinton, Hastert has a much lower public profile. Furthermore, where Gingrich sought to centralize power in his own hands, Hastert has broadened the leadership circle. For example, while Gingrich largely dictated the selection of committee chairmen, Hastert has left the task to the party's Steering Committee, which is composed of party leaders and regional representatives. Though Hastert has five votes on the Committee, he generally did not make his preferences known in advance when the Steering Committee nominated chairmen in January 2001, and his first choice was actually defeated for a handful of chairmanships (Cohen, 2001). Still, though Hastert's approach is more collegial, he has not hesitated to use the majority party's procedural advantages to push the Republican agenda and to stymie Democratic alternatives. Therefore, he has maintained much of the partisanship of the Gingrich era, but on a less centralized basis.

One unusual aspect of the Hastert Speakership is that the majority whip, Tom DeLay (R-Tex.), has at times overshadowed, and even defeated, the Speaker on important matters. The majority whip is typically the third most important party leader in the House, after the Speaker and the majority leader. But DeLay has his own power base as a leader of his party's conservative wing and at times acts independently. Indeed, DeLay was widely credited with rallying conservatives behind Hastert's selection as Speaker (Carney, Foerstel and Taylor, 1998). The most dramatic example of DeLay's influence occurred in April 2000, when he successfully lobbied fellow Republicans to defeat a House resolution endorsing US air strikes against Serbia in the conflict in Kosovo. Hastert had supported the resolution, and the Speaker's failure to overcome DeLay's lobbying suggested how much the Republican leadership has fragmented since the heady days of the Contract with America.

The House Committee system and the legacy of the Republican Revolution

Just as party leadership has become less centralized in the post-Gingrich era, the committee system is also making something of a comeback. Gingrich's tendency to bypass committees had irritated senior party members, and Hastert sought to encourage goodwill by promising to rely less on party task forces (Evans, 2001). As a result, committees, rather than task forces, are again writing most important legislation, as was the case in the pre-Gingrich era. Gingrich had argued that task forces provide the sort of flexibility required in a postindustrial era, but Republicans appear to have recognized the institutional benefits of reliance on a system of expert standing committees. Committee chairman have thus regained some of their status as important power brokers, though they remain accountable to their fellow party members. The shift back toward committee power was exemplified in January 2000 when Hastert sought to circumvent disagreements between the multiple committees with jurisdiction over prescription drugs legislation by creating a party task force to deal with this politically charged issue. The chairmen refused to go along with the task force idea and the separate committees continued to work on the legislation independently; it was then several months before they finally reached agreement on a proposal (Evans, 2001). Only two years before, legislation to reform health maintenance organizations had been sent directly to the House floor by a Republican task force, bypassing the committees with jurisdiction altogether.

That is not to say that all elements of the Republican Revolution have been jettisoned. The Republicans have maintained the shift in authority from subcommittee leaders to committee chairs. Furthermore, arguably the most noteworthy institutional legacy of the 1995 reforms was its six-year term limit on committee chairmen, which was first enforced in January 2001. Many of the chairmen had sought to repeal the term limits, but the Republicans voted overwhelmingly to stick with the new policy. This meant that the party Steering Committee had the opportunity to select thirteen new chairmen.

The term limits have numerous institutional implications. On the one hand, they may undermine committees' expertise and thereby weaken the committee system as a whole. With term limits looming, several experienced House Republicans chose to retire from Congress rather than return as rank-and-file members. These included John Kasich (R-Oh.), who had chaired the Budget Committee, and William Archer (R-Tex.) of Ways and Means (which handles all tax and trade bills), and Bill Goodling (R-Ill.) of the Economic Opportunities Committee. The term limits also may disrupt lobbyists' ability to develop stable ties to committee leaders.

At the same time, the term limits have offered important benefits to the majority Republicans. First, the term limits facilitate the party Steering Committee's ability to influence standing committees. In 2001, thirteen chairmanships were vacated. The Steering Committee has used its discretion over the selection of new chairmen to promote members who are most likely to pursue the party's agenda. The Republican Conference rules specifically state that the member designated by the Steering Committee for each chairmanship "need not be the member with the longest consecutive service on the committee" (Foerstel, 2000). For the first time, the Committee interviewed all prospective chairmen, grilling them on their plans for the committee and making sure that those plans were compatible with the party's goals. The Steering Committee did in fact violate seniority in a handful of cases, passing over moderates out of step with the party's conservativism, and also bypassing members who were believed to lack energy or competence. Second, the competition for chairmanships has had an important side-benefit for party members: the Steering Committee has let chairmanship candidates know that their fundraising for fellow Republicans will be considered in its deliberations. This has resulted in extremely aggressive fundraising efforts by candidates for chairmanships, helping the Republicans in their efforts to keep control of the House. Even after the new chairmen have taken office, several have continued their efforts to consolidate their power by raising money for their committee colleagues (Bolton, 2001).

Therefore, even as the highly centralized party leadership and weak standing committees of the early days of the Republican Revolution have proved impermanent, the Republican takeover has nonetheless left a significant institutional legacy for the House. Despite this, much of the reformist fervor of the Republican Revolutionaries has dissipated. The 73 freshmen Republicans elected in 1994 had formed the shock troops of the "Revolution," and were leading advocates not only of term limits for chairmen, but of such reforms as term limits for all members. But the House failed to muster the two-thirds majority required for a Constitutional amendment establishing a cap on how long members could serve in Congress, underscoring the limited success of the Republicans when it came to issues that threatened the prerogatives and power of all members of Congress. Since then, many of the most fiery of the freshmen Republicans have left the House in defeat, have retired, or have run for other offices, complaining about the difficulty of changing Washington. The remaining members of the class of 1994 appear to have become acclimated to congressional practices and are acting more like traditional lawmakers, moving up on committee hierarchies and trying to direct federal projects back home (Doherty and Katz 1998). In the 107th Congress (2001–2), five members of the class of 1994 are deputy whips, eleven are subcommittee chairmen, and one is a full committee chair.

The policy legacy of the Republican Revolution is similarly limited. The most noteworthy changes were the welfare reform bill of 1996 and the balanced budget agreement reached with President Clinton in 1997. The Republicans succeeded in slowing the growth of domestic spending initially, but by 2000, amid unprecedented budget surpluses, Congress adopted spending increases that rivaled or even exceeded those experienced during the heyday of Democratic Congresses. Furthermore, the federal departments targeted for elimination by the Republicans – Commerce, Energy, and Education – are still going strong. Perhaps nothing illustrates the dimming revolutionary ardor on Capitol Hill better than House Republicans' general acceptance of President George W. Bush's proposals for an increased federal role in education. One might argue that the Republicans saved their revolution – preserving their majority and capturing the White House – precisely by downplaying its most radical policy implications.

The Senate and the Republican Revolution

The Republican takeover of the Senate did not provoke such dramatic changes in 1995–6. It also proved less durable than the party's House majority, as Vermont Senator Jim Jeffords' surprise defection from the Republican party in May 2001 tilted the chamber back into Democratic hands. Still, the Republicans' stint in the majority has left a lasting legacy.

The Senate's Republican majority was dominated by conservatives, many of whom were veterans of the increasingly bitter partisanship that has characterized the House since the 1980s. These conservatives challenged the seniority system for determining committee chairmanships, complaining about the questionable loyalty of a handful of moderate committee chairmen, such as Appropriations Chair Mark Hatfield (R-Ore.) who cast the deciding vote to defeat the Balanced Budget Constitutional amendment in 1995. In response, the Republicans adopted rules specifying that the party's ruling body in the Senate – the Republican Party Conference – would vote on an official legislative agenda prior to selecting chairmen, providing a potential benchmark for evaluating the chairmen's loyalty. Furthermore, the Republicans adopted a term limit rule of their own for committee chairmen in September 1995, which would have forced several long-time chairmen to surrender their posts if the Republicans had continued to control the Senate through the 2002 elections. But Jeffords's defection cost the Republicans their majority status, shifting control of all chairmanships to the Democrats and thus precluding the implementation of the term limits. Still, the term limits would apply to a future Republican majority and therefore it is fair to conclude that the Senate has not been immune from the reforms instigated by the Republican revolutionaries of 1994.

In a further shift in Senate politics, the conservatives in control of the Senate Republican conference elected Trent Lott (R-Miss.) as majority leader following Bob Dole's departure to run for president in the summer of 1996. Lott had been an ally of Gingrich when he served in the House, and his ascension to the Senate leadership in summer 1996 signaled the Republicans' intention to run the Senate with a much firmer partisan grip. As leader, Lott exercised his prerogatives aggressively. For example, he often filed cloture motions to end debate on bills before a filibuster was even threatened. A filibuster occurs when senators use their right of unlimited debate to delay, and ultimately kill, a bill; adoption of cloture not only cuts off debate but also blocks nongermane amendments (that is, amendments unrelated to the bill itself). Since such amendments are one of the primary techniques used by the minority to bring its favored issues to the floor, early imposition of cloture threatened the Democrats' ability to offer their own alternative agenda. The problem for Lott, however, was that cloture requires 60 votes in the 100-member chamber, and the Republicans' majority was never that large. This meant that success in the Senate continued to require bipartisan cooperation. But Lott's efforts to shut out Democratic amendments tended to promote Democratic unity on cloture votes, making it extremely difficult to get anything done in the upper chamber. Lott often pulled bills when cloture failed, rather than attempting to negotiate an arrangement with the Democrats (Sinclair, 2001). The tenuous Democratic majority that took control of the Senate after Jeffords's defection faces the same difficult challenge of garnering the necessary bipartisan support for cloture in a fiercely partisan environment. Therefore, though partisan bitterness has increased in the Senate, the majority party remains more dependent on bipartisan cooperation to pass its legislative program than it does in the majoritarian House.

The persistence of member individualism also sharply limited Lott's leadership. Regardless of party, individual senators continue to insist on asserting their prerogatives under the Senate's rules and procedures. In addition to the right of unlimited debate, numerous senators use "holds" (threats of a filibuster) to delay – sometimes indefinitely – legislation and nominations that they oppose. When legislation does reach the floor, individual senators typically resist limitations on amendments, unlike in the House. Without the 60 votes needed for cloture, most major legislation requires delicate negotiations in search of a Unanimous Consent Agreement that satisfies individual senators' demands for consideration of their amendments yet also promises to bring an eventual final vote on the bill. Therefore, even as partisanship has increased, Lott was forced to rely on bargaining far more than command in making the Senate function (Smith and Gamm, 2001). The Democrats' leader, Tom Daschle of South Dakota, faces much the same set of constraints. The Senate authority structure that has emerged since 1995 is thus a curious mixture of heightened partisanship and still-vibrant individualism (see Sinclair, 2001).

The defection of the moderate Jeffords – who had become disenchanted by the increasingly conservative approach of his party's leaders in the Senate and in the George W. Bush White House – symbolized the extent to which individual senators retained their own power bases, independent of party ties. Indeed, one of Daschle's worries in his early days as majority leader was to ensure that none of his party's handful of conservative members would become similarly disenchanted and bolt to the Republicans.

Party voting in the Republican Congress

One of the most visible signs of the Republican Revolution was the rise in party voting that occurred in 1995–6. A party vote occurs when a majority of Republicans oppose a majority of Democrats. Though admittedly a fairly weak threshold – especially when one considers the near-perfect levels of party unity observed in many legislatures outside the United States – this measure is commonly used to track partisan trends in the USA. Figure 6.1 presents the percentage of all roll call votes in the House and Senate that were party votes from 1954 to 2000. The data show that party voting increased dramatically in both chambers in the 1980s and early 1990s, with one of the most noteworthy increases occurring in 1995 in both the House and the Senate.

Since peaking in 1995, however, the level of party voting has declined sharply, to levels more typical of the mid-1980s. For example, 73 percent of House roll calls were party votes in 1995, as compared to just 43 percent in 2000. The Senate experienced a slightly less dramatic but still noteworthy decline, from 69 percent in 1995 to 49 percent in 2000. Thus, in both chambers, fewer than half of all roll call votes currently pit majorities of the two parties against one another. Furthermore, the Republicans' success in holding their ranks together has declined, albeit modestly, on this shrinking subset of party votes. Figure 6.2 presents party unity levels on party votes. This is the percentage of members who vote together with the majority of their party on the subset of party votes. In 1995, approximately 93 percent of House Republicans sided with their party on party votes. This unusually high unity level declined to a still-impressive 86 percent in 1999 and 88 percent in 2000.

The decline in party voting derives partly from moderate party

Figure 6.1 *Percentage of votes where a mjority of Democrats opposes a majority of Republicans, 1954–2000*

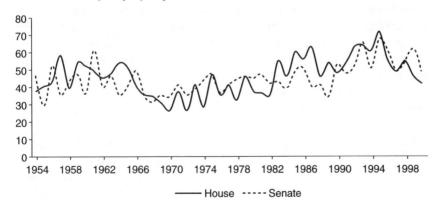

—— House ----- Senate

Figure 6.2   *Party unity in Congressional voting, 1954–2000 (%)*

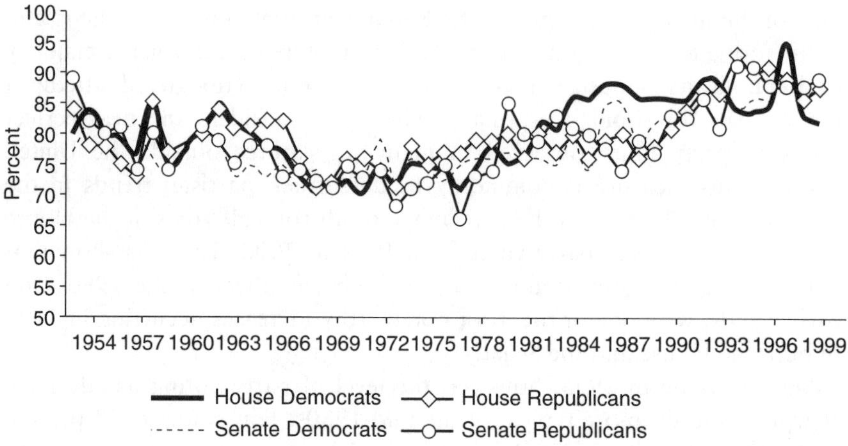

members' increased willingness to buck their leadership on important issues. Thus, House Republicans lost high-profile votes on campaign finance reform, new regulations on health maintenance organizations, and the environment in the 106th Congress of 1999–2000. The Republicans emerged victorious on 70 percent of all party votes in 2000, as compared to 88 percent in 1995, again suggesting the party's vulnerability as its unity and seat share have declined.

At the same time, lower party voting also results from deliberate strategic choices by Hastert and his fellow Republican leaders. Looking ahead to the 2000 elections, in which Republicans feared that their already-narrow majority was at grave risk, Hastert agreed to schedule votes on several issues that the Republicans had blocked in the past. As a result, the House voted on gun control, campaign finance reform, prescription drug benefits for senior citizens, a patients' bill of rights, and increased education funding. While Republican unity frayed on several of these issues, the votes inoculated vulnerable party members against Democratic charges that they were ignoring major concerns of voters. Meanwhile, these House-passed bills generally died in the Senate or in the conference committees appointed to reconcile differences in the House and Senate versions of proposed legislation. As a result, House Republicans gained the electoral benefits of voting for and even passing popular bills in their chamber, without conservatives having to endure the policy effects of undesirable legislation.

Lower party voting in the Senate also resulted in part from leaders' strategic choices. Republican leader Lott often blocked Democratic amendments that had been designed to embarrass the Republicans or to shift policy in a liberal direction. At other times, Lott simply removed bills from the floor when he lacked the 60 votes needed for cloture. The net result was that numerous potential party votes never occurred, even though deep partisan divisions over these issues remained beneath the surface.

Still, the decline in party voting is at least suggestive of the challenges facing party government in the contemporary context. Numerous commentators have noted the disconnect between the sharp partisanship and ideological polarization in Congress and the moderation of most voters (see, for example, Fiorina, 1999). This disjuncture has been rooted largely in the design of congressional districts: though the country as a whole is fairly moderate and is closely divided between Democrats and Republicans, most members of Congress come from districts in which their party has a safe majority (Jacobson, 2000). Nonetheless, both parties still have a few dozen members who come from districts that are not entirely in harmony with the ideological tenor of their party. These members become more important as the partisan balance on the Hill has grown ever closer. The result is that, on most issues, neither party can assume that it will be able to unilaterally push its programs through either chamber. This again is a major change from Gingrich's first hundred days and the triumphant passage of the Contract with America in the House of Representatives.

The rise of toss-up politics

An unintended, indirect legacy of the Republicans' 1995 takeover of Congress has been the rise of what can be called "toss-up politics" (see Mayhew, 1996). The United States has shifted from seemingly permanent and generally comfortable Democratic majorities to a much more volatile and evenly divided Congress. The party balance in the House has been quite close since 1995 and has edged closer following each of the past three elections. The 221–211 Republican majority in the 107th Congress (2001–2) is one of the narrowest divisions in US history. The Senate started out the 107th Congress dead even, which is something that has not happened for over a century. Only the tie-breaking vote of Vice-President Dick Cheney gave the Republicans official control of the chamber, and that control slipped away when Jeffords became an Independent midway through 2001. Perhaps nothing symbolizes the close partisan balance nationally better than the 2000 presidential election, which was decided by fewer than 1,000 votes out of the 6 million cast in Florida and 100 million votes cast nationally. Intensified party competition has important implications for congressional politics.

Unless there is an economic disaster for which one party is blamed, both parties can now reasonably expect switches in party control and a close party balance to persist for the next several years. This volatility could, in principle, create incentives for cooperation between the majority and minority parties. Today's majority party might allow some minority party influence, knowing that it could easily be in the minority in the next Congress. A norm of reciprocity could take hold amid the recognition of the majority party's insecurity. One major sign of cooperation occurred in the Senate in January 2001 when Democratic and Republican leaders agreed on a power-sharing arrangement reflecting the 50–50 seat split in the chamber. Republican leader Lott reluctantly agreed to Democratic leader Daschle's demand that the two parties have an equal number of seats on each standing committee. In exchange, Daschle withdrew his demand that the Democrats be allowed to share in committee chairman-ships. Lott also agreed not to block amendments by such methods as filing for cloture (Taylor, 2001a). The Republicans' willingness to accommodate the Democrats' demands suggested a keen awareness that the party's slender majority could easily slip away.

An alternative scenario, however, is for the highly-competitive race for majority status to give rise to increasingly nasty partisan warfare, as each side furiously fights to paint the other as out-of-touch with mainstream voters. Thus far, this has proven the main implication of toss-up politics. Therefore, even as party voting receded somewhat in the 106th Congress, partisan acrimony continued its long-term rise. Pitney (2001) reports two episodes that illustrate how the parties view themselves as engaged in political warfare. In June 1999, Representative Billy Tauzin (R-La) attempted to rally Republicans by distributing a videotape of himself dressed as General George Patton, standing in front of an American flag, and emulating the war hero's motivational speeches. Pitney quotes a Tauzin aide noting that "there's a symbolic significance in the fact that as we head into the 2000 elections, Republicans recognize they're in a polit-ical war for control of the House." Tauzin's selection as Chairman of the powerful Energy and Commerce Committee in January 2001 suggests that his understanding of the Republicans' strategic situation was not at all out-of-touch with his fellow party members. Furthermore, such bellicose views were by no means confined to Republicans. As the 2000 election neared, the usually mild-mannered Democratic leader Richard Gephardt (D-Mo.) took the martial theme further, showing up at a Democratic Caucus meeting dressed as a warrior from the movie *Braveheart*, wearing a breast-plate and face paint (Pitney, 2001). Even if one discounts such theatrics, the more general point is that the two parties' leaders, and many of their members, view the opposing party as an enemy in a protracted "war" for majority status.

While this may not sound all that different from normal party politics, it represents quite a departure from the behavior common between the 1920s and the 1970s, when the Speaker and minority leader were often close friends who sought to limit partisan strife (Peters, 1997; Schickler, 2001). In the contemporary Congress, Speaker Hastert and Democratic leader Gephardt rarely even talk with one another and they make little secret of their mutual animosity (Pianin and Eilperin, 2000). Such dynamics are reinforced by the fact that most members' only congressional experience has occurred during this era of fierce partisan warfare; fewer than one-third of current members had served in Congress prior to 1992 and half have arrived since 1994. This makes bipartisan agreements increasingly difficult to achieve, even on issues where the policy differences between the parties are not necessarily all that sharp. The Democrats believe they benefit politically by highlighting their differences with the Republicans, rather than by compromising on policy. The Republicans, meanwhile, show little inclination to bargain with Democratic leaders, preferring instead to develop programs to counter any Democratic talk of a "do-nothing" Congress (Evans, 2001).

Presidential-Congressional Relations in an Era of Partisan Warfare

George W. Bush entered the White House in January 2001 promising to end the partisan bitterness in Washington. Bush's ascension has had a substantial impact on presidential–congressional relations, but it seems unlikely to produce a major reduction in partisan warfare, particularly given the continuing close party balance in Congress.

After the Democrats' 1994 election debacle, Clinton confronted divided party control of Congress and the Presidency throughout his last six years in office. One result was a barrage of aggressive congressional investigations of alleged wrongdoing in the executive branch. These included well-publicized hearings probing the Whitewater scandal, fundraising abuses by Clinton, Vice-President Al Gore, and other Democrats in the 1996 campaign, and allegations of espionage at national weapons laboratories. The hearings that led to Clinton's impeachment were the culmination of this increasingly bitter relationship. Republicans hoped that Clinton's personal escapades would generate sufficient public disapproval to solidify their majority and propel their party to the presidency. But even when public opinion polls showed a noteworthy lack of enthusiasm for impeachment, House Republicans nonetheless pushed the process forward, believing (apparently correctly) that any damage to their party's image would be shortlived.

The numerous congressional investigations and bitter impeachment battle did not mean that Clinton and the Republicans could never work together on policy: for example, Hastert and Lott supported the

President's successful effort to grant China permanent most-favored nation (MFN) trade status. More generally, Republican leaders proved willing to work with Clinton when they believed it would help them retain majority status. In the months before the 1996 election, House and Senate Republican leaders concluded a series of deals with Clinton that produced legislation transforming the welfare system, increasing the minimum wage, and making health insurance portable when individuals switched jobs. Such legislation helped the Republicans avoid the label of a "do-nothing" Congress, while enhancing Clinton's reputation as an able leader. The only politicians hurt by these deals were Republican presidential candidate Bob Dole and Democratic candidates for Congress.

In the 106th Congress, House Republican leaders once again showed an interest in compromise with the White House. Fearing that their majority would otherwise be lost in the upcoming 2000 election, Hastert and his team remained flexible on such issues as the minimum wage and prescription drugs. House conservatives reluctantly went along with Hastert's efforts to find common ground with Clinton, believing that it would save the party's majority. News accounts noted that Hastert and Clinton had built a reasonably good working relationship, in contrast to Gingrich's far more confrontational dealings with Clinton. Hastert and Clinton even appeared together at an event in Chicago to promote tax incentives to spur community development in urban and rural areas with high unemployment. But unlike in 1996, Senate Republicans (incorrectly) believed their majority was safe and therefore were less willing to compromise with the White House. A top aide to a Senate Republican leader noted that "the House definitely wants accomplishments. They want bills signed. The Senate is less concerned with having bills signed. There will be a resistance on the Senate side to giving away the store in order to get accomplishments" (Taylor, 2000). Instead, Lott and his fellow Republican leaders argued that the Republicans should wait until their party gained control of the presidency, so that they would not need to compromise their conservative agenda.

The Bush presidency

Notwithstanding the controversies surrounding the 2000 election, George W. Bush's ascension to the presidency offered just this opportunity. For the first time since 1954, Republicans controlled the White House and both chambers of Congress. The shift to unified party government meant a much closer working relationship between the president and congressional leaders. Both Hastert and Lott adopted Bush's agenda as their own. Indeed, whereas divided party control had allowed House and Senate Republican leaders to pursue their own priorities, the shift to a Republican President has meant that party strategy is largely worked out in the White

House. A top Senate Republican aide noted in January 2001 that "we're still testing the waters to figure out who . . . is in charge . . . And we're learning quickly that it isn't us" (Taylor, 2001b). Deference to Bush also derives from the widespread belief that the Republicans' majority status will depend critically on Bush's popularity and accomplishments as President.

The shift from divided to unified party control had the biggest impact on budget deliberations. Under Clinton, budget battles extended throughout the year and often involved veto threats and warnings about shutting down the government. After the government shutdowns of 1995–6 resulted in devastating public relations defeats for the Republicans, Clinton generally had the upper hand in these negotiations. Between 1996 and 1999, the Republicans went along with the President's spending priorities in order to allow the budget process to conclude without further political damage (Alvarez, 2000). In 2000, the Republicans sought to avoid such presidential victories by passing their appropriations bills quickly. But in the end the Republicans could not reach an agreement with the White House over several spending bills during the regular session, and as a result resorted to a lame duck session after the November election. The final spending total was $10 billion more than Clinton had requested at the start of the budget cycle, a proposal that the Republicans had then attacked as excessive (CQWR, December 16 2000). The arrival of budget surpluses in the late 1990s had not led to a less confrontational budget process, but had allowed for significant spending increases.

Under Bush, the dynamics shifted considerably. The House speedily passed each of the components of the President's $1.6 trillion tax cut package, notwithstanding the vociferous objections of Democrats. House Republicans also passed a budget outline that closely reflected the new president's priorities. The evenly-divided Senate proved less accommodating as a handful of moderate Republicans cooperated with the Democrats to trim the tax cut. Nonetheless, Bush won a $1.3 trillion cut, which included virtually all of his main priorities. This victory suggested the persistence of partisanship in the budget process. Under divided party control, the Republicans had been forced to compromise with the Democrats and had failed to enact a major tax cut; but once in control of the White House as well as Congress, the Republicans were able to enact substantial changes.

This unified party control proved fleeting, however. Jeffords's defection brought the first era of Republican unified control to an end after a mere $5^{1}/_{2}$ months. Bush now has to contend with a Democratic Senate, with a narrowly Republican House, and with the presence of several maverick Republicans who have agendas of their own. (He also has to acknowledge the perspective of numerous moderates whose electoral concerns are paramount.) The narrow margins in the House and Senate gives mavericks and moderates in both parties considerable influence (Nather and Bettelheim, 2001). Among the Republicans, moderates have resisted efforts to scale back environmental laws, restrict abortion rights, and cut spending. Moderates are also organized, using the Tuesday Group as a regular meeting forum to plan strategy and to pressure party leaders to temper controversial conservative policy proposals. In reaction to the Tuesday Group's efforts to shape the Republican agenda, other party members formed the Conservative Action Team as a counterweight (Kolodny, 1999). The existence of these competing groups is indicative of Republican factionalism. Among Democrats, however, the Blue Dog Coalition, which consists of approximately 30 conservative House Democrats, has supported some Republican policies. Furthermore, Democrats are also divided between a Progressive Caucus that favors traditional Democratic positions on most issues and the centrist New Democrat Coalition. Democratic leader Dick Gephardt had managed to minimize these divisions in the 106th Congress, as Democrats submerged their differences in the name of winning back the House. But these burgeoning intraparty divisions present an opportunity for Bush, even as he has to manage his own party's split between moderates and conservatives.

In addition to such ideological cleavages, individual entrepreneurs can be expected to challenge Bush's agenda control. This is nothing new: the Senate, in particular, continues to house semi-independent operators who are as interested in promoting their own careers and issue positions as in working with their party. The best example is John McCain (R-Ariz.), Bush's opponent for the Republican nomination in the 2000 election. McCain demanded that Lott allow a floor vote on his signature issue, campaign finance reform, early in the 2001 session (see Chapter 18). Though Bush preferred that the issue not come up until well after his tax cut package (if at all), McCain threatened to force a vote and Lott agreed to schedule the debate for March 2001. Despite the objections of Republican party leaders, it passed the Senate. Therefore, though the arrival of unified party control initially promised more cooperative presidential–congressional relations, the shift to a Democratic majority in the Senate, the narrow Republican majority in the House, and persistent Senate individualism will limit Bush's ability to shape congressional deliberations.

Congressional partisan warfare: its roots and its future

One of the critical questions for the future of Congress is whether the partisan warfare will dissipate with the departure of such polarizing figures as

Clinton and Gingrich. The discussion thus far includes signs of both possi-bilities: party voting and centralized party leadership have declined from their peak levels, but bipartisan cooperation on key issues has proven elusive, to say the least. In order to assess the future of partisan dynamics in Congress it is necessary to consider the sources of the revival of parties and to evaluate whether these sources are likely to remain operative.

Conditional party government and the revitalization of parties

The most prominent explanation for the revival of parties emphasizes changes in their constituency bases. According to conditional party gov-ernment theory, majority party members will delegate power to party leaders when the members have similar policy preferences and when those preferences depart sharply from those of the minority party (Aldrich and Rohde, 1999; see also Cooper and Brady, 1981). As conservative Republicans replaced moderate and conservative southern Democrats in the 1970s–90s, and as liberal Democrats replaced northeastern liberal and moderate Republicans in the same period, the two parties' constituency bases became more internally unified and polarized from one another (Rohde, 1991; Polsby, 1997). Democrats now hailed from liberal districts, and Republicans from conservative districts. As a result, the Democrats became much more unified behind left-of-center policies and Republicans behind conservative policies. Under these conditions, party members benefit from centralizing power in the hands of leaders who will pursue their shared policy agenda.

From conditional party government theory, one would expect that parti-sanship would become less heated on Capitol Hill only if the majority party included a sizable number of members who come from districts that differ substantially from the districts of most party members. In other words, a Republican majority with a big faction of members from mod-erate and even liberal districts, or a Democratic majority with a large number of conservatives, would be unlikely to govern the House or Senate in a highly partisan manner.

Three caveats should be attached to this argument. First, the rise of par-tisan warfare in the Congress coincided with a long period in which the USA faced few, if any, external threats and in which foreign affairs and military policy were generally low priorities. The September 11 2001 ter-rorist attacks on the World Trade Center and the Pentagon transformed the issue agenda – and the more general political terrain – in ways that may encourage a period of increased bipartisan cooperation. Throughout much of US history, partisanship has tended to recede during wartime and other periods of intense foreign policy crises. Democratic leaders' quick moves to endorse President Bush's military response to the attacks suggest that this most recent crisis will likely be no exception.

Second, the House and the Senate differ in the potential success of aggressive partisanship. In the House, it is possible for a unified majority party to pass its agenda while shutting out the minority. In the Senate, by contrast, it is extremely rare for a majority party to have the 60 votes necessary for cloture. In addition, individual senators tend to safeguard their prerogatives and resist leaders' efforts to dictate an agenda. These factors constrain Senate party leaders, regardless of the level of constituent homogeneity and party polarization (Smith and Gamm 2001). Therefore, we should expect the Senate to continue to be fairly unruly, in spite of Trent Lott, Tom Daschle, and future majority leaders' best efforts to control the agenda.

Third, broader electoral calculations can also shape the degree of partisan warfare in Congress. The choice of Denny Hastert as Speaker in 1999 and his shift toward a more decentralized approach to party leadership was rooted less in a change in Republican unity or party polarization than in the Republicans' calculation that a less strident chief would help the party as a whole improve its image with the public (Dodd and Oppenheimer, 2001; Smith and Gamm, 2001). Similarly, Hastert's efforts to reach compromises with Bill Clinton were rooted less in a shift in House Republicans' ideological commitments or unity than in the Republicans' shared belief that legislative accomplishments were necessary to build a good party image. This suggests that partisan electoral calculations can, at times, soften partisan warfare.

Yet the permanent battle for majority status that is characteristic of "toss-up politics" also puts a premium on party members' working together to craft a message that will enhance their chances of gaining or retaining a majority. Instead of incumbents of both parties sharing an interest in passing legislation that will help all incumbents win re-election, members increasingly promote legislation that will help their party's collective reputation and sidetrack bills that will help the other party (Cox and McCubbins, 1993;Evans, 2001).

In sum, the bipartisan accommodations of the 1930s–70s were rooted in the anomalous situation of the Democrats' "permanent" majority and in the Democrats' fierce internal divisions. As long as neither party has a secure majority and both parties are reasonably unified internally, it may be that partisan warfare will characterize the US Congress for some time to come.

Chapter 7

The Supreme Court and the Constitution

TINSLEY E. YARBROUGH

The Supreme Court which George W. Bush inherited in 2001 was one still visibly shaped by the Reagan judicial agenda. Through federal bench appointments and litigation, Reagan had sought a constitutional counter-revolution against the civil liberties precedents of the Warren and Burger eras. For the 12 years between 1981 and 1993 Reagan and the elder Bush appointed nearly three-quarters of all lower federal court judges. They also changed the composition of the Supreme Court with the appointment of Reagan nominees Sandra Day O'Connor, Antonin Scalia and Anthony Kennedy, and of Bush nominees David Souter and Clarence Thomas. (Clinton by contrast appointed only two justices – Ruth Bader Ginsburg and Stephen Breyer – during his eight years in the presidency.) Reagan also elevated Nixon appointee William Rehnquist to be Chief Justice in 1986, thereby giving Rehnquist the center seat on the Court and an opportunity to place the stamp of his leadership on its jurisprudence.

The Rehnquist Court in perspective

Given his record as a member of the Nixon Justice Department and as an associate justice, Rehnquist had seemed ideally suited to lead the Reagan judicial revolution. Not only had he been one of only two dissenters in the landmark abortion case *Roe* v. *Wade* (1973); but he had also challenged the Court's incorporation of Bill of Rights safeguards into the Fourteenth Amendment's restrictions on state authority as well as other elements of modern civil liberties orthodoxy, including the broad construction of First Amendment bans on laws respecting the establishment of religion.

A White House bent on restricting national government power over the states would have found Rehnquist's conception of federalism equally appealing. (see Chapter 9). Rehnquist had spoken for the 5–4 majority in *National League of Cities* v. *Usery* (1976), invoking state sovereignty prin-ciples to overturn a congressional exercise of the commerce power for the

115

first time since 1936. Rehnquist had joined dissenters when *Usery* was overturned in *San Antonio* v. *Garcia* in 1985. Indeed, Rehnquist's conception of national power and federalism seemed more compatible with the anti-Federalist thinking of the founding era than with the Federalist views of the Constitution's most ardent supporters.

The appointments of Scalia and Thomas further advanced the conservative judicial agenda in the 1980s and they were even more likely than Rehnquist to support narrow interpretations of civil liberties and expansive notions of state governmental authority. Presidents, however, cannot always give effect to ideological preferences in their appointments; sometimes they are constrained by political considerations. Reagan's 1981 appointment of Sandra Day O'Connor resulted from a campaign pledge to choose the first woman justice, just as his nomination of Anthony Kennedy was prompted by his desire to avoid further controversy following the Senate's 1987 defeat of the Robert Bork nomination and the forced withdrawal of Douglas Ginsburg's name. Similar considerations apparently drove President Bush's 1990 nomination of David Souter, whose obscurity caused him to be dubbed the "stealth candidate." O'Connor and Kennedy have proved only moderately conservative and have become the Court's most influential justices. Souter, by contrast, has developed into one of the most articulate members of the Court's moderately liberal bloc. The appointment of Ruth Bader Ginsburg and of Stephen Breyer by Clinton brought two moderately liberal, judicial pragmatists to the bench and further complicated the Reagan–Bush judicial agenda.

As a result the Rehnquist Court has a decidedly mixed record to date (Yarbrough, 2001). While generally reluctant to expand the scope of privacy and other unenumerated rights accorded constitutional recognition, the Rehnquist Court has reaffirmed the essence of *Roe* v. *Wade*, if not its reasoning which used a trimester framework to determine the respective rights of the mother and the fetus. (see *Planned Parenthood* v. *Casey*, [1992]). The Rehnquist Court has also been relatively sympathetic to free expression and religious establishment claims, although the latter have caused vehement debates among the justices about the legitimacy of the criteria announced in *Lemon* v. *Kurtzman* (1971) to determine the constitutionality of laws which appeared to offend the establishment clause of the First Amendment. In free exercise of religion cases, however, the Court has virtually eliminated all judicial scrutiny of religiously neutral laws claimed to interfere with religious practice such as the ritual use of the drug peyote (*Employment Division* v. *Smith* [1990]; *City of Boerne* v. *Flores* [1997]). Moreover, like the Burger Court, the Rehnquist Court has usually given a narrow reading to constitutional protections in the criminal justice process, most notably in relation to the scope of the Fourth Amendment exclusionary rule (which excludes the use of evidence obtained in contravention of a suspect's constitutional rights), the so-called *Miranda* warnings (which require suspects to be advised of their constitutional right to silence and to have access to a lawyer), and in relation to capital punishment cases. And although the Rehnquist Court has thus far declined to overrule the use of race-conscious admissions by universities, the majority's distaste for affirmative action is obvious and reflected in its decision to subject federal as well as state affirmative action policies to identical and extremely strict criteria (*Adarand* v. *Pena* [1995]).

By contrast with its approach to these constitutional issues, the Rehnquist Court has been relatively consistent in its reaction to issues of congressional regulatory authority, state power and the scope of property rights. The Burger Court's 1985 rejection in the *Garcia* case of its own *Usery* precedent suggested that a narrow majority was inclined once again to leave judgments about Congress's regulatory powers primarily to the political arena. Beginning with *US* v. *Lopez* (1995), however, a narrow Rehnquist Court majority has been increasingly willing to subject to closer judicial scrutiny congressional statutes adopted under the commerce clause and to invalidate federal controls which appear insufficiently related to interstate commerce. In a related line of rulings the Supreme Court has also rejected congressional authority based on the commerce clause to force state officials to assist in the enforcement of federal policies (*New York* v. *US* [1992]; *Printz* v. *US* [1997]). Beginning with *Seminole Tribe* v. *Florida* [1996], yet another line of cases has significantly expanded the immunity of states from federal damage suits, even those initiated to secure state compliance with valid federal laws.

To dissenting justices and scholarly critics alike, such decisions smack of the pre-1937 *laissez-faire* Court's "dual federalism" construction of the Tenth Amendment with its artificial distinctions between "production" and "commerce" (only the latter of which fell within Congressional power) and between "direct" effects on commerce which Congress could regulate and mere "indirect" effects, which lay entirely within the states' sphere of authority. These decisions have not been the only ones to connect the Rehnquist Court to the Court's pre-1937 history. *BMW* v. *Gore* [1996], which struck down an Alabama jury's award of punitive damages as "excessive" and thus contrary to due process, is the closest the Rehnquist Court has so far come to resurrecting substantive due process – another favorite tool of the pre-1937 *laissez-faire* Court – in an economic context. But a Court majority's increasingly expansive reading of the Fifth Amendment's ban on uncompensated "regulatory takings," as well as the actual taking of private property by government mentioned in the Amendment's text, has served the same purpose of restricting government invasions of property rights and via a constitutional provision that, unlike due process, can only be invoked on behalf of property interests.

The Rehnquist Court's mixed response to civil liberties claims, its limited deference to Congressional regulatory powers, its expansive notions of state sovereignty and its growing protection of property rights are all reflected in very recent Court decisions. This chapter will examine such continuing major trends on the Court in more detail, before proceeding to analyse the implications for the federal judiciary of the transition from Clinton to George W. Bush. First, however, it is necessary to examine the decision of the 2000 term which brought George W Bush to the presidency and confirmed for many critics the suspicion that a majority of this Court's members are among the most ideologically and politically driven in its history.

Bush versus Gore

In 2000 the presidential election, the Electoral College for the first time since 1888 produced a presidential victor who had fewer popular votes than his major opponent. Presidents elected in the past without even a plurality of the popular vote have invariably been denied a second term, the legitimacy of their administrations forever in doubt. Republican Rutherford Hayes's 1876 victory was in some ways the most troubling of these anomalous results. Hayes not only garnered fewer popular votes than his Democratic opponent, Samuel Tilden; but a congressional commission, by a vote of eight Republicans to seven Democrats, awarded all the disputed electoral votes of four states, including Florida, to Hayes who was quickly dubbed "His Fraudulency." Ironically, given the circumstances of the 2000 election dispute, the commission also refused to examine whether votes in the states at issue had been properly counted. Such federal intrusion into a state's selection of presidential electors, the commission declared, would be an affront to state sovereignty.

Like Hayes, George W. Bush won the White House over Gore not merely by a minority of the popular vote (and one more Electoral College vote than the 270 minimum) but only through the decision of another federal agency, by a one-vote margin, to award Florida's 25 electoral votes to Bush. The decisive institution on this occasion – the Supreme Court – has traditionally been expected to remain aloof from partisan politics and had never before played a direct role in the outcome of a presidential election.

The intricacies of *Bush* v. *Gore, Bush* v. *Palm Beach County Canvassing Board* and the related suits growing out of the election dispute have already become the subject of extensive scrutiny (Dershowitz, 2001; Dionne and Kristol, 2001; Posner, 2001). Attorneys for Gore challenged the machine ballot count relied on by Florida's Republican secretary of state to certify the election in Bush's favour, seeking instead a manual recount in counties where evidence suggested sufficient inaccuracies in the machine count to award Florida's electors to Gore (see Chapter 2). When Bush appealed the decision of the Florida supreme court in the *Palm Beach* case to order manual recounts and extend the deadline for the submission of ballot counts to the secretary of state, the US Supreme Court unanimously vacated the state court ruling, remanding the case for further discussion. In a brief *per curiam* opinion (that is, an opinion of the whole court), the justices indicated uncertainty about the basis of the lower court's decision, and specifically the extent to which the state justices may have (impermissibly) invoked voting rights guarantees in the Florida constitution to limit the state legislature's authority under Article 2 of the Constitution to determine how the state's electors should be chosen.

While the *Palm Beach* case was pending, the Florida Supreme Court overturned a state circuit judge's ruling halting manual recounts in a related suit, concluded that there were sufficient uncounted legal votes to place the election outcome in doubt, identified a legal vote as any vote reflecting a clear indication of voter intent and ordered manual recounts to continue. By a 5–4 vote the US Supreme Court granted a stay of the state Supreme Court decision, thereby stopping the ballot recount. In dissent joined by Justices Souter, Ginsburg and Breyer, Justice Stevens accused the majority of violating the Court's traditional policy of refusing to become involved in issues committed by the Constitution to the political branches of government (that is, to Congress in the case of disputed presidential elections). Stevens saw no irreparable harm in the counting of every legally cast vote but tremendous damage to the nation and the credibility of the electoral process (not to mention the Supreme Court itself) if the majority's stay of the manual count, given the press of time, ultimately had the effect of a decision on the merits in Bush's favor.

Following oral argument, the same 5–4 majority (in another *per curiam* decision) reversed the Florida supreme court, holding in *Bush* v. *Gore* that the lower court's procedures for deciding voter intent permitted "arbitrary and disparate treatment" of voters contrary to the Constitution's equal protection and due process guarantees. As Justice Stevens had predicted, the majority also cited time pressures for refusing adoption of uniform standards and a continuation of the recount. The Supreme Court thus ensured that Florida's Electoral College votes – and the presidency – would go to Governor Bush.

A number of circumstances aggravated what one authority called the "vulgarly partisan" image which the Court's intervention in the dispute inevitably projected. Shortly after the decision, the usually taciturn Clarence Thomas sought to convince some schoolchildren that the Court was completely removed from politics. But news reports of Justice

O'Connor's indiscreet election night comment that what then appeared a Gore victory was "terrible" given her desire to retire from the bench hardly helped Thomas's case, and neither, whatever the formal conflict of interest requirements, did revelations that while the case was pending Thomas's wife was working for the Heritage Foundation (a conservative think tank) compiling files of possible appointees in a Bush administration. Equally embarrassing were revelations that Justice Scalia's son was working in the law firm of Theodore Olson, the lawyer who argued Bush's cause in the Supreme Court and who later was made Solicitor General by Bush.

Editorial cartoonists and television comedians had a field day. Reversing Mr Dooley's aphorism, more than one commentator announced that "the election returns now follow the Supreme Court". When Florida Governor Jeb Bush, the future president's brother, promised reform of his state's election machinery, one television comic quipped, "Why fix the election system when you can fix the Supreme Court?"

The Court's decision ended the election dispute and probably spared the nation a bitter confrontation in Congress, but it endangered its reputation. Justice Stevens put it best in a widely quoted passage from the *Bush* opinions when he commented that, although Americans might never know with complete certainty the identity of the winner of the 2000 presidential elections, the identity of the loser was "perfectly clear". It was "the nation's confidence in the judge as an impartial guardian of the rule of law."

The rebirth of "dual federalism"

Those who erroneously predicted the Court would refuse to intervene in Florida's election dispute rested their case primarily on the growing number of recent precedents which reflected the Court's considerable deference to state authority. The Court's break with that pattern in the election cases confirmed suspicions that the *Bush* majority were confusing political preference with legal obligation, although it is hardly likely to affect the general states' rights image of the contemporary Court. Indeed the Court's recent willingness to subject statutes adopted under the commerce clause to close scrutiny, expansive notions of state sovereignty, and broad readings of the Fifth Amendment's takings clause smack of the pre-1937 *laissez-faire* Court's jurisprudence and of economic due process.

In one 2001 case the Court avoided a constitutional ruling on the scope of the commerce power relative to state authority by narrowly construing the federal Clean Water Act to exclude from its reach intrastate waters used as migratory bird habitats (*Solid Waste Agency* v. *Army Corps of*

Engineers). The justices were not obliged to address federalism issues in rejecting a medical necessity exemption from the enforcement of federal drug laws against the distribution and possession of marijuana (*US* v. *Oakland Cannabis Buyers' Cooperative* [2001]). And in *Alexander* v. *Sandoval* (2001), a case challenging Alabama's English-only driver's license examinations, the Court declined to read the 1964 Civil Rights Act as authorizing individual suits against federally-funded policies if those policies had no discriminatory intent as opposed to a disparate impact on different social groups. In *US* v. *Morrison* (2001), however, a 5–4 majority invoked the *Lopez* precedent to invalidate provisions of the federal Violence Against Women Act. Dismissing a suit brought under the Act by a university student allegedly raped by two football players, Rehnquist rejected congressional findings as inadequate to establish a close connection between interstate commerce and gender-based violence which the Chief Justice concluded, was "in no sense of the phrase, economic activity." Neither would the majority uphold the law as an exercise of Congress's power to enforce the Fourteenth Amendment's due process and equal protection guarantees; under that Amendment, declared Rehnquist, Congress could regulate only *state* action, not the sort of *private* misconduct involved here.

In a brief concurrence Justice Thomas, an apparent philosophical soulmate of Justice McReynolds and other members of the pre-1937 Court, again rejected (as he had in *Lopez*) the power of Congress to regulate noneconomic activities, whether or not they had a substantial effect on interstate commerce. Commerce clause jurisprudence in general, Thomas argued, should be subjected to a thorough re-examination, a proposal which, if implemented, would cast constitutional doubt on a wide range of federal government responsibilities. As in *Lopez*, and other cases challenging the scope of congressional regulatory activity, Justices Stevens, Souter, Ginsburg, and Breyer dissented. Souter, joined by the others, recalled the many precedents extending the commerce power to all activities that, individually or in the aggregate, substantially affected interstate commerce. Congress needed only a rational basis for concluding that gender-based violence, or any other activity, exerted such an impact; and the factual findings Congress had amassed surely satisfied that rational standard. To Souter, the majority's approach resembled far more the "formalistically contrived" limitations imposed on congressional authority in the *laissez-faire* era than the substantial body of post-1937 case law which deferred to Congress's judgment on its regulatory power. The unfortunate history of the pre-1937 period, Souter added, had made it clear that politics, not the courts, should be the primary restraint on congressional power just as, in Breyer's view, Congress, not the courts, must remain primarily responsible for striking the appropriate state/federal balance.

Perhaps more potentially significant even than *Morrison* and other decisions invoking state sovereignty principles to restrict the reach of the commerce power are recent Rehnquist Court rulings expanding state immunity from private damage suits even to those brought to secure protection for federal rights. The Eleventh Amendment's text forbids federal courts to hear only suits brought against states by citizens of other states or foreign nations. Despite that language, the Supreme Court long ago construed the amendment to forbid also federal suits brought against states by their own citizens (*Hans* v. *Louisiana* [1890]). In *Seminole Tribe* v. *Florida* (1996) a 5–4 Supreme Court majority went further, denying Congress power under the commerce clause to authorize federal suits brought against states by Indian tribes to enforce federal law. This decision was followed by several in 1999 which invoked principles inherent in statehood, state sovereignty, federalism and what a dissenter termed a sort of natural or divine law more reminiscent of James I than James Madison to immunize states from damage suits brought in state courts to secure federal rights (*Alden* v. *Maine, Florida Prepaid Postsecondary* v. *College Savings Bank, College Savings Bank* v. *Florida Prepaid Postsecondary*).

In *Alden*, for example, a 5–4 Court dismissed a suit brought by Maine probation officers challenging the state's refusal to honor overtime provisions in federal wage laws. The majority agreed, however, that Congress could authorize federal officials (as opposed to the probation officers) to file suits against states to enforce rights protected by federal statute. As Justice Souter pointed out in dissent, such relief was more apparent than real, given the limits to federal litigation resources. By recognizing the immunity of states under such circumstances, Souter charged, the Court was abandoning the fundamental principle that the law provides a meaningful remedy for the violation of every legal right. Whatever the scope of the largely judge-made immunity doctrine, the dissenters argued, states were not sovereign entities clothed with immunity from private damage suits subjecting them to the provisions of supreme national law. As members of the union committed to the Constitution and the supremacy of national law, states could not disobey otherwise valid federal statutes, whatever the forum invoked to assure their compliance.

It is true that the Rehnquist Court has recognized an exception to the ban on private damage suits for cases where the argument is based on Congress's power to enforce the explicit restrictions on state action guaranteed in the Fourteenth Amendment, but that concession has been of limited value to plaintiffs. Thus in *Kimel* v. *Florida Board of Regents* (2000) a 5–4 majority dismissed a suit brought by state government workers under federal legislation preventing state as well as private age discrimination in employment. Speaking for the Court, Justice O'Connor conceded that Congress had intended to abrogate the states' immunity from suit in such cases. Pointing out, however, that the laws discriminating on age grounds were not constitutionally suspect (unlike laws based on race or color) and thus need only be rationally related to a legitimate state purpose, O'Connor concluded that the broad federal ban on age discrimination in employment exceeded Congress's Fourteenth Amendment enforcement authority. Similarly in *Board of Trustees* v. *Garrett* (2001) the same 5–4 majority dismissed federal suits brought against a state university under the 1990 Americans with Disabilities Act (ADA). Discrimination based on handicap, like age discrimination, need only have a rational basis, which is a less demanding standard than the requirements the ADA imposed.

Justice Souter in his *Morrison* dissent compared the majority's recent constructions of federal and state power to the pre-1937 Court jurisprudence but attributed the pre-1937 Court's rulings to the ideology of *laissez-faire* and the current Court's stance to a "conception of federalism." The recent and unprecedented flowering of the Rehnquist Court's jurisprudence on the takings clause, however, bears a striking resemblance to the pre-1937 Court's use of the doctrine of substantive due process to protect *laissez-faire*. Enlarging dramatically on Justice Holmes's largely forgotten assertion in *Pennsylvania Coal* v. *Mahon* (1922) that governmental control over private property taken "too far" constitutes a taking for which just compensation must be provided, or the regulation dropped, the Rehnquist Court has found "regulatory takings" in a variety of environmental and zoning contexts (for example, *Lucas* v. *South Carolina Coastal Council* [1992]; *Dolan* v. *City of Tigard* [1994]). Thus the Court has subjected to compensation requirements any regulation that amounts to a physical invasion of private property, deprives the owner of anticipated beneficial use, or is not closely related to the substantial societal interests it is claimed to promote.

In recent cases, the Court has taken its regulatory takings doctrine beyond controls over real estate to restrictions on personal property (*Phillips* v. *Washington Legal Foundation* [1998]; *Eastern Enterprises* v. *Apfel* [1998]), further underlining the links between its takings jurisprudence and the pre-1937 Court's use of substantive due process. Such connections are particularly interesting in view of the intense opposition of Justices Scalia and Thomas to the idea of substantive due process, despite their support for the Court's unprecedented expansion of the scope of the takings clause. Their position with respect to the two guarantees may not, however, be as surprising as it at first sight appears. The takings clause can be invoked only on behalf of property. Substantive due process has been used to protect not only economic interests but also abortion rights and other noneconomic freedoms in a manner which Scalia and Thomas reject.

The First Amendment

In contrast to the Rehnquist Court's distinctive approach to congressional and state regulatory issues, its decisions in the field of free expression and association have drawn on standards sculpted in the Warren and Burger eras, albeit with subtle modifications of doctrine and application. Where free expression and association claims have clashed with equality values, however, the First Amendment values have prevailed.

Partly perhaps because of its reluctance to make new law in this field, the Court has recently decided few expression and association cases. *California Democratic Party* v. *Jones* (2000) struck down California's 1996 adoption by voter initiative of the blanket primary method for party nomination of candidates for public offices on the grounds that the state's decision to allow voters to participate in the primaries of all parties regardless of party affiliation interfered with each party's associational right to choose its nominees for office (see also Chapters 3 and 19). In 2001 a divided Court extended its landmark 1976 decision in *Buckley* v. *Valeo* and upheld federal limitations on party campaign expenditures tied to particular candidates, equating such spending with the organizational contributions to campaigns that had long been subject to restrictions (*Federal Election Commission* v. *Colorado Campaign Committee* [2001]). In another case involving federal regulation of expression, a 7–2 majority construed federal copyright law favorably for freelance authors, refusing to allow publishers to place printed work in electronic databases without the author's permission (*New York Times Co* v. *Tasini* [2001]). In *Cook* v. *Gralike* (2001) the Court struck down a state requirement that ballots denote those Congressional candidates who opposed term limits. Although Justice Stevens, speaking for the Court, based his decision in *Cook* on the argument that such a requirement exceeded state authority to regulate the time, manner and place of Congressional elections, Rehnquist and O'Connor based their votes on First Amendment grounds. And in a 5–4 majority the Court held that a federal regulation prohibiting Legal Service Corporation lawyers from challenging welfare payments on behalf of poor clients also violated the free speech guarantee (*Legal Services Corp.* v. *Velazquez* [2001]).

In the controversial area of tobacco regulation, the Court at the end of its 2000 term struck down some, but not all, state restrictions on the advertising and sale of cigarettes, smokeless tobacco and cigars, invoking federal pre-emption and commercial speech doctrines. State regulations governing outdoor and point-of-sale cigarette adverts were pre-empted by federal controls over such advertising, according to Justice O'Connor; and provisions relating to advertising other tobacco products violated the freedom guaranteed commercial speech. However, the justices upheld provisions to prevent access by minors to tobacco which required that tobacco products be placed under counters and be accessible to customers only through a salesperson.

The rights of anti-abortion protesters have continued to split the Court's more conservative justices in recent years. In *Hill* v. *Colorado* (2000), the Court upheld a statute forbidding people to approach within eight feet of another person near a health service facility without the person's consent. Rehnquist and O'Connor joined Justice Stevens's majority opinion while Scalia and Thomas filed vigorous dissents upholding the First Amendment rights of abortion protesters. Justice Kennedy also dissented, arguing that the Court's decision conflicted with *Planned Parenthood* v. *Casey*, the 1992 case which upheld the essence of the *Roe* decision. While leaving the abortion option largely to the woman, *Casey* had recognized the serious moral questions surrounding abortion. By upholding restrictions on anti-abortion protests, Kennedy reasoned, the majority was limiting the opportunities for abortion opponents to participate in that moral debate.

More familiar divisions on the court reappeared in *Boy Scouts of America* v. *Dale* (2000) which concerned a clash between the associational rights of the boy scouts and a state's ban on discrimination based on sexual orientation. When a scout organization removed homosexual scoutmaster, the New Jersey Supreme Court had held the action contrary to the state's civil rights statute. The Rehnquist Court reversed the decision, by a 5–4 majority, holding that homosexual conduct was inconsistent with scout values, especially their requirement that scouts be "morally straight" and "clean." A state requirement that the scouts retain an avowedly homosexual scoutmaster conflicted with those values and thus unduly interfered with the organization's freedom of association.

The Rehnquist Court has recently decided only a few religion cases. Presumably, a narrow majority continues to embrace the position (most recently affirmed in *City of Boerne* v. *Flores* (1997) that religious practices must conform to religiously neutral drug, zoning and other laws, whether or not the regulations at issue promote the sort of compelling interest traditionally required of government burdens on religious liberty. Since unorthodox religious practices (such as the ritual use of the drug peyote) are more likely to run afoul of criminal laws than their mainstream counterparts, the Court's stance has narrowed considerably the scope of religious liberty. A different majority, however, has continued to take a strong separationist stance in religious establishment cases despite the complaints of Scalia, Thomas and Rehnquist that a proper reading of the First Amendment would permit considerable government accommodation of religion. Thus in *Santa Fe Independent School District* v. *Doe* (2000), a 5–4 majority struck down a public school policy permitting student initiated and led prayer before athletic events as impermissibly coercive. On the other hand, *Good News Club* v. *Milford Central School* (2001) held that public elementary schools, like their high school and public school counterparts, may not deny religious groups after hours access to school facilities available to other groups.

Criminal justice

Like the Burger Court before it, a Rehnquist Court majority has been most likely to side with the government in the criminal justice arena, expansively construing police powers of search and interrogation and imposing few restrictions on death penalty practices (see also Chapter 11). As several recent rulings attest, however, the Court has not been entirely predictable in its response to the claims of suspects and defendants. For example, Chief Justice Rehnquist has long been a vehement critic of the Fourth Amendment exclusionary rule and the *Miranda* doctrine because he thought neither was required by the Constitution, and both exacted heavy social costs by excluding reliable evidence from the courts and thereby undermining the criminal justice system. Yet in *Dickerson* v. *United States* (2000) Rehnquist spoke for a 7–2 majority in striking down a federal statute that made police failure to administer *Miranda* warnings only one factor to be considered by the courts in determining the validity of a confession. Rehnquist conceded that earlier cases had characterized the *Miranda* standards as judicially created safeguards whose extension to various stages of a criminal case depended on the degree to which it would serve as an additional deterrent to police misconduct. Noting, however, that *Miranda* was a state case over which the Supreme Court had no general supervisory authority beyond what the Constitution required, Rehnquist concluded that the *Miranda* warnings had "constitutional underpinnings" which Congress could not legitimately ignore.

During the 2000 term the justices handed down a decision in a death penalty case previously before the Court more than a decade earlier. In *Penry* v. *Lynaugh* (1989) the Court held that the execution of defendants who are mentally retarded but not legally insane did not violate the constitutional guarantee against "cruel and unusual punishment;" but it reversed Penry's conviction and sentence on the grounds that the trial judge had not specifically instructed jurors that they should consider mitigating factors relating to the defendant's background, character or the circumstance of the crime. In *Penry* v. *Johnson* (2001) the Court concluded that the penalty proceedings following the defendant's trial had not met that requirement.

At the end of the term, the Court also imposed restrictions on the authority of immigration officials to detain an alien subject to final deportation. Federal law provides that aliens can be held in custody during a 90-day removal period, but where necessary can be detailed or given supervised release after that date. To avoid the serious constitutional questions indefinite detention would create the Court held that aliens can be detained only for the period "reasonably necessary" to bring about their deportation. (*Zadvydas* v. *Davis* [2001]).

Equal protection

The Supreme Court's limited equal protection caseload over recent terms has focused primarily on governmental policies which are race-conscious, and especially on controversial congressional districting plans designed to increase minority representation in the House of Representatives. In *Shaw* v. *Reno* (1993) a 5–4 majority ruled that North Carolina electoral districts containing a majority of minority voters violated equal protection if they were so bizarrely drawn that they could only be the products of racial considerations. Later cases, including *Shaw* v. *Hunt* (1996), which was the North Carolina case's second trip to the Court, held by a 5–4 majority that majority–minority districting was invalid if motivated by predominantly racial, rather than political, considerations. But when a three-judge federal district court summarily invalidated the district plan enacted by North Carolina following the second *Shaw* decision, a unanimous Supreme Court reversed the decision (*Hunt* v. *Cromartie* [1999]), requiring a hearing on the issues in the trial court. And when, following that trial, the district court again ruled that race trumped politics in the adoption of the state's plan, the Supreme Court reversed the decision.

A trial court's finding of fact can be overturned on appeal only if found to be clearly erroneous. But speaking for a 5–4 Court Justice O'Connor, who had voted to strike down North Carolina's initial majority-minority plan, found only a "modicum" of evidence to support the trial panel's holding. O'Connor concluded that the state's decision to place large numbers of African-American voters in North Carolina's twelfth congressional district, the district at issue in the case, was just as likely to have been based on the heavily Democratic voting patterns of black voters, and the state's desire to protect incumbents, as on racial considerations. Justices Thomas, Rehnquist, Scalia and Kennedy dissented, emphasizing the traditional deference to be accorded to the factual findings of trial courts.

The most intriguing nonracial discrimination case of recent terms was *Saenz* v. *Roe* (1999) which struck down a California law that limited welfare benefits for new arrivals during their first year in the state. A number of controversial Warren and Burger Court decisions had invoked equal protection to invalidate residency requirements for welfare benefits, voting and medical care. Concerned perhaps about reviving the expansive approach to equal protection evident in these rulings, the Court in a 7–2 decision elected surprisingly to base its decision on the Fourteenth Amendment's long neglected privileges or immunities clause which had only once been used to strike down a state law and then in a precedent overturned five years later. Under the privileges or immunities clause, the Court concluded, a state could not distinguish at all between new and more established citizens with respect to benefits; and no challenge had been raised against the respondent's claim to be a California citizen. Rehnquist and Thomas, on the other hand, defended a state's right to use residence requirements to determine eligibility for benefits, arguing that there was little difference between the benefits at issue and others such as access to the divorce courts and university tuition where the Court had upheld the legality of residence requirements.

In a highly publicized case with equal protection implications decided on statutory grounds, the Court invoked the 1990 Americans with Disabilities Act to uphold the right of Casey Martin, a golfer afflicted with a degenerative circulatory disorder, to use a golf cart in Professional Golfer's Association tournaments contrary to the association's rules. ADA regulations, the Court held, prohibited the Professional Golfer's Association from denying Martin equal access to its tours, and the use of a golf cart, would not "fundamentally alter" the nature of the sport.

Unenumerated rights

The Fourteenth Amendment's equal protection guarantee was the Warren Court's favorite civil liberties tool and one more prominent in the Burger Court's constitutional legacy than its early efforts to confine its reach initially suggested (see *San Antonio Independent School District* v. *Rodriguez* [1973]). By contrast, the small number of equal protection claims in the Rehnquist Court's caseload reflects the current Court's reluctance to invoke the equal protection guarantee as a vehicle for giving constitutional recognition to additional substantive rights nowhere mentioned in the Constitution 's text. The current Court has also been generally reluctant to invoke substantive due process to recognize new rights. In *Bowers* v. *Hardwick* (1986) (decided in Burger's last term) a 5–4 majority refused to extend the right of privacy to homosexual sodomy, confining the scope of substantive due process to liberties "deeply rooted in this Nation's history and tradition." The Rehnquist Court has consistently affirmed the Bowers formula, refusing ,for example, to recognise a due process right to assisted suicide (*Washington* v. *Glucksberg, Vacco* v. *Quill*).

The Court's stance has, however, been more flexible than its rhetoric and certain of its rulings would suggest. Although a unanimous Court joined Rehnquist's opinion in the assisted suicide cases, a majority also indicated in separate opinions that the terminally ill are entitled, as Breyer put it, to "death with dignity" which (in certain circumstances) might require a physician's assistance. Despite the *Bowers* ruling, the Court in a 6–3 decision invalidated a state constitutional amendment forbidding laws against discrimination based on sexual preference (*Romer* v. *Evans* [1996]). A majority has continued to uphold the essence of *Roe* v. *Wade*'s provision of an abortion right; its approach, first announced in *Casey* v. *Planned Parenthood*, eliminates *Roe*'s rigorous trimester framework but prohibits "undue burdens" on a woman's decision to abort a pregnancy. In *Stenberg* v. *Carhart* (2000), for example, the Court in a 5–4 decision struck down a law forbidding "partial-birth" abortions.

Among the justices, Scalia and Thomas remain adamantly opposed to the concept of substantive due process, however, and the Chief Justice ordinarily extends considerable defence to government in such cases. *Troxel* v. *Granville* (2000) invoked the substantive due process rights of parents in overturning a law that granted judges broad discretion to award grandparents and "any other person" visitation rights considered to be in the child's best interest. Thomas concurred in the judgment but noted neither party in the case had argued that "our substantive due process cases were wrongly decided and that the original understanding of the Due Process Clause precludes judicial enforcement of unenumerated rights under that constitutional provision," a position Thomas obviously embraces. Dissenting, Scalia cited the limited precedential support for the Court's stance, rejected any judicial authority to define and protect such liberties, and cautioned against further extension of the parental rights at issue in the case.

Judicial appointments and the Bush presidency

Although judicial policy apparently played little role in shaping the choices of voters in the 2000 presidential election, the fundamental differences between the two candidates' likely approach to judicial nominations loomed large with their core constituencies and the media. When pressed, Bush offered Justices Thomas and Scalia as the type of judge he favored. Gore naturally had different ideas. The impact of a Bush or a Gore victory on the future of abortion rights was a subject of intense speculation (see Chapter 16); and the Supreme Court's intervention in the Florida ballot case underlined the probable impact of the election on the federal judiciary.

Even before the 1994 Republican takeover of Congress, President Clinton had leaned toward the appointment of centrist judges. This preference was consistent both with his moderate "new" Democrat politics and with his desire to avoid protracted Senate confirmation battles. A recent comparison of the appointees of Clinton, the elder Bush and Reagan shows that in criminal cases they were likely to vote against the defendant in 42.07 percent, 45.76 percent and 55.23 percent of cases respectively. By contrast the record of President Carter's appointees in such cases revealed that they were likely to vote against defendants 19.15 percent of the time. That pattern of continuity did not inhibit Senate Judiciary Chairman Orrin Hatch (R-Utah) in his determination to delay confirmation hearings at the end of the Clinton term to save lower federal court nominations for a Republican White House. Even when Rehnquist warned in the annual report of the state of the judiciary that the number of vacant seats on the federal bench was creating a crisis, placing blame on the Senate rather than on the judiciary, the situation barely improved. As his term began in 2001, President Bush had the opportunity to fill 89 lower court vacancies, with additional resignations anticipated in the near future.

On taking office, Bush also initiated a number of changes in the judicial selection process, most notably by eliminating the traditional role of the American Bar Association (ABA) in evaluating nominees. The ABA's Committee on Federal Judiciary had been reviewing and rating nominees and prospects for judgeships since the Eisenhower presidency; but, as the Reagan administration became increasingly concerned about the ABA's increasingly liberal position on abortion and other issues and about the ABA's preference for older judges with extensive trial experience (rather than the younger nominees and legal academics favored by Reagan), it shared with the ABA the names only of nominees rather than prospective candidates, thereby limiting the room for ABA influence. After some of the ABA's judiciary committee members found Robert Bork unqualified for a Supreme Court seat, relations between the administration and the ABA became even more strained. In a move to restore harmony, the elder Bush reinstated the practice of permitting the ABA to rate prospective nominees as well as those whose names had already been submitted to the Senate, and President Clinton continued that arrangement.

The new Bush administration, however, has decided to eliminate entirely formal ties with the ABA; and a White House spokesman has explained that no interest group should enjoy a special role in the selection process, even though the ABA has always emphasized nominees' professional credentials rather than their ideological leanings. At the same time the Federalist Society, an organization of conservative lawyers and academics which included Robert Bork among its trustees, has become an important source of nominees for judgeships and other administrative positions with the Bush administration. The new president also selected John Ashcroft, a defeated Missouri Senator with a strong anti-abortion record, as Attorney General, and Bush nominated as Solicitor General (the government's chief lawyer before the Supreme Court) Theodore Olson who had been Bush's lawyer in the election dispute and a strong critic of the Clintons' role in the Whitewater affair.

President Bush has had to be sensitive to the political situation in the Senate where, after a tie in the election, the Democrats gained a fragile control when Jim Jeffords (I-Vermont) defected, handing Senate control to the Democrats. The need to secure confirmation had caused the president to compromise somewhat on his first nominees to the federal court of appeals even before the Jeffords switch. For vacancies on the Fourth Circuit, the most conservative of the lower appeals courts, Bush chose two African-Americans initially selected for the posts by President Clinton. But he also nominated a number of prominent conservatives, including a leading advocate of restrictions on national authority over the states and a law professor who favored increased accommodation in church–state cases. The direction in which George W. Bush wishes to proceed in shaping the judiciary is thus becoming clearer, but political realities may limit his opportunities (at least until after the 2002 election).

Conclusion

The Rehnquist Court in recent years, as in the past, has continued to compile a mixed record. Justices O'Connor and Kennedy have remained its most influential justices with O'Connor (who wrote only one dissent in the 1999–2000 term) clearly the Court's dominant figure. Indeed more than one journalist has suggested that the current Court might be more accurately dubbed "the O'Connor Court" than the "Rehnquist Court."

O'Connor's prominence has a positive and a negative impact. Her moderate, pragmatic approach to issues to a large extent probably mirrors that of the nation generally. Her penchant for rulings tied closely to case facts, on the other hand, has prevented the development by the Court of a coherent body of doctrine and precedent.

This is not to suggest that the current Court has no clear image. To a greater degree perhaps than any of its predecessors, the Rehnquist Court seems committed to judicial supremacy over the coordinate branches and levels of government. Despite all their lip service to federalism, the separation of powers, and judicial self-restraint, most of the current justices appear entirely comfortable intervening in all manner of issues, challenging state as well as national power, and underscoring the Court's role as final arbiter of constitutional issues. Justice O'Connor clearly fits that pattern.

If, as is widely speculated at the time of writing, Rehnquist were to retire from Court to be replaced by O'Connor as Chief Justice, such trends would be likely not merely to be continued but to be strengthened by an O'Connor Court.

Chapter 8

Federal Bureaucracy and Public Management

B. GUY PETERS

Public management reform in the United States has not been as rapid or as extensive as that implemented in most other industrialized democracies during the past several decades. This relative absence of rapid change has been true despite the conventional wisdom of American citizens that the bureaucracy is bloated, inefficient, incompetent, and has almost any other negative attribute that might be applied to an organization. Further, even under several previous presidents seemingly committed strongly to reducing the size of the public sector and enhancing efficiency, relatively little had changed in the public sector. The federal bureaucracy that Bill Clinton inherited was hardly different from that left by Jimmy Carter. Perhaps most interestingly, despite a great deal of rhetoric and bureaucracy bashing, the Reagan administration was able to change rather little in the federal bureaucracy (Levine and Benda, 1988; Golden, 2000). In contrast to its previous history the federal government has in recent years lagged far behind state and local governments in modernizing its administration (Melkers and Willoughby, 1998).

That said, there were the beginnings of some significant change during the 1990s. The National Performance Review (the Gore Commission) launched by the Clinton administration has produced noticeable change in federal administration. Those reforms have had several consequences for the federal bureaucracy. One effect of the Gore Commission has been to reduce substantially the size of the federal public sector, although much of that downsizing can be explained by reducing the size of the Department of Defense. Also, the Gore reforms have increased internal democracy within federal agencies and reduced the burden of rules on managers. A second major reform effort, the Government Performance and Results Act (GPRA) was also adopted during the 1990s, and is beginning to affect the management of federal agencies, and their linkage to Congress and the budgetary process. Neither of these reform initiatives has produced rapid change and may take years to be effective, but they do represent significant attempts to produce change in government.

George W. Bush as public manager

George W. Bush is the first American president to have formal academic training in management in that he has a Master in Business Administration (MBA) from Harvard. He styles himself a manager, and his style while governor of Texas and during the first months in Washington has been to delegate most decisions (Sanger, 2001). That delegation enables him and his immediate staff to focus their attention on a few strategic issues at a time. Further, the preferred style of governing in this administration has been, to this point at least, from the top down with the expectation that decisions made in the White House will be followed in the departments. That style extends into the departments, with cabinet secretaries reporting that they also tend to manage from the top down, and also that they delegate extensively to their appointed staff.

This style of running American government like the CEO of a major corporation is in marked contrast to the more involved and participatory style of the previous occupant of the White House (Sanger, 2001); but it is familiar as a result of earlier efforts through the Hoover Commissions (1949, 1955) and the Ash Commission (1970) to make the president more of a manager. What remains to be seen is whether this leadership style can be as successful in Washington as President Bush believes it to have been in Austin. The sheer scale and complexity of the federal government and the decentralized structure of the federal executive branch make the task of any president difficult. By the summer of 2001 there were some complaints (even from loyal Republicans) that the detached, but yet top-down, style of governing coming from the White House did not appear to be working as well as had been hoped. Even after the events of September 11 2001 President Bush was seen as less personally involved than were other political leaders, such as Mayor Giuliani and Governor Pataki, although he may have switched from a managerial to a warrior style of governing.

At the beginning of his administration President Bush announced his goals for reducing the size of the executive branch swiftly and dramatically. He stated that he wanted to halve the number of senior and middle-level managers in the federal government, and also to expose about one-third of all federal employment to some form of competition from private sector providers. These proposed changes were not part of any integrated program of administrative reform but instead reflected a rather simple, ideological assumption about the excessive size and inefficiency of the federal bureaucracy. Less than six months into his administration, the President was forced to backtrack somewhat on the specific plans to reduce the size of the federal bureaucracy. (Barr, 2001). What had been very specific targets for downsizing the federal government have become more general goals of eliminating as many civil servants as possible and also of using the private sector as much as possible.

Barriers and boons for the President as manager

The problems that President Bush encountered in his attempts to pare the bureaucracy reflect some of the complexity of the federal government already mentioned. Slimming the federal government is always easier to advocate from outside government than when a president actually has to implement that downsizing. Politically, all the programs in the federal government have substantial support, or they probably would not have existed in the first place. Also, when the operations of government organizations are examined, some of the necessity for employing public servants and managers becomes apparent even to their critics. That having been said, however, a president also has more levers at his disposal to employ when attempting to make the executive branch of government work as he wishes than would the chief executive of most other democratic governments (see below). The President does confront a substantial managerial task when nominally in charge of the federal government. In addition to the 14 Cabinet-level departments of government there are also several dozen independent executive agencies that report directly to the President. Even for cabinet departments the managerial task is not as easy. Cabinet departments in the United States are composed of a number of agencies, many also headed by a political appointee. The political characteristics of the executive branch is such that each agency within a department has its own political constituency, and very often its own linkage to Congress and to powerful interest groups. These linkages are the basis of the familiar, if somewhat outdated, conception of the "iron triangle" – composed of an agency, a Congressional committee and an interest group – as the basis of government in Washington. These triangles, (for example a farming organization and the commodity program in the Department of Agriculture and a subcommittee of the House Agriculture Committee) divide government into a series of subgovernments and make coordination and coherence more difficult. The opening up of government through sunshine laws and the mobilization of groups such as consumers and environmentalists have weakened, but not totally eliminated, these symbiotic relationships in government (Heclo, 1978).

Federal agencies are in some ways responsive to the president but they also must respond to other political forces, such as interest groups; and they may be quick to mobilize those forces on their own behalf when confronted by a president or a cabinet secretary who has goals that may damage their position or their budget. Thus, America adopted the idea of a decentralized government composed of a number of quasi-autonomous organizations (Seidman, 1998) somewhat earlier than did other countries, and that choice continues to create a number of significant managerial problems for presidents and cabinet secretaries. Managing the response to domestic terrorism, for example, has involved approximately 40 federal agencies, and at least six coordinating organizations (GAO, 2001).

Public administration and executive politics in the United States are rather different from these features of government in most other industrial-ized democracies. Although largely different, there is a some common background in thinking about the role of bureaucracy in governing with the United Kingdom and other Westminster-style political systems. For example, the theory in both systems is that the career civil service should be politically neutral and be capable of serving any political party in gov-ernment. In addition to being politically neutral, the civil service is also assumed to be relatively uninvolved in making policy choices. This concept of neutrality and the willingness to serve any political master should give the President a major advantage in governing.

With those similarities come numerous factors that differentiate American public administration from other systems within this broad tra-dition (Peters, 2002). One factor in administration that clearly separates American government from most other industrial democracies is the large number of political appointments available to a President and his cabinet when they assume office. When President Bush took office in January 2001 he and his higher level appointees could look forward to the possi-bility of changing over 4,000 officials to public office, with political appointees going three or four layers down into the hierarchy of many federal organizations. "Looking forward" to making these appointments is perhaps a misstatement because the process of appointing officials and having them approved by the Senate has become increasingly grueling as partisan lines harden and the Congress becomes less willing to bow to the wishes of the White House. Still, in contrast to most chief executives in government, the American president and his Cabinet have a substantial capacity to select the individuals with whom they will work.

In addition to his appointment powers over the bureaucracy, the President has a large personal staff and a well-developed bureaucracy of his own in the Executive Office of the President (EOP). In addition to per-sonal staff in the White House Office, the EOP (see Hart, 1995) contains the Office of Management and Budget (OMB) that is the focal point of the allocation process of government and also central to attempts at improving internal efficiency in the system. The EOP also includes the National Security Council that provides the president with an independent source of advice on foreign and defense policy and can serve to counter advice coming from the Departments of Defense and State. The structure of advice on domestic policy has been more variable but the EOP always does contain some means of helping the president counter the weight of advice coming from the line departments. In short, unlike the executives of most governments the president has the ability to make up his own mind on policy (Peters, Rhodes and Wright, 1999).

The point about the Senate having to confirm Cabinet and subcabinet appointments points to another crucial difference: the role that the separation of powers plays in executive politics in the United States compared with that in most other countries. The American bureaucracy is subject to multiple lines of accountability. As components of the executive branch, federal organizations and their employees are directly responsible to the president. In addition, Congress has a number of powers over the bureaucracy, not least its power over the budget. Congress also exercises substantive oversight over federal programs and can shape the manner in which the agencies choose to implement programs, often including a good deal of micro-management of them (Gilmour and Halley, 1994). In addition, the courts are more active participants in oversight and accountability of the bureaucracy than in most Westminster systems. This judicial activity is based in part on the requirements for due process in procedures established by the Administrative Procedure Act of 1946 (APA) and its amendments (Kerwin, 2000). (The most significant amendments to the APA are perhaps the freedom of information requirements imposed by the Freedom of Information Acts of 1966 and 1974.) Judicial intervention is also based on the statements of individual rights, and other constraints on government, contained in the Constitution and the Bill of Rights.

Finally, following from the role of the Administrative Procedures Act and its sequels is the fact that American administration is distinctly open and participatory when compared to Westminster systems. For example, the APA mandates the opportunity for individuals or interest groups affected by proposed administrative rulings to make their views known in the process and also mandates that the administrative organizations make decisions that are not "arbitrary and capricious" given the information available to them at the time. Likewise, numerous public laws stipulate that government organizations hold hearings or provide other types of direct public participation so that the decisions made will have at least some opportunities for democratic involvement in the policy process.

Although large and in its own way democratic, the bureaucracy is not respected by the public. Americans in general are not very positive about government but the bureaucracy is even less respected, and more often the brunt of jokes and abuse. That having been said, citizens do support, and provide positive reports about, the programs that provide direct benefits to them. Likewise, although the public has negative stereotypes about the bureaucracy, they report that their actual encounters with "bureaucrats" are about as good as those with organizations in the private sector (see Peters, 2001). There have been numerous media reports of citizens being mistreated by the Internal Revenue Service (IRS), but the bulk of interactions with government appear to be positive. Indeed, the contradictory complaints of bureaucrats becoming the advocates of their clients and at times even ignoring the law are also common in the negative stereotypes of the bureaucracy.

The final point to make about the public bureaucracy in the United States is that most of it is not federal. Citizens like to complain about "big government" in Washington, but the federal component of the bureaucracy is small, and declining. In early 2000 the federal government employed 2.8 million civilian workers out of a total public sector of 20.2 million employees. (In that year there were also an additional 1.6 million uniformed "employees" in the armed forces.) This federal civilian employment, which is 10.4 percent of the total public employment, is down from 19 percent in 1980 and 17 percent in 1990. The taxing and spending of the federal government may be massive, and some of the regulatory interventions of the federal government, through organizations such as the Occupational Safety and Health Administration (OSHA) and the EPA, present problems for business. Also, the federal government utilizes state and local government bureaucracies to implement many of its programs, especially social programs, and this often makes such programs more complex than they might otherwise be. In terms of actual employment, however, the federal government is relatively small.

Reform and change

The perceived problems in public administration, often described in the United States through the litany of "fraud, waste and abuse", have produced a world-wide tide of reform (Pollitt and Bouckaert, 2000). The United States has had a number of prominent attempts at reform (Arnold, 1986; Light, 1997) of the federal bureaucracy, most inspired by the dominant business culture of the country. Other reforms, such as program budgeting, have attempted to instill greater rationality into a system that has been perceived to be dominated by politics rather than by economic or analytic logic. Other attempts at reform have been directed simply at reducing the size of government and its intrusiveness into the economy and society.

All the attempts at administrative reform have encountered political problems, and to some extent have been confounded by a culture of populism and individual rights. The political opposition to reform has been largely a function of the close links between interest groups, government agencies, and individual Congressmen and/or congressional committees. While the "iron triangle argument" linking these three actors is considered outmoded in some academic circles, it appears still to function in Washington. Thus any attempt to reform may be seen as an attack on an agency delivering valuable services to a particular constituency that is in turn protected by forces in Congress. Everyone loves reform in general but hates it when it affects their own services and benefits.

The focus of reform in the United States has been on performance and quality, as well as on political objectives such as generating greater involvement of clients and employees in federal policy decisions. During the Clinton administration the principal focus on reform was the National Performance Review (NPR), the Gore Report. At the same that the executive branch was pushing the NPR, the Congress adopted (in 1993) the Government Performance and Results Act that was an attempt to link budgets and other resources to the performance of government organizations on pre-agreed targets for those organizations. Interestingly, both of these reform agendas were based on long-term change in government, rather than on short-term results that might have had more immediate political impact.

National Performance Review

The Report of the Gore Commission stressed the need to "make government work better and cost less." The Gore Report was far from the bureaucracy bashing that has characterized much of American discourse on the public sector, including some by Clinton and Gore themselves; rather, the Report stressed that the bureaucrats themselves were not the problem in government. The problem with the federal government was perceived to reside in the heavily rule-bound and hierarchical organizational pattern within the federal government. These rules had been established for good reasons. Civil service laws were adopted to ensure merit recruitment and equal treatment of potential employees. Likewise, purchasing laws were designed to prevent favoritism and produce the lowest possible costs for public programs. Despite the good intentions, the perception of the Gore Commission was that these benefits were heavily outweighed by costs.

In addition to attacking the domination of rules, the NPR focused on the hierarchical nature of government organizations, and the failure of these organizations to involve their employees more effectively in making decisions. Without that involvement motivating employees may be difficult, given the failures of civil service pay and grading systems to provide financial incentives for outstanding performance. Thus, government was believed to be underutilizing a good deal of talent within government, and to produce the type of dispirited and uninterested employee that was the stereotype of public employees. The idea of involving workers in organizations is hardly a new idea in management but this idea received a more official sanction in this report than in the past. (Canada also adopted a similar approach to reform especially in the document entitled 'Public Service 2000'.)

The thrust of the Gore Report also has been referred to as "reinventing government." This concept of reinvention embodied some of the concept of greater involvement of public sector employees in their organizations that was behind the reforms more generally. As well as some of the deregulatory changes mentioned above, reinvention meant allowing government organizations to rethink what they were doing and why they were performing their tasks in particular ways. This was intended to be a bottom-up process in which all members of the organization were involved, with a group process being used to make decisions, in contrast to the usual hierarchical methods of imposing reforms from the top. This process often produced radical transformations of organizations (Thompson, 1999), with both the substance and the procedures of organizations being affected.

The members of the Gore Commission conceived of the implementation of these reforms as being a long-term process, involving at least the entire length of the Clinton administration to complete. That has indeed been the case, and the process of changing bureaucracy one organization at a time has been taking place for eight years. These changes were thought to require more time than the usual reform because they involved changing the way in which people thought about their jobs, rather than simply changing which organizations were grouped with which others, or changing the technical process by which decisions were to be made. Value change in any organization is more difficult than changing structure, but it is also likely to be more enduring if it is successfully implemented.

The evidence is that some organizations involved in reinvention exercises have been able to transform themselves rather completely, although there are also some notable failures. Some of the failures have occurred in organizations that already had strong internal cultures and therefore were resistant to change. The most notable failure has been the attempt to create Performance Based Organizations (PBOs). The federal bureaucracy has permitted agencies substantially greater autonomy than has been characteristic of most other industrial democracies, and the creation of PBOs was intended to make these organizations even more autonomous and to have their budgetary success more dependent upon their reaching targets.

These organizations would become in essence more market than government structures.

The Gore Commission was interesting politically as well as in terms of changes in public sector management. In the first place it was almost entirely generated and implemented by the executive branch. Congress became involved with reinvention only some time after the program was underway, and did not have the level of influence in the changes that might have been expected. In addition, Vice-President Gore attempted to use the (real and perceived) successes of these reforms as a part of his campaign for the presidency. It appears, however, that reinvention was much more important inside the Beltway than in the remainder of the country, and the Vice-President appears to get little credit for the changes that have been brought about (at least in part) by his activities.

In summary, the American public bureaucracy has been transformed substantially by the Gore Commission and its ideas. As noted, approximately one in six civil service positions available at the beginning of those eight years no longer existed at the end, and the style of management had been altered substantially. In addition, the rules that had bound the hands of managers prior to the reforms were relaxed substantially and the managerialism that has been part of the ethos of the system for years became more of a reality.

The Government Performance and Results Act

The GPRA was a Congressional initiative that was developed largely in isolation from the changes represented in the Gore Report. Although GPRA and NPR share the word "performance" in their titles, their ideas of performance, and how to produce better performance in the public sector vary rather markedly. The changes of NPR assume that performance will result from motivated people being liberated from the constraints under which they have had to labor in conventional public organizations. As already noted, NPR has a number of very positive assumptions about human behavior and especially about the commitment and dedication of public employees.

The Government Performance and Results Act, on the other hand, appears to assume that more immediate and tangible motivations may be required to make government organizations perform better (Radin, 1998). For any public organization perhaps the most immediate pressure is the annual budget; therefore GPRA attempts to link the actual performance of organizations with their budgets and to utilize more or less objective measures of performance as the means of driving the budgetary process. With GPRA reporting on performance becomes a standard part of the budget cycle, with Congress being able to determine how well its money is being spent and reward or punish organizations and their managers accordingly.

This general approach of using performance indicators as a part of the budgeting process was to some extent tried with program budgeting, but GPRA attempts to make the linkage even more direct. In addition, unlike program budgeting the Government Performance and Results Act empha- sizes the organization and its role in government, while program budgeting had focused on broad programs rather than the organizations that deliver services. This focus is in part a result of the emphasis of GPRA on the management of federal organizations. The performance indicators are used to demonstrate the success or failure of the organizations and to reward or punish them accordingly.

Implementing the Government Performance and Results Act has not been a simple task. The Act was passed in 1993 but required more than five years to begin to have any significant impact. As noted, GPRA depends upon the ability to identify and measure the performance of federal organizations. Measuring performance in government programs is a notoriously difficult task, given the amorphous nature of the outputs of many programs (see Ingraham and Moynihan, 2001). For example, pro- grams that create public goods, such as clean air, or whose performance might be measured by certain things not happening, including the FBI and major crimes, are at a particular disadvantage when measurement becomes a central aspect of allocation; thus attempting to develop measures of per- formance for all agencies of government was an extremely daunting task.

To provide as level as possible a playing field for organizations in the budgetary process, an elaborate mechanism for selecting indicators of organizational performance was developed. The legislation as implemented first required each federal agency to propose to Congress a performance plan containing a set of indicators, with the GAO (a Congressional organi- zation) serving as the arbiter in the process. The General Accounting Office took the role of judge seriously and returned a number of the plans to agencies for additional work, generally demanding greater specificity from the organizations. This initial stage of the process of performance management, requiring developing, revising and finally approving the per- formance plans, took several years and required a great deal of work from staff in the organizations and in central agencies.

As the process for implementing GPRA was developed, the general per- formance plans were to be supplemented by annual performance plans. These plans were to become a part of the process of budgeting. The extent to which the organization was able to meet the targets contained in the annual plan was used to assess the quality of management in the organiza- tion and the extent to which they should be rewarded or punished. The budget process has, since at least the inception of program budgeting, involved some attempts to measure the outputs of federal organizations. The GPRA process differs from the earlier efforts first in the creation of the performance indicators through a more or less consensual process. It is more difficult for agencies to complain about the application of those indicators when they have been involved in their creation. Further, the current process links those performance indicators more directly to the budget process, so that performance now should mean something in dollars and cents terms for the agencies. It is not entirely clear yet what good or bad performance will mean, but the connection is there in principle.

The Bush administration

As already noted, the Bush administration has come into office without any clear program for reforming public administration. Rather, there appears to be a general distrust of the bureaucracy and of "big government" that has been motivating attempts to change the federal government and its bureaucracy. The CEO model is at the heart of conceptions about change, implying that the reformed federal government would respond to the wishes of the President, and/or his cabinet secretaries. This is to some extent a restatement of the familiar politics-administration dichotomy that has been at the heart of traditional public administration in the United States (see Waldo, 1984). In that view the bureaucrats should be "on tap" and not on top and should respond rather slavishly to the wishes of their elected masters.

The management agenda for the Bush administration was to some extent established by the work of the Government Performance and Results Act, and especially by the Senate's Committee on Governmental Affairs (2001). Unlike the management reforms of the previous administration, much of the initial emphasis of the Bush White House has been on financial management, and the use of mechanisms such as for contracting out services, that could save money directly and that also would involve the private sector more intimately in providing public services. Contracting has hardly been unknown in American government, although it has not had the emphasis recently found in some of the other Anglo-American democracies, but during the first months of this administration there has been an extremely strong push toward greater use of contract mechanisms.

As well as those financial management challenges the Bush presidency has also inherited a growing problem of personnel management in the public sector, rather different from the targets of the previous reforms in this area. These emerging personnel problems are of two sorts. First, there is the problem of filling all the positions that are at the disposal of the president. The presidential appointments process has become increasingly cumbersome, with the need for background checks by the FBI, political vetting and then Congressional hearings (Felzenberg, 2001; Mackenzie, 2001). Even six months into the Bush administration there were hundreds of positions still unfilled, or filled on a temporary basis; less than half of the individuals put forward by the President had yet been considered by the Senate. This has meant that numerous federal organizations were not receiving the political direction that they might need, or that the administration would want.

The second part of the personnel problem is more basic, although given the preferences of the current administration it is perhaps not perceived to be as important as the ability to get their own people into office. This personnel problem is simply that federal employment has become a less attractive option than in the past. There simply are not the "best and brightest" coming into the federal service that there appear to have been in the past (Light, 2000a, b). The difficulties in recruitment are in part a function of economics, as federal pay levels have not kept pace with those in the private sector. Further, the declining prestige of federal employment, and government in general, deters many prospective employees from joining. The age structure of federal employment is such that a significant proportion of the existing staff will be retiring over the next decade.

Unlike in many previous administrations there is no clearly defined program for management change coming from the White House, but rather the more general emphasis is on reducing the level of federal employment. A great deal of the responsibility for implementing this generalized desire for reducing the size of the public sector resides with the leadership of the individual federal departments. For example, prior to September 11 2001 Secretary of Defense Donald Rumsfeld was in the process of implementing several programs for reducing administrative costs in a department that already has been downsized significantly, beginning at the end of the Cold War in the early 1990s. This program is irrelevant for the time being but it may yet mean that fewer person hours will be expended on defense issues, and more of those hours may be in the private sector. Indeed, one of the management debates during the first year of the Bush administration is how much contracting-out of public services should be permitted.

This restatement of the politics-administration paradigm represents a marked change from at least some of the ideas implemented as part of the National Performance Review. The participatory ideas that were at the heart of the Gore Report imply that public servants at all levels of the bureaucracy should have greater influence over their jobs and over policy, and if anything the lower echelons were to be differentially empowered. Likewise, the empowerment of more senior career managers as a part of the deregulatory aspects of the reforms gave those career civil servants a sense that they were to be assigned a larger voice in the making and exe-cuting of public policies. It may be more difficult than ever before to limit the influence of senior civil servants over policy, given that this sense of empowerment and involvement has been created. Thus, the Bush vision of a corporate managerial style seems counter to the ethos that had been built up over a decade of reform.

The management style of President Bush might appear more compatible with the ideas of the Government Performance and Results Act and the idea of performance has been, as noted, important in setting the manage-ment agenda. Even with that, however, there may be some potential prob-lems for the administration because of GPRA. The GPRA process was Congressionally motivated to give that institution, rather than the White House, greater control over the bureaucracy, and represents part of the longstanding institutional politics of the executive and legislative branches in Washington (Thompson, forthcoming). Further, the performance agree-ments that have been reached between the agencies and Congress represent the outcome of a long, and at times tortuous, process of negotiation. Any attempt on the part of an incoming departmental secretary to overturn these agreements on the basis of his or her ideology or whim is unlikely to be met with support either from Congress or from the agency. The man-agement process has, therefore, to some extent been locked in already so that it is more difficult for this (or any other) administration to govern in quite the top-down manner they might have wished.

The events in Washington and New York on September 11 2001 may well put the management agenda of the Bush administration on hold for some months, if not years, but has strengthened others. The reaction of politicians and the public has been to enhance the federal role in areas that previously had been private or contracted out, such as airport security. Also, the failures of organizations such as the FBI and the CIA became obvious, with demands for increasing their size and their powers as well as improving their management. On the other hand, the public and the bureaucracy appear more willing to accept a strong managerial role for the president. Further, the problems of the fragmented nature of American government – especially in the areas of immigration and security – became obvious and a strong, centralizing coordination strategy was adopted, with that coordination now coming from someone very close to the President.

Conclusion

Although the American president faces a daunting managerial task, he has more tools at his disposal than would the average CEO in a democratic government. The separation of powers, federalism and internal fragmentation within the administrative system itself makes the task of producing coherent policy action difficult in American government. Also, unlike other industrialized democracies, the managerial revolution in the public sector has had relatively little influence over federal management, although American state governments have been radically transformed over the past several decades. The President is left to use his appointment powers, his own substantial staff, and his powers of issuing executive orders to attempt to counteract some of the centrifugal trends within the federal policy-making apparatus. Further, although the separation of powers determines that the President can not make decisions on his own, it also ensures that Congress cannot act alone either, so that the President can usually block policies with which he does not agree.

The Bush administration has brought with it a set of familiar conservative assumptions about, and remedies for, the problems in the federal government. The assumptions are that the federal bureaucracy is too large, inefficient and cumbersome to provide the services needed by the population (and perhaps especially by business interests). The initial rhetoric of the administration stresses high-quality service delivery along with the cost-cutting, but what it does not do is stress the importance of recruiting and retaining the highest quality possible among the federal work force. The assumption is that people are part of the problem, and management systems are the solution. This is exactly the opposite approach from that guiding the reforms of the Gore Commission. These differences represent fundamental differences in approaches to public management in American government, which are closely linked with political parties and political ideologies.

Chapter 9

Federalism and Intergovernmental Relations

GILLIAN PEELE

When George W. Bush took office as the 43rd President of the United States, he brought to his new position governmental experience which had been gained primarily as Governor of Texas, a populous state with a distinctive history and culture. He also brought to the inner counsels of the Oval Office a team of personal advisers who had served him loyally during his period in the Governor's mansion. By so doing he was treading a career path which had become familiar in American political life where the post of Governor is seen as a major qualification for the presidency. Bush's background and his self-conscious celebration of his Texas associations once he reached the presidency serve as a useful reminder of the extent to which federalism gives American politics and policy-making a distinctive dimension which is at least as important as that provided by national level government in Washington.

The Constitution does not merely divide power vertically between the different branches of the federal government; it also divides power horizontally between federal government and the 50 states, creating a vibrant but complex system which displays enormous variety and contradiction. This chapter will focus on the changing federal balance within the United States and on the system of intergovernmental relations which underpins it. It starts by exploring why the fact that the United States is a federal system matters and proceeds to a discussion of the contemporary state of American federalism and intergovernmental relations, focusing particularly on the ways in which the balance between Washington and the sub-national tiers has been changing recently. It then proceeds to examine the implications of Bush's presidency for the wider federal system.

Why federalism matters

The fact that the United States is a federal system is of enormous importance for its public philosophy, for its decision-making structures and for the substantive policies which affect all areas of American life. Whether or not the states were correctly labeled "laboratories of democracy" when the history of many states in relation to civil rights for much of American history has involved a denial of democracy is a moot point. But there is no doubt that state government provides examples today of an enormous variety of policy preference. Oregon has developed a distinctive state medical system. It also has on its statute book a Death with Dignity law which allows physician-assisted suicide. Vermont recognizes same-sex marriages. Utah, as a result of the influence of the Mormon church, has long had strict drinking laws, although it finally (in 1990) lifted its ban on alcohol consumption in public, becoming the last state to do so; it then became the first state to ban the sale of cigarettes in vending machines. Some states make extensive provision for mother-tongue education; others do not.

The policy divergence between the states in such matters as family law, social policy and education is perhaps the most visible product of federalism. The division of powers and the existence of distinct political subsystems in the states has an impact also on the values of the American governmental system as a whole. The processes of American policymaking are deeply affected by the complex patterns of intergovernmental relationships in such areas as funding and regulation. Above all, the politics of the United States as a whole is profoundly shaped by the micro-politics of state and local arenas.

As far as the values of the American federal system are concerned it is evident that a system which allows substantial variation in the level or style of service provision will produce inequalities, inequities and anomalies. These may occur because a state chooses not to spend on a particular policy area or because a state's financial resources do not permit it to spend at the same level as other states. Such problems may occur even when the federal government is providing funding toward a service. For example, although Clinton's efforts to extend health insurance to poor children not covered by Medicaid produced a Children's Health Insurance Program (CHIP), many states did not use the money made available.

In terms of the policy processes the federal nature of the American system has enormous consequences. Most of the services which Americans consume are primarily the product of state and local, not federal, government. Although the federal government may wish to influence the standards of state provision in such matters as education, it can only do so to a limited extent by setting goals, offering subsidies or issuing regulations. State standards in such matters as environmental protection may vary significantly between states and may be higher than the federal standard. Federal policy usually requires state and local government cooperation for its implementation, which in turn generates divergent standards and styles of compliance (see Kraft and Scheberle, 1998).

The diversity of the states

The adoption of a federal system in 1787 reflected the diversity of interests within the infant Republic. As America enters the twenty-first century, the economy continues to display enormous regional differences, despite the heightened awareness of global economic trends. Within the regions the individual states display further economic diversity on such variables as per capita income, unemployment and percentages of the population in poverty. Although the poorest states in terms of median household income in 2001 (West Virginia and Mississippi) had apparently closed the gap on the richest (New Jersey and Connecticut), those states at the bottom of the scale have only half the median household income of those at the top.

Different states also contain different demographic mixes, display different cultural values, present different social problems and exhibit different political leanings and party traditions. Federalism permits – and, indeed, encourages – this diversity but in the process produces a seemingly bewildering array of political subsystems within the framework of the larger federal system.

The multi-faceted nature of the American federal system can be illustrated by the briefest of discussions of the different constitutions which govern the 50 states. While they all provide for an independent executive in the form of a governor, an independent judiciary, and (with the exception of Nebraska) a bicameral legislature, there is a startling variety both in nomenclature and power in these bodies. The states vary in the extent to which they provide their own protection for individual rights (sometimes in ways which are stronger than the federal Bill of Rights), make provision for other elective offices, operate electoral laws, construct budgetary procedures and create processes for revising the constitutions. State constitutions unlike the federal constitution have been frequently changed (see Chapter 19). Some states provide for direct democracy in the form of initiative, referendum, and recall (see Chapter 15). Some trends have marked a number of states in recent years – for example the tendency to overhaul bureaucracy and to strengthen executive powers over the budget – and historically we can identify a number of states which were self-consciously progressive in their effort to reform democratic structures through such innovations as the direct primary.

The formal constitutional position of the governor varies considerably across the states. In some states where the governor is the *only* elected member of the executive (such as Maine) or one of a small number of elected executive officials, power and accountability are concentrated and centralized. In other states, such as California and Texas, where there are a number of elected officials sharing power with the Governor, the governmental system is fragmented and decentralized.

Governors over the past few years have achieved a strengthening of their power and authority in relation to other elements of the state constitutional system. The rise of the mass media in particular has given governors, if they are able to use it, something of the ability to command attention and dominate debate which presidents have enjoyed at the federal level. Governors also have a number of weapons they can use in any conflict with the legislature. (Such conflicts occur frequently given that the states, like the federal government, regularly throw up divided party control.) All governors have the power of veto and have become increasingly likely to use it by comparison with a decade ago when a veto may have been seen as a sign of political failure (Mahtesian, 2000). In some states the governor has the line item veto; in others not.The line item veto is a device which enables the Governor to veto precise parts of bills, especially those which seem to involve unnecessary spending. Jesse Ventura, the controversial Independence Party Governor of Minnesota, in 1999 infuriated legislators by using a red pig stamp to signify his contempt for the pork-barrel items he vetoed, while Governor Pataki of New York in 1998 used the line veto on over a thousand legislative proposals (Mahtesian, 2000). Not surprisingly, the line item veto is a device which the President would like to have available but legislation designed to give it to him was found unconstitutional at the federal level in *Clinton* v. *City of New York* (1998).

There remain, however, substantial differences between the constitutional powers available to governors in their respective states and significant variations in political circumstance. It is perhaps worth noting as far as the relative strength of governors is concerned that Texas, where George W. Bush had executive experience, is a state whose governor has a weak role (Ivins and Dubose, 2000).

Significant differences also exist in the organization and power of state legislatures with respect to their size, their length of sitting and powers as well as, of course, in relation to their partisan composition. Some state legislatures, such as New Hampshire's, are large; legislatures in other states, even the size of California, are small. The period since 1990 (when California passed Proposition 140) has seen a national trend toward imposing term limits on members of state legislative assemblies as well as on other offices such as the governor. The term limiting of legislators at the state level inevitably changed the internal dynamics of many states' legislative bodies, increasing the number of novice legislators, reducing the level of expertise available to the legislature and creating new career paths for politicians (see also Chapter 19).

The position of many state judiciaries is affected by the varied selection methods in place. Many states elect their judges, often on a partisan basis. Other states use appointment, although the so-called Missouri Plan (involving appointment by the governor with a susbequent approval by voters after a specified number of years) is probably the most common means of selection. Recall (the removal of a judge after a petition and referendum) exists in some states, including California. The existence of a recall mechanism raises the possibility that a judge's continuation in office may be challenged if voters view his or her decisions as too liberal or too conservative. States may change their methods for selecting judges. Thus Florida, whose state judiciary played a key role in the controversies over the 2000 presidential election), had recently changed its judicial selection procedure and moved away from popular election.

In addition to structural differences between state governments, there are of course enormous differences of political disposition, party organization and culture among the several states. There are states with a distinctly progressive tradition such as Wisconsin, Washington and California; by contrast, there are states with a distinctly conservative character, such as Utah and the other Rocky Mountain states, as well as Texas. The southern states have an identity of their own, having been for long associated with segregation and hostility to civil rights; though those days have gone they still retain a common identity and a shared political disposition.

Local government

Inevitably these conflicts and complexities are further exacerbated when we look beyond the level federal relations strictly defined (the relations between Washington and the 50 states) and take in the bewilderingly fragmented dimension of local government. Local government is not mentioned in the federal constitution; but beneath the level of state government (and subject to each state's constitution) there exist in the United States some 3,000 county governments, some 19,000 municipal governments and some 16,000 townships, all with general (that is, multi-functional) governmental responsibilities. In addition, however, there are about 34,000 special districts, mostly with responsibility for a single function, such as fire protection or water provision. Of crucial importance there are the 13,000 independent school districts administering most (but not all) of the nation's schools (1997 Census on Government).

Funding

The financial relationship is of course crucial to the relationship between the different tiers of government. Each year the federal government spends large amounts of money on a variety of purposes (notably defense, social security, Medicaid and grants) and thereby effectively transfers resources to the states. It was estimated in 2001 that some $305.6 billion would be spent by federal government in grant aided assistance to the states (OMB, 2001). By the same token the federal government collects a large amount of money from citizens directly through various taxes, notably the personal income tax.

Not all states benefit from the flow of federal dollars. As a number of studies have shown some states are substantially in deficit, while others are in surplus as a result of federal spending. Thus a survey for Fiscal Year (FY) 1999 found that New Mexico, a relatively poor state, had the highest surplus in relationship with the federal government while Connecticut, a relatively rich state, ended up with the highest deficit (Taubmann Center, 2000). The overall impact of federal spending is something which is often hard to justify and which is indeed rarely discussed, despite the efforts of individuals, such as former Senator Moynihan, who have called for a new federal settlement to rectify the imbalances.

States are not the only recipients of federal monies. Indeed one authority has noted that by 1980 as many as 60,000 authorities qualified for direct government aid, compared with about 50 in 1960 (Walker, 2000). Since then, however, largely as a result of the Reagan years the proportion of federal aid which bypassed the states and went directly to other (mainly local) authorities has dropped (from 29% of the total in 1978) to 11.4% in 1994 and the number of recipient authorities has also dropped (Walker, 2000).

The states and local government raise their own revenues from a variety of sources, with sales taxes as a major source for the states and property taxes a major source for local government. Sales taxes present problems as a source of revenue because they are so volatile and liable to decline in times of economic recession. Some states, such as Tennessee which raises three-quarters of its revenue from sales taxes, are particularly vulnerable to an economic downturn. The variety of sales taxes in place at the state level has also come to seem anomalous in an age of e-commerce, prompting efforts by the states to produce greater uniformity in their tax systems, though as yet with little substantial effect. Table 9.1 shows the revenues and expenditures of state and local government.

The *form* which federal grants should take has long been at the center of debate about intergovernmental relations. The expansion of the federal role over the twentieth century was fueled by grants and other financial

Table 9.1   An overview of state and local government: revenues and expenditures (1996) ($million)

	State	*Local*
Revenues		
Intergovernmental	221,369	270,480
Individual Income Taxes	133,547	13,296
General Sales	139,363	29,709
Excises	66,752	13,123
Property Tax	9,974	199,467
Fees and Charges	144,747	169.225
Other	152,056	108,207
TOTAL	867,808	803,507
Expenditure		
Intergovernmental	252,005	8,198
Education	106,565	292,294
Health	51,243	59,471
Public Safety	57,081	68,090
Highways	47,548	31,545
Public Utilities	5,456	141,060
Debt Interest	25,410	33,502
Other	314,293	168,158
TOTAL	859,601	802,318

Source: *Statistical Abstract of the United States* (Washington, DC: Census Bureau, Department of Commerce, 2000).

incentives designed to promote federal policy goals. In 2001 OMB detailed 172 formula assistance grants which transferred money to the subnational government for various purposes as well as a host of other types of grant such as project grants and direct payments (OMB, 2001). Categorical grants were the favorite means of boosting money available for state programs which states would otherwise not have been able to afford but wanted to implement. These grants often carried with them bureaucratic burdens for the states as well as having distorting effects on state and federal spending. Since the Nixon presidency (1969–74) *block grants* have been seen as the remedy for many of the weaknesses of categorical grants because they allow states greater autonomy and flexibility in deciding their priorities. Reagan's projected swap of responsibilities with the states involved a much greater use of block grants which became a favored tool advocated by the governors in their search for flexibility in such areas as welfare reform. Block grants are now used in such areas as Community

Services, Social Services and Child Care. Clinton, although initially opposed to the use of block grants in entitlement programmes, acquiesced in their use in welfare. The Personal Responsibility and Work Opportunity Reconciliation Act (PRWORA) legislation of 1996 thus substituted a block grant known as TANF (Temporary Assistance for Needy Families) for a number of programmes (including Aid to Families with Dependent Children, or AFDC) which operated through matching grants. In theory this switch gave states greater freedom to adjust welfare priorities to their own specific circumstances than in the past. However, the block grant was linked to the cost of the AFDC program in 1994 and 1995, thus providing an incentive to states to cut costs on welfare because any savings which they make accrue to the states (Rom, Peterson and Scheve, 1998). How the legislation has worked in practice and how the states and federal government will approach the reauthorization of PRWORA is one of the issues which Bush will have to tackle in his first term.

Cities

Cities have always held a mirror to American social trends, identifying emerging social problems. Their government frequently presented special difficulties for the American federal system as cities defied state and other boundaries. Their association with the seemingly intractable problems of crime, homelessness, drug abuse, poverty, unemployment and infra-structure decay often made them politically unpopular with their state governments, which represented very different interests from those of the cities. Indeed, prior to the major reapportionment cases of the 1960s cities were often politically underrepresented by comparison with rural areas in the state legislatures.

The concentration of problems in America's cities – especially the older big cities such as New York, Boston, and Chicago – led in the 1950s and 1960s to the phenomenon of white flight to the suburbs which exacerbated the fiscal crisis of many American urban areas. However, the gloomy speculation about the future of American cities that was such a feature of the 1960s appears in retrospect to have been exaggerated (Banfield, 1970); in fact the 1980s and 1990s saw something of an urban renaissance and while that too was in many ways flawed, it at least underlined the capacity of many of America's cities to adopt new strategies to deal with a changing economic environment and the continuing appeal of city life for sections of the population (Rosenthal, 1980; Rast, 1999).

Not all cities are of the same type. The focus in the debates about the future of American cities tended to be on the older and larger cities. The variation in size of American cities is of course huge: New York and Los

Angeles each have over 10 million inhabitants by comparison with smaller and medium sized cities such as Salt Lake City, Rochester and Milwaukee. More important than size is the fact that, while some cities (especially the older cities of the northeast and midwest) have experienced decline and financial difficulty, others (notably in the south and west) have experienced growth and rapid development. In the case of the newer cities (for example, San José and San Diego in California or Houston and San Antonio in Texas) there has been a deliberate effort to cultivate new investment, to develop new partnerships with private sector firms and to make themselves more attractive in the new technologically driven (as opposed to industrially based) economy.

From the New Deal of the 1930s to Lyndon Johnson's Great Society initiatives of the 1960s, the federal government has enacted programs which were designed to cope with poverty and distress, and these have had a major impact on American cities. Programs aimed at the cities over the period 1933–68 also reflected the strong relationship between Democratic presidents and the Democratic cities; Republican presidents and Congresses by contrast had much less interest in developing an urban agenda. Not surprisingly therefore the period since 1980 has witnessed cuts in federal aid to cities on a number of fronts, including the abolition of Urban Development Assistance Grants (UDAGs). Programs of major interest to cities, such as housing and transport, have also suffered severe cutbacks. Some mayors have also argued that federal support for cities in the form of grants does not really help cities which need to devise their own strategies for economic growth based on entrepreneurial activity and development (Norquist, 1998; Goldsmith, 1997).

How easily cities can adapt to changing conditions is crucially dependent on leadership. Pressure groups such as the US Conference of Mayors can advise on and publicize strategies which might fuel a city's growth and development, but individual leadership is also crucial. Thus, for example, in San José mayoral leadership under Tom McEnery appears to have been a significant factor in developing the city's economic base (McEnery, 1994). In some cities the form of government is itself an impediment. Although the detail of the governance of cities varies enormously, three basic types of governmental structure should be noted. First there is the commission form of government where an elected council runs the departments of local government through a commission. Second, there is the mayor–city manager form where the mayor as a member of the council sets policy, but the city manager is responsible for administration. Finally, there is the mayor–council system in which the mayor and the council are elected separately.

Assessing the effectiveness of subnational government in shaping the delivery of services that are most vital to citizens in their daily lives –

including educational provision, penal policy, health care, transport and environmental protection – may involve a range of different authorities and structures. One of the most marked features of the politics of federalism in the period since 1981 (the Reagan era) has been an attempt to transfer functions away from federal government and back to the states. This so-called "devolution revolution," although by no means as straightforward as is sometimes claimed, has inevitably had knock-on effects for local government creating, what one commentator has called "second order devolution." Sometimes this devolution from state to local government has come about because the states have deliberately chosen to devolve policy responsibility to local government; sometimes it has happened because state-level funding for services has been curtailed and local government has had to pick up more of the burden.

A shifting federal balance

Enough has already been said to underline the fact that the relationship between the federal government and the states (and, indeed, the broader system of intergovernmental relations) is never static. The balance between Washington and the states shifted towards the federal government over the twentieth century, especially after the New Deal period of the 1930s. Not only did the range of federal programmes increase from the 1930s but the involvement and entanglement of the various levels of government became a marked feature of the system, whereas prior to the New Deal it was possible to see the responsibilities of the federal government and the states as separate and distinct. This interaction is captured in the famous metaphor of federalism being not a layer cake but a marble cake. The recent past – the period since 1980 – has seen efforts to simplify relationships, to restore autonomy to the states and to reduce the federal role. The period has also seen sustained academic and political debate about the proper distribution of authority within the constitutional system and the consequences of change. Before looking at where George W. Bush fits into this broader picture it is worth exploring why this renewed interest in the federal balance has occurred.

The first point that should be made is that the process of restructuring or readjusting the federal balance is a multi-faceted one which has come about as a result of a number of factors. By no means all of these factors involve a direct and straightforward wish to strengthen subnational government. Indeed the contemporary federal system involves a number of conflicting trends (Walker, 2000). The second point to emphasize is that insofar as we can detect a trend toward a stronger role for the states and a diminished role for the federal government the process has occurred incrementally across the period from 1980. The third point to note is that, although a revived role for the states has been an element high on the Republican Party's agenda, the eight years of the Clinton presidency also saw significant moves toward a strengthening of the states' policy role, especially in the area of welfare (see also Chapter 12).

So why has a shift in the dynamics of federalism occurred? One key reason is ideological and attitudinal. The last 20 years have seen a profound questioning of the role of government generally and renewed interest in the ability of the free market, private enterprise and the voluntary sector to produce solutions to social problems. Opposition to big government and doubt about the federal government's legitimacy benefited state and local government. In part this loss of faith in the policy-making capacity of Washington reflected a series of failures to get to grips with specific problems such the budget deficit, health care and welfare; in part it was the product of a more generalized discontent with national politics.

Matching the ebb of confidence in Washington-based policy-making capacity there was a marked increase in the self-confidence of the states in their own capacity to govern and to solve policy problems which had defeated the federal government. Take the case of health care. In the absence of a comprehensive national health care reform, states have experimented with their own different approaches to the multiple problems of health care provision. Minnesota, Tennessee and Wisconsin all developed their own responses to the problem of inadequate access to health care (Dukakis, 2001). Maine devised its own strategy for dealing with prescription charges, while Oregon developed a controversial health plan which entailed some rationing of medical procedures available on Medicaid (see Chapter 13).

Behind this renewed capacity at the state level there has been a series of reforms designed to root out the weaknesses of state institutions and personnel and to make the system more professional. Sometimes the new self-confidence of states flowed from self-confident political leadership, especially at the gubernatorial level where individual governors (such as Tommy Thompson in Wisconsin and John Kitzhaber in Oregon) became associated with important policy reforms. Sometimes strengthening of subnational governments flowed from structural reforms as state and local governments improved their managerial, informational and administrative capacity. Thus some cities such as San José and Oakland in California secured charter reforms giving greater power to the mayor in relation to the hiring and firing of staff and the development of a budget (Cain, Peele and Mullin, 2001). State governments, encouraged by their own governors and by their own representative bodies, reviewed aspects of their operations such as personnel and procurement policies. Undoubtedly there is now better monitoring of state government efficiency and a competitive culture of good government encouraged, for example, by the publication in *Governing* of league tables for the different states' performance on a range of criteria.

There were other reasons for the tilt away from Washington and the interest in greater policy autonomy for the state. The Republican Party embraced a new federal balance as part of its creed for ideological and self-interested, reasons especially after the Republicans captured the majority of gubernatorial positions in 1994. The problem of budget deficits limited Washington's enthusiasm for new domestic policy initiatives in the 1980s. Decentralization and deregulation were themes which resonated in the private sector and with the public in 1990s.

Above all, the representatives of the subnational government actively lobbied for change over the 1980s and 1990s. Particularly important was the National Governors' Association (NGA) which pushed for a number of changes in federal government practice on such matters as unfunded mandates (which placed federal burdens on state and local governments without paying for them), grant conditions (which imposed substantive and bureaucratic restrictions on federal aid) and pre-emptions, where Congress used its constitutional authority to override state legislation in a policy field. More ambitiously, the NGA initiated in 1995 a "federalism summit" designed to explore structural and constitutional reforms which could force Congress to reconsider a law if the states so desired, and which required Congress to make clear its constitutional authority for actions as well as for conditions attached to grants. While these ideas produced little concrete action they were indicative of the thinking of the NGA and other pressure groups on the intergovernmental stage, such as the National Council of State Legislatures (NCSL), the American Legislative Exchange Council (ALEC) and the Internation City/Country Management Association. Republican dominance of the NGA for the period after 1994 gave the NGA agenda a high salience in the Republican Party; and, although the governors were more pragmatic than many Congressional Republicans in the 1990s, mutual interest saw the evolution of a working relationship which has endured.

All three branches of the federal government were also themselves involved at different points in creating over the last 20 years a new federalism agenda. Early in his presidency. President Reagan had called for a major reallocation of government functions between the federal and subnational government and, although these swaps did not come into effect, the rhetoric of the new federalism took root. Although Republicans were most closely identified with the ideas behind the new federalism, development under Clinton underlined the extent to which the devolution revolution had gained a measure of cross-party support, although after 1994 Clinton was not the agenda setter. Clinton in fact signed into law a number of measures which had an impact on the federal balance. The Unfunded Mandates Reform Act (UMBRA) of 1995, the PRWORA of 1996 and the Balanced Budget of 1997 all radically changed the federal role in regulation and policy-making, while creating new opportunities for the states to pursue their own policy preferences.

Congress has regularly promoted legislation aimed at reducing the regulatory burden on the states and curbing the federal role across a number of policy areas. This trend became especially marked after the 1994 capture of Congress by the Republicans which generated a range of initiatives with implications for the federal system. Gingrich's Contract with America did not originally advocate empowerment of the states but a new federalist agenda was successfully urged on the Republican congressional leadership by the Republican governors who developed a close working relationship with the Congressional wing of the GOP.

Congressional inactivity also had an impact on the federal balance. When Congress proved unable to act in areas of high public concern (whether in relation to health care, welfare, or campaign finance reform) there was an incentive for the states to frame their own legislation. Thus alongside state innovation in health care provision there developed over the 1990s a range of state responses to welfare policy (see also Chapter 12). California legislated its own campaign finance reforms.

The Supreme Court in the period since 1980 also had a significant role in reshaping the federal environment. Federalism is at bottom a constitutional doctrine and the Supreme Court's interpretations of the relative powers of federal government and the states have, since 1787, carved the framework within which more informal and politics relationships have evolved. Before 1937 the Court took a highly restrictive view of the constitutional powers available to the federal government. From 1937, however, it became much more supportive of federal regulatory and legislative activity; so much so that many critics doubted whether there were any circumstances in which states' rights would be upheld. (During the Warren and Burger eras also the Court handed down decisions which had profound implications for areas such as criminal and electoral law with important consequences for state autonomy.) Under Rehnquist's leadership, a conservative-leaning Court has devoted serious attention to federal issues, especially the scope of the Tenth and Eleventh Amendments. Although there is still much disagreement about how far the Court has fundamentally changed its jurisprudence on federal issues, by handing down decisions such as *Lopez* (in which the Court struck down federal legislation regulating possession of firearms near schools as outside congressional authority) the Court has signaled that there are limits to federal legislative power and that states rights will obtain constitutional protection (see also Chapter 7)

The Bush agenda and federalism

Bush came to power proclaiming himself a "faithful friend of federalism" and, as a Republican with immediate prior experience of state government, it might be assumed that the federal balance will continue to shift away from Washington. Certainly Bush's administration drew heavily on the expertise of Republican governors and mayors. Tommy Thompson, the long-time Wisconsin governor who was responsible for much of the innovatory welfare reform that prefigured Clinton's 1996 PRWORA and who had been chairman of the NGA, was appointed Secretary for Health and Human Services. Christine Whitman, the former governor of New Jersey, was made head of the Environmental Protection Agency. Stephen Goldsmith, former mayor of Indiana, was made a domestic policy adviser with special responsibility for developing faith-based initiatives. Members of the Texas educational network were appointed to posts in the Department of Education to promote Bush's education agenda. And when, following the attacks of September 11th, Bush needed a "czar" for homeland security he called on former Governor of Pennsylvania Tom Ridge.

Yet a number of factors suggest that Bush's federalism agenda will be somewhat more complicated than might at first sight appear. First, changing the perspective from that of the state to the federal level is likely to have an effect. Thus on issues such as Medicaid and managed care – and, indeed, on other issues with implications for federalism and where the states and federal government may be at odds – Bush may find his views are altered by his new position.

Second, the Bush administration is inevitably responsive to the needs of business, the more so perhaps as recession looms. In recent years pro-business lobbies have been urging federal government to pre-empt state laws in areas such as consumer privacy where business favors uniformity rather than variety. In 1999 there were some 35 bills introduced into Congress which were aimed at pre-empting state laws mostly in the area of financial and telecommunciations regulation. Although in the 106th Congress (1998–2000) state and local governments tried to impose new guidelines on the Congressional legislation and agency rule-making processes (for example, by requiring federalism impact statements), only one of six bills actually became law. All the others failed, including the Federalism Accountability Act which would have implemented the states' manifesto on federal government pre-emption.The one that did pass into law – the Federal Financial Assistance Management Act of 1999 – directs agencies to streamline the administration of any financial assistance programme for which they are responsible (Weissert and Schram, 2000).

Third, in some areas drives to hand power back to the states may prove highly controversial. Although Bush wanted to transfer more power to the states in relation to pollution control, and indeed signaled a cut of $25 million in the EPA budget, an EPA Report issued in 2001 underlined weaknesses in pollution monitoring by the states, not least their tendency to avoid punishing polluters (Borenstein, 2001). And Bush was forced to withdraw his original nominee (Donald Scheregardus) as head of the EPA enforcement division because of doubts about his record while responsible for Ohio's environmental policies.

Fourth, Bush's conservative moral agenda conflicts in some areas with state autonomy. For example, Oregon's physician-assisted suicide law has been condemned by the federal government, and the Attorney General is at the time of writing trying to override it by invoking the federal power to control drugs. Oregon is suing the federal government, claiming that attempts to interfere with this law are unconstitutional because Oregon has the right to determine what counts as legitimate medical practice within its own borders.

Fifth, some key points of Bush's own policy agenda pose problems for federalism. Education is traditionally an area of state and local responsibility and limited federal jurisdiction. In the period since Jimmy Carter established a separate cabinet-level Department of Education, Republicans have consistently attacked its role and, as recently as 1996, urged its abolition. Bush's educational agenda aims to secure greater accountability of schools and to raise standards. It is an educational agenda in large part endorsed by both parties, although Democrats are opposed to the use of vouchers to enable parents to buy into private schools, a strategy which was promoted by Milwaukee mayor John Norquist and which had gained attention in recent years. Bush's educational policies have not been endorsed by the Republican governors, many of whom feared electoral retribution if the federal government imposed new standards on the states.

Finally, a changing political climate at the state level may make greater decentralization less than palatable to a Republican White House. There was, as noted earlier, a natural affinity between the Republican Congress of the post-1994 period and the Republican governors who dominated the NGA. The politics of intergovernmental relations will become more complex if the GOP hold on state governorships is reduced. When Bush entered the White House in January 2001, Republicans controlled 29 governorships compared to the Democrats' 19 (with two independent Governors). The Democrats took the two governorships (in Virginia and New Jersey) that were up for election in November 2001, thereby closing the gap. But the real test will be in 2002 when 36 states hold gubernatorial elections.

That said, Bush has thus far tried to maintain a pro-devolution image. He took his own federalism initiative early in the administration, announcing in February 2001 the creation of a new interagency working group (under the assistant to the president for domestic policy) in order to identify ways of promoting federalism and drafting a new executive order on intergovernmental relations. The working group, which Bush high-lighted in his first-year meetings with governors and state legislators, was required to report in six months.

To some extent the war against terrorism has worked against greater devolution, both by focusing attention on the federal government and highlighting policy areas such as security where federalism can produce dangerous inefficiencies and lack of coordination (see also Chapter 11). Equally, the economic situation itself may impose limits on the movement toward greater state and local autonomy. Clinton's second term saw a buoyant economy and a federal government surplus. As the economy edges into recession, this will have an impact on the ability of state and local governments to fund expenditures. Similarly, the cost of some items on the state and local government budget – notably education and Medicaid – have been rising rapidly. It was reported in 2001 that at least 17 states were having to adopt extraordinary measures to balance their budgets, and many others were in difficulties. To balance their budgets many states faced unpalatable choices between cutting programs and firing staff, putting up taxes, borrowing or cutting into their reserves. Borrowing is in turn dependent on credit ratings, which may be adjusted if the under-lying health of a state's finances is not good.

Conclusion

The relationship between the federal government and the states has always been a controversial one, and the last two decades have been no exception. What has been different however, has been the range and depth of efforts to recalibrate the federal balance and to prevent Washington and the federal government overwhelming state and local autonomy. Equally important have been the revitalization of subnational levels of government and the extent to which the rhetoric of the new federal order has com-manded support across the governmental system. Bush may expect, or indeed may want, to continue the rebuilding of a genuine partnership with the states. The evolution of the American system has, however, produced a complex labyrinth of relationships which are less than easily navigated. It is thus likely that although the American federal and intergovernmental system will continue to tilt away from Washington, change will be rela-tively slow and incremental, and the system will retain ambiguous, complex and frustrating features for those who have to work in it.

Chapter 10

Economic Policy

CHRISTOPHER J. BAILEY

Economic policy did not figure highly in the 2000 presidential elections. Five years of economic growth, rising productivity, increasing profitability, rising rates of investment, and falling inflation and unemployment rates, allowed both candidates to concentrate on developing plans to spend a soaring federal budget surplus rather than explain how they would manage the economy. While George W. Bush toured the country promoting a plan to cut taxes by $1.3 trillion, Al Gore sought to persuade the electorate of the virtues of his plan to increase spending, reduce public debt, and cut taxes by $480 billion. Traditional economic concerns rapidly began to intrude into the new administration's calculations, however, as evidence emerged early in 2001 that the economy might not be as strong as had been thought. Alan Greenspan, Chairman of the Federal Reserve Board, gave an early indication that all was not well when he told the US Senate Budget Committee on January 25 2001 that: "As far as we can judge, we have had a very dramatic slowing down [of economic growth]. We are probably very close to zero at this particular moment" (Martin, 2001a). Declining rates of economic growth, dramatic falls in share prices, rising levels of unemployment, and a growing energy crisis, suggested that the much-vaunted "new economy" of the 1990s had fallen prey to some very old economic ills. The terrorist attacks on the World Trade Center and the Pentagon on September 11 2001 pushed the economy further into trouble. Consumer confidence plunged, stock prices fell precipitously, unemployment rose, and a number of high-profile industries faced bankruptcy.

Evidence of an economic slowdown in early 2001 brought the difficulties of economic management into sharper focus than at any time since the early 1990s. The first difficulty lay in interpreting the meaning of various economic indicators. Some argued that the economic slowdown could be characterized as a U, others a V, and a few as a W. The first scenario suggested that the economy was heading for a "soft landing" followed by steady growth; the second scenario posited a rapid decline followed by equally rapid growth; and the third scenario predicted an iteration of rapid growth and decline. A second difficulty lay in choosing the appropriate policy tools to restore the vitality of the economy. Could monetary policy be relied upon to promote growth, or did the government need to employ fiscal tools to stimulate demand? Would large tax cuts or increased spending on the country's infrastructure be the best way to "kick start" the economy? Would de-regulation of the economy promote enterprise? Finding answers to these questions became even more pressing following the events of September 11 2001 as politicians struggled to alleviate the economic impact of the terrorist attacks. The final difficulty derived from the crowded institutional context of economic policy-making. No institution or individual has command over the tools of economic policy-making in the United States. Not only is power divided horizontally between the federal and the state governments, but it is also divided vertically between branches of government, and even within those branches.

Economic policy-making in the early years of the Bush administration bears witness to these difficulties. The sudden economic slowdown caught President Bush by surprise. Apart from a commitment to reduce the size of government and to promote free trade, Bush entered office with no coherent policy on the economy. He proved able to use the uncertainty about the economy in early 2001 to garner support for his tax-cutting proposals, and employed his executive authority to reduce some of the regulatory burden on big business, but failed to develop a package of policies worthy of any sort of sobriquet. In the absence of a clearly articulated alternative, the basic structure of economic management remained much the same as during the Clinton years. Political concerns meant that decisions about taxation and levels of government spending were made primarily on the basis of their allocative rather than economic impact. With fiscal policy remaining subordinate to budgetary politics, the primacy of monetary policy as the main means of managing the economy continued by default. Responsibility for tackling the uncertain economy resided with Alan Greenspan and his colleagues on the Federal Open Market Committee (FOMC) of the Federal Reserve Board. These arrangements were suddenly rendered inadequate by the terrorist attacks of September 11 2001. Recognizing that cuts in interest rates would be insufficient on their own to maintain economic stability, even Greenspan called for a $100 billion stimulus package to bolster the flagging economy. War revived the fortunes of fiscal policy.

The uneasy economy

The American economy performed exceptionally well throughout most of the 1990s. "Everything that should be up is up – GDP, capital spending, incomes, the stock market, employment, exports, consumer and business

Figure 10.1   *Key economic indicators, 1980–2000*

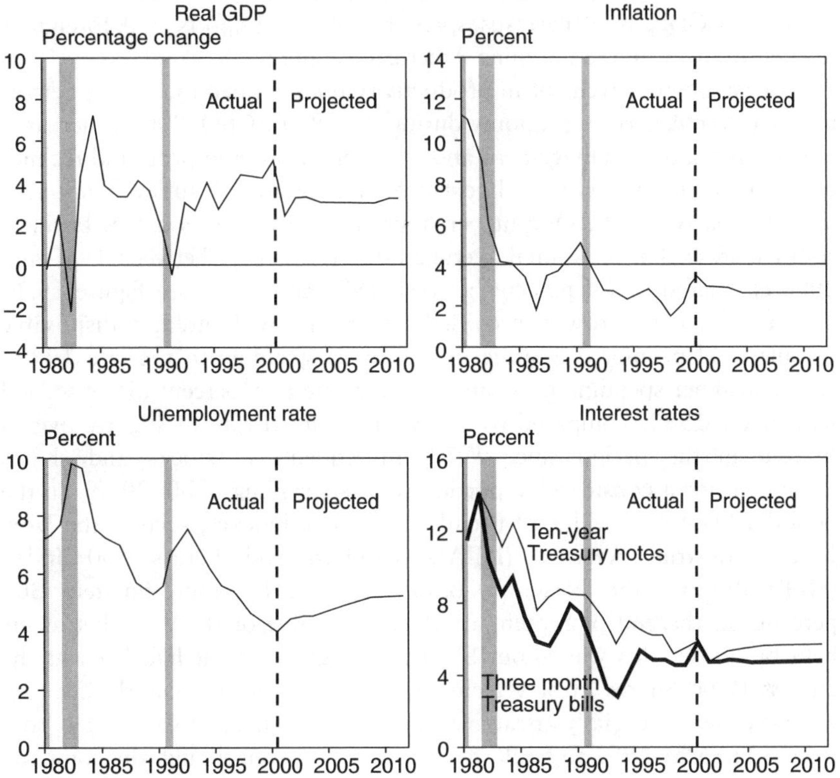

Source: CBO (2001).

confidence. Everything that should be down is down – unemployment, inflation, and interest rates," trumpeted Mortimer Zuckerman (1998) in an essay predicting a "Second American Century." Real GDP grew at a rate of approximately 3 percent per year from 1992 to 1996, 4 percent per year from 1996 to 1999, and reached 5 percent in 2000 (see Figure 10.1). These years of strong economic growth reduced the ranks of the unemployed to levels not seen since January 1970. The unemployment rate fell from 6.8 percent in 1992 to 3.9 percent in October 2000. Unemployment even fell among groups that traditionally failed to benefit from improvements in the economy. The unemployment rate for African-Americans fell from 14.1 percent in 1993 to 7.8 percent in 1999, and unemployment among Latinos fell from 11.3 percent to 6.5 percent (Glassman, 1999). Inflation also remained under control. The Core Consumer Price Index (CPI) averaged around 3 percent at the beginning of the 1990s, but had fallen to around 2 percent by the end of the decade. Only a worsening balance of payments appeared to give cause for concern. In the third quarter of 2000 the trade deficit reached a record $389.5 billion, or 3.9 percent of GDP, as Americans spent heavily on imports and foreigners flocked to invest in the booming American economy.

A dramatic improvement in productivity underpinned the strong performance of the American economy during the 1990s (CBO, 2001). Increased globalization, new management and labor practices, and profound technological innovation, served to boost productivity growth to levels not seen since the early 1970s. Output per hour worked in the nonfarm business sector increased at an annual average rate of 3 percent between 1995 and 2000 compared to 1.4 percent between 1973 and 1995 (see Figure 10.2). This productivity growth provided Americans with greater disposable income, and prompted a surge in consumer spending in the late 1990s. Real consumer spending grew at a average rate of 5 percent in the second half of the 1990s compared to an average annual rate of slightly over 3 percent in the period since 1973. Investments in stocks and shares accounted for a considerable portion of this spending (CB0, 2000). In the period 1994–99 the value of broad-based stock indexes, such as the Dow Jones Industrial Average (DJIA), Standard and Poor's 500 Index (S&P500), and the Nasdaq Composite, rose by approximately 300 percent. At the end of September 1999, the value of stock market assets held by households was about $9 trillion higher than it had been at the end of 1994. Shares in new technology companies, particularly dot.com shares, proved especially attractive. Amazon.com shares, for example, rose from $9 in May 1997 to $320 in January 1999, even though the company had never made a profit.

A dramatic improvement in the federal budget accompanied the economic growth of the late 1990s. Between 1995 and 2000 the budget moved from a $164 billion deficit to a $236 billion surplus, or 2.4 percent of GNP. Although part of the explanation for this improvement in the country's finances can be traced to action taken in the mid-1990s by the White House and Congress to reduce the deficit, the bulk of the improvement occurred because economic growth produced a phenomenal growth in government revenues. Revenues increased at an annual rate of 8.3 percent, much faster than the rate of economic growth, between 1994 and 1998. Individual income taxes accounted for most of this increase in revenue. From 1993 to 1998 the revenue from individual income taxes increased by more than 10 percent per year. The Taxpayer Relief Act of 1997 slowed this rate of growth in subsequent years, but it still exceeded the rate of economic growth.

The strength of the American economy in the late 1990s led a number of observers to conclude that various structural changes had produced a "new economy" that was immune to the problems that had traditionally

Figure 10.2   *Labour productivity in the nonfarm business sector*

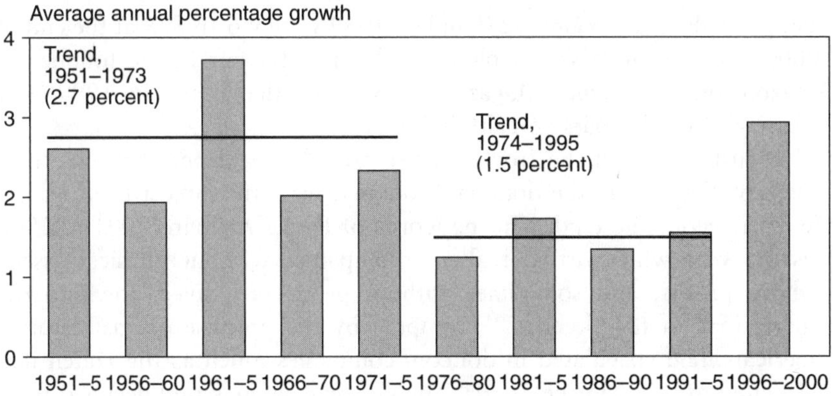

Average annual percentage growth

Source: CBO (2001).

plagued economies around the world (Jorgenson and Stiroh, 2000; CEA, 2001). Concerns about growth, unemployment, and inflation no longer appeared to be relevant as improvements in computers, the expansion of the Internet, innovation in financial markets, the development of new goods and services, an inflow of foreign capital, and cheap imports fueled an economy that seemed to grow ever stronger. "In a knowledge-based economy there are no constraints to growth," stated one analyst quoted by the *Wall Street Journal* (Krugman, 2001). Even Alan Greenspan proved willing to embrace a vision of a "new economy" in which improvements in productivity led to growth without fear of inflation or unemployment (Greenspan, 1997).

A fall in share prices in early 2000 punctured some of the euphoria surrounding the American economy. In the first two months of the new millennium the DJIA lost 11.9 percent of its value. Although subsequent gains in the next six months restored much of this lost value, further dramatic falls in the value of shares in September and November 2000 meant that the DJIA ended the year 6.2 percent lower than it had closed in December 1999. This was the first time since 1990 that the DJIA had closed a year at a lower level than where it started. Other stock indexes told an even bleaker story. The S&P500 Index fell 10.1 percent, which was its worst performance since 1977. The Nasdaq Composite fell 39.3 percent, which was its worst annual loss since its creation in 1971. Hardest hit were technology and telecommunications stocks. An estimated $3.3 trillion was wiped off the paper value of the hi-tech companies listed on the Nasdaq. Among the companies listed on the DJIA, AT&T and Microsoft had the largest price declines with losses of 65.9 percent and 62.9 percent respectively. These losses wiped a total of $390 billion off the value of Microsoft and an estimated $40 billion off the personal wealth of its founder, Bill Gates. The dot.com companies fared even worse. Yahoo shares, for example, valued at around $250 in late 1999 were worth $25 at the end of 2000. Amazon.com's shares plummeted similarly. Jeff Bezos, founder of Amazon.com and *Time* Magazine's "Man of the Year" in 1999, lost seven-eighths of his paper wealth in 2000.

The turbulence on the stock market provided evidence that the "new economy", especially the dot.com economy, was still subject to at least a few basic economic truths. In the words of Paul Krugman (2001): "2000 was the year when virtual reality – companies without physical assets, without profits, and sometimes without products – lived down to the expectations of the skeptics." Prompted by the promise of vast returns, Americans had speculated in dot.com companies much as the Dutch had speculated in tulips in the 1630s. The personal savings rate declined from just under 5 percent in the last quarter of 1997 to 1.5 percent in the last quarter of 1999 as Americans borrowed money to buy shares in the "new economy." In 2000 the personal savings rate became negative for the first time since the Great Depression. The burgeoning federal budget surplus of the late 1990s offset part of the decline in the personal savings rate, and helped to ensure that interest rates remained low, but the consequences of such high levels of private debt could not be postponed indefinitely. Rarely had Americans lived so far beyond their means.

The end of the speculative bubble of the late 1990s hit the dot.com economy first. Webmergers.com, an Internet consultancy company, reported that 210 dot.com companies went out of business, and 41,000 dot.com jobs were lost in 2000 (Campbell, 2001). Ripples from the burst bubble soon spread to the rest of the economy, however, as consumer confidence plunged. One index of consumer confidence compiled by the Conference Board, a private research group, plummeted to its lowest level in four years when it fell from 128.6 in December 2000 to 114.4 in January 2001 (Martin, 2001b). Unease about the economy led Americans to rein in their spending. Sales of goods and services declined markedly as a result (Smith and Alexander, 2001). New car sales, for example, were 7.6 percent lower in December 2000 than in December 1999. The specter of rising levels of unemployment inevitably followed. General Motors announced early in January 2001 that it would temporarily close eight plants and lay off 20,000 of its 388,000 workers. Chrysler also announced that it would close five of its 12 plants for two weeks. The unemployment rate rose steadily as other businesses followed suit. Unemployment reached 4.3 percent in March 2001 and 4.5 percent a month later (Uchitelle, 2001). The rise in unemployment in April 2001 was the largest single monthly increase since February 1991.

Increased unemployment levels provided confirmation that the

American economy had begun to slow down. Alan Greenspan had warned in December 2000 that various economic indicators suggested a dramatic decline in the rate of economic growth, but subsequent data released by the Commerce Department that showed an unexpected rise in retail sales had led to increased optimism about the future (Martin, 2001c). Treasury Secretary Paul O'Neill predicted in late March 2001 that economic growth for the first quarter of 2001 had risen by 0.75 percent (Knowlton, 2001). The unemployment figures for April 2001, however, suggested that such optimism had been misplaced. "These figures mean that the economy is right now at zero growth," said one analyst working for Deutsche Bank North America; "I don't see much of anything positive in this report" (Uchitelle, 2001).

A growing energy crisis exacerbated uncertainty about the future of the economy. De-regulation, a lack of investment in the infrastructure of energy production, and rising crude oil and natural gas prices in the second half of 2000, created energy shortages and price increases that threatened the well-being of the American economy. The crisis was felt particularly acutely in California. In January 2001 the state's two largest utility companies, Pacific Gas and Electric (PG&E) and Southern California Edison, warned that they could no longer meet demand for electricity and faced bankruptcy. Rolling blackouts and increases in the price of electricity in the world's fifth largest economy threatened to destabilize the entire economy. "California's crisis could magnify the downside for the whole economy. In the end the state's energy crisis could prove to be an unwanted wildcard for the American financial markets and the global economy at large," warned one analyst at Morgan Stanley Dean Witter (Alexander, 2001). Elsewhere in the country, consumer confidence fell further as the price of gasoline rose above the symbolic $2 per gallon mark.

The abrupt transformation in America's economic fortunes took the new administration by surprise. On August 3 2000, Governor George W. Bush told the Republican National Convention in Philadelphia that "the promise of prosperity" had never been so vivid for ordinary Americans. "America has a strong economy and a surplus", he announced, and it was time for the federal government to share it with the voters in the form of massive tax cuts. On February 8 2001, President Bush stood in the White House Rose Garden and stated that: "Americans are hearing, and some feeling, the economic slowdown . . . Consumer confidence has slumped, Many business leaders are worried. A warning light is flashing on the dashboard of our economy." Bush accepted responsibility for finding a solution to the problem. "My job is to lead. A President should not wait on events. He must try to shape them," he continued, "And the warning signs are clear. All of us here in Washington, the President and Congress, are responsible to confront the danger of an economic slowdown and to blunt its effects." The problem for President Bush lay in knowing what to do. Not only did economists have mixed views on the meaning of the economic slowdown and the effectiveness of potential solutions, but Bush also had to confront a crowded institutional landscape that restricted his scope for action.

The immediate response of President Bush to the economic slowdown was to reinvent his tax cutting proposals as an economic stimulus package. Representative Philip Crane (R.Ind.), a senior member of the House of Representatives Ways and Means Committee, had signaled the potential for such a change of emphasis late in December 2000. "Now that the economy appears to be slipping, tax cuts are even more important," he stated, "The economic case for tax cuts is that this is the absolute perfect time to cut taxes" (Ellison, 2000). President Bush moved quickly to act upon the cue provided by Crane. The conservative ideological content that had underpinned his earlier calls for tax cuts was quietly downplayed in favour of language that could have been penned by an unreconstructed Keynesian. "Today, I am sending to Congress my plan to provide relief to all income tax payers, which I believe will help jump-start the American economy," Bush told the public on February 8 2001. His rhetorical conversion to demand-side economics became even more explicit in a speech to the Kalamazoo Chamber of Commerce on March 27 2001. "We must put more money in the hands of consumers in the short-term, and restore confidence and optimism for the long-term. We need an immediate stimulus for our economy and a pro-growth environment for years to come," he informed the assembled businessmen.

Few economists believe that tax cuts offer the best means of managing the economy. The American Economic Association announced at its annual conference in New Orleans in 2000 that "the manipulation" of taxes is an unsuitable instrument for controlling the business cycle (Stelzer, 2001). This is because people tend to save rather than spend any "tax windfalls" they receive. "The problem with all these proposals is that the notion that tax policy this month can stimulate the economy next month is unrealistic at best," stated William Gale, an economist at the Brookings Institution (Stevenson, 2001). "If we could control peoples' behavior that well we wouldn't be in this situation in the first place," he continued. Even conservative economists doubt the effectiveness of tax cuts. "The problem with tax cuts is their timing," noted William Niskanen, Chairman of the Cato Institute, "They don't kick in in time to be a solution for economic weakness. That's the awkward thing" (Ellison, 2000).

The skepticism voiced by economists counted for little among senior members of the new administration. Virtually all proclaimed a belief that tax cuts would stimulate demand and ensure that the economy did not slide into recession. Behind this rhetoric lay an awareness that emphasizing the potential stimulus of the tax cuts offered the best way of overcoming congressional opposition to the proposals. The close partisan division of the 107th Congress (2001–2) meant that Democratic votes would be needed to enact the president's tax proposals. Reinventing these proposals as an economic stimulus package provided President Bush with the best means to sell his main policy priority to wavering Democrats. Constant reference to the need to stimulate the economy gave Bush a way to navigate the crowded institutional context of economic management in the United States.

The crowded institutional context of economic management

A crowded institutional context compounds the problems of economic management in the United States. Control over fiscal, monetary and regulatory tools is not only divided between the federal and state governments, but also between and within the branches of the federal government. These institutional arrangements mean that the president has no control over some tools of economic management, and must negotiate about the employment of others. The conflictual nature of economic policy means that such negotiation is usually fraught and difficult. Opinion is often divided both on the efficacy of various fiscal tools as means of controlling the economy, and the desirability of the way that they redistribute resources. The result, as President Clinton found when he tried to secure passage of an economic stimulus package in 1993, is frequently deadlock (Bailey, 1999).

The US Constitution gives primary control over the tools of economic management to Congress. Article 1, Sections 7, 8, and 9 grant Congress the power to tax and spend. Article 1, Section 8 gives Congress the power "To borrow money on the credit of the United States." Authority "To regulate Commerce with foreign Nations, and among the several States, and with the Indian Tribes" is similarly provided in Article 1, Section 8. These grants of power do not mean, however, that Congress has exclusive control over the management of the American economy. Not only do the states retain taxing, spending, and regulatory powers, but Congress has also delegated much of its "operational authority" to manage the economy to other institutions (Gosling, 2000: 31). Congress ceded virtually all power over monetary policy when it created the Federal Reserve Board in 1913. The Federal Reserve has the authority to set interest rates without any need to secure the agreement of either Congress or the president. Congress ceded further power with enactment of the Budget and

Accounting Act of 1921. This gave the president a central role in shaping fiscal policy by requiring him to submit an annual budget to Congress. Enactment of the Employment Act of 1946 cemented the president's central role in economic management. The Act requires the president to submit an annual report to Congress on the state of the economy.

The divided nature of American government restricts the president's ability to manage the economy. Although the president's responsibility to submit an annual budget to Congress allows him to shape the fiscal agenda, congressional acquiescence to the president's spending and taxation plans is very rare. On one famous occasion President Reagan even sent the budget to Congress in an ambulance and proclaimed that it was "dead on arrival." Presidents lack even nominal leadership over monetary policy. The president has no power to compel members of the Federal Reserve Board to do his bidding. A seven-member board governs the Federal Reserve. The president appoints the members for staggered 14-year terms, subject to Senate confirmation, and cannot remove members once appointed. Even when presidents manage to secure support in Washington for their policy preferences, the budgetary and regulatory authority of the states may still frustrate efforts to manage the economy.

A number of institutions have been created to help the president meet his budget setting and economic management responsibilities. The Budget and Accounting Act of 1921 created a Bureau of the Budget situated within the Treasury Department to help the president draft the budget. This Bureau was moved to the EOP in 1939, and was renamed the Office of Management and Budget in 1970. The Employment Act of 1946 created a three member Council of Economic Advisors (CEA) to provide the president with economic expertise. Staffed primarily by professional economists, the CEA offers the president a source of advice on broad macro-economic issues. Presidents have also used the Treasury Secretary to obtain advice on tax policy and wider economic issues. The role of the Treasury in collecting taxes, borrowing money, and managing the national debt means that the Treasury Secretary is well placed to play a significant role in crafting economic policy.

The way that presidents have used these institutions has varied over time (Gosling, 2000). Some have tried to centralize economic policy advice in one person. President Nixon relied upon Treasury Secretary George Schultz for advice and appointed him assistant to the president for economic affairs. Others have employed a more collective approach. Presidents John F. Kennedy and Lyndon B. Johnson created an informal economic advisory committee made up of the Treasury Secretary, the Chair of the CEA, and the Director of the OMB. Presidents Ford, Reagan, Bush, and Clinton formalized the collective approach of the

Kennedy–Johnson era by creating new coordinating institutions. Ford created an Economic Policy Board (EPB), Reagan and Bush used an Economic Policy Council (EPC), and Clinton established a National Economic Council (NEC). All of these institutional units had a broader membership than the informal committees used by Kennedy and Johnson. The membership of the NEC, for example, consisted of virtually the entire cabinet, the Administrator of the EPA, the Chair of the CEA, and presidential assistants for economic and domestic policy. Chaired by Clinton, the NEC was intended to coordinate both policy advice and policy implementation across the executive branch. President George W. Bush has eschewed the formal framework established by his immediate predecessors, and relied instead upon a few trusted individuals for economic advice. He appointed Lawrence Lindsey, a former governor of the Federal Reserve, as assistant to the president for economic policy and director of the NEC. Other advice at the beginning of his administration came from Vice-President Dick Cheney, Treasury Secretary Paul O'Neill, and OMB Director Mitchell Daniels. All had considerable experience of working within Washington, DC, and close ties with big business. Only two members of the CEA, Chairman R. Glenn Hubbard and Mark B. McClellan, had been appointed some nine months into the new administration.

The nature of the economic advice given to presidents has changed over time. In the decades following the end of World War II the prevailing economic orthodoxy insisted that governments should use fiscal tools to manage aggregate demand within the economy. Propounded most famously by the British economist John Maynard Keynes, the central idea of demand-side economics is that governments should use their powers of taxation and spending to boost demand when recession looms, and to reduce demand during periods of inflation. The dominance of Keynesianism began to collapse during the 1970s as high inflation and high unemployment challenged the idea that governments could manipulate aggregate demand to resolve economic problems. Keynesianism's demise allowed two alternative means of economic management to gain credence. Monetarists such as Milton Friedman of the University of Chicago posited that governments should employ monetary tools, primarily interest rates, to control the money supply. The argument is that high interest rates restrict the growth of credit in an economy and dampen inflationary tendencies, while low interest rates promote economic growth by making it cheaper to borrow money. Supply-side economists, such as Arthur Laffer of the University of California, argue that governments should use the tax system and de-regulate the economy to promote an enterprise culture. The central idea is that government regulations and high tax rates for upper-income earners act as a disincentive to invest. A more recent orthodoxy suggests that governments cannot effectively manage the economy; the argument is that government action is more likely to exacerbate economic problems than solve them.

Large federal budget deficits in the 1980s and 1990s accentuated this sense that governments cause economic problems. Critics claimed that the level of federal debt led to high interest rates, a decline in funds available for private investment, a reliance upon foreign capital, and interest payments that reduced the government's capacity to respond to more pressing concerns (Krugman, 1994). Although not all economists agreed with this prognosis (see Eisner, 1994), public concern about the size of the deficit contributed to a profound change in the nature of fiscal politics in the United States. Use of the tax system and government spending as tools of economic management was largely forgotten as deficit reduction became the priority of presidents and Congress. Budgets were designed to reduce the deficit rather than promote economic growth, full employment, or low inflation. A series of budgets enacted during the 1990s that increased taxes and cut government spending finally eradicated the budget deficit in 1998. An era of budget surpluses, however, did not presage a return to economic management by fiscal means. Debates about how to spend the budget surplus simply replaced debates about how to eradicate the budget deficit.

The preoccupation with budget politics during the 1990s left primary responsibility for economic management to the Federal Reserve Board. Under its Chairman Alan Greenspan, the Board's FOMC pursued an active policy of making minor adjustments in interest rates to control fluctuations in the economy. From 1994 to 1998 the Board raised interest rates on a number of occasions to tackle the threat of inflation. Worries that a serious financial crisis in East Asia in late 1998 might cause economic problems in the United States caused it to alter direction and reduce rates, but Greenspan's fears that the economy showed signs of overheating led to a rise in interest rates in 2000. The Board reacted to signs of a slowing economy in 2001 by successively reducing interest rates. Interest rates were cut seven times in the first six months of 2001 in an effort to produce a "soft landing" for the economy. Remarking on the role played by the Federal Reserve, the chief economist at Lehman Brothers highlighted the shift in responsibility for economic management: "I'm old enough to remember when fiscal policy was used to stabilise economies; now it is monetary policy. And it isn't even monetary policy – a half point off rates is neither here nor there – it's more a laying-on of hands" (Smith and Alexander, 2001).

The politics of surplus

The existence of large federal budget surpluses during the late 1990s and early years of the new millennium changed the nature of budgetary politics in the United States. Predictions that accumulated surpluses would total $5.6 trillion by 2010 laid to rest the arguments about deficit reduction that had characterized budgetary politics since the mid-1980s, and raised new questions about how the surpluses should be spent. Four options dominated discussions (Gosling, 2000). First, the Treasury could buy back government securities and reduce the burden of interest payment needed to service the national debt. In 2000 the annual net interest payable on the national debt stood at $215 billion, or 12.2 percent of federal budget outlays for that year. Second, the surpluses could be used to finance tax cuts. In 1999 the federal government took 11.6 percent of the country's GDP in individual and corporate income taxes compared to 9.7 percent in 1990. Third, the surpluses could be used to expand government spending. Limits on discretionary spending during the 1990s restricted the development of new federal programs and created a backlog of infrastructure improvements. Finally, the surpluses could be saved to help meet rising entitlement costs. Analysts estimated that the Social Security Trust Fund would have an annual cash deficit of $766 billion by 2030.

Support for these proposals divided very much along partisan lines. On the one hand, most Republicans believed that the surpluses should be used primarily to finance tax cuts. Partly this was because they believed that the surpluses should be returned to those who had earned them. "[O]ur Treasury is full and our people are over-charged," declared President George W. Bush when introducing his proposal to cut taxes on February 8 2001, "Returning some of their money is right, and it is urgent," Partly it was because they believed that tax cuts would help limit the size of government. Lawrence Lindsey, President Bush's chief economic adviser, told the January 6 2001 "Evans, Novak, Hunt & Shields Show" on CNN that: "I think the key here is that, when Congress has money, it will spend it. That is a point we made repeatedly during the campaign." On the other hand, most Democrats tended to argue that the surpluses should be used to finance infrastructure improvements. Few politicians of either party appeared willing to set aside substantial portions of the surplus to deal with the long-term problem of Social Security.

The results of the 2000 elections complicated the politics of the surplus. Although President Bush had campaigned on a tax-cutting platform, and the Republicans had retained their majorities in Congress, Bush's contested mandate (and the GOP's wafer-thin majority in the Senate) made it unlikely that a significant tax cut would be enacted. The economic slowdown, however, gave Bush an opportunity to reinvent his proposal as an economic stimulus package. In remarks on February 5 2001, he stated that: "I strongly believe that a tax relief plan is an important part of helping our country's economy recover. And I think expediting money into people's pockets is going to be the key ingredient." Shifting ground in this way allowed him to court the votes of conservative Democrats who might otherwise have voted along partisan lines. Even more audaciously, Bush also sought to sell his proposal as a means to help Americans faced with rising energy prices. At a news conference on May 11 2001 he stated: "I'm deeply concerned about high gas prices. To anyone who wants to figure out how to help the consumers, pass the tax relief measure as quickly as possible."

The tax proposal that Bush submitted to Congress on February 8 2001 included provisions to replace the current federal income tax rates of 15, 28, 31, 36, and 39.6 percent with a new rate structure of 10, 15, 25, and 33 percent, doubled child tax credit to $1,000 per child, abolished the federal estate tax, reinstated a 10 percent deduction for double-income couples, and expanded charitable deductions. The White House estimated that a typical family with two children would receive at least $1,600 in tax relief per year if the proposal were enacted. President Bush claimed in a speech made on February 5, 2001 that:

> This is real and practical and helpful, when at this time many Americans need it. Sixteen hundred dollars will pay the average mortgage for a month. Sixteen hundred dollars will pay for a year's tuition at a community college. Sixteen hundred dollars will pay the average gasoline costs for two cars for a year. And $1,600 will buy the average California family 24 months' worth of electric power.

The total cost of the tax cut was calculated to be $1.6 trillion over ten years.

Constant claims by the administration that tax cuts were needed to provide a stimulus to a slowing economy structured congressional reaction to Bush's proposals. Debate centered on the size and timing of the tax cuts rather than their need. While most Republicans rallied around President Bush's proposals, most Democrats argued for smaller and more immediate tax relief. Democrats also wished to ensure that sufficient money was available to fund education programmes and other infrastructure plans. The House passed a tax bill in March 2001 that included most of the president's proposals, but action in the Senate proceeded at a slower pace. A budget deal negotiated between the White House and congressional leaders in early May 2001 agreed a compromise that reduced taxes by $1.35 trillion over ten years, but also gave an immediate $100 billion in immediate tax cuts to help boost the economy, and authorised nearly $2 trillion in spending for FY 2002. A budget resolution incorporating the compromise passed the House on May 9 2001 on a 221–207 vote. Six Democrats voted for the measure and three Republicans voted against it. The budget resolution passed the Senate a day later on a 53–47 vote. Five Democratic senators voted in favor of the resolution: John B. Breaux of Louisiana, Max Baucus of Montana, Ben Nelson of Nebraska, and Zell Miller and Max Cleland of Georgia. Two Republican senators voted against the resolution: Lincoln Chafee of Rhode Island and James M. Jeffords of Vermont.

The Budget Resolution is a nonbinding planning tool that sets guidelines for tax and spending legislation. Senator Breaux, who delivered the Democratic votes that secured passage of the measure, alluded to this fact when he admitted to colleagues: "This is an imperfect document. But it is written on paper; it is not written in concrete" (*Congressional Record*, May 10 2001). Passage of the Budget Resolution was important, nonetheless, for two reasons. First, it showed that President Bush could hold Republicans together to advance his agenda through Congress. Second, it meant that any tax bill that fit within the parameters established by the Resolution could be passed by a majority vote in the Senate and could not be filibustered. With the Senate divided 50–50, the Republican leadership would not have been able to gather the 60 votes needed to end a Democratic filibuster on the tax bill. Trumpeting passage of the Budget Resolution, White House spokesman Ari Fleischer claimed that: "Now that House and Senate have acted, it's clear that the economic recovery package that the president has talked about is on the way" (Rosenbaum, 2001a).

On May 16 2001 the House re-approved the tax bill that had passed in March 2001 to meet the constitutional requirement that money bills originate in the House of Representatives. The bill passed on a 230–197 vote that largely followed party lines. No Republican voted against passage, while 13 Democrats voted in favor. The Senate finally approved a tax bill on May 23 2001 on a 62–38 roll-call vote. The 50 Republican senators were joined by 12 Democrats in voting for the bill. Final passage occurred on May 26 2001 when both chambers approved a conference report. The bill provided tax cuts of $1.35 trillion over ten years, and incorporated most of the elements sought by President Bush. The bill established a new 10 percent tax rate to provide an immediate rebate of $300 per person, created a new rate structure of 15 percent, 25 percent, 28 percent, 33 percent, and 35 percent to be phased in over five years, reduced and eventually abolished the federal estate tax, and phased in tax breaks for married couples. The bill also accommodated liberal demands that low-income groups benefit in some way by making child credit available to families that did not earn enough to pay federal income taxes.

President George W. Bush signed the tax cut into law on June 7 2001. "Tax relief is a great achievement for the American people," Bush proclaimed; "Tax relief is the first achievement produced by a new tone in Washington, and it was produced in record time." The president's success in securing passage of his primary policy goal came at a price, however. The emphasis on tax cuts contributed significantly to Senator Jeffords's decision to become an independent and end the Republican Party's majority status in the Senate. Although Jeffords voted for final passage of the tax bill, he expressed serious misgivings about the direction of policy in negotiation with the White House. The struggle over the tax bill also weakened the partisan allegiance of two other Republicans: Senator John McCain (R-Ariz.) and Senator Lincoln Chafee (R-RI). Furthermore, loss of the Senate placed a serious question mark over whether the agreed tax cuts would be sustained. "I know we're going to revisit it," declared new Majority Leader Senator Tom Daschle (D-SD) in his first press conference; "I just know that at some point that reality is going to come crashing down on all of us, and we're going to have to deal with it" (Rosenbaum, 2001b). Democratic leaders also made clear their intention to challenge the limits on government spending established by the Budget Resolution. Senator Kent Conrad (D-ND), the new Chair of the Senate Budget Committee, described the Republican budget as a "fraud" that set artificially low spending limits in order to pay for the $1.35 trillion tax cuts (Shenon, 2001). Even House Republicans began to revisit spending limits as they realized that favorite agencies and projects would be underfinanced in the budget. Eleven Republicans on the House Appropriations Committee voted with the Democrats just a week after President Bush had signed the tax cuts into law to add $150 million in emergency assistance for apple growers. "A lot of apples are grown in a lot of members' districts," reported Representative C.W. Young (R-Fla), Chair of the Appropriations Committee (Shenon, 2001). Republicans also voted to increase spending on natural resources programs and energy research beyond the levels sought by Bush.

The economics of terror

Evidence that President Bush's tax cuts had failed to revive the American economy became available in early September 2001. The Federal Reserve reported a decline in consumer spending as Americans reduced their levels of debt. More than $200 billion was saved in the first eight months of 2001 compared to a total of $75 billion in 2000. "The new story is less spending and less borrowing as households get their finances back in shape to weather the downturn," commented the chief economist at Decision

Economics (Pearlstein, 2001). Fewer than one in five households proposed to spend their tax rebate, according to a poll conducted by the Survey Research Center of the University of Michigan. The fuel that had propelled the economic growth of the late 1990s had all but run out. Sluggish consumer demand led to falling sales, reduced profit, and rising levels of unemployment. On September 7 2001 the Department of Labor reported that the unemployment rate had risen from 4.5 percent in July to 4.9 percent in August.

Any residual optimism about an "autumn rebound" for the economy was swept away by the terrorist attacks on America on September 11 2001. Consumer confidence plummeted in the immediate wake of the attacks. The Conference Board's index of consumer confidence fell to 97.6 in September 2001, the largest drop since the Gulf War, as Americans grew increasingly pessimistic about the health of the economy (Stewart and Elliott, 2001). Unease about the future led to a further decline in consumer spending. Hardest hit was the airline industry, which announced 120,000 job losses in the two weeks following the attacks, but virtually all major retailers reported falls in sales. Bloomingdale's and Macy's suffered a 40 percent fall in sales, hotels in Las Vegas announced $100 million in cancelled conference bookings, and Walt Disney's shares fell by 25 percent amid fears of fewer visitors to its theme parks. The DJIA suffered its biggest decline since the Great Depression while the value of the shares of seven of the top 100 Nasdaq companies fell below $1.

Fears that the terrorist attacks threatened to push the American economy into a full-blown recession prompted Alan Greenspan to call for enactment of a $100 billion stimulus package on September 26 2001. Greenspan argued that a $40 billion emergency spending package (including $15 billion for the airline industry) already approved by Congress might not be sufficient to bolster a faltering economy. Partisan disagreements soon emerged, however, about the shape of such a package. Both Republicans and Democrats supported further tax cuts but disagreed over who the recipients should be. Democrats argued that tax rebates should be given to low-income households while Republicans wished to restrict tax cuts to those who paid income tax. The Bush administration further argued that a cut in corporate income tax rates would improve the earnings, cash flow, and competitiveness of American industry. Democrats countered that increased spending on the country's infrastructure and financial support for specific industries damaged by the terrorist strike offered a better way forward. All agreed that decisions on taxation and spending needed to be based on economic rather than political calculations.

Conclusion

The terrorist attacks on New York and Washington, DC, changed the context of economic policy in the United States. Not only did they push a faltering economy closer towards recession, but they also placed primary responsibility for economic policy-making back in the hands of politicians. Alan Greenspan's call for an economic stimulus package revealed an awareness of the limits of monetary policy that had not been admitted for almost a decade. Whether President Bush and Congress can respond to this challenge is a moot point. Recent battles over taxation and spending have typically involved political rather than economic calculations. President Bush's successful effort to re-invent his tax-cutting proposal as an economic stimulus package was a decision based upon political rather than economic imperatives. Like the struggles to reduce the deficit that had dominated the 1990s, the decisions over taxation and spending taken before September 11 2001 were not made on the basis of their likely fiscal-policy effects, but on how they affected important constituencies and promoted partisan advantage. The need to fight a war on terrorism and combat a looming recession suggests that economic calculations will probably play a greater role in the determination of fiscal policy in the near future.

Chapter 11

Law and Order

ROBERT SINGH

The US Constitution was established, among other goals, to "insure domestic Tranquility," "provide for the common defense" and "secure the Blessings of Liberty." In striking at all three, the terrorist attacks on New York and Washington of September 11 2001 caused political debates on America's domestic security to enter a new era. For criminal justice policy-makers, traditionally preoccupied by crime, firearms violence, and the "war on drugs," the audacious and devastating attacks posed fundamental questions about the nature of homeland security in the twenty-first century. As such, the strikes added the most powerful impetus and immediacy to reassessing a longstanding American dilemma: the appropriate balance in an open democratic society between extensive civil liberties and "big government" interventions to minimize threats to domestic well-being and public order.

Even prior to the attacks, the politics of law and order graphically encapsulated the broader ambivalence Americans harbor toward the federal government: simultaneously eager for its benefits and protection but wary of its reach. Public concern about the consequences of untrammeled individualism traditionally accorded the American state an important – though neither a monopolistic nor centralized – role in the preservation of life, liberty and property. Support for individual self-defense translated into the most heavily and legally armed civilian population in the world whilst increasingly punitive public policies against lawbreakers brought about the world"s largest prison population. Against these security concerns has been pitted a pronounced respect for individual civil liberties, protections for the accused, and privacy rights.

This balance has always been tested. Although terrorism has mostly been an alien presence in the continental United States, lawlessness has been as much a constant in American life as the rule of law has been fundamental to American democracy. But to many citizens, America remains subject to an excess of laws and a dearth of order. Although official statistics noted a marked decrease in crime rates from 1995 to 2001, for example, those rates remained three times higher than during the 1950s and lethal violence represented a notable exception to the downward trend. Rational and dispassionate discussion, however, has only rarely distinguished criminal justice policy in recent years. Instead, in an electoral environment where the vulnerability of public officials invariably yields a risk-averse approach to campaigning and where divided party control of the federal government often militates against policy innovation, the public rarely encounters clear or forceful arguments against populist approaches to crime and punishment. With politicians of both main parties fearful of being labeled "soft" on crime, traditionalist Americans have proven remarkably effective in achieving their preferred punitive policies, despite the limited effectiveness of those policies in deterring or combating crime.

The chapter is organized around four broad themes. First, the nature of the American law and order regime is explained. Second, the relative absence of issues of crime and punishment from the 2000 elections is analyzed. Third, the three mainstays of recent political conflict on criminal justice policy – firearms, capital punishment, and drugs – are assessed. Finally, the implications of the terrorist attacks for homeland security and American political culture are considered. The Bush administration's response demonstrated the willingness of Americans to endorse a new balance between collective security and individual freedoms. However temporary this may be, it both reflects and advances broader trends in recent criminal justice politics.

The governance of crime

Law is a unique resource of government and the capacity to enforce the law and punish its transgressors is crucial to government's effectiveness. As Peters (1993) notes, "Citizens may obey speeding laws most of the time, but the prospect of a policeman hiding with a radar set makes compliance more probable." But the governance of crime and punishment in America is shaped by two forces that make for immense administrative difficulties: a vast, complex and growing web of federal, state and local laws and a large and highly fragmented network of law enforcement agencies.

The content of constitutional and statute law on crime has traditionally married extensive protections for the rights of the accused with highly punitive policies for those found guilty of violating laws. More than half of the rights enumerated in the Bill of Rights directly concern crime and punishment. Safeguards in the Fourth through Eighth Amendments specify how government must behave in criminal proceedings. Federal judicial interpretations of these constitutional protections required radical changes in the conduct of local and state police forces and courts after 1953, such that federal courts have often been accused of tilting the balance of justice in favor of criminals and against the police, prosecutors and crime victims.

Substantial variance still exists, however, in the administration of criminal justice across American states. For example, the right to a jury trial in criminal cases – guaranteed by the Sixth Amendment – was applied to the states in *Duncan* v. *Louisiana* (1968) but, although the Supreme Court mandates a minimum of six jurors, it permits jury sizes to vary from state to state (in contrast to the 12 jurors specified for federal cases). Neither has the Court imposed on the states the federal requirement of a unanimous jury verdict for conviction. By contrast, the Sixth Amendment's guarantee of right to counsel is binding on all states (though even here the extent to which effective counsel is guaranteed varies dramatically). Although the Rehnquist Court has partially eroded protections for criminal defendants, it has thus far refused to overturn the landmark *Miranda* v. *Arizona* (1964) decision thus keeping intact the rule of thumb that police officers should read the rights of the accused to suspects (see also Chapter 7).

Once convicted, however, criminals now confront particularly harsh penalties. Though still devoted to punishing past crime, the criminal justice system became increasingly concerned with preventing future crime through mass incarceration during the 1980s and 1990s. Habitual offender statutes, like "three strikes and you're out" laws, sentenced repeat offenders to life imprisonment after their third felony conviction. "Truth in sentencing" laws effectively abolished prison parole. "Mandatory minimums" reduced federal judges' discretion when sentencing felons. Jurisdictional reforms lowered the age at which juveniles could be tried as adults, increasing the available terms of imprisonment beyond those of juvenile court. Gang membership and recruitment became criminalized. "Megan's Law" statutes required community notification of convicted sex offenders, whilst "sexual predator" statutes provided for civil detention of offenders who remained dangerous at the conclusion of their criminal term. Sentencing guidelines also increased the sentence of offenders with a prior criminal history, these being statistically the most likely to re-offend.

In order to enforce such penalties and combat crime, a massive federal enforcement complex has developed. In the aggregate, the federal regime is made up of a bewildering array of agencies – 148 in total –but primary responsibility for law enforcement is fragmented among 14 (see Table 1). Excluding prosecutors, approximately 80 percent of federal law enforcement personnel are involved in three functional areas: criminal investigation and enforcement (43 percent), maintaining prisons and other correctional facilities (21 percent) and police response and patrol (16 percent). In total, $26 billion is spent annually on law enforcement priorities by the federal government, in addition to that of states and localities.

Table 11.1 *The 14 primary law enforcement agencies (financial year 1998)**

Department and Agency	Personnel	Budget** (in millions)
Department of Justice		
Federal Bureau of Investigation	11,710	$1,911.0
Drug Enforcement Administration	4,246	674.0
Immigration and Naturalization Service	17,573	29.0
United States Marshals Service	2,924	43.4
Federal Bureau of Prisons***	28,390	70.9
Department of the Treasury		
Bureau of Alcohol, Tobacco, and Firearms	1,775	317.2
Internal Revenue Service	3,292	415.9
United States Customs Service	11,910	2,591.0
United States Secret Service	3,613	500.0
Department of Agriculture		
United States Forest Service	614	48.9
Department of the Interior		
Bureau of Indian Affairs	307	78.5
Bureau of Land Management	196	14.7
National Park Service/Rangers	1,596	58.6
National Park Service/U.S. Park Police	601	60.0
Total	88,747	$6,813.1

* Federal personnel authorized to carry firearms, execute search warrants, and make arrests.

** Dollar amounts refer to personnel costs for those authorized to carry firearms.

*** The Federal Bureau of Prisons personnel figure represents present employees who meet annual firearms qualification requirements and are currently certified.

Source: Commission on the Advancement of Federal Law Enforcement Survey, 1999.

Enthusiasm for the increasingly punitive measures these agencies police is powerfully reinforced by the mechanisms of popular accountability in American government that encourage populist appeals on crime and punishment. Not only state and federal legislators but also many law enforcement officers – including district attorneys and many state and local judges – are elected officials. Consequently, from presidential candidates to district attorneys, most candidates for public office are loath to challenge the strongly traditionalist views of most American voters on crime.

Majoritarian preferences have therefore strongly influenced the criminal justice system to prioritize punishment over prevention, treatment and rehabilitation.

The politicization of crime

Crime first emerged as a partisan issue in 1964 but it was Richard Nixon in 1968 who popularized the term "law and order." The mid-1960s to the mid-1970s combined steep crime increases with a doubling of the homicide rate, political assassinations, major urban riots, drug use and extremist political violence. Politically, the most influential explanations imputed rising crime and urban disorder to a growing (and disproportionately black) "underclass." "Law and order" rapidly became a shorthand signal to millions of white voters about broader questions of social disorder, authority, morality, responsibility and race. One result was that criminal defendants who, in the years preceding the civil rights revolution of the 1960s, had been subject to arbitrary authority and random cruelty completely lost their public status as victims by the 1980s. Public concern shifted from victims of egregious law enforcement to victims of criminal violence. Another result was that the politics of crime and race became inextricably linked.

At no point was this more vivid than 1988. Exploiting the notorious Willie Horton campaign advertisement (featuring the face of a convicted black rapist who had been temporarily released from prison in Massachusetts and then raped a white woman and murdered her husband), the elder George Bush declared that, "on no other issue is my opponent's philosophy so completely at odds with mine, and . . . the common sense attitudes of the American people, than on the issue of crime." Accusing the Democratic Party candidate and Massachusetts governor Michael Dukakis of having left the "clear-cut path of common sense" and become "lost in the thickets of liberal sociology," the salience of the crime issue helped Bush to reverse his opponent's lead in the election and capture the White House (Edsall and Edsall, 1991).

Despite the association of law and order appeals with Republicans, however, it was the Democrats who enacted the Safe Streets and Crime Control Act of 1967 and the Crime Control Act of 1968, which together made millions of federal dollars available to law enforcement agencies to strengthen their forces and modernize their equipment. In 1992, Bill Clinton's embrace of a strongly punitive stance on crime – supporting capital punishment, refusing as governor of Arkansas to grant clemency to Ricky Ray Rector (a mentally retarded black death row inmate), and pledging to put 100,000 police on the streets – returned the Democrats to the Johnson era and in office extended the nationalization of law enforcement and the incarceration of even non-violent lawbreakers.

Federalizing Crime

When the Republic was founded, fewer than a dozen crimes were federal offences. Currently, over 3,000 exist. More than 40 percent of federal crimes have been designated so since 1970. These range from the heinous (terrorism) to the absurd (disrupting rodeos). Even in the 12 states that have abolished capital punishment, federal prosecutors can now seek capital sentences for certain crimes as a result of legislation enacted in 1994 and 1996. So extensive is the present body of federal criminal law that no conveniently accessible list of all federal crimes exists, but pressure to continue the federalizing efforts – to include crimes of violence against women, pregnant women and fetuses ("unborn victims of violence") and to extend "hate crime" laws – remains intense. (The current federal hate crime law was passed in 1968. It allows federal prosecution of crimes that are based on the victim's race, color, religion, or national origin. But the federal government can get involved only if the act occurs while the victim is on federal property or engaged in one of six federally protected activities, such as voting.)

The increasing federalization of crimes traditionally left to states and localities has reflected and reinforced the "punitive paradigm" on crime and punishment. This process nonetheless exacerbates long-standing problems of strategy and coordination among federal law enforcement forces. The report of an independent federal commission on improving law enforcement in 2000 concluded that profound coordination dilemmas confront law enforcement agencies. It is frequently unclear which organization has responsibility for handling specific types of crime, a problem compounded by the federalizing tendencies that spread federal resources too thinly whilst threatening the establishment of the type of national police force that America has always avoided. With new criminal and security threats from terrorists (international and domestic), the globalization of crime in narcotics, prostitution and money-laundering, and advanced computer technologies that assist cyber-crime, such problems have become especially pronounced security concerns for policy-makers.

"Fortress America"

No liberal democracy embraces mass incarceration with the fervor of the "land of liberty." Approximately one in 142 Americans is currently in prison, an increase from one in 218 at the beginning of the 1990s. America imprisoned its two millionth lawbreaker in 2000. With approximately 5 percent of the global population, America possesses 25 percent of the global prison population, the highest incarceration rate in the world, at a cost to the taxpayer of $40 billion each year (approximately $20,000 per prisoner). America's rate of 690 prisoners per 100,000 people is over five times that of the UK. The figures represent a six-fold increase over the number of prisoners in 1970, when American crime rates were consider-ably lower (Downes, 2001).

Prisons represent the pre-eminent symbolic guarantor that law and order will be enforced. If crime falls, prisons gain the credit, but if crime rises the case is made that existing provision is insufficient. Only one-quarter of admissions to American prisons, however, are for violent crime. Moreover, the notion that building more prisons is the best way to reduce crime lacks reliable empirical support. Since 1992, the states locking up the most people have not been the ones where crime has dropped most dramati-cally. In Texas, for example, the crime rate dropped 35 percent from 1991 to 1998, while the imprisonment rate increased by 144 percent. But far smaller increases in imprisonment rates in states such as California (52 percent) and New York (24 percent) accompanied even larger reductions in crime (36 percent and 43 percent, respectively). Overall, the 30 states with the smallest increases in incarceration rates (averaging 30 percent) had larger crime reductions (17 percent) than the 20 others where incar-ceration rates increased an average of 72 percent and crime fell by only an average of 13 percent. Although such statistics are at best crude indicators of policy effectiveness, they suggest only a tenuous connection between mass imprisonment and domestic security.

Even with this decline, the violent crime rate remains more than three times higher than during the decade following World War II. The aggra-vated assault rate is nearly four times higher. Although media reports cele-brated the drop in crime to the levels of the late 1970s, they typically failed to note that these rates tripled those of the 1950s. The crime rate has also begun to increase again in some larger cities, such as Los Angeles. Beyond this, dead-bolted doors, security-staffed apartments and "gated" commu-nities condition a pattern of fortified American life wholly unlike that of prior eras.

The 2000 elections

Although most Americans appeared insouciant about their prison complex, law and order was widely anticipated to figure prominently in the 2000 elections. Governor George W. Bush had established a national profile as zealously pro-capital punishment and anti-gun control. Under him, Texas achieved a record for the number of executions carried out by an individual state in a single calendar year (40, out of a nationwide total of 85, in 2000). Several state-level moratoriums on executions were instituted in 2000, whilst public concern over lax firearms regulation was expressed in the largest-ever mass protest for gun control, the "Million Mom March" in Washington, DC of May 16 2000. But despite references to these issues during the three presidential debates, crime and punishment proved "dogs that didn't bark" in the elections.

Crime's marginal status was the result of four factors. First, the Clinton administration had achieved a broad policy consensus – "punishment, prevention, and policing" – that offered attractive features to Americans across the political spectrum, with harsher penalties and an expansion of capital crimes linked to additional investment in programs to prevent crime and increased efforts to combat violence against women. Strategically, by mobilizing supportive organized interests in state and local institutions – law enforcement officials, clergy, judges, anti-drug and community-based groups, and police associations – the administration forged a broad coalition that proved difficult to challenge concertedly from either the left or right.

Second, the sharp reductions in official crime figures decreased the electoral salience of "law and order." This is not to suggest that American insecurities about public order had disappeared or that criminologists agreed on the key causes of the reduction. Nonetheless, the decline confirmed to many Americans the effectiveness of existing approaches and heightened the electoral risks for candidates of challenging established policies.

Third, neither George W. Bush nor Al Gore sought directly to exploit law and order issues for fear of alienating key swing voters with more moderate positions than their own. Not since Ronald Reagan had the Republican presidential nominee proven so stridently traditionalist on guns and capital punishment. But in an especially close election, Bush's priority was to downplay these issues or risk appearing a callous rather than a compassionate conservative. Gore, by contrast, could not afford to exploit these issues without forfeiting the support of culturally conservative and marginal voters in key Electoral College states where support for gun ownership and capital punishment remains robust (some claimed that, even with such an approach, Gore's gun control position cost him crucial support in traditionally Democratic states such as West Virginia).

Fourth, despite policy disagreements on firearms, Bush and Gore shared more in common on criminal justice issues than any two main party candidates since 1960. Admittedly, some differences existed. For example, Gore called for mandatory drug testing in state and local prisons and expanding drug treatment programmes within the institutions, spending $500 million in annual federal grants to match state expenditures. Gore also backed passage of the Hate Crimes Prevention Act that would expand the definition of "hate crimes" and permit federal prosecution. Bush, by contrast, argued that all violent crime could be defined as a form of hate crime and that existing laws should be equally applied across the board. More significantly, though, both Gore and Bush supported more police on the street and neither opposed capital punishment or the "war on drugs." Both also supported a Victim Rights Amendment to the US Constitution that would give crime victims the right to testify at sentencing hearings and be notified when a prisoner's release is imminent.

Gun control

America possesses the world's most heavily and legally armed civilian population. Most estimates place the number of privately owned firearms at approximately 250 million. Although most Americans do not own guns, one in six owns a handgun. By 2000, most states had enacted laws to allow licensed citizens to carry firearms concealed, hidden either on the person or in a vehicle. (In "shall issue" states, applicants automatically receive a license unless the state can provide compelling reason why they should not; in "may issue" states, the onus is on applicants to explain their reasons for wanting a license.) Not only do many Americans discern no conflict between private legal gun ownership and public order, but millions view the former as the means to preserve the latter. With firearms representing "freedom's insurance policy," proposals to regulate them invariably stoke intense political opposition.

Gun politics has featured two constants since 1968: crisis moments when, in the aftermath of notable gun violence incidents, demands are voiced for new federal controls; and the dominance of gun rights groups such as the NRA (Spitzer, 1995; Bruce and Wilcox, 1998; Dizard, Muth and Andrews, 1999). The regulatory regime on firearms comprises relatively few federal controls. Most of the 20,000 laws regulating the manufacture, distribution and sale of guns exist at state and local level, but these tend to be weak in character. Moreover, despite passage of the Brady Bill in 1993 and a temporary ban on 19 assault weapons in 1994, Republican control of Congress from 1995 to 2001 frustrated further federal legislation. Gun rights groups" donations increasingly rewarded Republicans over Democrats, a function of their incumbency advantage in Congress, majority status and conservative ideology (Singh, 1999). At state level, the popularity of concealed carry laws reinforced the *de facto* privatization of

American security to the citizen and the apparent logic of "more guns, less crime" (Lott, 1998).

The years after 1998 nonetheless opened a "window of opportunity" for gun control advocates. Successive gun atrocities, many involving children as both victims and perpetrators, heightened public attention. In particular, the massacre at Columbine High School in Littleton, Colorado, on April 20 1999 (where two teenagers killed 14 students and a teacher), appeared a turning point, energizing a new activism by gun control forces.

That window of opportunity, however, was rapidly and decisively closed. Gun control activism – alongside litigation threats by trial lawyers and federal and local authorities against gun manufacturers – prompted a powerful response from Republican elected officials and gun rights groups. In 1999–2000, the 106th Congress declined to act on proposals to impose a three-day waiting period so that police could run background checks on would-be buyers at otherwise unregulated gun shows. Bills to ban the importation of large-capacity ammunition clips and to require child-proof trigger locks also failed. By the summer of 2001, Florida became the twenty-sixth state in two years to enact legislation protecting gun manufacturers from lawsuits, one month after a unanimous New York Court of Appeals had ruled that victims of gun violence could not sue gun manufacturers. In the twelve months following Columbine, the NRA's membership increased from 2.7 to 3.4 million, and was estimated to have passed the 4 million mark for the first time in 2000 when Charlton Heston was re-elected to its presidency for an unprecedented third time. With Bush's victory, Moses appeared to have led his followers to the promised land of a Republican administration and Congress that guaranteed no new federal gun regulations. A survey of Washington political operatives for *Fortune* in May 2001 magazine saw the NRA displace the American Association of Retired Persons as the most influential lobbying force on Capitol Hill (Sarasohn, 2001).

Unlike most criminal justice issues, the electoral politics of guns offered a clear contrast between the leading presidential candidates in 2000. Bush had signed concealed carry legislation in Texas in 1995 and in 1997 approved an amendment extending this to places of worship. He opposed mandatory gun registration but supported stronger enforcement of existing gun laws, increasing the age for handgun possession from 18 to 21, and requiring instant background checks at gun shows. Bush also stated that he supported voluntary efforts to equip handguns with child safety trigger locks and would sign mandatory trigger-lock legislation if passed by Congress (an unlikely occurrence).

Gore's position, by contrast, consolidated the Democratic Party's emergence since 1993 as the party of gun control. Although the Vice-President echoed Bush in advocating increased penalties for gun-related crimes and raising the age for handgun possession, he supported expanded background checks and banning "Saturday Night Special" handguns. Gore opposed loosening existing limits on concealed weapons and endorsed child safety locks, photo licensing for handgun purchases and background checks for all firearms sold at gun shows. But the need to win key Electoral College states in which gun use is high – especially Michigan, Ohio and Pennsylvania – strongly tempered Gore's embrace of gun control as a campaign priority.

Although Bush's pro-gun stance may have cost him some suburban votes in the presidential election, 48 per cent of voters were gun owners in 2000, an increase from 37 percent in 1996. However, the year 2000 also saw gun control groups achieve several victories in Senate races and ballot initiatives. The defeat of Senator John Ashcroft (R-Mo.) was as much a success as his subsequent appointment as Attorney General was dismaying to pro-control forces. "Americans for Gun Safety" spent approximately $2.8 million in Colorado and Oregon on ballot initiatives that required background checks to be administered on prospective buyers at gun shows, overcoming intense NRA opposition to the measures.

That gun control should remain weak as gun massacres became increasingly routine perplexed and angered many Americans. Deaths from gun violence in the 1990s exceeded 30,000 annually, with suicides the largest category. The message of Bush and other conservatives – that gun violence was more a result of the absence of the Ten Commandments in schools than the legal presence of guns in almost half of all American households – was derided by gun control advocates. But the conflict over firearms remains complex as well as emotive for several reasons. Guns involve core features of American political culture: liberty, constitutionality, federalism, rights and responsibility. Compounding these are the contested empirical data on the criminological effects of widespread gun ownership. Stark as the absolute figures of gun violence are, the overwhelming majority (more than 98 percent) of the many millions of Americans who own guns use them responsibly: they do not cause crimes, murder, commit suicide or have accidents with them. Moreover, although official figures exist for gun violence victims, no reliable figures are available for the numbers deterred by the use, or threatened use, of guns. Gun rights groups therefore have a powerful case that there is nothing inherently problematic about widespread legal access to firearms.

Much of the intensity of the political conflict therefore arises from the sharply divided lenses through which firearms regulation is viewed. For gun rights groups, firearms represent a fundamental part of American culture, securing individual freedom and property rights; ownership is protected as an individual citizenship right by the Second Amendment – a position supported "unequivocally" in 2001 by Attorney General Ashcroft (charged with enforcing America's gun laws) despite court rulings to the contrary over the prior half-century. Owners of assault rifles, semi-automatics and other firearms are not fringe elements on society's margins but participants in a long-running constitutional argument over the meaning and nature of individual liberty. But for advocates of stronger controls, as Daniel Lazare puts it, America is now "a congested, polluted society filled with traffic jams, shopping malls and anomic suburbs in which an eighteenth-century right to bear arms is as out of place as silk knee-britches and tri-cornered hats" (Nelson, 2001). On this approach, the gun rights case represents a fatally flawed amalgam of mistaken history (Bellesiles, 2000), erroneous constitutional interpretation (Henigan, Nicholson and Hemenway, 1996), and blind ignorance of the public health consequences of legalized access to firearms and the ease with which gun producers evade new laws (Diaz, 1999).

Whether the current regulatory regime induces insecurity or promotes order, citizen access to firearms remains a mainstay of American political culture. Fear of government as well as criminals (and now terrorists) fuels such a passion for firearms that many Americans find it incredible that progressives who condemn police brutality and racism nonetheless seek to concentrate more coercive power in the hands of the state rather than the citizen. Belief in the Second Amendment remains a potent force among public opinion but gun control (unlike capital punishment and drugs) remains an issue where most Americans – who consistently support stronger federal controls – are denied their preferences in public policy by a politically vociferous and skilful minority. Indeed, such is the gun rights lobby's success that when, in May 2001, President Bush declared "Project Safe Neighborhoods," calling for 113 new assistant US attorneys and 600 new state and local prosecutors to assist in the enforcement of existing firearms laws, many gun control advocates reluctantly embraced this position as the best for which they could hope.

Capital punishment

Bush's election heightened international attention to America's capital punishment regime. In his six years as governor (1995–2001), 152 convicted murderers were executed in Texas. In a notorious interview with *Talk* magazine in 1999, Bush parodied the pleas of a female death row inmate to spare her life. The governor's insistence on the complete reliability of his state's justice system appeared either naive or disingenuous, exhibiting a conservatism that played well in the Lone Star state but generated profound concern elsewhere in America.

The only industrialized nation other than Japan to allow and implement judicial killings, capital punishment is currently legal in 38 American states and for the federal government. Executions in 2000 declined by 13 percent from the previous year but remained high at 85. Almost 90 percent of these occurred in the South. Of the 38 death penalty states, 24 carried out no executions and only three outside the South (Arizona, California and Missouri) conducted any. Texas, with 40, accounted for almost as many executions as the rest of the 49 states combined.

Like gun control, a shift in public policy was suggested by new developments in capital punishment politics. The year 2000 was the most significant single year affecting death penalty opinion in America since 1972 (when the Supreme Court declared capital punishment unconstitutional in *Furman* v. *Georgia* only to reverse itself four years later). High-profile releases of innocent prisoners from death row, news reports on flaws in the administrative process, and adverse election-year attention to Texas exerted strong pressure on public authorities to re-examine the death penalty. From the declaration in January 2000 of a moratorium on all executions in Illinois by George Ryan, a pro-death penalty Republican governor, to the Clinton administration's postponing the first federal execution in almost 40 years in September 2000, doubts about the process grew considerably. In 2000, the New Hampshire legislature passed a bill abolishing capital punishment that was vetoed by its Democratic Governor.

The US Constitution allows but does not require capital punishment. The Fifth and Fourteenth Amendments expressly permit "deprivation of life" providing this occurs according to "due process" of law. Although the Eighth Amendment prohibits "cruel and unusual punishments," this was intended to prohibit barbaric punishments rather than the death penalty as such; to restrict the methods of implementation rather than outlaw the principle. Two key constitutional problems therefore shape capital punishment politics. First, does the Eighth Amendment take its meaning from prevailing public sentiment (as the Supreme Court declared in *Trop* v. *Dulles*, 1958) – in which case it merely restates majority opinion rather than protects vulnerable minorities – or is there some independent, timeless content to it? Second, does the existing administration of capital punishment meet the requirements of due process, equal protection and the Sixth Amendment's guarantee of adequate legal counsel?

If the constitutionality question rests on public support, this is currently less robust than previously. An American Broadcasting Corporation (ABC) poll in January 2000, for example, found that 64 percent of Americans supported the penalty, a decline from 77 percent in 1996. Former death penalty supporters have also joined long-time critics in raising concerns about the capital punishment system being "broken," including staunch conservatives such as Pat Robertson, Oliver North and

George Will. But most Americans still support capital punishment, despite such concerns.

A more plausible constitutional case lies in the denial of due process, equal protection, and adequate counsel, where arguments against the fair and equitable operation of the system are powerful: a nonexistent deterrent effect, arbitrary sentencing, racial and class bias, and wrongful executions (Bedau, 1997; Sarat, 2001a). The revelations in May 2001 that the FBI had not brought important evidence to the trial of the Oklahoma bomber, Timothy McVeigh, suggested that if even such a high-profile case could reveal major procedural errors, the likelihood of this occurring lower down the system is high.

The racial bias in the system also provokes particular disquiet. Of the 98 inmates (all men) executed in 1999, 61 were white, 33 were black, 2 were Native Americans and 2 were Asians. Despite the fact that nationally whites and blacks are murder victims in approximately equal numbers, 83 percent of the victims in cases resulting in executions in 1999 (and 76 percent in 2000) were white. A study by the Department of Justice of the federal death penalty, released in September 2000, found that 80 percent of the cases submitted for federal death penalty prosecution also involved minority defendants and that 80 percent of the federal death row comprised minority inmates. Despite the Supreme Court ruling that jurors in capital cases could only be removed for "race neutral" reasons (*Batson* v. *Kentucky*, 1986), both prosecuting and defending legal teams deliberately seek to influence the racial composition of capital juries with views to their likely verdicts (McFeely, 2000). The composition of the key actors in the process also displays an overwhelming white dominance: of 1,838 criminal justice officials responsible for deciding whether to seek a capital sentence (in 1998) across the 38 death penalty states, only 22 were black and 22 Latino.

Although capital punishment is a peripheral part of the criminal justice system, its political symbolism exerts a powerful force as a proxy for crime and punishment more broadly. A profoundly religious people, most Americans concur in the views of many theocratic regimes that some crimes exist for which a life sentence is an insufficient punishment. Not only did most states restore the penalty after 1976, but the judicial system echoed the elected branches' approach in becoming increasingly punitive from 1987. Key court decisions rejected the argument that a racially biased system was unconstitutional (*McCleskey* v. *Kemp*, 1987) while upholding the constitutionality of juvenile executions (*Stanford* v. *Kennedy*, 1989) and victim impact statements at trial (*Payne* v. *Tennessee*, 1991). Concern for victims' rights has become so pronounced that 34 of the 40 Texas executions in 2000, had the victims' families present. Four defendants who were under 18 at the time of their crime were executed in 2000 and 25 of the 38 death penalty states allowed the execution of mentally-retarded prisoners.

The European Union, the Pope, the United Nations, Amnesty International and other human rights organizations made strong objections to many of these executions. America was sued successfully in the International Court of Justice by Germany for executing two of its citizens in Arizona who were not informed of their rights under the Vienna Convention. But international pressure is unlikely to achieve change whilst domestic American opinion remains supportive.

Despite recent concerns, the number of crimes eligible for death has increased whilst the opportunity for appeals has diminished. The 1994 crime bill created 60 additional federal crimes subject to capital punishment (including certain drug offences). The 1996 Anti-Terrorism and Effective Death Penalty Act – a response, in part, to the Oklahoma City bombing of 1995 – sharply restricted death row appeals by extending recent Supreme Court decisions limiting access to the judiciary. Death row inmates are now allowed only one appeal in a federal court within six months of their initial sentencing. In addition, states that allowed but did not practice capital punishment have resumed judicial killings. In 1999, Ohio had its first execution since the Supreme Court reinstated the death penalty in *Gregg* v. *Georgia* (1976). Tennessee carried out its first in 2000.

America enjoys a settled jurisprudence on capital punishment, federal courts that demonstrate reinvigorated respect for "states' rights" and local, state and federal elected officials for whom supporting the death penalty appears a prerequisite of re-election. Admittedly, "only" 49 executions occurred in the first nine months of 2001, a reflection of heightened public concerns, increased judicial scrutiny and the "backlog" executed over 1999–2000. During the 106th Congress, Senator Patrick Leahy (D-Vt) also called for the passage of the "Innocence Protection Act" to ensure access to DNA testing and better legal representation for defendants facing the death penalty. But widespread political support for such reforms is better viewed as seeking the reinforcement rather than the dismantling of America's capital punishment system.

Drugs

As Downes (2001) notes, "It is a peculiar irony of American exceptionalist mythologizing that the right to bear arms, which harbour the potential for instant lethal violence, is regarded as sacrosanct, whilst the right to bear drugs, whose potential is rarely so, is regarded as taboo." Many Americans who view a ban on firearms as unenforceable do not extend that logic to drugs – despite the precedent of Prohibition – where the punitive paradigm on crime has been especially emphatic and ineffective. Senator John McCain (R-Ariz.) epitomized the federal government's approach when he said of Senate efforts to increase the military's role in combating drugs supply that, "This is such an emotional issue – I mean, we're at war here – that voting no would be too difficult to explain" (Bertram, Blachman, Sharpe and Andreas, 1996).

The war has been one of America's longest and least successful, failing to stem the supply of drugs whilst perpetuating organized crime and contributing substantially to the nation's prison population. For example, the massive expansion in women prisoners (from 39,000 in 1985 to almost 150,000 in 2001), three-quarters of whom are imprisoned for nonviolent offences, is largely due to punitive drugs laws. Internationally, America has become increasingly involved in Colombia's civil war whilst, in April 2001, US forces shot down a "drugs" plane in Peru that turned out to have been carrying missionaries. The effects on drug supply and consumption, however, have been minimal. Drugs have never been easier for Americans to obtain, with prices lower, purity higher and experimentation among schoolchildren more pronounced than ever.

Successive administrations have acknowledged that the root of the drugs crisis is domestic demand but the focus of policy has been to stem the supply of a commodity that millions of Americans crave. Illegal drug sales have held steady even while the imprisonment of drug offenders has soared to 75 percent of all those entering federal, and 35 percent of those entering state, prisons and jails. Roughly half of America's two million prisoners are serving time for small-time drug deals and other non-violent crimes. The Drug Enforcement Agency's record of drug seizures (at about 10 percent of total supply) is comparable to the Prohibition Bureau, which at no time seized more than 5 per cent of the quantities of liquor entering America from 1919 to 1933.

The racial aspects of the drugs war have also reinforced the disparate social impact of America's criminal justice system. With powder cocaine a drug popular among professional whites, while "crack" is almost exclusively the drug of black ghetto youths, it is the latter who suffer disproportionately since the penalties for crack are far higher than for powder cocaine. While a disparate racial impact exists, it is unclear that there is a discriminatory intent behind the policy. The same sentencing standards apply to people of all races convicted of dealing in cocaine. However, some critics question whether Congress – still an overwhelmingly white institution – would have passed such a law if its effect was to treat whites more severely than blacks.

Even if no clear intent exists, the results are powerfully negative for minorities. Only 11 percent of drug users are black, but blacks constitute almost 37 percent of those arrested for drug violations, over 42 percent of those in federal prisons for drug violations, and almost 60 percent of those in state prisons for drug felonies. At current incarceration levels, black men have more than a 1 in 4 chance of going to prison during their life-times, while Latino males have a 1 in 6 and white men have a 1 in 23 chance. Around 54 percent of blacks convicted of drug offences are sentenced to prison, against 34 percent of whites convicted of the same offences. The impact extends beyond criminal justice into the political arena: 1.46 million black men of a total black male voting population of 10.4 million have lost their right to vote due to felony convictions (Wright and Lewin, 1998). According to The Sentencing Project, a Washington-based organization that researches criminal justice issues, a total of 4.2 million Americans were not allowed to vote in the 2000 elections because they were in prison or had prior felony convictions. Of those, more than one-third (1.8 million) were black, amounting to fully 13 percent of African-American men.

As a result of its inability to stem drug supply and consumption, the racial inequities that plague its administration, and its contribution to America's prison population, critics of established drugs policy now exist across the political spectrum. Among conservatives, Milton Friedman, William Buckley and George Schultz have deemed the existing approach futile and have endorsed partial decriminalization of drugs. Bush's victory raised the prospect that a pragmatic conservative president might expend political capital – in a fashion that a Democrat would find difficult – to confront the failed drugs policies of his six predecessors since Nixon first made drugs a national political issue. But this receded sharply with the appointment of John Walters – a prominent proponent of the war in the 1989–93 Bush administration – as the new "drugs czar" in the spring of 2001. In maintaining a repressive regime predicated on a King Canute-like refusal to accept the inevitability of American demand for, and foreign supply of, drugs, the Bush administration remained "singularly indifferent to the lessons of the past" (Behr, 1998).

The racialization of crime

With blacks and Latinos disproportionately represented among the disadvantaged sections of society, their disproportionate presence among both the perpetrators and victims of crime – as well as in prison and on death row – is disturbing but unsurprising. For many whites, this reinforces an association of minorities with crime whilst, to many nonwhites, the figures suggest instead that American justice is anything but color-blind.

Recent events have done little to disturb these distinct racial prisms. In February 2000, for example, a jury acquitted four white New York City policemen of murdering a young unarmed African immigrant, Amadou Diallo, after they had fired 41 bullets as he stood in the vestibule of his Bronx apartment building. None of six alternative charges brought by the prosecution (including manslaughter, homicide and reckless endangerment) stuck. In 2001, the FBI joined an investigation in Los Angeles into allegations that anti-gang police officers acted like gangsters themselves (lying, stealing and shooting without cause). The shooting of an unarmed black man by a white police officer in Cincinnati, Ohio, in April 2001 prompted two days of race riots and city curfews. For most Americans, criminal justice and race remain inextricably interwoven. The latest addition of Arab-Americans – despite their mostly Christian faith and many professional occupations – to this macabre mosaic was one important consequence of 2001's terrorist atrocities.

Homeland security

America has struggled with terrorism of one kind or another for decades but only rarely on its own shores. Domestic terrorism has come full circle since the 1960s, with anti-government violence once dominated by radical leftists (such as the Weathermen) now more the province of far right activists (such as McVeigh). At the international level, terrorist attacks on American targets during the 1990s became simultaneously less frequent but more lethal. The car bomb at the World Trade Center in 1993, the Oklahoma bombing and the sarin gas attack in Tokyo of 1995 heightened domestic security concerns, especially in regard to nuclear, chemical and biological weapons of mass destruction. Movies such as *Arlington Road* (where the FBI headquarters in Washington, DC, is blown up in an extremist right-wing plot) and books such as Richard Preston's *The Cobra Event* (featuring a biological attack on New York) reflected such concerns.

The attacks of September 11 2001, however, crossed a threshold. Not only did they occur on American soil with no warning, against major landmarks, and with thousands of innocent lives lost, but the weapons employed were practical and symbolic mainstays of American life: conventional commercial aircraft turned into unconventional missiles. Moreover, some of the suicide hijackers had even gained flight training in America.

Government responses combined an emphasis on stringent efforts to identify and bring to justice the perpetrators and their associates with commitments to preserve civil liberties. But whatever the length, nature and results of the war against terrorism declared by President Bush, domestic affairs were to be profoundly tested by the administration's new priority. Attorney General Ashcroft declared terrorism to be a "clear and present danger." Unlike traditional wars between states, however, four aspects made this threat a particularly demanding challenge and entailed changes in American life whose scope and duration cannot easily be anticipated.

First, only the most draconian and "un-American" measures could prevent a terrorist threat to the continental United States from recurring. The terrorist attack was long in preparation, its supporting network was elusive and hydra-headed, and it exploited the openness – and hence vulnerability – of American society. The increasing sophistication of terrorists in terms of technology, operations and financing poses severe challenges to federal, state and local law enforcement agencies. American intelligence had anticipated and prepared for attacks using chemical and biological weapons, but not aircraft. Faced with a combination of "low-tech" methods and high-tech means of organization – mobile phones, the Internet, voice mail – authorities confronted an entirely new type of "enemy within" as well as outside America.

In sending to Congress proposals to strengthen the Immigration and Naturalization Service, establish penalties to punish those harboring terrorists, and increase federal surveillance and intelligence capacities, the Department of Justice pursued an active and broad agenda. The president's proposal to establish an Office of Homeland Security within the White House also represented explicit recognition of the necessity of bureaucratic rationalization of over 40 agencies with roles in national security. (As a result of jurisdictional divisions and turf disputes between the Department of State, law enforcement and intelligence-gathering agencies, for example, some of the terrorists had gained entry visas to America despite being on FBI suspect lists.) Whether, how, and how rapidly this would address the endemic fragmentation and traditional competition between key law enforcement and intelligence agencies, however, remained unclear.

Second, the new legislative measures generated deep disquiet among some Americans fearful of the erosion of traditional civil liberties and rights. With extensive and complex statute laws and judicial rulings regulating questions of privacy rights, searches and seizures of private property, and rights to fair trial, the very foundations of America's constitutional democracy posed obstacles to attempts to enhance the domestic security state. According to an ABC News–*Washington Post* poll of September 29 2001, however, large majorities of Americans (racing from 69 to 95 percent) supported additional police powers to combat terrorists with wiretapping, voice mail and e-mail surveillance, the admission of foreign intelligence evidence that would normally be illegal in US courts, the sharing of grand jury information with intelligence services, and allowing the government to detain indefinitely foreigners suspected of terrorist links. Reflecting the fears of the libertarian right (as well as some on the American left), David Boaz of the Cato Institute observed: "We've always known that if you put the Bill of Rights up for a popular vote, it would probably lose" (Milbank and Morin, 2001).

Whether the new measures would secure both congressional approval and constitutional muster remained uncertain; but the judiciary has tended to defer to the elected branches in times of national security threats, and the Rehnquist Court is only rarely accused of insufficient conservatism.

Third, the terrorist strikes demonstrated the globalized networks that support such action. An effective national response necessitated international coordination, not merely military and diplomatic but also through intelligence, law enforcement and financial measures to erode the capacity of terrorists to operate in America. As successive commissions reiterated, however, the capacity of an inherently fragmented state to meet such challenges was questionable, even if the political will to do so was unequivocal.

Fourth, the combination of these factors raised a more profound concern about the future of America's political culture. American history has been punctuated by periods of profound illiberalism, especially (though not exclusively) during periods of crisis and war. From "red scares" after World War I through the internment of Japanese-Americans in World War II to attacks on "subversives" during McCarthyism and the wiretapping of anti-war and civil rights activists during the 1960s, the Constitution's guarantees have faced constant challenge. Moreover, although officials from the president down warned against attacks on Arab-Americans and the FBI vowed prosecution of such hate crimes, many violent acts occurred against them (and other ethnic minorities) in the aftermath of September 11.

Few Americans objected to the prospect of new delays and checks at airports or tightened airline security. The extension of the federal government's reach into the most private areas of citizens' lives, however, represents a far more contentious proposition for a generation more disposed to view national government as a source of social problems rather than solutions. Ironically, the more that civil liberties are eroded, the more that extremist paranoia of an oppressive federal government among America's far right and left may be stoked still further. However, the ABC–*Post* poll revealed that, for the first time in three decades, most Americans said they trust the federal government to do the right thing "just about always" or "most of the time" which is double the percentage of April 2000 and more than three times the proportion of 1994. How far such a change, and the shifting priority accorded security and individual liberties it reflects, proves enduring rather than ephemeral will remain inextricably tied to the fate of the anti-terrorist campaign itself.

Conclusion

It is often said that America is a violent society. Certainly, criminal activity in pursuit of the material wealth that the American creed makes central to individual self-worth represents an important negative aspect of the "double-edged sword" of American exceptionalism (Lipset, 1996). Recent concerns about capital punishment and drugs have assisted a slight shift in mainstream opinion. Some states, such as California, have also seen successful direct democracy initiatives legalize marijuana for medical use and establish rehabilitation centers rather than prison for drug offenders. But the scope of such changes should not be exaggerated. Without a sea-change in public opinion, the prospects for rationality to trump emotion in public policy on crime and punishment remain slim. The unprecedented tragedy that befell America on September 11 2001 appears likely to reinforce strongly the ranks of an armed citizenry intent on punishing law-breakers and seeking new ways to wage effective punitive campaigns on those – from organized crime syndicates and drugs barons to terrorists at home and abroad – who threaten American lives, property and collective security. To "insure domestic tranquility" in an entirely new chapter in the "American experiment," the toleration of significant and long-lasting abridgements of the "blessings of liberty" may prove a price most Americans are reluctantly willing to pay.

Chapter 12

Social Policy

FIONA ROSS

When George W. Bush was finally declared the winner of the 2000 presidential election, liberals feared that his preference for helping the poor through faith-based and voluntary initiatives rather than government programs could have a devastating effect on poverty levels, especially in times of recession. The new President's "compassionate conservatism" signaled a policy agenda founded on the standard conservative principles of low taxes, reduced regulation and smaller government combined with a social agenda that favored self-reliance over government redistribution and support. According to Bush and like-minded conservatives, the Great Society strategy of "throwing money" at the poor had failed to relieve poverty or promote personal responsibility. On the contrary, it had encouraged a passivity and dependence among the poor, further isolating them from mainstream America. Wasteful government programs had also had the effect of undermining civil society more generally. Ineffective state paternalism, therefore, needed to be replaced with a new reliance on individuals, families, faith-based groups and local communities. In cases where state intervention was deemed to be absolutely necessary, the lower units of local government should be the first port of call.

Despite President Bush's commitment to compassionate conservatism, his scope for shaping the social agenda is likely to be limited by inheritances from the Clinton years and by future electoral considerations. His pledge to increase the rights of patients *vis-à-vis* their health care providers is a hold-over from the Clinton years. And, regardless of the President's preference for state over federal initiatives, his attempt to regulate the managed care industry is set to override more rigorous state laws. Likewise, George W. Bush has pledged his support for huge federal programs such as Medicare, and during the 2000 campaign he promised to provide new, expensive coverage under this program.

The new president has also inherited a loose consensus on the crisis-ridden nature of the American pension system, popularly known as Social Security. His Commission to Strengthen Social Security has been charged with devising a plan to meet his campaign pledge to add consumer choice and responsibility to the pension system via private investment accounts.

Though promising to secure the future of this massive federal program, however, the President's $1.3 trillion tax cut, combined with the worsening economy, seems likely to have the opposite effect. Despite vowing not to use off-budget Social Security revenues to meet budgetary shortfalls, most analysts expect President Bush to do so. With respect to income support policies for the poor, the mainstream of both the Republican and Democratic parties have accepted that the work of welfare reform was completed following radical overhaul in 1996.

This chapter seeks to provide a context for recent developments in social policy. First it provides an overview of the main federal social programs in the United States. Second, it examines key social policy developments during the Clinton years. The chapter pays special attention to the 1996 overhaul of the American welfare system and discusses the consequences of this radical reform, particularly the shift to a fully developed system of workfare and the imposition of benefit time-limits. Third, the chapter considers competing explanations for recent developments in social policy, examining the comparative importance of economic, demographic and political pressures in driving change. Finally, it concludes with a discussion of the issues most likely to dominate the social policy agenda over the next decade.

Welfare American style

The United States does not attempt to engineer equality of result among its citizens through extensive government programs, and it does not seek to ensure that all Americans enjoy a similar quality of life. The country had to suffer the collective desperation of the Great Depression before it introduced the national anti-poverty programs that many other affluent societies had long considered necessary and just. Though most of these initiatives incrementally expanded over the years, and the 1960s brought a fresh wave of social policy innovation, America has never been comfortable with the idea of a "welfare state." The federal government, often in conjunction with the states, provides numerous benefits and services that ease the lives of many Americans, ranging from low-budget nutritional programs for pregnant/nursing women to massive entitlements, such as the health and pension systems for the elderly. However, the wide disparities and omissions in programmatic coverage, particularly in the areas such as health care, maternity leave, and sick pay, remain startling to many European observers.

The very concept of government assistance poses a philosophical dilemma for a society that favors individual responsibility, equality of opportunity and risk-taking over the welfare state's attempt to create greater equality of result and contain the risks of the market place. While polling data indicates that Americans are willing to help the needy and most agree that structural forces contribute to individual hardship, they rarely accept that market imbalances, unemployment, or inadequate education constitute insurmountable barriers to self-sufficiency. Consequently, poverty derives in part from the behavior and choices of the individual. Cope (1997) makes note of this fact by pointing to the titles of state welfare reform initiatives, such as Colorado's "Personal Responsibility Project," Missouri's "Families Mutual Responsibility Plan" and Georgia's "Personal Accountability and Responsibility Project." Handler (2000) summarizes the American ethos well when he writes: 'Failure of the "able-bodied" to support oneself and family is considered a *moral* fault. Moral fault, in turn, is broader than failure to earn; it incorporates other forms of so-called deviant status and behavior. Hence, it becomes easier to blame the victim rather than address structural issues.'

The mantra of individual responsibility with respect to work and poverty has been articulated more explicitly since the Republican Party gained control over both Houses of Congress at the 1994 midterms. Following the electorate's rejection of liberal values (and Democratic incumbents) just two years into Clinton's first term, many pillars of the New Deal have come under threat. Major entitlements, programs that guarantee benefits to anyone who meets the eligibility criteria, have been retrenched and the economic, social and reproductive behaviors of the poor are increasingly subject to stringent monitoring, a system of regulation which Lawrence Mead (1996) refers to as "the new paternalism."

It would be misleading, of course, to imply that all social programs now confront a hostile political environment. There is significant variation in support for social benefits depending on whether they are insurance-based or income maintenance measures that bear no link to contributions. For the most part, it is the low-cost, high-stigma forms of income maintenance that have undergone restructuring. A cross-party consensus has emerged, encouraged by the scientific research of policy "experts," that government "hand-outs" foster dependency (King, 1999). As a result, these programs have found few powerful defenders in Washington. While noncontributory benefits have always been severely means-tested and targeted at the "deserving" poor, such as the disabled, elderly, children and their parents/guardians, eligibility criteria have become increasingly restrictive during the last decade. For individuals not falling within these selective categories, the only means of public support is general assistance, a highly conditional form of temporary (often emergency) help provided at the discretion of the state governments.

There is also some variation in support for income maintenance measures depending on whether they provide cash or noncash aid to the needy.

Reflecting America's unease with the choices and behavior of the poor, the most costly forms of public assistance are "in-kind" benefits, such as Medicaid (the federal-state health insurance program for the poor). Indeed, the only popular form of cash assistance is the Earned Income Tax Credit (EITC), which provides a tax rebate for the *working* poor. In the most radical shift in social policy during the Clinton administration the main federal cash welfare entitlement, AFDC, was terminated in 1996. Largely a Republican initiative, but embraced by Clinton just months before the election, the PRWORA ended six decades of the cash guarantee to poor mothers with children under 18 years of age. The $23 billion federal-state program was replaced by a block grant to the states, TANF. This was the first time such a large-scale entitlement had been reduced to a block grant. Not only did the legislation create a fully developed system of workfare, but it departed radically from previous initiatives by imposing severe time-limits upon the receipt of benefits. The transition from AFDC to TANF affected one in seven children, 5 million families and a total of 14.5 million Americans.

Table 12.1 summarizes the major social programs provided in part or whole by the federal government. It lists the number of recipients and the total (federal, state and local) expenditure each consumes.

Despite the pervasive misinformation regarding the cost and beneficiaries of public assistance for the poor, insurance-based benefits for the elderly are both hugely expensive and suffer from more severe internal programmatic imbalances. Indeed, several high-cost programs have proved to be remarkably resistant to restructuring. The retirement system, popularly known as social security, is the single largest item in the federal budget, followed by Medicare, the health insurance program for the aged, blind and disabled. Together these programs will devour over $680 billion in 2002 and show no signs of slowing ($452 billion will be spent on social security and $226 billion on Medicare). Both entitlements confront long-term instabilities deriving from a combination of demographic trends, social changes and medical developments. An aging population, combined with an expansion in early retirement and increased longevity into old age, place obvious stress upon the health and pension sectors. These programmatic tensions are set to become more pronounced once "baby boomers," the 76 million Americans born between 1946 and 1964, begin to retire from 2010 onwards.

The graying of America would be less important for social security were it not for the fact that the pension system operates on a "pay-as-you-go" basis, whereby current retirees are supported by the payroll taxes of current workers. At present, there are more than three workers for each retiree. By 2030, there will be just over two. At this point, 20 percent of the population will be seniors and the fund will only be able to pay bene-

Table 12.1   *Social benefits in the USA 1998*

	Recipients (1,000)	Total expenditures ($millions)
Insurance-based benefits		
Social Security		
Retirement	30, 284	258,885
Disabled	6,326	51,331
Survivors	6,820	75,309
Medicare	38,825	216,600
Income Maintenance		
Cash Aid		
"Welfare" TANF/AFDC	8,770	21,513
Supplementary Security income	7,199	33,601
Earned income tax credit*	58,197	25,3000
Non cash Benefits		
Food Stamps	21,000	22,384
Housing†	4,295	20,013
Job training	1,099	3,857
Medicaid	41,360	177,364

*   Refunded portion.
†   Low-income housing assistance and low-rent public housing.
Source: Derived from *Statistical Almanac* (2000) and the US Census Bureau, *Statistical Abstract of the United States* (Washington, DC: Department of Commerce, 2000).

fits at about 75 percent of their full rate. Much the same applies to Medicare, except this huge entitlement is experiencing faster growth rates owing to the soaring costs of health care that derive from new technologies and expensive prescription drugs. Despite these pressures, the widespread popularity of social security and Medicare, together with their large and zealous constituency and the organizational power of the American Association of Retired Persons (AARP), has continued to buffer both programs against austerity politics. Indicative of social security's political strength, President Clinton anointed the Social Security Administration with independent agency status in 1995.

The Clinton years

The first term: big promises, mixed results

Clinton entered the White House in January 1993 with an ambitious social agenda. By 1996, after four years in office, the first two working with a Democratic Congress, the last two with staunchly conservative GOP majorities in the House and a more moderate Republican majority in the Senate, the results were mixed. The centerpiece of the Clinton agenda was a system of universal health care. The spectacular collapse of this plan over-shadowed important achievements, such as the 1993 expansion of the EITC, the Family and Medical Leave Act (granting employees up to 12 weeks of unpaid leave for family and medical reasons), a rise in the minimum wage from $4.25 to $5.15 per hour and improved regulation of the managed care industry. This last assured new mothers of a minimum 48 hour postnatal hospital stay (the aptly named "drive through baby bill"), increased the flexibility of health insurance with the "portability" bill, and required mental health to be treated in the same way as physical health. The significance of these laws should not be under-rated when we consider that not one of the 50 managed care bills before Congress during the first session of the 105th Congress was enacted (Carey, 1997). While managed care firms have become notorious in America for controlling costs and maintaining profits by limiting treatments and, according to some reports, imposing gag-rules on doctors (whereby patients are not informed of expensive medicines and procedures that might benefit their health), Congress is generally loath to interfere with the private health insurance schemes that cover 161 million Americans.

These initiatives, of course, only benefited those who already enjoyed health insurance. Likewise, the expansion of the EITC only affected those who had jobs. By the time Clinton departed from the White House, 42.6 million Americans were without any form of health insurance. This figure represented an increase of more than 4 million in the ranks of the uninsured since the "health care" President assumed office in 1992. Moreover, a far cry from his liberal agenda for universal health coverage, the defining issue of Clinton's first (and second) term turned out to be the radical over-haul of the federal welfare system. Anxious to respond to the conservative mood of the country and in need of a major domestic achievement, Clinton embraced a largely Republican vision of welfare restructuring (albeit after two earlier presidential vetoes). During the course of the 1992 campaign for the White House Clinton had pledged to "end welfare as we know it." With his failed health reforms in danger of defining his presidency, Clinton needed a major domestic initiative to underpin his bid for a second term in office. His initial vision for reforming AFDC was considerably more moderate than the measure he eventually endorsed on August 22 1996. However, a fully fledged system of workfare was central to his welfare agenda and when the President signed the legislation he was keen to point out that it did meet many of his key aims. As the defining social policy initiative of the last eight years, let us take a closer look at this legislation and its consequences for work and poverty in America.

Welfare overhaul

The PRWORA mandates that an individual can only receive welfare assistance for five years during their entire adult lifetime (counting from its enactment). Within two years of receiving welfare, claimants must work. At state discretion, this period can be reduced or abolished, forcing welfare recipients to work immediately (an option that a number of states have taken advantage of). Participation in community service is now mandatory after two months of receiving benefits. States have a high incentive to enforce work mandates for two reasons. First, each state was obliged to demonstrate that 35 percent of welfare recipients were working for a minimum of 20 hours per week by FY 1997 (three-quarters of two-parent families for a minimum of 35 hours per week) otherwise it could have its grant cut by 5 percent the following year and by an additional 2 percent for each year of non-compliance (up to a total of 21 percent). These figures must rise to 50 percent of welfare recipients working for a minimum of 30 hours per week by FY 2002 (90 percent of two-parent families for a minimum of 35 hours per week). To date, all states have reached their targets. A second reason for cooperation from the states is that they continue to receive the same block grant from the federal government irrespective of their caseload.

In order to compel welfare recipients to comply with the PRWORA's work mandates, a family's benefit can be reduced pro rata for each day an individual does not work. At state discretion, the sanction may exceed the pro rata penalty to include the full denial of benefits. Medicaid coverage can be terminated for adults (but not their children) who do not fully comply with the work requirements. The law also stipulates that no person between the age of 18 and 50 (without children) can receive food stamps for more than three months in a three-year period. It tightens eligibility criteria for Supplemental Security Income (SSI, a cash benefit targeted at the poor aged, blind and disabled) for a number of groups, including disabled children and legal immigrants.

It is important to recognize that the PRWORA was designed to change the behavior of the poor more than reduce the cost of welfare, which constituted just 1 percent of the federal budget. Believing cash assistance to encourage teenage pregnancy and lone parenthood, lawmakers decided to allow the states to impose family cap policies on welfare recipients whereby children born on TANF can be excluded in the calculation of family benefits. They also wrote a number of paternity enforcement provisions into the law. Any "felon" convicted of drug-abuse offences (which Handler reminds us amounts to the possession of a little marijuana in some states), may be denied benefits for their entire life (Handler, 2001). The legislation requires any parent under the age of 18 to live in an adult-supervised setting. The states have also been offered financial incentives to promote sexual abstinence, marriage and cut out-of-wedlock births.

As part of the balanced budget agreement of 1997, Clinton amended some aspects of the legislation early in his second term. The President never intended to reverse the PRWORA's main conditions and, as noted, he fully accepted the principle of workfare. At most, Clinton sought to provide a number of supports to help people move from welfare to work with greater effectiveness, ease the law's impact on legal immigrants and restore some of the cuts in food stamps. While the President was unable to restore most of the cuts in food stamps, he did manage to establish $3 billion fund to assist the states in their job-placement efforts. Disabled children who lost their SSI benefits under the PRWORA were assured of medical coverage and $1.5 billion was allocated to finance a Medicaid program for the poor. Republican lawmakers also accepted that legal immigrants who were resident in the United States prior to the PRWORA's enactment could qualify for SSI, regardless of when they became disabled. This U-turn had much to do with the fact that GOP governors from politically important states with high immigrant populations, such as New York, were growing increasingly anxious about the social, financial and electoral implications of the PRWORA. Of the 500,000 legal immigrants affected by the changes to SSI, 16 percent (80,000) were concentrated in New York (Carney, 1997). The administration also offered welfare recipients further work-place protections via a Labor Department directive which stipulated that people enrolled in workfare schemes had to be covered by federal labor laws, such as the Civil Rights Act and the Americans for Disability Act, and enjoy the same basic legal rights as other workers, including equal health and safety standards, minimum wage levels, and overtime pay regulations (Katz, 1997b). Overall, approximately $13 billion in welfare-related spending was restored. The incremental revisions softened the harshest elements of America's welfare experiment.

The impact of the Welfare Act on the states depended upon whether they had been granted a federal waiver when the legislation was signed. Around 75 percent of the states were already running their own welfare experiments when AFDC was dismantled (most of which entailed time limits, work requirements and benefit restrictions). The PRWORA, however, institutionalized a highly fragmented, coercive and paternalistic system of workfare across the entire nation. Critics pointed to the absence of systematic evidence regarding the legislation's consequences for work and poverty. Many states had only been granted waivers since Clinton had come to office and could hardly provide conclusive evidence of workfare's success. Lesson-drawing from atypical Wisconsin, a state with comparatively low unemployment and few inner-city problems, proved to be politically inviting for national and international policy-makers alike despite the fact that Tommy Thompson's radical reforms (founded on the principle of dismantling the whole welfare system) were never subject to rigorous evaluation (Mead, 1996). Moreover, while Wisconsin had slashed its welfare rolls by 75 percent in less than 18 months, according to one report, "nearly two out of three former recipients had lower income than during the three months before they left welfare" (Children's Defense Fund, 1998).

The legacy of welfare overhaul: work and poverty

Early predictions concerning the effects of overhaul differed widely. Within a year of the legislation's passage, supporters were celebrating plummeting welfare rolls while opponents predicted frightening rises in poverty and homelessness. The caseload has dropped by 50 percent since the PRWORA was enacted and close to 30 percent of welfare recipients who remain on the rolls are working (Handler, 2001). Explanations for this dramatic fall vary. In May 1997, the Council of Economic Advisors claimed that over 40 percent of the drop could be attributed to economic growth, state welfare experiments could claim credit for around 30 percent of the fall, and measures to boost employment, such as the increase in the EITC, were responsible for the other 30 percent (Katz, 1997c). Irrespective of government policy, the welfare caseload was expected to fall as the economy gained strength following the recession of the late 1980s and early 1990s. After reaching an all-time high in 1994, the number of people claiming welfare had been in a systematic decline before overhaul.

Most policy experts agree that the full impact of welfare overhaul on work and poverty will only be clear under less prosperous conditions. Welfare recipients are typically short on competitive skills and usually the first victims of economic swings (65 percent of welfare recipients do not have a high school education). The dramatic early decline in the welfare rolls has already leveled off as those with the weakest skills and highest barriers to employment remain jobless. Estimates suggest that these people will be inadequately qualified for 90 percent of all positions created over the next five years (Handler, 2001). Even the 10 percent of vacancies that are suitable in terms of low-skill requirements may be inaccessible for other reasons. Indeed, education is just one of several critical barriers that prevent the least employable Americans from entering the workforce. Many of these people also lack basic job skills and a high proportion suffer from depression and drug-related problems. Recognizing this fact, the majority of states have decided to take advantage of federal provisions that permit them to exempt up to 20 percent of their caseload from the PRWORA's work mandates/time-limits, and six states are planning use state funds to support welfare recipients with multiple employment barriers beyond the five year limit (Handler, 2001).

Forcing welfare recipients to work, of course, has always proved less taxing than enabling them to maintain their positions. In order to stay employed, welfare recipients often require health insurance, social support, and, above all else, adequate child care. In many cases, mothers are required to work once their infant is just 12 weeks old. The cost of high quality childcare is prohibitive for most women leaving welfare and the majority of "leavers" are relying on relatives who may be ill-qualified to care for children. Despite the fact that the PRWORA created the Child Care and Development Fund to help cover the costs of childcare and thus enable women to work, Handler (2001) reports that up to 80 percent of those leaving welfare have not received any such subsidy. Part of the explanation for this high figure is that close to 40 percent of ex-welfare recipients are actually not employed (71 percent of those with multiple employment barriers: Handler, 2001). These mothers have left the welfare rolls for other reasons, including sanctions (the majority of states have imposed stricter sanctions than those required under the PRWORA: see Handler, 2001). One study that examined families in Utah who had their benefits terminated for reasons of noncompliance reported that 23 percent could not participate for transportation reasons; 18 percent cited childcare as the main reason; 43 percent reported health problems and another 20 percent cited a mental health issue (Children's Defense Fund, 1998). Another study of Minnesota found that "penalized families were twice as likely to have serious mental health problems, three times as likely to be judged to have low intellectual ability, and five times more likely to have family violence problems compared with other recipients" (Children's Defense Fund, 1998).

It is important to bear in mind that the welfare caseload is simply one indicator by which to evaluate the success of overhaul. Quality of life indicators, including poverty rates, teenage pregnancy and out-of-wedlock birth rates and health coverage must also be considered. The Congressional Budget Office, an independent source of advice, estimated that 77 percent of single teenage mothers draw on welfare before their first child is five years of age and a high proportion remain dependent on government assistance for long after that. They are no longer able to do so. Yet indicative of the simplicity of linking government programs such as AFDC to the reproductive behavior of adolescents, it is noteworthy that the teenage birth rate had already fallen by close to 12 percent since 1991. And, perhaps not surprisingly, teenage mothers are just as likely as before the PRWORA not to marry, with the percentage of out-of-wedlock births to adolescents hovering around 75 percent.

The evidence regarding poverty is mixed. After sharply rising during the 1980s and into the early 1990s, poverty rates have declined in recent years (a trend that preceded overhaul but has not been arrested by the new welfare law). The percentage of poor Americans fell from 12.7 percent in 1998 to 11.8 percent one year later. Altogether 32.3 million Americans are living in poverty, compared with 34.5 million in 1998 (US Census Bureau, 2000). Not since 1979 has the country seen such "low" poverty rates. Every racial and ethnic group has experienced an improvement in their economic well-being. In 1999 the poverty rate for African-Americans stood at 23.6 percent (compared with 26.1 percent in 1998). For Hispanics, it was 22.8 percent (down from 25.6 percent in 1998). In 1999 child poverty fell to its lowest level in two decades. It dropped by 2 percent just between 1998 (18.9 percent) and 1999 (16.9 percent).

Yet these figures remain alarming. It is also worth noting that the depth of poverty has not been alleviated. Close to 14 million Americans earn less than 50 percent of the poverty line and approximately 24 million people are classified as "near poor" in that they earn less than 150 percent of the poverty line (Handler, 2001). Poverty rates remain severely racially imbalanced (black Americans suffer more than treble the rate of whites), and data on poor families (as opposed to individuals) reveal an increase in poverty for some groups since 1998. Furthermore, poverty levels have declined at a far slower rate than the fall in the welfare caseload, suggesting that work is failing to lift many people out of poverty. Female-headed families (those most affected by welfare overhaul) continue to experience over four times the poverty levels of married-couple families, regardless of whether a family member is in paid employment (US Census Bureau, 2000). Close to a third of these families are poor (a massive 67.9 percent where there is no worker present) and they comprise over 53 percent of all poor families.

One of the chief explanations as to why the drop in the welfare caseload has not brought a proportionate decline in poverty is that the low-wage labor market, where the vast majority of welfare recipients find jobs, has stagnated despite America's economic boom. The bottom 20 percent of households have lost 12 percent of their after tax income (inflation adjusted) since the late 1970s and $1,200 on their average annual income alone since 1997 (reducing it from $10,000 to $8,800: Handler, 2001). Moreover, the poorest fifth of households leaving welfare for work have suffered an average annual income deficit of $577 as their wages have failed to compensate for lost benefits (Handler, 2001). Those with incomes between 75 and 112 percent of the poverty line, the second poorest fifth of welfare leavers, have lost $1,460 on average for the same reason. The jobs that welfare recipients find (mostly in the service industry, sales, clerical, food preparation) tend to be unstable, they are often part time, lack benefits, and most leavers will find themselves unemployed several times after leaving welfare. As Handler (2001) reminds us, leavers do not find a solid career and work their way up the employment ladder to affluence: they remain poor. A 1998 report by two advocacy groups, the Children's Defense Fund (CDF) and the National Coalition for the Homeless, found that many families who moved from welfare to work lacked the three most basic necessities of life: food, shelter (or stable housing) and medical care. The CDF's summary report notes "a proliferation of inadequately-paid employment; and signs of rising hardship for many families leaving welfare." Cuts in the food stamp program and cash assistance benefits have also contributed to this situation.

Before overhaul, many social conservatives predicted that charities would fill the vacuum left by the federal welfare guarantee. Some argued that welfare retrenchment was one means of reinvigorating the historically important role of Christian giving in America that had long been undermined by state welfare (Wolpert,1997). The evidence does not lend credence to these claims. Charities are unable to fulfill a broad welfare function. They are heavily reliant on government grants, their finances are usually extremely limited, and donations tend to be geographically concentrated with little respect for need (most giving occurs in affluent communities with the least demand for charity). Wolpert (1997) concludes: "The evidence about charitable giving . . . shows that even if individual, foundation, and corporate donors were to retarget virtually all their contributions to relief of immediate social needs, the total amount of giving would not make a noticeable dent in the shortfall resulting from the federal cuts." On top of these practical concerns rests a point of principle: namely the switch from a welfare system founded on a conception of social rights (albeit a very weak one), to forcing the poor to rely on the mercy of others.

With respect to health care coverage, the PRWORA allowed welfare recipients to remain insured under the Transitional Medicaid Assistance program for up to a year after they enter the workforce. However, the number of uninsured Americans has swelled following its enactment. Once the direct connection between welfare and Medicaid was terminated in 1996, enrollment in the health insurance program dropped for the first time in decades, a fall that neither Democrats nor Republicans welcomed. According to the Kaiser Commission, close to one million adults and a further million children were struck from the Medicaid rolls between 1995 and 1998 (Nather, 2000a). While the rise in the number of uninsured poor Americans has been arrested with programs such as CHIP (the state children's health insurance program created as part of the 1997 Balanced Budget Act), insurance rates remain below par. With few jobs at the low end of the labor market offering health coverage, it is perhaps not surprising that close to 50 percent of women, and 30 percent of their children, have no insurance after a year off welfare (Nather, 2000a).

Part of the explanation for the drop in Medicaid enrollment resides with the complexity of America's highly fragmented and contingent benefit system. The US safety net resembles a jungle of federal and state rules that shift with selective retrenchments, expansions and changing regulations. Texas boasts a total of 17 Medicaid programs, including one for claimants who died between submitting an application and acceptance into the program (Nather, 2000a). Adjustments to one part of the system, therefore, often leave caseworkers confused over linkages between benefits. Not only do caseworkers now have to place the least employable Americans in jobs, they also have to figure out which health insurance schemes apply to whom (some families have one child covered by Medicaid and another insured under CHIP). *Congressional Quarterly* reports that many people leaving welfare have not been informed that they can still apply for Medicaid, CHIP, food stamps and childcare for the very reason that caseworkers are unable to grasp the complexities of the programmatic changes.

These administrative confusions, of course, may be the natural teething problems that accompany any major overhaul. *If* these organizational anomalies are ironed out, *if* the overhaul experiment stands the test of recession, *if* welfare recipients can find stable positions, *if* work lifts them out of poverty, and *if* children do not suffer from the contingencies of poverty and poor childcare in the process, then America's new welfare system may look that much stronger.

Clinton's second term: small promises, small results

Clinton's second-term agenda can best be described as incremental. This said, the second term was not devoid of social policy initiatives. He did amend elements of the PRWORA as part of the 1997 balanced budget deal and the same agreement slashed Medicare spending by $112 billion over five years. The bulk of this sum came from cutting payments to health care providers (hospitals, nursing homes, managed care plans, doctors). By 1999, however, lawmakers had agreed to restore $16 billion of these cuts over 5 years following a vigorous and extremely costly campaign by medical groups, and the fiscal 2001 omnibus bill delivered a further $35 billion to providers over five years. The balanced budget deal did postpone the insolvency of Medicare Part "A" (which pays for hospital care and is financed by payroll taxes) mainly by shifting payment for home health services to Part "B" (which pays 80 percent of out-patient services and is financed by patient premiums and general revenues). A number of small-scale cost-containment initiatives were also introduced, including a pilot program allowing 390,000 pensioners to buy medical savings accounts.

On social security, Clinton managed to shift the debate during the second session of the 105th Congress although little was achieved in terms of policy change. Partisan conflict over whether social security was actually in crisis (as opposed to whether this was simply a GOP ploy to retrench the program) retreated and a loose consensus emerged concerning the nature of the pension crisis if not the solution. Two years of discussion on the future of social security, however, culminated in the most marginal of changes—and one that had absolutely no effect on the program's solvency. During the second session of the 106th Congress, lawmakers repealed the "earnings test." This provision was a remnant from the high unemployment era of the Great Depression when lawmakers sought to encourage the working elderly to retire by curtailing the amount they could earn while receiving social security. Seniors who decided to work had their benefits cut but were recompensed in full at a later date. Consequently, the repeal – limited to 65–69 year olds – had no long-term financial effect.

Of more substance, health care for the poor was incrementally improved during the 105th and the 106th Congresses. The Balanced Budget Act of 1997 created CHIP, a state grant in excess of $20 billion to provide health care for poor children (paid for by raising cigarette taxes by 15 cents per pack). While providing coverage for two million uninsured children (and 1.5 million others), the program initially proved more limited than lawmakers had hoped largely because it was inadequately promoted (Adams, 2000). Responding to this problem, the omnibus spending bill for FY 2001 allocated a further $300 million to improve enrollment. In 1999 Congress voted to cover the health insurance benefits of disabled people who return to the labor force in an effort to remove one of their key workplace barriers (the federal disability register lists around eight million working-age Americans). The second session of the 106th Congress also brought a children's health bill (dealing with mental and physical health, drug problems and childcare), and it passed a measure that sought to encourage the states to treat poor women with breast or cervical cancer under Medicaid. In response to reports that workfare had led to a deficit in health care, the omnibus spending bill for FY 2001 provided $700 million to cover an additional year of Medicaid benefits for welfare recipients who enter the workforce.

The public housing system, dating from the New Deal, was overhauled during the second session of the 105th Congress after divisions within the GOP had stalled the measure several times. Following the trend towards devolution in social policy, much decision making power was transferred to local public housing authorities and funding was consolidated into block grants. During the same Congress, lawmakers also merged over 60 federal job training and vocational education programs into three block grants. Again, the legislation provided the states with much greater authority to shape their own schemes. It also allowed recipients to devise their own personal training and education agenda (see CQWR, November 14th 1998).

Clinton's second term brought no significant anti-poverty programs or income-support initiatives for the poor. The 2001 omnibus spending bill attempted to revitalize poor urban and rural communities by providing tax incentives for investors. Of far more importance, repeated efforts to increase the minimum wage by $1 per hour failed in 1998, 1999 and again in 2000. During the second session of the 106th Congress, both the House and Senate passed bills to raise the minimum wage, but they specified different timetables for doing so and conferees were unable to reconcile the two bills.

In summary, while the second Clinton presidency was not without effect, there were no initiatives to compare with the overhaul of the federal welfare system in 1996.

Explaining developments in social policy

Political scientists usually argue that restructuring safety nets is difficult owing to the electoral popularity of social supports, the institutionalization of existing policy structures and the power of organized interests attached to the status quo. Consequently, elected officials must be pushed into change by demographic pressures, economic stresses or programmatic maturation (when programs cease to fulfill their intended purpose and the costs of continuing down the same route are too high). Thus political leaders, we are told, will not voluntarily restructure social supports if they can avoid so doing. Clearly in the case of AFDC this was not true. Unlike social security and Medicare, the program was not plagued by economic or demographic pressures. Compared to the 23 percent of federal spending devoted to social security and the 12 percent spent on Medicare, AFDC was a low-cost, small-scale program consuming just 1 percent of the federal budget. Moreover, even if one accepts that the demands of globalization require a more flexible, competitive labor force and, by extension weaker safety net policies, this can hardly explain the retrenchment of a highly residual and means-tested program that was targeted at poor women with dependent children. While a fully developed system of work-fare provides capital with a cheaper and more pliant labor force, overhaul in the United States was driven more by ideology than international capital flows. Above all else, Americans wanted to see welfare recipients put to work. Voters objected to providing people with even meager benefits in the absence of obligations (the average welfare payment was $6,000 per annum).

Programmatic stresses, particularly the belief that AFDC was hurting welfare recipients rather than helping them, did play an important part in the overhaul. Clinton explicitly stated on numerous occasions that AFDC no longer served its purpose, arguing that the federal welfare program had become a way of life for generations of Americans rather than a temporary hand-up in times of need. That 7 percent of Americans were claiming government assistance and about 50 percent of these people were on and off the welfare rolls for the best part of a decade, was evidence of the program's failure (some estimates actually put long-term dependency as low as 15 percent: see Handler, 2001).

It is hard to disentangle these programmatic problems from the basic unpopularity of an entitlement that was overwhelmingly associated with black single mothers. Indeed, as the program's constituency changed over the years, so did its popularity. As Handler (2001) comments: "Starting in the late 1950s and 1960s . . . [its constituency changed] from largely white widows to divorced, deserted, and disproportionately never-married women as well as families of color. Welfare was now a 'crisis'." The pervasive misinformation engulfing the entitlement also did much to undermine its support. Kuklinski *et al.* (2000) report extraordinarily high levels of public ignorance concerning welfare provision, culminating in a distinct anti-welfare bias. Up to two-thirds of respondents in their Illinois study were misinformed regarding the percentage of black people on welfare and 90 percent provided incorrect answers when asked about the portion of the federal budget spent on welfare (which proved to be the most important predictor of their preferences).

In contrast to welfare for the poor, social security and Medicare are victims of demography and the beneficiaries of politics. Programs suffering the most severe demographic, economic and programmatic stresses have escaped major reform simply because politics is more important than "objective" trends in determining social policy outcomes, at least in the short and medium term. It is worth remembering that the very concept of an "era of austerity" cannot be detached from political choices. The emphasis placed on balancing the budget during the Clinton years certainly limited the amount that could be spent on government programs in practical terms, yet this emphasis itself was a political choice and one that previous Republican administrations had little regard for. Indeed, the budget deficit was only defined as a pressing political issue when Ross Perot made it the centerpiece of his third party candidacy in 1992.

If political choices lie at the heart of developments in social policy, we need to understand how choices change. It is important to appreciate how programs that appear to be "untouchable" for decades can quite suddenly seem ripe for retrenchment. With respect to workfare, it is worth recalling that when the Family Support Act of 1988 was under consideration many of the Democrats who supported the PRWORA just eight years later routinely referred to workfare as "slavefare" (Katz and Cloud, 1996). Moreover, prior to the GOP takeover of Congress in January 1995 even many Republicans expressed serious reservations about dismantling AFDC as an entitlement. The misinformation and racist stereotypes engulfing public assistance just mentioned, together with influential policy experts asserting that welfare was more of a problem than a solution, not only lowered the political risks of overhaul, but rendered restructuring a prime credit-claiming election-year issue. Sweeping change in the United States is usually contingent upon a decisive rejection of existing arrangements and, in the case of welfare reform, no defensive coalition of interests emerged to support the status quo. Even welfare recipients and liberals who resisted overhaul did not necessarily support AFDC. Of course, the apparent success of the state experiments in cutting their welfare caseload legitimized terminating the federal entitlement.

Bearing in mind how quickly choices can change following prolonged periods of policy stability, social security and Medicare may prove to be less politically robust over the next few years than they seem at present. It is worth remembering that the health and pension sectors have only recently been framed as crisis-ridden. As noted earlier, during Clinton's first term the public debate on social security concerned whether or not the system was in fact broken. Now few question whether the pension program is in dire straits and the debate has moved on to which rescue options are most appropriate and politically acceptable. For a number of years now, surveys by the AARP have revealed that Americans are losing faith in social security. One poll indicated that just 27 percent of workers were confident about social security's future (Katz, 1997a). Another survey found that 55 percent of people accepted the statement "in theory, social security is still a good idea but I doubt that this country can afford it anymore". As more Americans obtain private pension coverage through the work place and greater affluence brings new expectations that workers should invest to maintain themselves in retirement, the voters' stake in social security may be weakening.

Much the same applies to Medicare. Until recently, it had always been a political truth that Medicare's constituency – 38 million well-organized Americans – rendered it immune to all but the most incremental changes. Over the years, the parties wrestled over who is the program's greatest advocate, especially during election season. The 2000 presidential race saw candidates Bush and Gore promising to provide new drug coverage for seniors under Medicare, despite the costs.

Yet, when the expense of extending benefits has been passed on to seniors, experience suggests retirees prefer lower benefits to higher premiums. In 1988 Ronald Reagan signed the Medicare Catastrophic Coverage Act after the measure won the approval of huge majorities in Congress. The following year lawmakers were compelled to reverse the legislation after the elderly decisively rejected better benefits when accompanied by higher costs. The measure so infuriated retirees that constituents of Dan Rostenkowski (D-Ill.), a former representative who led the reform effort, ran him out of a meeting at the seniors citizens' center while calling for his impeachment, and blocked his car so that he had to take flight on foot (Mintz, 1997). Moreover, though a majority of seniors continue to reject some of the radical reform proposals advocated by the AMA, they are less opposed to others. A rise in the age of eligibility from 65 to 67 years is broadly unpopular with the elderly. This proposal was rejected by about 66 percent of respondents in recent polls. However, means-testing the program, a concept with which Americans are comfortable, attracts considerable support. About 60 percent of respondents accepted the idea of charging people with an annual income over $40,000 higher health care costs (Langdon, 1997). As a consensus develops on the need for major reform, more fundamental change can be expected.

To summarize, ideas that are unthinkable for prolonged periods of time can quickly become acceptable. Once the political debate about social policy begins to shift, the range of feasible choices can change remarkably rapidly. An emphasis on the political determinants of social policy does not mean that objective pressures are irrelevant; rather, it suggests that economic and demographic tensions tend to interact in a secondary way with the ideas and expediencies of politics.

The future of American social policy

Few changes in the new welfare system can be anticipated in the near future, especially given that the mainstream of both main political parties are deeply committed to the principle of workfare. Perhaps the fact that this concept has a long historical legacy in the United States has encouraged its precepts to become quickly embedded. For the consensus supporting workfare to collapse, critics of the law will have to provide insurmountable evidence that the new status quo is failing on several fronts: with respect to work, poverty, health, out-of-wedlock births, and teenage pregnancy. In no sense does this imply that the current system represents the "end of history" in terms of income support policy for the poor. Wolpert (1997) notes the irony that this "severe brand of tough love and paternalism ... is reminiscent of 19th- and early 20th-century experiments in Social Darwinism whose failures helped provide the rationale for post-Depression entitlements and the emergence of modern welfare programs." If and when recession takes its toll, however, the bipartisan agreement that has legitimized the idea of workfare, and perhaps even made an ideology out of workfare, is unlikely to suddenly break down. The immediate future of TANF, of course, is not guaranteed in that Congress is obliged to reauthorize the program, as well as food stamps and the Child Care Development Fund, in 2002. In the unlikely scenario that lawmakers refuse to renew these programs, the states could find themselves grappling with a whole new range of problems, and ones that could even compel the governors to demand renewed intervention from the federal government.

Most likely, however, is that health care will dominate the social policy agenda over the next decade. There is a struggle in the health sector between three antagonistic issues: cost containment, incremental expansions in the number of insured Americans, and improvements in the quality of health insurance for those who already enjoy coverage. With respect to cost containment, America spent $1.1 trillion on health care in 1998. Estimates suggest that the country can expect to pay twice that amount by 2008 as health care spending climbs to 16.2 percent of GDP (Nather, 2000b). Though the rate of growth in health costs was contained during the Clinton presidency, cost containment is in a constant battle with new expensive drugs, technological improvements and, soon, the graying of the baby boomers. In the short term, providers may have to accept more cuts (they still make significant profits from Medicare and Medicaid). In the longer-term, there is a good possibility, as argued above, that seniors will chose Medicare restructuring over higher premiums.

Since the tragic events of September 11th, social policy issues have fallen sharply down the presidential agenda. The war against terrorism appears set to override the bulk of the Bush administration's domestic agenda. In the words of Dan Barlett, White House communications director, "We're not meeting with members of Congress on the patients' bill of rights. We're meeting with intelligence committees about the war effort" (Sanger and Bumiller, 2001). Domestic policy initiatives in the immediate future will most likely be a response to circumstance. For example, claims on state unemployment insurance rose to their highest levels in almost a decade in aftermath of the attacks. For states suffering a 30 percent-plus hike in unemployment, Bush has pledged full federal funding for 13 additional weeks of unemployment benefit (on top of the usual 26 weeks), and created a $3 billion fund to help states assist the newly unemployed.

On a broader level, the trend in social policy for the poor in recent years, and one that we can expect to continue for the foreseeable future, has been toward the increasing devolution, regulation and privatization of the American safety net. More policy and financial authority have been transferred to the states, and the new paternalism provides private companies with fresh opportunities to determine benefit eligibility, verification, monitoring, and sanctions. In 1995, GOP lawmakers attempted to restructure Medicaid along with AFDC. Clinton objected strenuously to the possibility of losing Medicaid as an entitlement and exercised his presidential veto power. It may only be a matter of time, however, before the states gain greater control over health insurance for the poor in the form of block grants. With the value of a unified federal safety net losing support even among liberals in Washington, social policy provision in America will begin to look more localized, more fragmented and more uncertain.

Chapter 13

Health Care Policy

STEPHEN LINDER AND PAULINE ROSENAU

To analyze the politics of health care in the first decade of the twenty-first century is to confront not just one policy problem but many. Before identifying the most serious issues concerning health care within the United States at the current time, however, it is important to set the discussion of the most pressing contemporary issues against three features which explain and shape American health policy. The first is the piecemeal and fragmented character of the American health care system and its heavy dependence on insurance and the private sector. The second distinctive feature of the American system is the extent to which policy is developed within the context of a federal system in which the states are increasingly key players (Hackey and Rochefort, 2001). Third, the United States' distinctive approach to health care is often explained (and sometimes justified) by reference to broader notions of American exceptionalism. These accounts, while not always entirely convincing, have the merit of pointing up a number of features of the wider political system which have an impact on health care and also help to explain why the American health care system seems to diverge so markedly from the provision found in other advanced democracies.

A piecemeal and fragmented system

American health care is fundamentally a patchwork system which relies heavily on insurance and the private sector. Although governments – at both the federal and the state level – have developed important regulatory and policy-making roles, many of the most important problems are debated in terms that assume the insurance industry will remain central to health care delivery. Issues of cost, of managed care (in which patients are confined to a set group of health care providers rather than having complete freedom of choice) and of quality are bound up with the core questions of payment and reimbursement. There is indeed in today's debates an echo of the arguments at the end of the nineteenth century as Americans address the challenge of what insurance schemes governments and private sector employers will support and what the role of government should be in the process. By comparison with the Progressive era, however, when reformers recoiled from free-market economics and emphasized sickness funds and philanthropy, today's reformers in both parties, influenced by "third way" thinking, generally endorse market-based solutions and embrace private insurance markets and competition in health planning. Although there are some public insurance funds in America (such as for flood insurance) insurance is, for the most part, a *private* commodity in the United States and it is purchased through compulsory wage deductions and contracted for by employers (Brown, 2001). Typically now the insurance contracts are not directly with providers but through managed care organizations such as Health Maintenance Organizations (HMOs) which offer employers some promise of cost restraint.

Reliance on private insurance, of course, produces anomalies and imperfect coverage; and it has been left to government to make provision for the groups (such as the poor, the retired and, more recently, the children of the working poor) excluded from these arrangements and to fill other gaps such as coverage of pharmaceutical expenditures. Yet the process of expanding coverage has occurred only slowly, and currently about one person in every six in the United States has no medical coverage of any kind.

Federalism and Health Care

The fact that the United States is a *federal* system also has a major impact on health policy. The relationship between the federal and the state governments is a fluid one and the decade of the 1990s saw a strong shift towards greater state autonomy in a number of policy fields including welfare (see also Chapters 9 and 12). At the same time the states themselves, notwithstanding Clinton's first term effort to find a federal solution for health care, have developed new and innovative policies and taken advantage of their freedom of action to tailor health service programmes to their own needs. Health care is thus not the same in California as it is Oregon or New York. There are strengths and weaknesses in this diversity; but the important point to note here is that the variations produced by federalism further complicate an already fragmented system

Exceptionalism

Finally, we need to recognize that the health care system in the United States diverges from that of other comparable countries, not least because of its odd conjunction of a huge level of health care expenditures with a relatively small governmental role. Various accounts attempt to explain this exceptionalism. Some accounts stress the institutional factors which affect health policy, notably a fragmented political system which inhibits policy initiative (Weissert and Weissert, 1996; Bodenheimer and Grumbach, 1998). Some accounts, especially case-based studies, emphasize the role of interest groups in policy-making and specific factors such as personality and timing (Marmor, 1970). Such accounts argue that policy events, when they do occur, result from a peculiar constellation of actors and circumstances that cannot be replicated. Not only, is the American system "exceptional" therefore, but the events within it are also. A third kind of exceptionalist argument focuses on ideology. Such accounts also underline the pervasive mistrust of government in the United States and the strength of conservative or neo-liberal values in a culture which gives heavy emphasis to private initiative and self-help (Morone, 1990). When government does assume responsibility for a public function, it does so incrementally and as a last resort (Oliver, 1999).

Against this background it is possible to examine some of the major controversies in relation to contemporary health care, although we shall have reason to return to the characteristics of the system as a whole at the end of the chapter.

Access to health care services

Health insurance and the insurers

The health sector in the USA is so enormous that one would not think access might be a problem. There were 3,140 health insurers serving the group and individual health insurance market in the USA in 1997 according to the Academy for Health Services Research and Health Policy, Health Insurer Database. But health insurance is not a right in the United States and there is no national program to provide access to universal health insurance. Since possession of health insurance is the best predictor of access to health care and close to 44 million Americans (about 18 percent of the population) are without health insurance, this patchy coverage constitutes a major problem. The position in part results from the fact that the USA has a much lower percentage of total health spending from public sources (44 percent) than do most other modern Western industrialized countries, including France (76 percent) and Britain (84 percent) (according to OECD data published in *The Economist*, March 3 2001).

The level of uninsurance for health services varies a great deal from state to state. In 1999, 24 percent of Texans were without health insurance but only 8–9 percent of those living in Minnesota and Hawaii had this problem. The majority of those without health insurance say that they are uninsured because insurance is too expensive. (Interestingly, unpaid medical bills are the second most common reason why individuals in the United States plead bankruptcy.) Seventy-five percent of the uninsured say that are in poor health (*Journal of the AMA*, October 23 1996). The situation is especially serious for individuals with serious and disabling illnesses, such as cancer.

About half of those without health insurance obtain care at their own cost and pay for it themselves, a process known as out-of-pocket expenditure . The very poor and the very sick sometimes get care at an emergency room or are eligible for Medicaid (a program financed jointly by state and federal government funds that is targeted to the very poor). But even those with higher incomes sometimes find it difficult to purchase health insurance on their own or through their employer if they have been sick in the past (for example, a cancer survivor), or if they have a known genetic predisposition to serious disease or illness, or some other pre-existing condition. Sometimes health insurance is issued with the qualification that such pre-existing conditions are excluded from their insurance coverage for various lengths of time, or even permanently.

Access to health care is further restricted in several ways. Many insurance plans are inadequate and do not cover essential services such as prevention and screening. Some have what is called a low lifetime cap for certain services. This means that coverage ends when the patient requires more than, for example, 60 visits during their lifetime to a mental health care provider. Financial lifetime caps are common. For example, health insurance policies may end when the cost of the patient's care exceeds $100,000. Patients with this type of health insurance are considered to be *underinsured*.

Factors other than insurance affect access. Access is also restricted by geography. Americans who live in rural areas have fewer doctors and hospitals than those in urban areas. Many of the poor neighborhoods in American's urban centers similarly have no hospitals and doctors nearby. Residents of these areas have to depend on public transportation to get to health providers which can be a difficult and time consuming process. Medical providers, and pharmacies are unlikely to locate centers and stores in poorer areas because they cannot make a profit in these communities. Individuals from various ethnic groups and those who are recent immigrants often find access restricted because of cultural and language barriers.

The role for employers

Most people in the USA who have health insurance obtain it through their employer. Except in the state of Hawaii, however, there is no legal requirement for employers to provide their employees with health insurance. Employers do receive an incentive, by way of a reduction in taxes. from the government to provide health insurance to their workers but this incentive is not great enough to permit all employers to provide health insurance. Small businesses, new businesses, or enterprises that involve risky work are less likely than large, well-established companies to provide their employees with health insurance. As a result, most of those without health insurance in the USA are among the employed. According to the Employee Benefit Research Institute, 80 percent of the uninsured are associated one way or another with a working family member, yet they do not have insurance.

For those workers with health insurance, in most cases the employer pays for only part of the cost of a health insurance policy and the employee must also pay part of the cost in the form of a "co-payment" or "deductible" designed to discourage use of the benefit. In the past many employers provided employees with the opportunity to purchase health insurance for their spouses or partners and their children. This employment benefit is disappearing and fewer employers offer it today compared to the past. The advantage of having employer-provided health insurance is that employers who purchase health insurance coverage for their employees are usually able to negotiate substantial cost reductions because of the volume of individuals involved.

The role of the states: the Employee Retirement Income Security Act, CHIP, and Medicaid

States are limited as to what they can do to provide access to health insurance. These limits are not only financial but also legal. A federal law, The Employee Retirement Income Security Act (ERISA), pre-empts the area of retirement and health benefits policy-making and legislation to the federal government. The courts have interpreted this law in ways that limit the power of the states. Under ERISA states may not tax health insurance plans to use the revenue from such a tax to provide health insurance for the poor. For many years also ERISA was interpreted by the courts as prohibiting Americans from suing their HMO for malpractice if that plan was paid for by their employer under a self-insuring arrangement. State courts have attempted to get around the federal ERISA law. Over time the Supreme Court seems to be signaling though a series of cases that it will not permit ERISA to hinder all state-based regulation of health care delivery in the future.

The greatest expansion of health insurance in the USA has come in the area of health insurance benefits for children. The State Children's Health Insurance Program, or SCHIP, also called the CHIP program, was initiated by the Congress as part of the Balanced Budget Act of 1997. It involves the states but requires that the states follow rules set up by the federal government (very flexibly in this case) concerning eligibility and benefits. In return the federal government pays a part of the cost for the program. Despite the fact that CHIP has extended health insurance to between 2 and 3 million children, the number of uninsured children continues to increase in the USA and now stands close to 11 million.

One reason for this large number of uninsured children is that so many of them live in families that are not poor enough to qualify for the US health care program for the very poor called Medicaid. The US Medicaid program that covers many adults and children is similar to CHIP in the sense that the federal government and the states share responsibility for it. Medicaid covers about 36 million people with very low income. It includes some services to the aged, the blind and other disabled Americans with limited ability to pay for their own health care.

The federal role: Medicare

The American Medicare program was enacted by Congress in 1965. It is a federal government program that provides those 65 and over, close to 40 million people, with universal, comprehensive health insurance. The adoption of this legislation was perhaps the biggest expansion of American health care in the twentieth century. However, Medicare has large and increasing deductibles and co-payment provisions which mean that the elderly poor pay a large part of their total retirement income for health services and medication. Medications were not included in the original legislation, and this is now a problem because the elderly are the largest consumers of medicines of various sorts. As a result of this omission, many elderly people dependent on Medicare go without needed medication.

Paying for health care services

Health care costs

Health care costs are high and increasing in all of the industrialized countries, but, according to World Health Organization (WHO) data, the USA has the highest per capita health expenditure in the world ($4,187). By comparison per capita health care costs are $1,303 per person in the UK, $2,369 in France, $1,783 in Canada, $1,730 in Australia, $1,855 in Italy, and $2,373 in Japan. Yet on quality the USA was ranked 37th according to WHO in 2000. The UK was ranked 18th, France was first, Canada was 30th, Australia was 32nd, Italy was ranked second, and Japan was 10th. Thus, contrary to many American assumptions, the high cost of health care in the USA cannot be accounted for by better care or better health outcomes. For example, citizens in almost all of the above-mentioned countries on average have more doctor visits than do US patients. Those in other countries benefit from lower infant mortality and better life expectancy with only a few exceptions. The obvious conclusion is that Americans are not getting their money's worth for their health care dollars.

The reasons for the cost increases in the health sector in the USA and the rest of the industrialized countries are complex. Among the most important explanation is the skyrocketing of medical technology costs, and especially the cost of pharmaceutical products. Another reason is that the population in the industrialized countries is aging; because older people use more medical services there is an increasing total cost to the health system.

Between 1990 and 2000 prescription drug expenditures have grown faster than any other component of the US health care dollar according to the Kaiser Family Foundation. This same time period saw the expansion of direct advertisements by pharmaceutical companies targeted to the population via television commercials in order to argue that such marketing expenditures are greater than the overall amount spent by the companies on research. The increase in prescription drug costs is also due to increased utilization. Congress has failed to react to this problem with legislation; but several of the US states are actively attempting to control these rapidly rising costs by organizing purchasing pools, including multi-state pools, and by demanding rebates and discounts from the pharmaceutical manufacturers for the cost of medication paid for by the states. States pay a large share of medications destined for those in Medicaid, but each state is also responsible for the pharmaceutical benefit program for its own employees, and this may involve hundreds of thousands of individuals.

There are a number of relatively painless ways to reduce health care costs in the USA. These involve improving quality and reducing waste. Global budgets and all-payer systems (where fees are set uniformly for various services by the government), such as that of the state of Maryland, can successfully control hospital costs. When these types of experiments are limited to a single state, however, they seldom succeed in the long term because health service providers relocate across state borders to neighboring states, thus avoiding such cost controls. Solutions to cost control that involve such direct government intervention are also out of tune with the general American policy approach that depends on the market rather than the government. The state of Oregon has gone in a different direction and instituted a system of medical rationing that involves the government. This program is not without problems; but it has succeeded in eliminating some wasted resources. In brief, it provides health services to the poorest 20 per cent of the population by ranking medical procedures and not reimbursing providers for those services that are without efficacy.

Quality control could reduce waste in many areas. It is, unfortunately, assured in a large part of the USA via the legal system. In the end, using the judiciary for this purpose increases costs. Malpractice insurance purchased by doctors is indirectly passed on to payers resulting in overall cost increases for the health system of about 7–8 percent. Lawyers are paid in malpractice cases on the basis of whether they win for a plaintiff or not (contingency fee basis). This method of payment encourages frivolous claims in the USA by contrast with many other countries where such methods of paying lawyers are not allowed in the health sector and the cost of malpractice insurance is consequently lower. Research suggests that, in the end, the American judicial system does a poor job of compensating those who suffer from errors in medical practice. The prevalence of errors in the medical care sector that add to overall costs is enormous. No effective policy to remedy for this situation is even beginning to be formulated.

Contracts and competition: health maintenance organizations and preferred provider organizations

Failing broader, comprehensive health system reform in the early 1990s, market competition to control costs and improve quality was introduced as a last resort. It may be premature to evaluate the success of this experiment but overall the results so far have not measured up to promise and American health care costs have not been brought into line with those of other industrialized countries. Initial cost reductions of about 5 percent were a one-off affair and have not been sustained. The market-driven move to managed care in the US health system set up a system of health maintenance organizations (HMOs), preferred provider organizations (PPOs) and point-of-service organizations (POSs) designed to provide efficient health care and control costs at the same time. Traditional indemnity health insurance that pays *all* of the physician and hospital charges has almost disappeared. The HMOs place the most limits on patient freedom of choice. They require patients to choose a primary care physician who acts as a gatekeeper to control the patient's visits to specialist health professionals without a referral. PPOs offer patients greater direct access to specialists but include strong financial incentives to use specialists who gave fee discounts to the insurance company. POSs combine features of both HMOs and PPOs. They include several layers of physician networks that may be very complicated but in the end patients may, at substantially increased cost, go to any doctor and at least part of the bill will be reimbursed. Today restrictions on physician access designed to control costs are being called into question, not least because they are very expensive to administer. In addition, the patients themselves demand more freedom to choose their doctors directly.

HMOs, PPOs, and POSs all have some type of review mechanism to monitor physician care of patients. Physicians, for their part, have become more efficient at manipulating the system to circumvent efforts by health maintenance organizations and insurance companies to control how they practice medicine. A survey indicated that most doctors were willing to lie about a patient's condition to the insurance company in order to obtain what the doctor felt was needed care for the patient. Health economists such as Uwe Reinhardt are doubtful whether the radical reductions in lengths of hospital stay that market competition accomplished result in cost savings.

There is no evidence of sustained quality improvement throughout the US health system resulting from market competition. Market-based reform has not expanded health insurance coverage but has rather, directly or indirectly, increased the number of underinsured and uninsured Americans. Medical research and education have suffered and medicine's social mission has declined.

For-profit versus nonprofit payment: does it matter?

Part of the American experiment with market competition has also involved a test of the relative performance of "for-profit" and "nonprofit" health care providers. If quality of care, cost of care, access to health services, and the amount of charity care provided are accepted as performance criteria, then the weight of evidence over the last two decades in the United States does not testify to the superiority of the for-profit model. A synthesis of all 123 studies comparing for-profit and private nonprofit providers since 1980 in a wide range of health sector services indicates that the nonprofits were judged superior 57 percent of the time, the for-profits only 12 percent, and the rest (31 percent) other found no difference or results were mixed. Health policy that encourages private for-profit health care services in the United States as an alternative to private nonprofit provision of health services may thus be misguided.

Other controversies

Prescription drug coverage

Many employers who provide health insurance for their employees also offer prescription drug coverage in some form as well. Usually this involves the employee paying part of the cost which is called a co-payment. This co-payment can vary between a few dollars to as much as $40 per prescription. Proposals to formulate a prescription drug benefit for the elderly underlined the differences between the American political parties regarding health sector reform. While both parties agreed that the government should pay for the prescription program, the Republicans proposed that any such program be administered by private sector insurance companies and HMOs, giving the elderly a choice of programs through a voucher system. This was expected to encourage competition within the private sector and to require senior citizens to become critical consumers. Republicans also seek to limit government's role in such a program. The Democrats, by contrast, prefer that the program be integrated into the over-65 Medicare programs, and that it be closely regulated to control costs. During the 2000 election campaign, Al Gore proposed a pharmaceutical benefit program that was progressive and redistributive from the rich to the poor, while the Republican proposal was much less so. Grounds for agreement between the parties were evident, as both parties' plans assumed that the government would be responsible for the costs of the program and that it would be voluntary (that is, available to all Medicare beneficiaries if they were willing to pay part of the cost).

The pharmaceutical benefit for the elderly provides yet another illustration of how lobbyists for private groups in the USA play a substantial role in health care policy formulation. Industry lobbyists sided with the Republican Party, strongly opposing any role for government beyond financing the benefit. Their fear was that government would exert its purchasing power to demand deep discounts or would move to regulate the price it paid for medications. The bill extending these benefits failed in 2000, but remains on the Democratic Party's agenda.

A patients' bill of rights

Some form of a patients' bill of rights has been central to the American health policy agenda since the late 1980s. Issues of confidentiality and informed consent formed the early core of these proposals. The rights demanded expanded over the next decade to include protections against medical error and against denial or restriction of coverage by managed care organizations. The expansion of patients' rights was fueled, in part, by the public's reaction against the cost-saving restrictions imposed by managed care plans, and their willingness to sue these plans in court for damages. In the mid-1990s, HMO enrollees in Georgia and California won huge cash awards in suits claiming that their health plans had wrongfully denied or delayed necessary medical care. In June of 2000, however, the Supreme Court (in *Pegram* v. *Herdrich*) denied a plaintiff's claims against her plan's administrator, and invited Congress to set guidelines for managed care administrators in lieu of court action. By then, 45 states had enacted some form of patients' rights legislation. Not all of them favored patients, however. Some state legislation placed limits on the available monetary damages, and others restricted standing or limited available remedies in state and federal courts.

The Republican Congress in 1999 itself failed to pass a patients' bill of rights. By an Executive Order that year, however, President Clinton authorized a bill of rights for patients covered by all federal programs, including Medicare, Medicaid and the Veterans Administration. The key features of this federal patients' bill of rights were confidentiality and privacy protections, information disclosure, and a right of patient involvement in treatment decisions. Although President Bush has not rescinded these rules, he has weakened a few of the enforcement provisions. A broader Patients' Bill of Rights, still pending in Congress, would extend these rights to the majority of the population covered by private insurance and add provisions for grievance and appeals, access to emergency care, and special protection against having cost-savings steer medical decision-making. The debate is now turning on liability issues and patients' access to the courts for relief. As in some state versions, monetary damages could be capped and the liability of either the plans or of employers funding the plans could be limited. Without the ability to sue for enforcement, the effect of any set of rights will be seriously attenuated for patients. On the other hand, any extension of rights that is enforcible creates new financial risks for the insurers and employers alike.

This approach to patient rights is perhaps the one area in which the United States can claim a unique contribution to the international exchange of health policy ideas. Rather than making the transition to tax-funded social insurance, the USA may well be charting the course for the juridification of health care policy under the auspices of court-enforced rights claims. Beyond statutory and regulatory statements, juridical language and logic now appears in a number of registers in the USA, ranging from technology assessment to clinical ethics. The question is whether these developments will find a place among social insurance regimes in other countries where human rights claims are already well established.

Apart from the issue of patients' rights and the juridification of health care, few ideas from the American system have been exported to other systems of health care, and health provision in the United States remains obstinately distinctive. Whether this difference should be celebrated, as some writers on its exceptionalism claim, or regretted for the extent to which it has caused the United States to lag behind its peers, remains a contested issue. What is not contested is the extent to which the weaknesses of the existing system now present a formidable challenge to American policy-makers.

Chapter 14

Foreign and Security Policy

DAVID WILLIAMS

The horrific events of September 11 2001 produced the most significant foreign policy challenge to the United States in a generation. The way America responds to the death of over 3,000 of its citizens will be a defining moment in its relations with the world. At the time of writing the full ramifications of America's response to the attacks are unclear. It seems likely, however, that American policy will be played out within the tension that has characterized American foreign policy since the end of the Cold War. This tension runs through party politics, public opinion, relations between Congress and the executive, and through the broader public debate about American foreign policy. At base it is over whether the post-Cold War world requires active engagement with world affairs and coop-eration with other states, or whether it provides an opportunity to disengage and pursue a more unilateral foreign policy. In one sense this is a continuation of the old dispute between "internationalism" and "isola-tionism" which has been a recurrent theme in American foreign policy. But the options open to foreign policy-makers today are now not nearly so stark and so simple, largely because the world has become more a complex and interconnected place.

The Clinton administration was guided by a particular vision of American foreign policy that had at its heart the ideas of "engagement" and "enlargement." The basic thrust of the policies was to expand the community of democratic and economically open states, and to expand the reach of international institutions that embodied the administration's broadly liberal approach. These policies were not simply the result of the Clinton administration being more "internationalist" in its inclinations; they also resulted from a recognition that they served America's political, economic, and security interests both at home and abroad. The Bush administration came to office promising a redefinition of America's foreign policy. Many of its early actions suggested it was much less inclined toward international cooperation. The withdrawal from several interna-tional treaties, the pursuit of NMD, the so-called "son of Star-Wars" program, and the move from seeing China as a "strategic partner" to a "strategic competitor" all indicated a more unilateral foreign policy stance.

Even before September 11 these policies were causing the Bush administration problems, as they seriously complicated relations with Russia, China and Europe, and aggravated many smaller states. As America searches for international support for its response to the attacks, and as it needs international cooperation in its fight against terrorism, so the administration may be pushed toward a more cooperative foreign policy stance.

This chapter is organized into three sections. The first section discusses the debates within America over its role in world affairs. The second section reviews the Clinton administration's foreign policy in the areas of security, economic issues and multilateralism in order to highlight the policies Bush inherited. The final section traces the changes that have taken place under the Bush administration, and the chapter concludes with a discussion of its response to the terrorist attacks.

Searching for a role

By any conventional measure America is the most dominant state in international politics (Kapstein and Mustanduno, 1999). America has a position of military dominance in international politics that has rarely been achieved by any state. It has more combat ships available than Russia and China put together, and it has an overwhelming predominance in aircraft carriers, the most potent form of conventional military power. In addition, it has a massive lead in the development and utilization of sophisticated military weapons. Its past strategic rival, Russia, has seen its once large, but technologically inferior, military capacity crumble alongside that country's economy. Another traditional American antagonist – China – is increasing its military spending, but it still spends *less* in monetary terms than the United States on its armed forces, and less per soldier than almost any Western state. It is not just in the military sphere that America has assumed a position of extraordinary relative dominance. America is still the largest economy in the world, and during the 1990s it experienced an unprecedented period of economic growth. The world has never been more organized along American lines. The international economic institutions it helped set up and sustain, such as the International Monetary Fund (IMF), the World Bank, the World Trade Organization (WTO), and the North Atlantic Treaty Organization (NATO), have reached unprecedented influence. Many of the former communist states have been assimilated into these institutions, and even China has recently reached an agreement with the WTO (after joining the IMF and the World Bank in the 1980s). America's broadly liberal economic and pro-democratic values have never been as widely accepted (in rhetoric at least) as they are today. Even China has signed up to the United Nations Conventions on Human Rights.

Foreign policy-making is always a tricky business because of the myriad of competing pressures on decision-makers and, despite its dominance, the world remains a potentially dangerous place for America, as the terrorist attacks so vividly showed. What is striking, however, is that debates over America's role in the world are characterized by internal divisions that at face value do not reflect this dominant position in international affairs.

The end of the Cold War has seen the search for a set of principles that can guide American foreign policy. Part of the difficulty with this has been the intense disputes over quite what the post-Cold War world actually looks like. For some it is characterized by "globalization." For all its rhetorical appeal this is a rather opaque concept, but it is generally taken to mean that all states are being enmeshed in increasingly transnational or global processes and problems (Clark, 1997; Scholte, 2000). The globalization of financial markets, the massive expansion of international trade, global warming, the spread of consumerism ("McDonaldization"), and of course the emergence of international terrorism, are often pointed to as indicators of this process. For others the end of the Cold War has seen the revitalization of the "liberal international order" established by America at the end of World War II. This is characterized by the spread of democracy and liberal economic regimes, the rejuvenation of international organizations and increasing international cooperation. These visions are countered by those who see a more dangerous world emerging after the Cold War. For some this involves a "clash of civilizations" whereby ideological conflict between communism and liberal capitalism is replaced by "civilizational" conflict between the "west" and "Islam" (Huntington, 1996).

These alternative visions imply different roles for the United States. For some, America should embrace globalization for the economic benefits it brings and because it leads to the spread of liberal and democratic values, but should also recognize that international cooperation is necessary to tackle the problems associated with it which range from global warming to international crime and weapons proliferation. For others, America should embrace its role as the dominant state in international politics, and revitalize its commitment to a liberal international order based on democracy and free trade (Kagan, 1999). This would involve actively spreading democracy, human rights and economic openness, and leading humanitarian and peacekeeping operations in war-torn states. The justification for this latter view is that there are economic benefits to be gained, and also that a world of democratic and liberal states is a more peaceful world (Doyle, 1995). This analysis provokes fierce criticism. One argument is that the active spread of American values will increase tension as other cultures come to resent their imposition (Huntington, 1996). Other critics assert that humanitarian intervention is "foreign policy as social work" and has no part in a foreign policy directed toward America's vital interests (Mandelbaum, 1996).

The political parties in America are also divided over foreign policy. Within the Republican Party in particular there are a number of distinct foreign policy views (Kitfield, 1999; Rose, 1999). These differences were especially evident in the latter stages of the Clinton administration. First, there is a broadly internationalist wing of the party, reflected in the policies pursued by former president George Bush. These Republicans wish to see America engaged with the world, pursuing its values and security through building and sustaining alliances and coalitions (Zoellick, 2000). In contrast to this, there is a neo-populist and isolationist wing of the Party. This faction has become more influential with the arrival of a new generation of Republican congressmen with little or no interest in foreign affairs and with little experience of the world outside the Unites States. Its influence is reflected in the accession to positions of power of senators such as Jesse Helms (R-NC), until recently Chair of the Senate Foreign Relations Committee (Kitfield, 1999). Helms, for example, has said that "the UN is looked on with disdain by the American people," and that the UN poses a threat to "American sovereignty" (Kull, 1999; Helms, 2000). The Democratic Party is also divided over a number of issues, although the divisions are less profound than those in the Republican Party. Broadly speaking Democrats are agreed on the need to pursue an internationalist foreign policy, which includes supporting international organizations. There are differences, however, over some sensitive issues. One is free trade, where Congressmen with labor union support were distinctly less enthusiastic about the NAFTA treaty than the Clinton administration. Another is relations with China, where left-leaning Democrats were against granting MFN status to China, and against allowing China to join the WTO.

The American public too is divided on foreign affairs, although not as much as one might imagine; and despite a more "isolationist" sentiment in Congress, there is no evidence that the public has changed in its attitudes towards foreign policy since the end of the Cold War. There remain splits over the extent of America's commitments in the world, the extent of America's duties to others, and divisions between Americans in the north and south (and west) and between skilled and unskilled workers. But the latest evidence from a think-tank study indicates that Americans are generally in favour in principle of some kind of internationalist foreign policy (Kull, 1999). When asked if America should "take an active part in world affairs," respondents said "yes" by a margin of 2 to 1, and nearly three-quarters of respondents thought that America should do its "fair share in multilateral efforts." In general, Americans seem to view the UN in a favorable light (*contra* Jesse Helms) and are broadly supportive of contributing troops to UN peacekeeping operations. As with all public opinion surveys, however, the answer you get depends on how you ask the questions. In addition, it is also clear that American public opinion can change quickly when a sentiment they are theoretically in favour of is translated into actions that lead to casualties, the most obvious example being Somalia where the death of a number of Army Rangers led to a rapid withdrawal of American troops.

These debates will no doubt continue. They are an indication of the divisions within American politics and society not just over the details of foreign policy, but over basic questions of America's role in the world. These divisions have been reflected in the different foreign policy orientations of the Clinton and Bush administrations.

Assessing Clinton's foreign policy

The two words most used by the Clinton administration to describe their foreign policy goals were "engagement" (or "selective engagement") and "enlargement". As Madeleine Albright described it, this meant the administration would "take actions, forge agreements, create institutions, and provide an example that will help bring the world closer together around the basic principles of democracy, open markets, law, and a commitment to peace" (Albright, 1998). The main intellectual thrust behind this was that security interests, economic interests, and the promotion of American values were all linked together. One example of this was the commitment to support and promote democracy. The administration saw this as desirable in itself, but they also thought that democracies were less likely to go to war with one another, so that the more democracies there were in the world, the more America's security was enhanced. Another example was in dealings with China. Here the aim was to integrate China into the world economy and the international economic institutions. Such integration, it was argued, would make China less likely to challenge American security as China would have economic interests at stake in maintaining economic relations with the West.

The other recurrent theme in Clinton's foreign policy was globalization. Clinton himself said that "everything from the strength of our economy, to the safety of our cities, to the health of our people depends on events not only within our borders but half a world away". The events of September 11 have shown this to be a remarkably prescient statement. Dealing with the opportunities and problems associated with globalization chimed with the ideas of engagement and enlargement. It implied a need to engage in cooperation with other states and international organizations as the only way of harnessing and shaping the forces of globalization to the benefit of America. So, for example, it meant international economic cooperation in order to open markets to American companies, and it meant cooperation in dealing with international environmental problems which no one state can solve alone. As already noted, globalization is a rather vague concept but, in theory at least, this idea combined with engagement and enlargement provided a set of ideas to guide foreign policy-making. Like many administrations before it, however, the Clinton administration faced a number of difficulties in implementing these ideas, not least because of opposition from Congress, particularly during Clinton's second term.

Security issues

The most significant example of engagement and enlargement in the security field was NATO expansion. NATO had been the cornerstone of Western security since its foundation in 1949, and it represented the most institutionalized and most powerful military alliance ever constructed. The decision to pursue a policy of opening NATO up to states of the former communist bloc was a radical change, because it signaled a shift in the role of the alliance. The rationale for NATO expansion was most usually expressed in terms of providing support for, and helping to entrench, the new democracies in Eastern Europe, and thereby enhancing regional stability. NATO expansion can be seen as an innovative response to the collapse of the Warsaw Pact (the Communist bloc's military alliance) and the Soviet Union. In these new conditions, it was argued, NATO needed a different role and a fresh rationale. Alongside expansion was a new willingness on the part of NATO, encouraged by America, to use its formidable military resources in "nontraditional" conflicts such as in the former Yugoslavia and Kosovo, where NATO warplanes engaged in extensive bombing campaigns.

The expansion of NATO was not without its critics, however. In particular it was argued that expansion strained the cohesion of the alliance and antagonized Russia. NATO was founded on the idea of mutual assistance. If any member state was attacked, the other member states would do what they could to defend that state. With a clear enemy (the communist bloc) and a clear threat this idea retained its power. In theory this applies to the new members of NATO (Poland, Hungary, the Czech Republic) but there remain doubts about the extent to which America would see its soldiers die to defend these states from external aggression. NATO expansion also took place in the face of opposition from Russia. Indeed, it was one of the key areas of dispute between Russia and America during the Clinton presidency. The Russians saw it as a direct military threat to themselves, and as a sign of American involvement in areas that had traditionally been part of the Russian sphere of influence. The fact that NATO expansion was achieved is a good example of presidential leadership in foreign policy. Clinton and his National Security Adviser, Anthony Lake, were the key players in pushing NATO expansion in the face of bureaucratic and congressional opposition. Also important were pressure groups, particularly the Polish lobby which campaigned vigorously for expansion. Finally, NATO expansion won the day because of support from Democrats who viewed it as making good on the promises of engagement and enlargement, and Republicans who saw it as an opportunity to assert American leadership and influence in the region.

The Clinton administration was also highly activist in terms of military deployments, and the bulk of these deployments were of a nontraditional kind, involving American military forces in peacekeeping and humanitarian missions. The obvious examples here are the missions in Haiti, the former Yugoslavia, and Kosovo. The other noteworthy examples of the use of military power were the unilateral Cruise missile strikes against Osama Bin Laden in response to what the administration saw as his involvement in the American embassy bombings in Kenya and Tanzania. These strikes proved very ineffective, and this fact has had a important influence on the Bush administration's response to the attacks on New York and the Pentagon. This military activism complicated relations with both Russia and China, both of whom saw in this an aggressive American foreign policy outlook and a direct threat to their own interests (particularly as Russia had a long-running civil conflict of its own in Chechnya). Dealing with Russia was made easier by the fact that it relied heavily on American financial support, and by the fact that the administration was actively engaged in assisting the Russians in dismantling their nuclear missiles. Dealing with China was complicated by the other pressures on China–America relations and by Congress. The administration opposed a congressional "Taiwan Security Enhancement Act" that would have required America to upgrade its military relations with Taiwan (something which the Chinese objected to very strongly). Also at play was the desire on the part of the administration to see China accede to the WTO, and more generally to open China's markets to American business.

Economic issues

The Clinton administration put a great deal of emphasis on economic issues, particularly free trade, again under the guiding principles of engagement and enlargement. The administration oversaw the creation of NAFTA in 1993, against opposition in Congress and from labor unions. The White House also signed a record number of international trade deals. To coordinate foreign economic policy-making the White House established a "National Economic Council" as a complement to National Security Council. This was a sign not just of the importance of economic issues but also of the fact that the Clinton administration saw economic and security issues as being interrelated. The Clinton administration was also highly activist in other economic areas. It led the response to international financial crises in 1994 and 1998. In both cases the US Treasury was instrumental in putting together rescue packages to be overseen by the IMF. In 1998 it also defeated Japanese plans for an Asian Monetary Fund and so ensured America's continued dominance in the area of international economic relations.

The Clinton administration was hampered in its ability to pursue the free trade agenda by the refusal of Congress to grant fast-track negotiating authority to the President. Indeed, some have argued that in the face of opposition from liberal Democrats, Clinton backed off from the free-trade agenda in his second term. The one notable exception to this retreat was the passing of legislation to clear the way for China's membership of the WTO. Clinton faced opposition from both left of center Democrats and some Republicans; but he succeeded in part due to support of major business lobbies. Towards the end of his Presidency, Clinton was also heavily criticized for trying to appease domestic protest groups at Seattle by seemingly accepting the need to integrate labor standards into the free trade regime (something opposed by the WTO and, indeed, by most developing countries). It is important to note, however, that the Clinton administration's success in the area of free trade was helped enormously by the continued strength of the American economy. There might have been much more domestic political opposition, especially from labor unions, if the American economy had been experiencing a recession during Clinton's second term.

Multilateralism and humanitarianism

As part of the Clinton administration's broadly internationalist outlook, it embraced the idea of humanitarian action – at least up to a point. The most obvious example is Kosovo where America led a NATO bombing campaign to stop the expulsion of Kosovo Albanians by Serbian forces. The campaign was successful to the extent that it achieved the objective of getting the Serbian forces to withdraw from Kosovo. Some have questioned the "humanitarian" nature of this mission, and it is true that there were at least some security interests at stake, particularly regional stability. More plausibly it seems there was a genuine desire to stop the expulsions, and that NATO rather boxed itself into a corner over the appropriate strategy. Having expected the Serbians to back down in the face of threatened air strikes, the alliance was forced to fulfill its promise when the

Serbians continued their activities. Despite this, the Clinton administration could claim with some legitimacy that it had lived up to certain humanitarian ideals, as it also could in its dealings with Haiti.

Balanced against this are questions about the legality of the intervention (under international law) as it was not clear it was authorized by the UN Security Council. Of course intervention would not have been authorized because of Russian and Chinese opposition to what they saw as a dangerous precedent. The military campaign soured relations with Russia and China, and Chinese opposition increased after its embassy in Belgrade was accidently targeted by Allied bombers. The campaign also only received lukewarm support in Congress, and there was very little support for the deployment of American ground troops. Congressional opposition to humanitarian military deployments (including peacekeeping operations) and the more general anxiety about the public's attitude to military casualties were both considerations in the case of Rwanda, where America did not support strengthening the UN mission. The humanitarian justification in the Rwandan case was overwhelming (nearly one million people were killed in Rwanda, compared to about 20,000 in Kosovo), yet the administration did not act.

A final point of contention between the Republican Congress and the Clinton administration is worth noting, as it goes to the heart of the disputes between Congress and the administration. Congress and the President were frequently at loggerheads over funding for the non-military aspects of America's foreign policy institutions. Between 1991 and 1998 there was a 25 percent decline in the international affairs budget (State Department and related agencies). The State Department's budget was 20 percent less in 1998 than it had been in 1993, and during this time it had to close more than 30 embassies and consulates and cut 2,000 employees. Funding for foreign aid also fell under the Republican Congress, especially in the period 1994–96. The United States Agency for International Development (USAID) cut staff and closed 27 overseas missions. There was also a growth in arrears owed to the United Nations, from $287 million in 1992 to $1.4 billion in 1996. Congress passed unilateral legislation reducing America's share of UN peacekeeping costs from 31 percent to 25 percent. Funds for the Multilateral Development Banks (such as the World Bank) were cut by 33 percent between 1995 and 1996. Senator Jesse Helms (R-NC), along with Congressman Joe Scarborough (R-Fla), went so far as to attempt to get the United States to withdraw from the UN completely. All of this frustrated the Clinton administration as it undermined engagement and enlargement. Madeleine Albright argued that this reduction in the nonmilitary aspects of America's foreign policy capability reduced American influence as "a force for peace . . . detracts from our leadership on global economic issues . . . [and] makes it harder for us to exert leverage on the contributions of others" (Albright, 1998).

Assessing the Clinton legacy

It is too early to come to any well-rounded conclusions on the success or failures of the Clinton administration's foreign policy. Given the debates over America's role in the world it is no surprise that there have been plenty of critics of Clinton's approach. Some have argued the Clinton administration lacked a coherent foreign policy guided by an overarching vision, while others criticized the administration for conducting too many operations in areas outside of America's core interests (Mandelbaum, 1996); and yet others have argued that the Clinton administration was not concerned enough about pursuing a policy guided by liberal values. Being criticized from both sides of the political spectrum is a sign that the administration embraced the necessary pragmatism that Madeleine Albright argued should always be part of American foreign policy (Albright, 1998).

The Bush administration

In terms of rhetoric some of the early statements of the new Bush administration were little different from those of the Clinton administration. In his first address to Congress, Bush said that he wanted to promote "a distinctly American internationalism." "We will work for free markets and free-trade and freedom from oppression," he said, and "we will promote our values and we will promote peace." Despite this rhetoric, the Bush Administration initially embraced a much more aggressive and unilateral foreign policy. The obvious examples here were the new attitude toward China, the pursuit of NMD, and the withdrawal from the Kyoto Accord on climate change. It remains to be seen if this more aggressive and unilateral foreign policy will be able to secure the cooperation and partnerships America needs to manage international problems. The difficulties the Bush administration faces are not just to do with relations with other states. Also likely to be problematic are relations with Congress, where there are already indications of opposition to Bush's foreign policy stance, and the economic ramifications of pursuing NMD as the American economy teeters on the brink of a recession.

Security issues

The most high-profile security issue that faced the new administration was dealing with the fall-out from the decision to develop NMD. NMD is a system designed to shoot down incoming ballistic missiles. There are massive technical difficulties in producing an effective system, as it requires the ability to launch an interceptor rocket from a ground station to hit an incoming warhead traveling at several thousand miles an hour. Beyond these problems there remain severe doubts about the actual usefulness of such a system. As currently proposed, the system would not be able to prevent a full-scale attack from a major nuclear power. The justification for such a system is, then, that it will protect America from surprise attack by so-called "rogue states" which might develop a long-range missile capability. Often mentioned in this regard are North Korea, Iraq, and Libya; but even here the logic is unclear. Any state that launched such an attack would be annihilated. While the leaders of some of these "rogue states" no doubt see America as a mortal enemy, it is highly unlikely that any of them would be prepared to risk that result. This is the traditional logic of deterrence and it renders NMD pointless (at least in providing for American security).

The most telling argument against NMD is that it would not prevent "unconventional" low-technology terrorist attacks of the kind seen on September 11 2001 and it is precisely this kind of attack that these "rogue states" are more likely to undertake. It remains to be seen what will happen to the NMD program in the aftermath of the September 11 attack. Clearly those attacks will lead to a re-assessment of the security threats facing America. There are, however, many senior politicians and Pentagon officials committed to the NMD system, particularly Donald Rumsfeld, the Defense Secretary; and there are congressmen who see economic benefits for their districts from the program. The decision to pursue NMD had deleterious effects on relations with China, Russia, and America's European NATO partners in the early months of the Bush administration.

Relations with China were strained before the Bush administration came to power. The Kosovo campaign, and the accidental bombing of the Chinese embassy in Belgrade, had alarmed China. It is important to note that these episodes, combined with NMD, meant that China saw America as a potential security threat to itself and to its interests. It saw the USA as a country willing to use military force in areas traditionally beyond its sphere of influence, and one that was deliberately upsetting the traditional logic of nuclear deterrence. US strategic moves in fact added impetus to the expansion of Chinese military spending. On top of this the Bush administration initially used a different rhetoric in its dealings with China. It talked of China as a strategic competitor rather than a strategic partner, a change that reinforced China's sense of insecurity. Tensions over Taiwan added to the already difficult relations. At one point Bush seemed to abandon the longstanding, and quite deliberate, ambiguity over the extent of American commitment to the defence of Taiwan by saying that the United States would do "whatever it took" to defend the island if Taiwan were attacked by China. This approach was subsequently retracted by Dick Cheney, but it reinforced China's view of America as a potentially severe threat to its security. Complicating relations further was a dispute over arms sales to Taiwan. The White House approved the biggest package of arms sales to Taiwan in over ten years (even though it fudged the issue of the sale of the advanced submarines) which absolutely infuriated the Chinese who see Taiwan as rightfully part of China itself. There were yet other issues complicating relations with China, including American pressure over China's human rights record, the detention of a number of American citizens on suspicion of spying, and America's criticisms of China's supply of technology to Iraq. As America searched for international support for its response to the attacks of September 11, tensions in the China–US relationship have receded into the background. The administration now no longer talks of China as a "strategic competitor." It seems likely, however, that these tensions will re-emerge in the future.

Relations with Russia have also been complicated by NMD. The pursuit of NMD requires breaking the Anti-Ballistic Missile (ABM) treaty jointly negotiated by America and the Soviet Union in 1972; and Russia is adamantly opposed to NMD deployment. In addition to this, Rumsfeld in particular has been critical of Russia over the supply of technology to other states. However, the long-term prospects for relationships with Russia are not nearly so bleak as with China. Russia desperately needs American aid and support for renewed IMF loans. The pursuit of NMD also added to the strains on relations with Europe. Both Germany and France are opposed to the NMD system. Britain is in a very difficult position, because as America's key ally it will be expected to support the system, and the number of radar bases in Britain will be key to its successful operation. On the other hand, it seems that there is very little support for the NMD system within the British government or in the Labour Party. Relations with Europe have also been complicated by the debate over the development of a European rapid reaction force, which also seems to divide the Bush administration. Rumsfeld has expressed concern that a European force would undermine the coherence of NATO, while Colin Powell (the Secretary of State) has said (in public at least) that he has no such worries. At the bottom of this issue are more general strains within European–American relations. The Americans have always said they want Europe to shoulder more of the burden of providing for its own security, particularly when it comes to operations within Europe. When viewed from Europe, however, it seems the Americans want to dictate the terms of any enhanced European security force.

Economic issues

Bush proclaimed that one of his administration's highest priorities was the expansion of the free trade agenda. If Bush is going to do this he needs fast-track authority to protect any negotiated agreement from amendment when it eventually comes before Congress for approval. This demand was a central theme in his election campaign and was reiterated in his first address to Congress. However, as with Clinton, Bush faces serious obstacles. There are the usual pressures from environmental and labour groups, and the American public is divided over the benefits of free trade. A poll in early 2001 showed that by 48 percent to 34 percent Americans think free trade is bad for the economy (*Washington Post*, March 18 2001). Bush also faces opposition to the granting of fast-track authority from within his own party. The last time the House of Representatives voted on the issue in 1998, 71 Republican congressmen voted against allowing Clinton fast-track authority. These Republicans were a mixture of Southern and Western conservatives and moderate Republicans in districts with a strong labor union presence. The House is even more closely divided now than it was then.

The other big economic matter confronting the Bush administration's foreign policy is the state of the American economy (see Chapter 10), as NMD is likely to cost up to $60 billion. Alongside the development of NMD the administration is also conducting a Strategic Review in order to rationalize and re-orientate the US military; and it has promised increased defense spending, possibly by as much as $6 billion. At the same time, the American economy is on the verge of a recession, and combined with the costs of responding to the terrorist attacks on New York and Washington, DC, additional defense spending raises the question of whether the Bush administration will be able to fund its foreign policy objectives without massively increasingly the government deficit (something Republicans in Congress have adamantly opposed in recent years). If America does slip into a recession, there is likely to be more domestic opposition to further free trade deals.

The abandonment of multilateralism?

Beyond NMD there were other indications that the Bush administration was intent on pursuing a more unilateral foreign policy. The most high profile of these was the withdrawal from the Kyoto Accord on climate change, signed by Clinton in 1997. This accord called for industrialized countries to reduce emissions of greenhouse gases by an average of 5.2 percent from their 1990 levels by 2012. The rationale for withdrawing was that the Accord itself was badly negotiated and would not lead to an effective reduction in the global level of greenhouse gas emissions. Whatever the truth of this argument, withdrawal reinforced the perception that the Bush administration was less committed to multilateral solutions to global problems, especially when American business interests were at stake. Withdrawal from the Accord led to international condemnation, particularly from European countries and from Japan, where the Accord had been agreed. America's withdrawal threatened the entire process of international agreement on climate change. After the international outcry the administration appeared to soften its stance a little by agreeing to join climate change talks in Bonn, but it still remains adamantly opposed to the Kyoto Accord.

Another indication of Bush's move toward a less multilateral foreign policy were the initial commitments to reduce overseas troop deployment, especially noncombat missions such as peacekeeping forces. The former Yugoslavia has been mentioned as a area where American troops may be withdrawn from their peacekeeping role; and Rumsfeld has indicated that he wants to withdraw American troops engaged in the peacekeeping operations in the Sinai (supporting the Israel–Egypt peace agreement). It remains to be seen how this will work in practice, and the initial indications are that the administration is changing its stance, partly as a result of pressure from America's allies. Balanced against this, Colin Powell promised "strong support for the work of the UN," and said that that the days of acrimony between Congress and the UN were over. It is very far from clear that this is actually the case. As Congressman Joe Scarborough (R-Fla) said, "any republican president who expects the House members and probably the newer members of the Senate to merrily go along and rubber-stamp" his national security polices "will be very disappointed" (quoted in Kitfield, 1999).

The pursuit of a more unilateral foreign policy has created opposition at home and abroad. At home it generated an unprecedented attack from the Senate Majority Leader Tom Daschle (D-SD). Daschle said the pursuit of NMD and withdrawal from the Kyoto Accord were "very divisive," and that the Bush administration was isolating America and in so doing minimizing its influence. When asked about this, Senator Lieberman (D-Conn.) said Daschle was "absolutely right . . . President Bush has begun to follow a unilateral foreign policy that has separated us from our allies." Abroad, apart from the vocal condemnations of NMD and of the withdrawal from Kyoto, there were other indications that the Bush foreign policy was causing an international backlash. America was voted off two United Nations panels, one on drug control and the other on human rights. Such action is only a gesture, of course, but it is a significant one. A State Department spokesman said: "I think it is fair to speculate there may be issues related to how we handled ourselves."

Responding to September 11 2001

The response to the worst terrorist attack ever perpetrated on American soil is the most significant foreign policy challenge in over a generation. In terms of the problems associated with any of the possible responses, it may even be the most difficult set of foreign policy decisions that any American government has been forced to take. The consequences of any kind of military action will be hard to foresee and hard to control. One of the problems confronting Bush's foreign policy team is what kind of military options are likely to be available. After the Gulf War and the experience of Somalia, Colin Powell articulated what has become know as the "Powell doctrine." This doctrine asserts that America should only commit combat troops when vital national interests are at stake, and when other avenues such as diplomacy have been exhausted. If troops are committed, they should have clearly defined political and military objectives and have the support of the American people and Congress (Powell, 1992). There is at the moment public support for military action and there are vital national interests at stake. The problem lies in relating military action to clearly defined political objectives. The use of military force is a very blunt instrument in the fight against terrorist groups. In addition to having limited utility, the use of military force raises the question of how long the American public will tolerate large numbers of American military casualities or the civilian casualties that might result.

The Bush administration is also facing a dilemma over the balance between cooperation with other states and unilateral action. At the moment there is still a high level of international sympathy for America and broad, but largely unspecified, support for some American military action. In the medium term the key to combating international terrorism is clearly international cooperation with other states in terms of sharing intelligence, tracing money and controlling arms flows. This approach will require the cooperation of states in Europe and the Middle East, as well as Russia. If the Bush administration wants this kind of cooperation to continue it will undermine a more unilateral foreign policy as all of these states will have their own sets of priorities which the Americans will need to take into account. In the short term, however, while there is clearly a lot of domestic support for military action, this could cause international support for America to dwindle. Russia is supportive of America's response to the attacks. They see new opportunities for cooperation with America, and they have their own problems in dealing with Islamic groups in Chechnya. Concern about stability in Central Asia and about American aggression will, however, make Russia very wary of large-scale military action by the United States. In Europe too there are anxieties about the extent to which America should engage in a large-scale military operation.

With the exception of Britain, most European states are anxious about the possible loss of civilian lives in such a venture and also again about American unilateralism. NATO has taken the unprecedented step of invoking the mutual assistance clause, but it remains to be seen how much support NATO members will continue to give America, as the conflict drags on. With regard to these states the problem for America is to balance desire for short-term action against the desire to ensure these states cooperate with America in the long run.

Perhaps most difficult of all is dealing with the countries of the Middle East. Many of these states are allies of America, but many of them also have domestic political concerns of their own, as sections of their populace are anti-American, if not sympathetic to Islamic militancy, and these internal concerns are bound to limit the support and cooperation they offer to America. Pakistan is in the most obvious difficulty. There is case for arguing that one of the main objectives of many Islamic militant groups is to destablize the more moderate (or what they see as un-Islamic) regimes in the region. There is an obvious danger that American military action will in fact produce just this result and not only reduce the possibility of the medium-term cooperation in the fight against terrorism, but also create a whole new set of foreign policy problems.

Finally the Bush administration has to deal with the dilemma between security and economic imperatives. Clinton was right when he said that global processes affect America's economy, the health of its people and the safety of its cities. What Clinton did not say was that there are trade-offs in dealing with global forces. Economic globalization has the potential to threaten America's security as people, money, weaponry, and information move more freely. But dealing with this has economic implications precisely because it is necessary to control more strictly the movement of people, money, and weaponry. Ultimately this is the great dilemma facing America and, indeed, all states today. Until the attacks on New York and Washington, DC America had not directly confronted the malevolent aspects of globalization. Now that it has, some very hard choices will have to be made.

Chapter 15

Direct Democracy

ELISABETH GERBER

One aspect of American politics that may be easily overlooked by people outside the USA is the use of *direct democracy* (or "direct legislation"). Direct democracy refers primarily to the use of *initiatives* and *referendums*. Although some people also consider the recall in which citizens force a special election before the end of an official's term as a form of direct democracy, this chapter concentrates on processes which allow citizens to vote directly on laws rather than on the early dismissal of their representatives (see Cronin, 1989). In direct democracy, regular citizens – as opposed to elected representatives – pass laws by voting on ballot propositions. The difference between initiatives and referendums derives from where the propositions originate. Initiatives are proposed by ordinary citizens who must circulate petitions and collect a pre-determined number of signatures to qualify their measure for the ballot (this number varies from jurisdiction to jurisdiction). Referendums are proposed by legislative bodies. They are then either placed on the ballot automatically or are forced on to the ballot by citizen petition. Initiatives and referendums can be used to pass state constitutional amendments or statutory legislation.

In recent years, many of the most controversial political debates in the USA have taken place over ballot initiatives. For example, in 1994, voters in California passed an initiative statute that prohibited the provision of most social services to illegal immigrants. The measure, Proposition 187, sparked a national debate over immigration policy, polarized the California electorate, mobilized unprecedented numbers of foreign-born citizens to vote, particularly Latinos, and probably caused the then Governor, Pete Wilson, to overcome a huge public opinion deficit and win re-election. Recent statewide measures to ban same-sex marriages, legalize marijuana, try juvenile criminals as adults, and allow physician-assisted suicide have all been passed by initiatives.

Direct democracy is used in most modern democracies, typically to decide matters of major national importance such as the adoption of a new constitution or membership in an international organization. The most frequent European user of direct democracy is Switzerland, which held 102 national initiative or referendum votes between 1992 and 2000 (Initiative

Figure 15.1 *Citizen initiatives by state 1992–8*

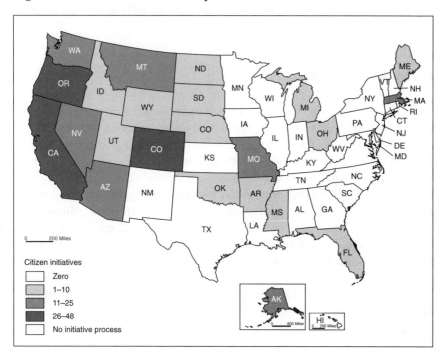

and Referendum Institute, 2001b). In the USA, there is no national initiative or referendum, making direct democracy unique to states and localities. No fewer than 27 American states allow some form of direct democracy, with 24 allowing the direct initiative. All states except Delaware allow or require citizen approval of constitutional amendments proposed by the state legislature, and thousands of counties, cities, towns, townships, villages, and other localities allow some forms of direct democracy. Frequency of usage varies greatly across states, as shown in Figure 15.1.

Understanding how American direct democracy functions is important for a number of reasons. First, many laws are made this way, and they embody some of the most salient and controversial public policy debates in contemporary American government. Second, direct democracy affects other areas of government by constraining the activities of policy-makers and elected representatives. As an example, many people believe that the tax limitation initiatives passed in a number of states in the late 1970s and early 1980s fundamentally changed the way state and local governments function by restructuring the way taxes were raised and allocated between levels of government (Sears and Citrin, 1982). Third, understanding direct democracy provides insight into other questions about American government, such as citizen competence, the role of organized interest groups, and the influence of money, that are more difficult to isolate in the context of representative government.

Historical context

Since their colonial beginnings, the American states have struggled with the problem of how to balance direct and indirect citizen participation in government (see also Chapter 19). In understanding this struggle, it is important to be clear that American democracy is, and always has been, fundamentally a representative democracy, where citizen participation is largely limited to electing representatives. Layered upon that basic structure of representative democracy, many governments throughout American history have allowed their citizens additional, more direct forms of participation. During the colonial era, this participation often took the form of town hall meetings, where all eligible residents – that is, white adult male property owners – participated in debating and enacting legislation. In some colonies, direct participation also took the form of popular ratification of state constitutions and popular ratification of the US Constitution (see Cronin, 1989).

By the time of the Constitutional Convention of 1787, deep cleavages had emerged between several of the framers on the appropriate role of citizen involvement in the proposed government. On one side of the debate was Thomas Jefferson, who forcefully advocated expanding citizen participation in government, albeit with important restrictions on who would be eligible to participate (again, limited to white adult male property owners). Jefferson envisioned a new nation organized around small agricultural communities where all citizens would be involved in government decision-making. On the other side of the debate was Jefferson's fellow Virginian, James Madison. Madison advocated a much more limited role for citizen involvement. In his republican government, citizens would be limited to electing their state legislators and members of Congress. Even the election of US Senators and the President would be indirect, through the state legislatures (for Senators) and the Electoral College (for the President). In the end, advocates of limited participation prevailed, with the resulting Constitution providing little role for direct citizen involvement in the new government.

A century later, many of the "republican" features of American government came under fire from Populist and then Progressive reformers. Emerging in the 1880s, the Populists were concerned with the social, political, and economic consequences of industrialization. One of their proposed reforms was to introduce direct legislation as a mechanism for passing laws that advanced populist ideals such as public ownership of industry, currency reform, and so on. While their ideas were viewed as quite radical by many mainstream Americans, the Populists' advocacy of direct democracy placed the issue on the national reform agenda.

Then, around the turn of the century, a new reform movement – the Progressive movement – emerged as a serious, legitimate political force. The Progressives were concerned with what they perceived as the social ills of their time, particularly government corruption, economic consolidation, and a decline of morality (concerns that many reformers still articulate today). The Progressives held that in addition to providing a way to pass reform legislation, citizen (that is middle-class) participation in government was of inherent value, in and of itself. Their preferred mechanism for this participation was the initiative and referendum. Through election of sympathetic state legislators, a public relations blitz, and a lot of luck, the Progressives succeeded in pushing the adoption of direct democracy through 19 states by 1918.

Over the following decades, reformers in a number of states used direct democracy to pass election reform, tax reform, economic regulation, and social/moral legislation. However, despite the promises of its progressive champions, most modern observers agree that the legislative advances made in the early years of direct democracy were quite modest. By the mid-1920s, the progressive wave had largely subsided and few initiatives were making their way to state ballots. Over the next several decades, a handful of states added the direct democracy option to their state constitutions, but usually with little fanfare or national notice. In short, after a flurry of activity in the first two decades of the twentieth century, direct democracy was rarely used for most of the century and had a minimal impact on state policy (although less is known about its impact on local policy).

Then, in the late 1970s, something dramatic happened. Figure 15.2 shows the number of initiatives appearing on the ballots in three states and nationwide during each decade since 1900. No one is exactly sure what happened in the 1970s to trigger this dramatic change. Most likely it was the result of a confluence of many factors, including increasing gridlock and unresponsiveness in state legislatures, the establishment of broad-based citizen interest groups whose large numbers made direct democracy a natural political vehicle, and the emergence of policy entrepreneurs who seized upon direct democracy as a way to force new issues on to the political agenda. Whatever the exact causes for the re-emergence of direct democracy in the late 1970s, it is clear that the consequence has been a dramatic restructuring of the political landscape in several states.

Figure 15.2   *Number of initiatives, by decade*

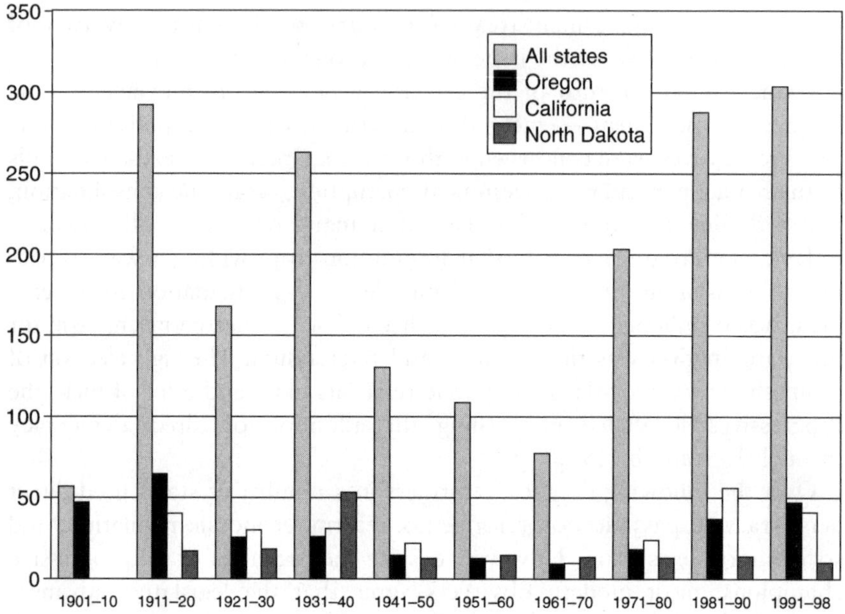

Recent trends

Behind the figures showing an enormous increase in the use of direct democracy are several important, interconnected trends. One major trend is the huge increase in the cost of initiative campaigns. Table 15.1 shows the total amount of campaign spending and the average cost of initiatives and referendums over the last several election cycles in one state, California. California is somewhat unique in that the sheer magnitude of campaign spending far exceeds that in other states. However, we see the same sort of trend, in terms of an enormous increase in costs over recent decades, in most other states as well.

Clearly, ballot measure campaigns have become more expensive. These increasing costs result from a number of factors. One has to do with the increasing cost of qualifying initiatives for the ballot. In all states, initiative proponents must collect a pre-determined number of signatures (usually of registered voters) to qualify an initiative for the ballot. These signature requirements are typically a percentage of the number of voters who cast ballots in the last gubernatorial or other statewide election race, ranging from 2 percent in North Dakota to 15 percent in Wyoming. In all but the smallest states, this translates into hundreds of thousands of signatures.

Table 15.1   *Spending on California statewide propositions, 1992–2000*

Year	Number	Total spending	Average spending
1992[a]	13	$31,408,222	$2,416,017
1993[b]	7	19,902,797	2,843,257
1994	19	48,503,076	2,552,793
1996	27	141,274,345	5,232,383
1998	21	247,305,548	11,776,455
2000[c]	8	133,525,061	16,690,633

[a]   Through October 1992, general election measures only.
[b]   Through October 1993, general election measures only.
[c]   Through December 31, 2000, general election measures only.

These sheer numbers mean that proponents cannot rely strictly on volunteers to collect these signatures, and instead employ professional signature gatherers. The use of paid signature gatherers has generated substantial controversy and has been the subject of numerous recent lawsuits (see Garrett, 1995 for a discussion of these suits). For our purposes, the practice is important because it has increased the cost of qualification. In California, the going rate is about $1 per signature. With over 850,000 valid signatures required to qualify a constitutional initiative, and additional signatures usually collected to insure against invalidation of fraudulent, incomplete, or improperly completed petitions, proponents must collect (and pay for) up to 1 million signatures.

These qualification costs are just the beginning. A second factor underlying the increasing cost of initiative campaigns is the nature of campaign advertising. Initiative proponents have come to rely more and more on paid advertising, especially television commercials and direct mail. For any given campaign, the total cost will depend on many factors, including the nature of the issue (what do voters already know about it?), the election environment (is it a special, primary, or general election?) and the opposition's strategies (how much do they spend, and do they use television and direct mail?). In the end, most successful initiative campaigns in most states cost their proponents millions of dollars.

These skyrocketing costs have contributed to a second major trend. After a high point in the late 1980s, there has been a significant slowing of usage nationwide and in the states where initiatives and referendums are most common. This slowdown is probably due to the poor performance of many expensive initiatives at the polls. In the 1988 elections in California, for example, proponents and opponents of five competing insurance initiatives spent a total of $80 million (in 1988 dollars). Only one of the five initiatives passed (Proposition 103), and this was the measure on which the least was spent and on which the opposition targeted much of their resources. After spending millions of dollars and watching their propositions go down in defeat, potential initiative proponents no doubt began to understand that for most policies, direct democracy just is not a very good investment.

A third major trend has to do with the kinds of measures that qualify for the ballot. Over the last decade, the measures that made it to the ballot have increasingly dealt with social policy issues. It is useful to distinguish between three types of issue contained in ballot measures (and in all types of legislation): political reform, economic policy, and social policy. Political reform measures attempt to restructure government and the nature of political relationships. They include things like term limitations, campaign finance reform, changes in the roles and responsibilities of elected officials, changes in electoral laws, and so on. Economic policy measures attempt to restructure economic relationships. These measures tend to deal with taxation and the regulation of specific economic actors or activities. Social policy measures attempt to restructure social relationships. They deal with issues such as civil rights and civil liberties, restrictions on access to abortion, gun control, medicinal marijuana, same-sex marriages, physician-assisted suicide, and so on. Of course, many initiative propositions, like all other types of legislation, deal with several issues simultaneously, such as increasing taxes and earmarking those taxes for specific expenditures. This is true despite the fact that many states have "single subject" requirements that limit the number of subjects covered in a single ballot proposition. For example, California's Proposition 99 of 1988 increased the state's tax on tobacco products (economic policy) to pay for a range of health-care related social policies. Numerous states have increased taxes on gasoline specifically to pay for transportation projects.

Recent research by Tolbert (2001) shows that, in the period from 1980 through 1996, over 17 percent of all statewide ballot initiatives dealt with social policy issues. While this proportion is roughly the same as the proportion of social policy initiatives appearing between 1900 and 1920, the total number of statewide initiatives has increased dramatically in recent decades, meaning that the *number* of social policy initiatives has increased as well. There are a number of reasons for this trend. One reason is social: as American society becomes more affluent, citizens become less concerned with bread-and-butter economic issues and focus more on quality-of-life social issues. Numerous studies have documented this change toward more social issues on the American political agenda (see Inglehart, 1977); it stands to reason that a similar change would take place in the kinds of issue that qualify as ballot initiatives. A second reason for a greater emphasis on social issues is political: initiatives often deal with issues that legislatures have neglected to take up. Legislative bodies tend to avoid issues that are polarizing or that cut across partisan lines. Many social issues have these characteristics, and when policy advocates support the sorts of issue that make legislatures uncomfortable, they may have no options but to circumvent the legislature and appeal directly to the voters.

A fourth major trend is that many of the issues that now qualify for the ballot are highly controversial. In some ways, this trend is a direct consequence of the increasing incidence of social policy issues; these issues, by their nature, tend to be emotionally charged and polarizing. In addition, a number of other developments contribute to the controversial nature of many recent ballot propositions. As described above, successful initiative campaigns in most states cost millions of dollars. Initiative proponents must mobilize vast resources to qualify and effectively campaign for a statewide initiative. These resources include both financial resources to pay the costs of qualification and advertisement, as well as other resources such as expertise for drafting the measure, volunteers to circulate petitions and engage in campaign activities, free media coverage, and so on. Because mobilizing resources involves getting people to make voluntary contributions to public goods, proponents (and opponents) will find it easier to mobilize these resources when people feel strongly about an issue (see Olson, 1965; Walker, 1991). Emotional issues such as gun control, abortion, physician-assisted suicide and the like may trigger this form of political action.

A second reason initiatives tend to deal with controversial issues is because of the nature of modern direct democracy campaigns. Unlike regular legislation, where elected representatives debate proposed legislation on the statehouse floor and in the proverbial smoke-filled rooms, direct legislation campaigns are highly public events. Because proponents and opponents must appeal directly to voters, the debate literally takes place in people's living rooms, or wherever their television sets are located. In addition to driving up costs, media such as television and direct mail determine the kind of information people have. Specifically, to attract voters' attention, campaigners have an incentive to frame their policy debate in stark, polarizing terms. Thus, even if the issue itself is not particularly controversial, the need to attract attention and provide a take-home message forces campaigners to frame issues in more polarized terms.

Controversies

Public opinion evidence shows that direct democracy is extremely popular among Americans. A recent poll of 992 adults, sampled from across the country, found that 68 percent favor the initiative process in their state, compared to less than 14 percent who oppose it (Rasmussen Research, 2001). Additionally, 58 percent favor establishing a similar process at the federal level, while only 21 percent oppose it. Despite this public support, the process attracts a great deal of controversy wherever it is used, and it has been the subject of attack by political reformers in many states. Much of this controversy revolves around the following questions about how the process works and how it affects other areas of the political system.

Citizen competence: do voters make good laws?

One of the most common criticisms of direct democracy is that regular citizens are incapable of making good laws. Critics argue that voters lack the information, reasoning capacity, or motivation to understand and decide complicated public policy propositions (see Donovan and Bowler, 1998). They note that many ballot propositions, particularly in the area of economic policy, are long and complex, and often deal with technical issues that are unfamiliar to most voters. They observe that when asked simple questions on surveys, most citizens reveal extremely low levels of substantive information about politics in general, and about ballot propositions in particular. Even when citizens are familiar with the issues they are voting on, critics argue that their decisions are self-interested, short-sighted, and fail to take into account the impact of their decisions on other aspects of policy and government.

This line of criticism raises an important question: what do citizens need to know to make good decisions? Does the fact that they lack much substantive information about ballot propositions – a fact that virtually no one disputes – necessarily mean that they will make bad decisions? The answer to these questions largely depends on what one means by "good" and "bad" decisions. If one takes the term "good decisions" to mean decisions with which one agrees in substance, then it is really the preferences of the citizen lawmakers, and not their capabilities, that matters. If one takes the term "good decisions" to mean political decisions that systematically take into account all of the possible costs and benefits of a particular choice, to the individual and all others affected, then few citizens could be expected meet this standard. However, in response to this conclusion, one might question whether this standard can reasonably be met by any decision-makers, including professional bureaucrats, interest group advocates, or elected representatives themselves, and conclude that it cannot. Thus, if we apply a more realistic standard and ask whether citizens can make the same sorts of decisions as the policy-makers who make most policy decisions, the answer changes. Most social scientists now agree that under reasonable conditions, citizens can use cues, information shortcuts, and available information to make "informed" decisions: that is, the same sort of decisions they would make if they had all of the information available at the time they are making the decision (Lupia, 1994; Donovan and Bowler, 1998; Karp, 1998). In other words, most analysts concur that citizen competence *per se* is not a major problem in the practice of direct democracy.

Quality of legislation: do amateurs write good laws?

A second criticism, related to the first, is whether regular citizens (and interest groups) write "good" legislation. As above, the answer to this question depends largely on the definition of "good" that one employs. If we interpret the term "good legislation" to mean whether a piece of initiative legislation achieves some normative standard, such as fairness or equity or liberty, then it is not at all clear whether the process produces good or bad legislation. As previously, an important comparison is whether direct legislation produces legislation that is better or worse than the legislative process, and in what ways. This comparison represents perhaps one of the most difficult theoretical questions in modern political philosophy – what political systems produce the best legislation – and it is far from resolved.

If we interpret the term "good legislation" in more practical terms, to mean whether the laws that qualify for the ballot have clear language that is both constitutional and likely to result in the policy outcomes intended by the proponents, then the question is easier to answer. Most scholars would conclude that citizens do not, in fact, write good legislation by this definition. Most successful initiatives are challenged on legal grounds. Of those that are challenged, most are overturned, in part or in their entirety (Miller, 1999). Only a small fraction survive the legal challenges and, even for those that survive, proponents often complain that bureaucrats and other policy-makers were able to re-interpret the language to implement policies different from those intended when the initiative was written (Gerber *et al.*, 2000).

Why do citizens write legislation that is ambiguous, unclear, or unconstitutional? In some cases, the reason is a lack of experience. There are no restrictions on who can write initiatives: authors of initiative propositions need not be lawyers, bureaucrats, or politicians with experience writing legislation, and they do not even need to have any specialized knowledge of the area in which their legislation falls. Of course, in some cases, initiative proponents do have this expertise, but there is no requirement that they do, and occasionally initiatives qualify for the ballot that are truly the product of amateur legislators.

In other cases, initiative proponents are fully capable of writing clear or constitutional legislation, but they do not. In these cases, the cause of unclear or unconstitutional language may be political expediency. It may be difficult or impossible to pass initiative legislation that is clearly written and highly detailed since such legislation provides a much clearer target for opponents (see Alvarez, 1997). Thus, proponents may believe their only option is to pass a vague or ambiguous law, and take their chances in the courts. It is also important to note that most laws passed by legislatures are also challenged in the courts, reinterpreted in the executive branch, or rewritten in the legislature. In this context, the main difference between regular legislation and initiative legislation is that it can be extremely difficult to make minor changes or improvements to initiatives after they pass. Most states and localities restrict amendments to initiatives after they pass, and so the consequences of "bad" legislation may be more lasting (see Dubois and Feeney, 1992).

Minority rights: does the majority tyrannize minorities?

A third criticism is that direct democracy allows a political majority to tyrannize against a political minority or minorities. This criticism follows directly from the majoritarian logic of direct democracy: proponents need only obtain the support of the slimmest majority of voters – 50 percent plus one – to pass initiatives and referendums, even over the strong objections of the large opposing minority. The fear is that a single group will comprise the minority across many issues, and that their rights and interests will be systematically undermined by the majority. This line of argument dates at least to the founding era, when Madison and his contemporaries worried that the poor masses would pass legislation that stripped the country's economic elite of their power. In recent years, concern has turned to the vulnerability of racial and ethnic minorities in the face of a white voting majority, although some authors contest this analysis. (Gamble, 1997; Donovan and Bowler, 1998; Frey and Goette, 1998).

There is some evidence that states and localities that use direct democracy pass different laws from otherwise similar places that do not. Specifically, policies in direct democracy cities and states more closely reflect the (estimated) preferences of the majority of the electorate than do policies in places that prohibit direct democracy (see Gerber, 1996). For this effect on policy to translate into tyranny of the majority, however, there must also be polarization of preferences. In other words, for whites to use direct democracy at the expense of nonwhites, it must be the case that whites hold similar policy preferences, that nonwhites hold similar preferences, and that the preferences of these groups differ. Recent research shows that neither whites nor nonwhites tend to vote as cohesive blocs, but rather that there is a great deal of heterogeneity within these segments of the electorate (Hajnal, Gerber and Louch, 2001). This line of research further provides no evidence that racial and ethnic minorities systematically lose out in direct democracy votes at the state level, although this may be more problematic in smaller communities where there is greater homogeneity within racial groups (Donovan and Bowler, 1998).

Money: do wealthy interest groups dominate?

Earlier in this chapter, we noted the tremendous increase in the cost of direct democracy campaigns. This trend has fueled a fourth criticism of the process: only wealthy special interest groups can use direct democracy. Ironically, these wealthy special interests are precisely the same sorts of interests whose influence over the state legislative process Progressive reformers sought to circumvent through the adoption of direct democracy (Gerber, 1999).

Clearly, money is an important factor in modern direct democracy. Only interests that can amass substantial sums can qualify their initiatives for the ballot and compete for the voters' attention and support (Garrett, 1999). However, it is also clear that while money is necessary for success in passing initiatives, it is not sufficient (Garrett and Gerber, 2001). Recent research shows that the initiatives that are most likely to pass are not those on which proponents spend the most money (Lowenstein, 1982; Owens and Wade, 1986; Smith, 2001); the initiatives that are most likely to pass are those proposed by broad-based citizen interest groups. These groups can rarely match the financial resources of economic interest groups; when they can mobilize sufficient resources to qualify their measures and engage in some basic campaign activities, however, they are often successful. Their success shows that it is not money that dominates the process, but rather the ability to appeal to a broad coalition of voters.

Representative government: does direct democracy undermine the legislative process?

Finally, critics argue that direct democracy undermines the legislative process. Not surprisingly, this criticism often comes from legislators themselves who complain that initiatives prevent them from doing their jobs. They (and others) argue that direct democracy affects them in at least three ways. First, citizens may pass laws that directly restrict what legislators can do. Many political reform measures limit the resources that legislators and other policy-makers have at their disposal (Tolbert, 1998). Other initiatives, particularly economic policy measures, mandate certain expenditures or earmark certain revenues, thereby leaving legislators with fewer options and less discretion. Second, citizens may pass laws that indirectly constrain legislators. When voters pass laws in a particular policy area, it may be difficult or impossible for legislators to amend, revise, reverse, or otherwise change policies in that area (Gerber 1998, Gerber and Hug, 2001). Third, the presence of direct democracy may lead legislators to do things that they would not otherwise. Specifically, legislators may pass laws they would not otherwise in order to pre-empt initiatives that they (and their constituencies) find particularly unattractive (Gerber, 1996).

Clearly, initiatives affect legislative behavior in these ways. The unresolved question, however, is whether these effects on the legislative process improve or undermine representative government. The Progressive reformers envisioned direct democracy as a way of checking an unresponsive legislature; reasonable people disagree about whether these checks are for the better or the worse.

Future developments

It is difficult to predict the future of direct democracy in American states and localities. In many places, reformers have pressed to limit the power of initiatives and referendums by making it more difficult to initiate, qualify, campaign for, and defend direct legislation. Overwhelming public support, however, implies that direct democracy is here to stay, in some form, for some time to come. In addition, there are a number of developments that have recently appeared on the political horizon.

National initiative or referendum

Periodically, advocates call for the adoption of a national initiative and/or referendum. Polls consistently show strong support among the voting public for the idea of a national initiative or referendum (for example, 58 percent of respondents in a 2001 poll supported the idea, while only 21 percent opposed it: Rasmussen Research, 2001). Despite the popular appeal of such a proposal, however, adoption of national direct democracy would require the passage of an amendment to the US Constitution. Since elected representatives from the major political parties tend to strongly oppose direct democracy, most observers concur that the current political configurations in the US Congress and most state legislatures make this possibility highly unlikely.

Internet voting

Several states are considering proposals to allow for voting for candidates for political office over the Internet. In California, several efforts are moving forward: the Secretary of State recently convened an Internet task-force charged with developing recommendations on how to implement Internet voting; the state legislature passed a measure that was subsequently vetoed by the Governor; and several groups proposed initiatives that failed to qualify for the ballot. Other states, such as Washington, are seriously considering proposals for Internet voting and, in 2000, Arizona used Internet voting in the state's Democratic primary (Chernay, 2000). Advocates of direct democracy see the Internet as a natural mechanism for increasing citizen participation in lawmaking as well. Opponents point to the problems of unequal access to Internet technology and the potential for fraud as issues that must be resolved before Internet voting in ballot propositions could become a reality.

Conclusion

Since its adoption at the beginning of the twentieth century, direct democracy has become an important part of the political landscape in a number of American states and hundred of localities. Direct democracy allows citizens the ability to directly pass or nullify legislation and constitutional amendments. As such, initiatives and referendums offer voters an opportunity to shape public policy that is unique in the American context. Direct democracy empowers different interests from those empowered by traditional legislative politics. It creates different opportunities for political access and engenders powerful and often passionate support and opposition. Many Americans feel highly ambivalent toward the process: they hate it because it brings politics to their attention, and may produce policy outcomes that they oppose. At the same time, they cherish the process because it provides what many voters believe is an essential check on the legislative process.

Chapter 16

Religion and Morality

SUSAN B. HANSEN

Religion is highly salient in American politics today. Candidates for President routinely invoke the Deity in their speeches and discuss political issues in moralistic terms. Religious groups are increasingly active at all levels of the political system as they attempt to mobilize voters, select candidates, and appoint judges who share their beliefs. Religious beliefs figure prominently in public-policy debates over issues as diverse as school choice, abortion, foreign policy, and gay rights. Early in 2001 the Bush administration established an Office of Faith-Based Programs in the White House and planned federal subsidies to religious institutions as agents for the delivery of services such as welfare, job training, and abstinence education (see also Chapter 12).

Although religious issues may be highly salient, religious influence is seldom the definitive or dominant factor with respect to public opinion, voting behavior, or public policy. Its limited influence is due in part to the diversity of religious beliefs and institutions in the US Religious influence is also constrained by broader cultural trends that endorse individual freedom, self-expression, and the pursuit of happiness rather than transcendent moral values. Finally, because of the complex American political system with its many veto points, religious influence is likely to be limited to a geographical area dominated by one particular religious perspective. And because American society is highly mobile, even areas such as Utah and the Bible Belt have found the earlier religious hegemony of Mormons and Southern Baptists challenged by the influx of immigrants from other parts of the USA.

This chapter will first describe some contemporary trends in religious affiliation, beliefs, and voting behavior in the United States before considering the current impact of religion on political elites and public policy. It concludes with a review of recent assessments of the role of religion on American politics and especially the influence of the Religious Right, a term used for a broad movement of conservatives who espouse traditional moral and social values. This movement has undergone substantial organizational change in the last 25 years. It first attracted extensive public attention when the Reverend Jerry Falwell founded The Moral Majority in

1979, which he led until 1989. The Moral Majority was succeeded by the Reverend Pat Robertson's Christian Coalition, which grew out of his failed 1988 Presidential campaign and (under the executive directorship of Ralph Reed) developed close ties with the Republican Party and became a powerful political force.

Trends in American religiosity

Although the United States was founded largely by Protestants, secularization and generations of immigration have produced highly diverse patterns of religious affiliation, as Table 16.1 shows. Roman Catholics, although still a minority, constitute the largest single denomination. "Mainline" Protestants (Episcopalians, Methodists, Presbyterians, and Lutherans), were historically dominant and remain a sizeable percentage of American believers, but their numbers have shrunk considerably since 1960. Evangelical Protestants are a sizable and fast-growing group and by 1990, evangelical Protestants outnumbered "mainline" Protestants in the USA by 28,000,000 to 26,000,000 (Utter and Storey, 1995). There is a distinction between evangelical and "mainline" Protestants: evangelicals are distinguished by pietistic rather than liturgical religious beliefs and most claim to be "born again" Christians (that is, to have had a life-altering conversion experience as adults). Fundamentalists, a subset of evangelicals, tend to believe in the literal interpretation of the Bible and to accept the truth of Christian doctrines unquestioningly. Evangelicals and fundamentalists are the mainstays of the Religious Right, but it also draws support from "mainline" Protestants, Roman Catholics and Orthodox Jews who espouse traditional moral values, even if they differ on theology.

Beyond the older denominations, a number of newer religious groups (such as Mormons and Jehovah's Witnesses) are attracting increased numbers of adherents. The proportion of Jews has declined slightly since the large influx of immigrants between 1880 and 1920, and again after World War II; nevertheless, more Jews reside in America than in Israel. But as of 2000, Muslims outnumber Jews in the United States (Tarjani, 2001). Only about 10 percent of Americans claim to have no religious affiliation or to be atheists.

American society appears to be fairly religious according to several conventional indicators from the Gallup Poll (Table 16.2). The proportion who say they attend church or synagogue weekly peaked in the 1950s, but declined only slightly in the 1980s and has increased since then (Gallup, 2001). However, religiosity (indicated by attendance at worship) is far more prevalent among older rather than younger Americans. Church or synagogue membership remains high, and only a minority of Americans

Table 16.1   *Religious affiliation in the USA (%)*

	1960	1980	1990	2000
Protestant	73	61	56	58
Evangelical	25		24	
Mainline	41		24	
Black	7		8	
Roman Catholic	20	28	25	26
Jewish	3	2	2	2
Other	2	2	6	4
None	2	7	11	10

Source: Adapted from *Gallup Poll Monthly*, March 2000, p. 60. The more detailed Protestant breakdown for 1960 and 1980 is from Kellstedt and Green (1992), p. 56, based on National Election Study data.

accept the view that religion is "old-fashioned" with no relevance to today's problems. Over 45 percent of Protestants claim to have been "born again," a perspective shared by almost all of the recent candidates for president in the United States and by every President of the United States since Jimmy Carter.

Americans are far more likely than citizens in other industrialized democracies to believe in God and Heaven, to pray, and to attend worship services regularly. Only about 50 per cent of Danes or Swedes report belief in God, and less than 20 percent of people in France, the UK, or Norway attend church weekly. Only citizens of the Republic of Ireland or Northern Ireland exhibit levels of religiosity comparable to those of Americans. The 1991 World Values survey found that the United States was virtually the only country where the vote in national elections was essentially unrelated to a measure of belief in God (Wald, 1996). This reflects the lack of variance on that measure among Americans, and the split in many European countries between religious and secular political parties. Data from the Gallup Poll also indicate that, as of June 2000, "the church or organized religion" was an institution in American society in which respondents expressed high levels of confidence. Religion thus ranked well above banks, political institutions, the police, business, labor, or HMOs. However, the 2000 ranking (53 percent) demonstrates considerable decline since 1973, when 66 percent of Americans voiced "a great deal" or "quite a lot" of confidence in religion. This trend may be another indicator of the growing secularization of American society, but may also reflect the numerous scandals (theft, fraud, pedophilia, sexual indiscretions) that have

Table 16.2   *Religiosity of the American public (%)*

	1980	2000
Consider religion very important in their lives	55	61
Member of a church or synagogue	69	67
Attend worship services regularly (weekly or monthly)	53	60
Believe in God	95	86
Pray regularly	89	—
Believe in Hell, Day of Judgement	71	79
Believe religion can answer today's problems	65	68
Religion is old-fashioned	15	19

Source: Adapted from *Gallup Poll Monthly*, December 1999.

afflicted many religious denominations since the 1980s. Of course such indiscretions have received intense coverage by the mass media. As considerable research has found, newspaper and television reporters tend to be far less religious than most Americans; and sinful behavior by ostensibly moral religious or political leaders makes very good copy.

However, the religiosity suggested by these poll responses is countered by other evidence. Seventy-five percent say a religion "other than their own" offers a true path to God, with a majority of these stating that this other path is equally as good as their own. Increasing tolerance is also evident in views of interfaith marriages. Approval of Catholic–Protestant marriages increased from 63 percent in 1968 to 79 percent in 1983; the comparable figures for marriages between Jews and non-Jews rose from 59 to 77 percent (Mayer, 1992). Support for fundamentalist views of the Bible as the "actual word of God to be taken literally" declined from 65 percent in 1963 to 40 percent in 1984 (Mayer, 1992). While 48 percent claim to rely on God and religious teachings in deciding how to conduct their lives, almost as many (45 percent) say they more pay attention to their own views and those of others. This secular perspective is more prevalent among men, younger Americans (65 percent of those 18–29), and those living on either coast (Newport, 1999).

Despite the organizational efforts and increasing prominence of the Religious Right since the 1970s, the general public has become increas-

Table 16.3   *Political preferences of evangelical and mainline Protestants versus those with no religious preference (%)*

	Evangelical Protestant	Mainline Protestant	No religious preference
Republican	39	37	17
Conservative	50	38	24
Vote for Clinton, 1992	35	39	54
Oppose legalizing marijuana	81	74	48
Extramarital sex is wrong	85	80	62
Homosexuality is a choice	63	38	27
Support abortion for any reason	33	47	67
Support school prayer	74	58	29
% divorced	16	15	21

Source: Adapted from 1994 General Social Survey (*N*=2919), cited in Utter and Storey, (1995).

ingly skeptical of many of its most cherished precepts. Although Americans remain more puritanical than most Europeans with respect to sexual matters, acceptance of premarital sex, of recreational drug use, and of homosexuality have all increased since the 1960s, especially among younger voters. Although birth rates to teenagers have declined since 1990, the proportion of out-of-wedlock births to women of all ages continues to increase. The majority of Americans still support the availability of abortion under at least some circumstances; even Catholics support abortion rights (Moore, 1993). Opinion polls show strong general support for prayer in public schools, but this drops precipitously when people are asked who should compose or deliver those prayers. Efforts to ban Hallowe'en or teach creationism do not have widespread support. And despite strenuous efforts by the Religious Right to "Take Back Vermont," that state re-elected most of the officials who had supported legislation legalizing civil unions for gay and lesbian couples (Sneyd, 2000). The growing public acceptance of what the Religious Right abhors as "moral relativism" or "secular humanism" has contributed to the intensity of their campaigns to change both public views and the nation's laws. Its strategy of trying to define gay rights as "special rights" (and hence constitutionally novel) is indicative of such efforts (Mookas, 1998).

However, the overall trend toward more tolerant or secular attitudes within the United States is counterbalanced by the strength and persistence of traditional religious views, especially among adherents of the Religious Right. Table 16.3 contrasts the political and social views of evangelical Protestants, mainline Protestants, and people with no religious preference. Mainline Protestants differ little from their evangelical brethren with respect to party identification, their 1992 vote, their views on the acceptability of extramarital sex, or divorce rates. But mainline Protestants are considerably more accepting of legalizing marijuana, abortion rights, and homosexuality, and are much less likely to support school prayer than are evangelicals and fundamentalists. The most striking differences, however, lie between these religious groupings and those with no religious preference, who take an individualistic or liberal position on all of these issues. The latter group of "seculars" is far less likely be Republican or conservative (Utter and Storey, 1995). The Religious Right's efforts to raise funds and mobilize supporters is, by contrast, fueled by its adamant opposition to "secular humanist" viewpoints, nontraditional life styles, and liberal sexual mores.

Religion and American voting behavior

A generation ago, most political analysts considered religious affiliation to be one of the bedrock predictors of voting behavior. Roman Catholics and Jews were overwhelmingly Democratic; mainline Protestants were overwhelmingly Republican. The Solid South, coterminous with the Bible Belt and Southern Baptist predominance, was also Democratic, although turnout rates by both whites and African-Americans were low. In fact, the 1960 election remains the one where religious factors had the strongest impact compared to other predictors of voting behavior (Kohut *et al.*, 2000).

Since the 1960s, much has changed. Significant numbers of Roman Catholics and Jews are now voting Republican, as are most Muslims. Mainline Protestants are now somewhat more Democratic. The Solid (Democratic) South has largely disappeared: Georgia is now the only Confederate state which has yet to elect a Republican governor or legislature. The major change, however, has been the rise of the Religious Right as a major political force. Before the 1960s, many fundamentalist and evangelical churches emphasized personal salvation rather than political involvement, and not voting was common among these groups (Peele, 1984). But conservative Christians were galvanized into action by several factors, including the 1973 *Roe* v. *Wade* abortion decision, opposition to feminism and the Equal Rights Amendment, and what many groups saw as a dangerous decline in moral values.. The rise of the Religious Right was also facilitated by the advent of direct-mail solicitation, which proved highly successful at raising funds and mobilizing a geographically dispersed group of adherents. Many of these were members of "mainline" denominations disgruntled by the ordination of women and the involvement of their churches in liberal social causes (Wald, 1996).

How have these activities been reflected in voting behavior? Kohut *et al.* (2000) show that throughout the 1970s and 1980s the influence of religious tradition was much lower compared to demographic factors than it had been in 1960. In the 1990s, however, the importance of religion increased considerably. The Religious Right (well-organized through Ralph Reed's leadership of the Christian Coalition) became even more closely entwined with the Republican Party at state and national levels, while secular voters (perhaps in reaction to the rise of the Religious Right) became even more supportive of Democratic candidates. Over this same time period, both Roman Catholics and Jews became somewhat less Democratic, but mainline Protestants remained largely Republican.

Exit-poll data on religious voting in the presidential elections of 1992, 1996, and 2000 are shown in Table 16.4 (based on Dionne, Pomper and Mayer 2001). Blacks (largely Protestant, although no separate breakdown for this group is available for 2000) have become even more firmly wedded to the Democratic candidates. Also, as Kohut *et al.* (2000) found, black Protestants and seculars are the only groups in American society whose voter turnout has increased during the 1990s. Catholic voters have become considerably more Republican in voting patterns, a trend deliberately fostered by the Bush campaign in 2000 (Lizza, 2001). The same is true of white Protestants and Jews. There is a gap of about 40 points in the Republican direction between the Religious Right and other voters in 2000; over 80 percent of the Christian right voted for George W. Bush.

Clearly Americans of different religious persuasions vote differently, but are their religious beliefs the causal factor? Or is religious affiliation simply a surrogate indicator of differences in education, race, region, or social class? Kohut *et al.* (2000) control for a variety of other demographic and political factors and find that religion remains a significant predictor, although the amount of variance explained by religious factors alone is quite small. But religiosity (indexed by frequency of attendance at worship services) remains a better predictor of political opinions and behavior than do religious beliefs.

It is also striking to note the absence of analysis of religious factors in several accounts of the 2000 election by political scientists. Dionne, Mayer and Pomper (2001) has no index entry for religion, and makes only passing reference to the Christian right. A special issue of *PS* (March 2001)

Table 16.4   *Religion and presidential voting, 1992–2000 (%)*

	2000		1996			1992		
	Gore	Bush	Clinton	Dole	Perot	Clinton	Bush	Perot
White Protestants	34	63	36	53	10	33	47	21
Blacks	90	8	84	12	4	83	10	7
Catholics	49	47	53	37	9	44	35	20
Jews	79	19	76	16	3	80	11	9

Note: Totals may not add to 100% because of rounding.
Source: Adapted from Pomper, 2001, p. 138.

stressed aggregate factors as predictors of Presidential votes. In that same issue, Stone and Rapoport credit Ross Perot's third-party movement with making American Presidential and Congressional elections more competitive, but do not analyze Perot's appeal (or lack thereof) to any religious groups. Jacobson's (2001) analysis of voting behavior in 2000 notes in passing that churchgoers were more likely to vote Republican. Wirls (2001) reaches the same conclusion, stressing the importance of regional and rural/urban divisions:

> despite the relative moderation of both presidential candidates and their general avoidance of culturally divisive issues, the voters for the major parties nevertheless formed two fairly distinct and familiar camps, with a predominately white, rural, and religious Republican constituency at odds with a more secular, urban, and racially diverse Democratic core.

But analyses in the popular media often take a different slant. As Lizza (2001) states of the 2000 election: "More than by age, race or gender, the electorate was split in half by religion – or, more precisely, by religiosity . . . the more you attend church, the more likely you are to vote Republican."

A full analysis of the impact of religious factors on voting in 2000 must await the analysis of in-depth survey data. Since the 1980s, the Michigan election surveys have greatly expanded their questions on religion, and can now code religious denominations to reflect the fundamentalist or evangelical beliefs which best predict sympathy for the Religious Right (Kellstedt and Green 1992). Scholars will therefore be able to ascertain whether Kohut *et al.*'s (2000) finding of increasing religious influence on voting holds for 2000, or whether Niemi and Weisberg (2001) are correct in concluding that cleavage politics, based on social class or group attachments, is declining in importance as candidate and issue factors become more salient as predictors of voting behavior.

Parties, candidates, and church involvement in elections

In 1960, John Kennedy tried to minimize the impact of his religion on his policy positions, and took pains to distance himself from the Vatican. However, his Roman Catholicism was widely noted in the media, and is credited with inducing many Southerners to vote Republican for the first time in their lives. But an increase in religion-based voting in the 1990s may reflect growing efforts by parties, churches, and religious interest groups to mobilize voters and endorse candidates who shared their views. Carefully staged prayers at party conventions, party platforms, and speeches are designed to appeal to voters on the basis of their religious beliefs.

The Roman Catholic hierarchy sharply ratcheted up its political activity during the 2000 elections, in part as a consequence of the National Conference of Catholic Bishops' 1998 resolution making a ban on abortion the top political priority of the Church (Conn, 2001). The Roman hierarchy's tactics included using homilies to highlight the issue, publishing diocesan newspaper articles calling for the faithful to vote "pro-life," and questioning the credentials of Al Gore and other pro-choice Democrats. Thousands of voter guides were also distributed to parishes, listing candidates' stands on issues of interest to Roman Catholic voters. But some feared the risk of creating an anti-Catholic backlash by these highly publicized efforts to influence the election, and most Catholics apparently resisted the bishops' appeals. According to a poll conducted by Catholics for a Free Choice, six out of ten Catholics oppose statements from the bishops supporting candidates, 70 percent believe the bishops should not use the political arena to articulate moral viewpoints, and two-thirds believe abortion should remain legal (Conn, 2001). A majority of American Catholics also support the death penalty, despite the Pope's strong opposition to it.

After George Bush was criticized for making a speech at the anti-Catholic Bob Jones University, the Republican Party established a well-funded Republican National Committee Catholic Task Force to win Catholic votes for Bush. The GOP asked Philadelphia's Cardinal Anthony Bevilacqua to give the benediction on prime-time television on the last night of the 2000 Republican convention (Conn, 2001). The bishops lauded Bush's support for vouchers for private and parochial schools and for federal aid for faith-based social services, but appeared to ignore

Governor Bush's frequent use of the death penalty in Texas, a violation of the church's Consistent Life ethic. The Bush campaign did increase its percent of the Catholic vote, but voters in many northeastern states with large Catholic populations voted for Gore, who garnered 49 percent of the Catholic vote (compared with 47 percent for Bush and 53 percent for Clinton in 1996.)

African-American pastors also took an active role in the 2000 election, as they had done ever since the civil rights movement of the 1960s. They offered their pulpits to (mostly Democratic) candidates and urged their parishioners to register and vote, in many instances explicitly urging a Democratic vote. This clergy activism may account at least in part for the strongly Democratic vote by African-Americans in 2000, since they voted even more strongly for Al Gore than they had for Bill Clinton in 1992 or 1996. However, although many African-Americans did vote in 2000, their overall turnout remained well below that of Catholics, Jews, or white members of the Religious Right. In fact, African-Americans and Hispanics in Congress have come out against the proposed McCain–Feingold campaign finance reforms that would ban the use of "soft money," since they have found it extremely useful for ethnically targeted get-out-the-vote drives (Mitchell, 2001). The Religious Right opposes campaign finance reform for the same reasons, and was vehemently hostile to McCain in the 2000 Republican primaries (Abramson, 2000). McCain reciprocated by lambasting the "evil influence" of such celebrities of the Religious Right as Pat Robertson, although this attack on Robertson and his allies hardly helped McCain win Republican votes, especially in closed-primary states (Dionne, Mayer and Pomper, 2001).

The Christian Coalition continued the voter-mobilization efforts it had made since its founding in 1989 to reverse what Pat Robertson has called the "moral decay that threatens our great nation." Over 40 million "Congressional Scorecards" were mailed to members and circulated in churches, showing votes by all members of the Senate and House on "issues critical to the family." This Scorecard urged Christians to register and vote, but included a disclaimer that it was for "informational purposes" only. The Christian Coalition was thus able to claim that it was not trying to influence election outcomes and did not advocate the election or defeat of any candidate, or endorse any political party. Ratings on the Scorecard were not to be taken as a commentary on the personal faith of individual members of Congress.

The Christian Coalition was thus apparently trying to stay within IRS guidelines, which prohibited partisan political activity by tax-exempt organizations. Nevertheless, the IRS, in response to a lawsuit filed by Americans United for the Separation of Church and State, imposed a sizeable fine on Pat Robertson's campaign organizations for violating IRS rules during Robertson's unsuccessful 1988 campaign for President. Americans United and other groups such as the American Civil Liberties Union (ACLU) are considering further legal action against the high levels of church involvement in partisan politics in recent elections.

The 2000 election was remarkable in several other respects. Although religious issues like abortion were generally avoided by the candidates, the personal faith of the candidates was very much in evidence (Woodward, 2000). References to God in 2000 election material exceeded that in any recent election. Both Bush and Gore spoke frequently of their "born-again" status, and the religious and moral views of the first-ever major-party Jewish candidate for vice-president, Senator Joseph Lieberman, received intense media coverage. Except for a few anti-Semitic Internet sites, Lieberman's religion did not appear to be an issue. In fact, polls reported that Americans were now more willing to vote for a Jew or a Catholic than an atheist for President.

Whether or not the candidates' expressions of faith reflected true religious commitment may be open to question; but the religious discourse of political candidates in 2000 did resonate with Americans' own expressed beliefs in God and the Bible, and with their views on morality and the efficacy of prayer. And it meshes well with recent survey data: 51 percent of voters in 2000 thought religion should play a bigger role in public life, and only 12 percent thought it should have a smaller role (Woodward, 2000). In the wake of the various scandals surrounding the Clinton administration, "morality" ranked high on the list of issues the public considered crucial in the campaign, although opinions on this and on the Clinton scandals were highly partisan. Al Gore's selection of Lieberman as his running mate was widely perceived as an attempt by Democrats to defuse the impact of the Clinton scandals and impeachment (Edwards, 2000). However, the Jewish Anti-Defamation League and other prominent political actors were critical of Leiberman's frequent references to God, the Bible, and his faith. Critics felt that politicizing religious belief tempted politicians to "messianic delusions" and "corrupted faith" (McCarthy and Burris, 2000).

Government support of religious activity

Thomas Jefferson used the phrase "wall of separation" to describe church–state relations in America, but the precise relationship between religion and government has been subject to continued litigation over where the constitutional boundaries should be drawn (see also Chapter 7). Religious institutions enjoy tax-exempt status, upheld by the Supreme Court's 1971 *Walz* decision, although more recent decisions have limited tax exemption for income-producing church properties such as gymnasiums and beauty salons. The openness and decentralization of the American political system encourages the involvement of religious groups in politics, but the degree to which they do so varies greatly by denomination and issue (Wald,1996). Churches and synagogues thus have a long history of activism on a variety of causes, from Prohibition to civil rights to anti-war protests. And chaplains in the armed services are funded under the defense budget.

However, direct government assistance to religious institutions or organizations has long been subject to the "*Lemon* test." Based on that 1972 Supreme Court decision, direct financial support was not allowed unless the primary purpose of such support was not religious. Thus taxpayer monies could provide buses for parochial school children because this improved child safety, not because it provided direct funding to their schools. By the 1980s, however, the "*Lemon* test" no longer provided clear guidelines, and a split 2000 *Mitchell* v. *Helms* decision by the Supreme Court further expanded the domain of permissible public assistance to parochial schools (Greenhouse, 2000).

The Mitchell decision also suggested a possible trend toward eventual Court approval of school vouchers (government grants to parents for use in any school, public or private). Vouchers are strongly supported by the Roman Catholic Church, by Republicans, and by conservatives critical of the condition of American schools. They are also advocated by members of the Religious Right who are seeking public support for the many "Christian academies" established in recent years. Vouchers are also increasingly popular with African-Americans distressed by the conditions in many urban schools. Vouchers are, however, strongly opposed by teachers' unions, whose influence in California in 2000 helped defeat an initiative supporting school vouchers. A definitive ruling on the constitutionality of vouchers has yet to be issued; cases are pending in the 2001–02 session of the Supreme Court. But federal district courts in several states have struck down vouchers designated for religious schools as a violation of the First Amendment.

Another exception to the *Lemon* test was federal funding ($250 million in 1996) for "chastity education" programs developed to try to reduce high rates of teenage pregnancy and premarital sex. Advocates claimed that these programs provided useful information and social support to help teenagers avoid intercourse; critics claimed that federal monies (much of which went to religious institutions) were being used to proselytize.

With the election of George W. Bush in 2000, major new initiatives were instituted to channel government funding to religious organizations. These efforts were spearheaded by a new "Office of Faith-Based Programs" in the White House, directed by former Indianapolis mayor

Stephen Goldsmith. The monies were to be used to augment social-service programs (literacy, childcare, gang intervention, assistance to the unemployed) being run by churches and synagogues. Such programs would be eligible for federal funding even if they actively promoted religion. Advocates argued that such "faith-based" programs were often more successful than government agencies in delivering services, reforming criminals, and improving people's lives (Chavez, 2001), but critics feared that recipients of such services would be subject to religious proselytizing. Members of some religious organizations themselves expressed concerns that government regulations and oversight would distort their missions (Hutcheson, 2001). A sharp racial division also emerged; many African-American clergy in the inner cities welcomed federal financial assistance for their chronically underfunded social programs, while wealthier white churches were more likely to fear unwelcome government intrusion (Goodstein, 2001).

Conclusion

Religion is increasingly salient in many aspects of American politics. As we have seen, religiosity (in the sense of church/synagogue attendance rather than affiliation) plays an important role in voting behavior in the 1990s. Although Jews and Catholics have become more diverse in terms of voting, the Religious Right has consolidated its support for the Republican Party, and now dominates grassroots party organizations in a significant number of states. Republican presidential, senatorial, or gubernatorial candidates ignore the influence of religion at their peril. Religious language, symbols, and values also play a considerable role in public discourse; candidates are now increasingly likely to invoke God in their campaigns and to make frequent statements as to their own religious beliefs and values.

However, the impact of the Religious Right in elections is more likely to be decisive in low-turnout primary, local, or off-year elections, due in part to its success in mobilizing its adherents to go to the polls. As Rozell and Wilcox (1995) have shown, Religious Right candidates tend to be more successful when they run as "stealth" candidates, or disguise their religious views as support for "family values." Yet American religiosity is counterbalanced to a significant degree by diversity, particularly in large urban areas. The Religious Right may be influential in the rural Bible Belt, as are Catholics in Louisiana and Mormons in Utah; but the electoral successes or policy impact of these groups is considerably reduced in the presence of countervailing cultures of belief. Gray and Lowery (1996) argue that we should not assess interest groups individually but in terms of their position in the group system. And in a hugely diverse country, policy or political dominance by any particular religious perspective (no matter how well organized) is unlikely to endure.

Three examples illustrate this lack of impact. First, in a low-turnout, off-year election, a majority of seats on the Kansas State School Board were won by adherents of the Christian right. The Board promptly required the teaching of Bible-based creationism rather than evolution in the state's public schools. But this innovation was strongly criticized by parents and teachers, and the offending Board members were all defeated in the higher-turnout Presidential election of 2000 (Simon, 2001). Second, Hallowe'en was banned as "Satanic" by the Religious Right majority on the Woodland Hills, California School Board. But as Gallup Polls have shown, over 80 percent of American households give out candy on Hallowe'en, and the Board's decision was reversed when parents and children in costume packed a School Board meeting.

And third, despite strong pressure from Roman Catholic bishops and the Religious Right, the Bush administration has been hesitant to try to limit abortion rights, because this is not popular in areas like California, the northeast, and among suburban women (Lizza, 2001). Bush's controversial choice for attorney general, John Ashcroft, survived his confirmation hearings only after declaring *Roe* v. *Wade* "settled law" and promising to uphold limits on protests at abortion clinics. Bush was strongly pressured by the Religious Right and the Pope to prohibit the use of embryonic stem cells for federally-funded medical research, despite the prospects such research offers for conditions such as Parkinson's disease and diabetes. But in August 2001 Bush nevertheless approved continuation of research on stem-cell "lines" already in existence, a decision which infuriated many on the Religious Right but was strongly supported by public opinion (Seeley and Bruni, 2001). The Bush administration did, however, cut off funds for international family planning soon after taking office.

As Wald (1996) noted, American religion, by remaining independent of the state but reserving the right to pass judgement, has avoided becoming an adjunct of the political system. It can thus remain unscathed "when the political system itself is in dispute" (Wald, 1996). But when churches actively enter the political fray, even if doing so helps to mobilize religious adherents, their leaders may indeed undermine religion. The National Election Studies "thermometer ratings" show that approval of the Moral Majority, the Christian Coalition, and Christian fundamentalists is more negative than positive, and ranks well below African-Americans, liberals, and the women's movement (Zinni, Rhodebeck and Mattei, 1997). Gallup Poll data on confidence in American institutions also bears this out. Before 1985, churches and organized religion consistently ranked first in public confidence. Since that time, they have steadily lost ground to the military as the most trusted American institution.

Chapter 17

The Media

TIM HAMES

The relationship between the media and politics in the United States is intimate. It is also complicated. There is no such thing as a single media in this vast country. While politicians cannot project themselves and their policies except through one outlet of the media or another, usually television, they are not prisoners of these outlets. Indeed, as many observers of the American media have ruefully observed, the media requires news to cover just as much as politicians require that coverage. The intense competition among those who provide that coverage has made the news itself a more valuable commodity and made access to political operatives yet more important. This chapter will highlight two main areas. The first, and the most substantial, relates to the recent developments within the industry itself. This section of the chapter will chart the rise of cable television and the increasing irrelevance of local television networks as outlets for serious political news. It will also note the entry of the Internet into this market but concludes that cyberspace has not yet become a serious rival to the more conventional media outlets. Despite this, however, the overall theme of this section will be that in the course of less than a decade extraordinary change has been recorded. The second segment of the chapter will concentrate on the nature of political coverage, most notably coverage during election campaigns. It will argue that relatively little change has been witnessed in this arena. The candidates are, on the whole, capable of framing their campaigns in a manner of their choosing, often to the intense frustration of those attempting to cover the contest. The focus in any political race remains "Who is winning?" rather than "What would they do if they won?" The particular and peculiar role of the media in the 2000 presidential election, and its extraordinary aftermath, will be the subject of critical inspection.

Americans and their political information

The bulk of this chapter will be devoted to television. This concentration is justified because the majority of Americans receive most of their political

Table 17.1   *Sources of political news (%)*

All-News Cable Television	35
Network Television	28
Newspapers	22
Radio	12
Don't know/None /Others	3

Source: Eve Gerber, 'Divided We Watch', *Brills Content* (February 2001).

information from this source. This has long been true but this consistency masks a remarkable shift in preference among television networks which merits further discussion. When asked towards the end of the election season in 2000 which outlet voters considered to be their primary source for political news, the responses shown in Table 17.1 were recorded.

These statistics understate the extent to which television is really the primary force in the media. There are a large number of television viewers who receive virtually *no* other information from any other source. There are few newspaper readers or radio listeners who are not partly influenced by television. Furthermore, those who claim to obtain most of their information from newspapers are drawn disproportionately from generations who were born before television came to dominate American life. Some 30 percent of senior citizens rely on newspapers for the majority of their political news compared with only 16 percent of voters aged 30 or younger. It is also the case that those Americans who claim to be at least "somewhat interested" in current affairs are more likely to draw their information from television than any other option.

As a vehicle for political campaigns to attempt to attract votes, the television screen is dominant. The money spent on political commercials in 2000 exceeded all records. As Table 17.2 reveals, it doubled in the course of the Clinton presidency. Expenditure was especially stratospheric in 2000 because a booming economy meant that competition for television space was even more fierce than usual. Television stations are obliged, by

Table 17.2   *Political advertising revenue (television)*

1988	$227,900,000
1992	$299,623,400
1996	$400,485,900
2000	$665,000,000

Source: Television Bureau of Advertising, 2001.

federal regulation, to sell air time to candidates at a somewhat discounted rate but no such restriction is placed on what they can charge political party organizations or interest groups who wish to broadcast their message. In the last few weeks of the campaign political advertisements constituted 10 percent of all commercials. The candidates collectively spent less than the automobile industry during this period but more than firms in the fast food, alcohol and telecommunications sectors of the economy (Wayne, 2000). While many individual media commentators are devoted supporters of campaign finance reform in the United States, the senior executives at the companies which employ them have every reason to be satisfied with current arrangements.

The alternatives to television are not, it should be conceded, inconsequential actors. There are still 1,750 daily newspapers published in the United States which employ some 56,400 journalists in their newsrooms. The overwhelming majority of cities and towns in the United States (98 percent) have, however, but one daily newspaper. Most American newspapers therefore concentrate on local or state news and do not maintain expensive bureaus in Washington, DC, let alone distant foreign capitals. The "national" news published by the typical American daily newspaper is therefore drawn from wire services such as the Associated Press (AP) or the United Press International (UPI). Most international material is drawn from agencies such as Reuters. There are only a handful of newspapers which devote really extensive resources to national political matters or foreign coverage. These include the *New York Times*, the *Washington Post*, the *Los Angeles Times* and the *Wall Street Journal*. Technological advances have made it possible for newspapers such as these to be available in many cities outside of their traditional catchment areas, but sales in such locations are still very modest.

The US newspaper industry is supported by a wide range of magazine publications. About 11,000 such titles appear on a weekly basis. In 2000, according to the Publishers' Information Bureau, an astonishing 286,932 pages of advertising appeared in these publications, raising some $17.6 billion in revenue. The market for magazines devoted to current affairs is, however, very limited. The leading journals in this field – *Newsweek* and *Time* – have been obliged to devote a larger share of their pages to news features, notably "human interest" stories, rather than what would once have been regarded as mainstream "hard news," in order to maintain circulation.

The 1980s witnessed the revival of radio as a political medium. This resurgence was inspired by the development of talk radio programmes. These remain the principal device for political discussion in this theatre. This has produced a distinct ideological pattern in this sector. Self-described conservatives are far more likely than self-labeled liberals to tune into radio talk shows. Indeed, a remarkable 65 percent of such conservatives claim to listen to at least one hour of talk radio every week. In sharp contrast, 57 percent of liberals never listen to talk radio at all and a substantial section of the minority who do tune in listen to National Public Radio (a network which conservatives have often accused of being biased against them). The ideological and right-wing character of talk radio means that it is more likely to reinforce existing partisan positions than make converts. Political strategists therefore tend to advertise here with the objective of mobilizing and motivating core supporters to cast their votes on election day.

The rise of cable

The truly striking changes in the American media over the past decade concern the rise of cable television, the eclipse of traditional national networks, and the demise of serious political discussion on local television stations. As Table 17.1 indicated, a plurality of Americans (35 percent) now obtain the majority of their political information from cable networks. This shift has occurred since the 1996 presidential election when it is estimated that only 21 percent of Americans awarded cable television such prominence. The melodrama surrounding the extremely close and then immensely controversial presidential election in 2000 appears to have reinforced the dash towards cable. As a Pew Trust Report confirmed, cable television outranked both network and local outlets as the primary source in both the pre-election and postelection phases (Hall, 2001). The Pew study also found that 83 percent of those who said that they were at least "somewhat interested" in the election result got their news primarily from television. More to the point, 41 percent of those who were checking the developments in late November (2000) said that they were tuning to cable news, compared with 30 percent who were watching local news and 23 percent who cited network news as their primary source.

The impact on the network news has been little short of catastrophic. The evening news broadcasts and the heavyweight Sunday morning political programmes are being watched by an ever-dwindling number of Americans. This means that the candidates can afford to pay them less attention. Advertisers have observed their falling ratings with the inevitable result that budgets for these kinds of programmes have been slashed. To add insult to injury, the 2000 campaign reinforced the trend for politicians to appear on almost every sort of programme except the traditional news shows. Bush and Gore rarely appeared personally on such revered programmes as 'Face the Nation' or 'Meet the Press' but would make time for the breakfast shows, for television talk shows such as that fronted by Oprah Winfrey, and for late-night comedy shows hosted by the likes of Jay Leno and David Letterman.

Changes within cable

The rise of cable does not mean that one network dominates political coverage. A decade ago, the Cable News Network (CNN) was the only company operating in this field. It had built its reputation on the basis of its performance during the Gulf War. The costs of attempting to compete with it seemed to be prohibitive and it became an extremely profitable franchise. That monopoly has been ended by the arrival of the Fox news network and MSNBC. The former actually matched CNN's ratings in October 2000 before the election melodrama worked to the advantage of the established market leader. The arrival of competition alone cannot, though, explain the difficulties that CNN has encountered. The declining appetite of Americans for international news – at least until the terrorist attacks of September 2001 created a sudden surge of interest – is part of the explanation. A further twist came with the merger of Time-Warner (CNN's parent company) with America On-line. That deal was reached shortly before the point when the boom in "new economy" shares turned into an equally dramatic bust. CNN suffered as a consequence.

CNN remains, however, the most impressive of the three companies in size and scale. It has 150 full-time correspondents and 42 overseas bureaus. When a truly huge political story (such as the Afghanistan war) emerges, requiring serious resources to cover it properly then CNN is unsurpassed. But it is now maintaining its market share primarily because, as Table 17.3, demonstrates, more American households have access to CNN than to either of its rivals.

The network cannot afford to assume that it will always hold this advantage. The overall number of viewers for CNN fell by 5 percent in the course of 2000 while the numbers watching MSNBC soared by 51 per cent and the audience for Fox rocketed by an amazing 132 percent during this

Table 17.3   *Access to cable news networks*

CNN	81 million homes
MSNBC	61 million homes
FOX	57 million homes

Source: John Cook, "CNN's Free Fall", *Brills Content* (April 2001).

period. There are two further factors of interest at work here: the nature of the programming at Fox and MSNBC and the character of the audience which Fox has started to attract.

When CNN first started to broadcast from Atlanta in 1980 it consisted of constant news bulletins. The philosophy of the network was that "the news is the star," and international news dominated proceedings. This has become an increasingly difficult formula to sustain, and consequently MSNBC has placed much more weight on domestic business and personal investments. CNN has felt obliged to respond in kind. Fox devotes most of its prime-time coverage to what might be described as news comment rather than news broadcasting. The news of the day provides the material for lively discussion and disagreement. CNN has again been obliged to depart from its original philosophy. In the crucial 8–11pm slot CNN now airs a mere 30 minutes of conventional news broadcasting. It fills the rest of the time with programmes hosted by prominent personalities such as Wolf Blitzer, Larry King, and Bill Press. This shift is partly a response to viewer preference but is also dictated by cost. Talk is relatively cheap compared with the production of specific programmes from overseas locations. There is the strong suspicion that cable television is blurring the line between news and entertainment. This process is being encouraged by the social profile of the typical cable news viewers. In contrast to the early years of all-news programmes when the typical audience consisted of highly-educated enthusiasts for in-depth news coverage, the most loyal supporters of cable television news today are apparently the least educated consumers of news. They do not want much political information, but when they seek it they prefer to turn to an outlet where it is constantly available rather than organize themselves around the 30-minute evening slots provided by the mainstream networks.

One other aspect of Fox's coverage should be highlighted. Many of its leading personalities, notably Bill O'Reilly, host of the popular programme, 'The O'Reilly Factor', are willing to express stridently conservative opinions on camera. There is increasing evidence that Fox is becoming the channel of choice for committed Republicans. An astonishing 18 percent of self-identified conservatives name Fox as their favored media outlet compared with a mere 3 percent of liberal activists. It is a matter of debate as to whether it is healthy for a news channel to be so identified with one part of the political spectrum.

The decline of local television

If cable television news is booming then local television news is, alas, moving in the opposite direction. Politics does not sell here. The typical local news broadcasts consists of a combination of crime stories, tales of bizarre incidents and individuals, consumer news, personal health and diet, sport, the weather and local traffic conditions. When politics is included it is covered in a superficial fashion. The prominence of the presidential race in 2000 meant that, according to a survey conducted by the Project for Excellence in Journalism, only 8 percent of all stories broadcast on local news outlets touched upon the contest. (Rosenstiel, Gottlieb and Brady, 2000). This meant that politics ranked second behind crime in terms of coverage. But, as the survey team, noted some 93 percent of these stories were about the "horse race or tactics of the campaign as opposed to what the candidates stood for and how their proposals might affect people locally. And 95 percent of the stories were either wire-feeds or the station going to a staged campaign event" (see also Chapter 2).

A vicious cycle appears to have been reached in local television. The majority of networks have experienced a decline in ratings for their news programmes since 1990. Advertisers soon discover this and move their funds elsewhere. Budgets are cut and the most expensive elements of the broadcast are axed. It is usually cheaper to buy in national news feeds or send a single cameraman to the scene of an incident without a reporter than it is to maintain a large newsroom. Investigative reporting has thus all but disappeared from local television news. Coverage of events during the presidential campaign now consists of little more than some introductory words from the local newscaster and a clip which lasts, on average, for eight seconds: barely the length of a short sound bite. The end result is a predictable and repetitive form of television. This drives away more viewers, especially the younger ones, from the network because it removes the very elements that attract viewers – especially local items. That in turn means that what coverage exists of local political issues is broadcast to an ever-smaller audience. The inadequate nature of local television news is a major factor in the increased popularity of the cable networks.

The limits of the Internet

Enthusiasts for the Internet hope and believe that it will become the outlet for intense coverage of political issues. This faith is not without foundation. About 40 percent of American households in 2001 had access to cyberspace. A respectable proportion of Internet users will search for political news this way. These individuals are, however, a distinct subsection of all Americans. They tend to be the youngest and best-educated voters. An estimated 16 percent of those aged 30 or under and 14 percent of college graduates surf for news on ten occasions or more in any week (Gerber, 2001). They also tend to be somewhat more liberal than the average

Table 17.4 *The Internet and vote choice (%)*

	1996	2000
Has an impact on vote choice	31	43
No impact on vote choice	69	55

Source: Pew Research Center.

American. Candidates and parties have invested huge resources into their websites and constructing e-mail address lists. The consensus among campaign professionals is, nonetheless, that very few undecided voters can be found or converted this way. This sense of frustration was neatly captured by Michael Cornfield, an expert in this field, when he protested that "The 2000 cycle produced one disappointment after another: net persuasion, advertising and discussion were outright flops, while news outreach, fund raising and volunteer mobilisation fell short of expectations" (Cornfield, 2001).

This assessment is perhaps unduly sweeping for a medium still in its infancy. The numbers of Americans who claim to be influenced by what they encounter on the web is impressive. About one-third of adults will either browse for or inadvertently discover political news on the web and the percentage who assert that they have been affected by it is, as Table 17.4 confirms, increasing.

The Internet also had an impact on several aspects of the 2000 elections. George W. Bush, who decided not to follow voluntary federal restrictions on how he could raise and spend funds, responded to criticism of his decision by posting the names of his financial contributors on his website. In the aftermath of the New Hampshire Primary, John McCain had some notable success in raising campaign funds through the Internet (see also Chapters 3 and 18). In the closing stages of the campaign various websites were established to allow supporters of Al Gore and Ralph Nader to "trade" their votes so that the Democrats would not be harmed in the most important battleground states. The Gore campaign was first alerted to election day problems in parts of South Florida through the Internet. It was also able to establish that the vote in Florida was far closer than the television networks were announcing by reference to the official Florida election website. The practice of politics might not have been revolutionized by technical innovation, but it has not been unaffected.

The Internet is not poised, though, to threaten seriously either television stations or major newspapers. Indeed, most of the major providers of news on the web are either themselves television networks (such as cnn.com) or newspapers (for example, nytimes.com). A major independent news agency based on the Internet alone has yet to evolve and it would be very expensive to create one. The demise of dot.com mania on Wall Street makes it unlikely that such an enterprise will be undertaken shortly.

New outlets, old coverage

The internal character of the American media has altered dramatically over the past two decades, but the content of the coverage does not seem to have changed as rapidly. Political coverage continues to focus disproportionately on the White House over either branch of Congress or the Supreme Court. There is a certain ritual to the manner in which all elections, but particularly presidential elections, are covered. The early stages of the contest are dominated by speculation as to who will emerge to challenge those that the media has anointed the front-runners. Much more attention is devoted to personality at this stage than to policy considerations. The frenzy of the primary season itself is predominantly portrayed as a story of a front-runner stumbling and (usually) then recovering (see Chapter 2). A political close-season then follows during which the pundits fill the time by endless, often pointless, speculation concerning the vice-presidential nomination. This is followed by the two conventions which are now events designed entirely to impress the television audience. The formal campaign then starts on Labor Day (the first Monday in September) when opinion polls and journalists engage in speculation about the likely outcome of the election campaign. The staging and interpretation of the televized debates then assumes importance. The final month of the battle is covered in similarly breathless fashion.

This means that the candidates and campaigns are normally effective at shaping their own coverage. Mistakes will certainly be highlighted when they occur but by and large the contenders are able to stick to their preferred scripts and fend off more inquisitive inquiries. The Bush–Gore contest had a certain familiarity about it. The two front-runners ran highly risk-adverse campaigns, sticking with a few set themes that had been carefully tested by their pollsters. When they wanted to avoid the press they did so. Al Gore managed to dodge a formal press conference for five consecutive months while on the campaign trail. The two conventions were simply advertisements for the candidates and the three debates were less than informative. Policy was addressed, if at all, in a cursory fashion. Much the same could be said for every other political contest in the United States fought on television.

The most distinctive feature of the television coverage of the election in 2000 was polling day itself and the five weeks of uncertainty which came afterwards. The various networks have saved money in recent years by pooling resources for exit polling and the early analysis of results. One organization, the Voter News Service, provided all this information. The television stations made a series of dreadful mistakes in their handling of this political data. The pivotal state of Florida was called first for Al Gore, then retracted, and next for George W. Bush, a decision which in effect awarded him the presidency. That decision had to be renounced as well but the perception that the Republican had in some sense been the President-Elect was to prove a significant asset for him in the course of the 35-day struggle for the White House which the Supreme Court finally settled in favor of the Governor of Texas. The Vice-President was cast as a bad loser when he had a perfectly respectable case to make in Florida and led the national vote tally by some 350,000 ballots. In the aftermath of this debacle, a bipartisan commission led by former Presidents Gerald Ford and Jimmy Carter produced a series of recommendations which would radically alter the manner in which television networks cover future elections. It remains to be seen whether any of them will be adopted.

Conclusions

The principal conclusion of this chapter is paradoxical. The chapter has argued that, while Americans are finding their political news in different parts of the media, the basic product itself remains consistent and, most critics would assert, rather unsatisfactory. There is, thanks to cable television, far more comment than before but this discussion revolves around quite familiar aspects of the political process. The basic format for the coverage of a presidential election is, despite the new technology, not dissimilar to that of the contests of 1980 or 1984. Americans can receive as much or as little information on policy matters as they wish to uncover but the majority of the electorate choose to focus instead on the perceived personal qualities of the contender. Television certainly augments and encourages that process. There is the fear that the qualities required for effective electoral campaigning are fundamentally different from those needed for effective administration.

These concerns are not unique to the United States but they are still significant. They are raised in the aftermath of every election campaign but show no sign of resolution. The media invariably hold their own inquest and agree that they should be less interested in the "horse race" and more concerned by the details of the programmes put forward by candidates for public office. This resolution invariably collapses with the arrival of the first opinion poll of the season. The most intriguing media strategy of recent years was that adopted by Senator John McCain in 2000. He desperately needed favorable publicity and knew that the news media were irritated by the restrictions placed on them by other candidates. McCain therefore decided to be open, constantly accessible to reporters and willing to speak candidly on the record. He received exceptionally favorable coverage as a reward. That was not enough to deliver him the Republican nomination. It might, however, have set a precedent which other presidential aspirants in future contests will yet wish to emulate.

Chapter 18

Campaign Finance

ALAN GRANT

The 2000 elections again broke new records in terms of campaign expenditure: around $3 billion were spent by candidates for the presidency and for Congress, almost half as much again as the $2.2 billion in 1996, with a further billion dollars being used for state election campaigns (Marcus, 2000). The booming economy, the closeness of the races for the presidency and for the control of Congress and memories of the weak enforcement of existing regulations in the 1996 campaign all contributed to the spiraling levels of monies raised and spent in 2000.

Evidence of the increasing use of "soft money," funds donated mainly to political parties by wealthy individuals, corporations, trade unions and other groups without any restrictions on the amounts contributed, provided fresh momentum to the movement arguing for a reform of the nation's campaign finance legislation. The presidential bid by one of the leading proponents of such legislation, Senator John McCain of Arizona, and the hugely effective fund-raising efforts of his rival for the Republican Party nomination, Governor George W. Bush of Texas, also served to highlight the issue during the 2000 campaign season. When McCain, along with his co-sponsor, Senator Russell Feingold of Wisconsin, successfully piloted the Bipartisan Campaign Reform Act of 2001 it raised the prospect of the most far-reaching overhaul of campaign finance laws in almost three decades passing Congress. This chapter examines the background to the vexed question of campaign finance reform, the way reform proposals were modified in the late 1990s to address new concerns, and in particular it looks at developments since the beginning of 2000.

The 1970s reform legislation

To understand the current debate on the issue it is necessary briefly to refer to the last major reforms to the campaign finance system which were passed in the 1970s (Sorauf, 1992). In 1971 Congress passed the Federal Election Campaign Act (FECA). This established a fund to provide for the public funding of presidential campaigns which would come into effect in 1976. Following the Watergate scandal, sweeping amendments were passed to the Act in 1974 in an attempt to clean up election campaigns and limit the influence of wealthy contributors. The reforms included caps on donations to candidates' campaigns by individuals, PACs set up by pressure groups, and by political parties; limits on overall spending in campaigns for federal office; the extension of public funding in presidential elections to the nominations process whereby candidates would receive matching funds from the taxpayer when they had raised private donations on a broad enough basis; and the creation of a new agency, the FEC, to enforce the regulations. At the same time Congress rejected the idea of extending public funding to congressional campaigns.

However, in 1976 in the case of *Buckley* v. *Valeo* the Supreme Court declared that major parts of the legislation were unconstitutional because they conflicted with the First Amendment rights of both candidates and citizens. Accordingly, the Court ruled that it was unconstitutional to impose mandatory limits on campaign spending because high spending levels in themselves did not have the potential for corruption. It also struck down limits on how much candidates could spend of their own money, and restrictions on spending by independent campaigns for or against particular candidates.

In the same judgment the Justices supported voluntary spending limits as a condition for receiving public funding in presidential elections as well as limits on the amounts which individuals, PACs and parties could contribute to campaigns. The *Buckley* decision has been much criticized but, with the failure of attempts to pass a constitutional amendment which would allow Congress or the states to limit campaign expenditure by law, any reform proposals have to be drafted in the light of the principles enunciated by the Court or in the hope that the current bench will take a different view from that which decided the 1976 case.

In 1979 Congress passed further legislation which permitted political parties to raise and spend money for "party-building" activities (see also Chapters 3 and 19). It was hoped that new sources of money, which could be given without any limits by individuals, businesses, trade unions and other groups, would help finance registration drives and voter mobilization efforts, as well as pay for generic party publicity and administrative overheads. This "soft money" (as opposed to the "hard money" regulated by the 1974 legislation) was not intended to be used to support the campaigns of individual candidates, but by the late 1990s, was to become the most criticized and controversial area of campaign spending. In fact one expert study found that in the 2000 elections state and national parties together spent only 8.3 per cent of their soft money on voter mobilization and other traditional party-building activities, while the largest expenditure, 38 per cent, was used for television and radio commercials and direct mail campaigns in support of individual candidates (Brennan Center for Justice, New York, 2001). Dealing with the unintended consequences of the 1979 Act and closing a major loophole which has subsequently been exploited by the parties to directly support their presidential and, in recent years, even their congressional candidates has become the major preoccupation and top priority for reformers such as McCain and Feingold.

Reform proposals in the 1990s

Before the emergence of soft money as a key issue in the mid-1990s, critics of the campaign finance system had focused on a number of concerns: the escalating costs of campaigns and the need for constant fund-raising by legislators; the advantages which incumbent members enjoyed, allowing them to raise money more easily than challengers; the influence of "special interests," symbolized by the growth in the number of PACs; and the unfairness created by allowing wealthy candidates to spend their own resources without any limits (Grant, 2000). Therefore most legislative proposals in the early 1990s, usually promoted by Democrats, included provisions to cap campaign expenditure by the introduction of "voluntary" spending limits with some public funding or subsidy to encourage compliance and to reduce the amounts PACs could donate, or even to ban them altogether. Opponents of these measures, mostly Republicans, argued that public funding was both objectionable in principle and impractical in the light of the huge federal budget deficits at the time; and also that imposing spending limits discriminated against challengers who needed to spend more than incumbents to become well-known to the electorate. They also argued that restricting PACs was an unconstitutional infringement of citizens" First Amendment rights (see also Chapter 7).

In 1993–94, with President Clinton replacing George Bush in the White House, Democratic congressmen had a golden opportunity to pass a reform bill. However, differences between Senate and House Democrats over the details of the bill – for example, on the issue of PAC contributions on which House members were far more dependent than their Senate colleagues – led to a fatal delay in agreeing terms and the Republican minority in the Senate filibustered the proposal in the run-up to the 1994 midterm elections. For the Republican leadership which took control of both houses of Congress in January 1995, the issue was one that did not have wide public appeal and one where change might threaten the party's newly won majority status. In July 1995 Speaker Newt Gingrich declared that there was "zero pressure" for action (*Washington Post*, 1995), and this remained true even after the 1996 elections when some of the most egregious infringements of the law became apparent and the use of soft money rose dramatically.

Despite the efforts of the leadership, a minority of Republicans in the House began to work with the Democrats to support a bipartisan proposal submitted by Christopher Shays (R-Conn.) and Martin Meehan (D-Mass.). The House voted in favour of the bill by 252–179 in 1998 and 252–177 in 1999, with around 60 Republicans supporting the legislation. However, the Republicans enjoyed a 55–45 majority in the Senate and, moreover, the party leadership had available a weapon that their House counterparts lacked: the filibuster. On several occasions in the mid to late 1990s the bills proposed by Senators McCain and Feingold failed to muster the necessary 60 votes to end debate, even though they had majority support for the bills. They had the backing of 53–54 senators (all 45 Democrats and 7–8 moderate Republicans) but no further progress could be made before the 2000 elections.

In September 1997 McCain and Feingold had drastically reduced the scope of their reform bill in the hope of improving its chances of passing the Senate road block. It was stripped of most of the provisions which had formed the basis of comprehensive reform bills in the past in order to concentrate on what now seemed the most pressing problems. Gone was the attempt to cap campaign spending in recognition of the fact that there was no chance of public funding being made available. Also deleted were the restrictions on PAC donations as PACs were no longer seen as quite the threat they had appeared in the past: the number of registered PACs had stabilized during the 1990s to just under 4000, they did at least contribute regulated hard money, and the real value of the $5000 maximum donation had depreciated by almost two-thirds since it was set in 1974 (Grant, 1995). Although the revised bill did contain some other provisions its main purposes were to ban entirely soft money contributions to political parties and to introduce new regulations affecting issue advocacy commercials which mention a candidate by name in the run-up to an election.

The soft money issue

The introduction of public financing of presidential election campaigns was supposed not only to have ended the dependence of candidates on private donations but also to have effectively capped expenditure by the voluntary agreement when candidates accepted taxpayers' money. The 1979 legislation resulted in $22 million of soft money being spent by the parties in 1984. In the 1995–96 election cycle soft money expenditures by national party committees had risen to $263 million and in 1999–2000

Table 18.1   *Hard and soft money donations and the political parties ($ million)*

	1991–2	1993–4	1995–6	1997–8	1999–2000
Democrats					
Hard money	155.5	21.1	210.0	153.4	269.9
Soft money	36.3	49.1	122.3	91.5	243.1
Republicans					
Hard money	266.3	223.7	407.5	273.6	447.4
Soft money	49.8	52.5	141.2	131.0	244.4
TOTAL	507.9	446.4	881.0	649.5	1,204.8

Source: Federal Election Commission, quoted in *CQWR*, 10 March 2001, p. 525.

almost doubled again to $487 million, with the Democrats and Republicans each spending approximately half of this sum, a proportion of which was used in support of their presidential candidates. The amounts involved dwarfed the $67.6 million of public money given to each of the two main party candidates for the general election campaign. For more information on donations, see Table 18.1.

The 1996 campaign had demonstrated the extent to which the party leaders would go to raise money from wealthy supporters. President Clinton gave numerous speeches at fund-raising dinners while also raising money by holding coffee mornings and inviting guests to stay overnight at the White House. Vice-President Gore's success in raising an estimated $40 million also damaged his reputation as it was alleged that some of his activities bordered on illegality. What is more, there were blatant breaches of the requirement that soft money should not be used to support presidential candidates directly. The FEC auditors found that such activities broke the conditions of public funding and recommended that the parties be fined by withholding a portion of the tax monies due; but the Commission itself, split evenly on party lines, refused to take action (Carney, 1999).

In addition to the Republican and Democratic National Committees (which have a broad remit to promote their parties' interests nationally) and the two parties' House and Senate Campaign Committees also dramatically stepped up their efforts to raise soft money in 2000, despite the fact that their sole purpose for existing is to elect candidates for federal office. A number of individual candidates also established their own soft money committees and accounts, including Hillary Rodham Clinton who raised $9.7 million toward her successful bid to become New York's junior senator.

The major argument in favour of banning soft money contributions is that they are corrupting the system by allowing wealthy individuals and special interests to circumvent the hard money limits and to use the parties as intermediaries in their efforts to buy influence with politicians. John McCain described the system as one of "legalised bribery and legalised extortion" (Marcus and Cohen, 2001). Corporate contributors include many companies which have interests in regulatory legislation before Congress. In 1996 some 20 individual citizens contributed at least $250,000 in soft money; in 2000 the number increased to 78. Some political scientists have argued that the parties could easily finance their activities from the increasing amounts of hard money they raise and that banning soft money would force them to broaden their base of grassroots contributors.

Opponents of a ban argue that to do so would irreparably damage the ability of the political parties to play an active role in elections and strengthen the position of pressure groups even further. For many years political scientists lamented the decline of parties because they believe that these organizations perform valuable functions for the political system as a whole. In recent times there has been a revival in their fortunes and many believe that soft money has played its part in this development. Opponents of the McCain–Feingold bill therefore believe that it would hamstring the parties' ability to raise money to support their candidates, particularly challengers who have problems in raising money from other sources, and to mobilize voters on election day. Some also contend that soft money has only become so significant because of the unwillingness of Congress to raise the hard money limits for individual donations from the $1,000 per election set in 1974.

Issue advocacy commercials

One of the most controversial trends in recent elections has been the huge increase in issue advocacy commercials. Thus it was estimated that $509 million was spent on issue advertisements in the 2000 campaign, approximately a third of it by the political parties and the rest by various pressure groups (Willis, 2001). These commercials on the face of it discuss issues in the campaign and may attack or praise a candidate's stand or vote on the issue. Unless they "expressly advocate" the election or defeat of a candidate, the Supreme Court held in the *Buckley* case that they could not be regulated by campaign finance laws. There are therefore no limits on how much groups may spend on issue advertisements, and corporations and trade unions which are banned from giving directly to campaigns can spend as much as they like through this medium in support of (and in opposition to) particular candidates. The groups sponsoring the commercials do not have to reveal who is paying for them and their costs do not have to be reported to the FEC, with the exception of those paid for by political parties.

McCain–Feingold's supporters argue that the commercials are a sham; that their real intention is to influence the outcome of elections and that they are in practice virtually indistinguishable from regular campaign commercials as far as the public is concerned. They see the use of such advertisementss as a loophole through which vast *de facto* campaign contributions pass unregulated in each election year. The reform bill as introduced in the Senate therefore banned unions and corporations from buying issue advertising on television or radio which mentions candidates by name within 30 days of a primary or 60 days of a general election. Other groups which buy issue advertisements would be subject to new disclosure rules on the funding of such commercials.

The proposals have been attacked as a serious infringement of First Amendment rights which would not be sustained by the Supreme Court. A wide range of pressure groups from across the political spectrum (including for example the ACLU and the Christian Coalition) joined forces to argue that they must be allowed to raise issues in campaigns even if the politicians would prefer to control the agenda and not discuss them. They also contend that the public has a right to know where a candidate stands and what his or her record is on the issues, although many politicians claim that these commercials often distort the real facts about their views. Many of the groups opposing this provision also object to having to report to the FEC when they plan to use independent expenditures to purchase airtime and to disclose the names of those citizens whose contributions have helped pay for the commercials.

Important recent developments

Supreme Court decisions

The Supreme Court has made decisions in recent years upholding some of the basic tenets of the *Buckley* case. In 1998 the Justices confirmed the principle that spending limits could not be placed on candidates' campaigns in a case involving elections to Cincinnatti City Council. In January 2000 the Court again backed limits on individual contributions to campaigns by 6–3 in *Nixon* v. *Shrink Missouri Government PAC*.

In June 1996 the Court had ruled that political parties have a right to spend as much as they wish in congressional races as long as they do so independently of the candidates, placing parties in the same position as PACs. However, in the June 2001 decision in *FEC* v. *Colorado Republican Federal Campaign Committee* the Court upheld by 5–4 strict spending limits on how much parties could spend in coordination with their candidates (Lane, 2001). The majority argued that allowing parties to spend unlimited amounts could give wealthy donors a chance to evade contribution limits and the opportunity to exercise improper influence over candidates. This case only involved hard money but, given the fact that legislation based on McCain–Feingold proposals would be bound to be challenged as to its constitutionality, supporters of a ban on soft money drew encouragement from the Court's ruling, which they felt showed sympathy to their arguments about potential corruption. With hard money spending limits confirmed, the decision also made it more likely that Democratic legislators would support a ban on soft money; many had been worried that their party was not as effective in raising hard money as the Republicans and that they would be left at even greater disadvantage if unlimited spending had been allowed.

Passage of the first campaign finance legislation since 1979

In June 2001 Congress passed a new campaign finance law for the first time in more than two decades, albeit it one with very limited scope. It required that certain groups with tax-exempt status ("527 groups" after the section in the IRS code) which are involved in political campaigns file financial reports with the IRS and disclose the sources of their funding. Attention was focused on these organizations when a group called "Republicans for Clean Air," formed by two Texas businessmen, ran attacking commercials against McCain on environmental issues before key presidential primaries. Subsequently McCain took the lead in introducing a new law to regulate 527 groups' activities which passed both houses overwhelmingly (Foerstal, 2001b).

The 2000 election campaigns

The 2000 campaigns highlighted a number of the ways in which money is raised and spent in US elections, quite apart from the huge increase in soft money and the use of issue advertising. George W. Bush decided early on that, faced with the self-financed billionaire Steve Forbes in the Republican primaries, he would reject the matching federal funds which would be on offer because he did not wish to be limited to particular levels of spending overall or in individual states. By doing so he would avoid the financial problems Robert Dole faced when seeing off the Forbes challenge in 1996.

With the advantages of his name and his father's contacts and mailing lists of donors, Bush was able to raise phenomenal amounts of hard money contributions of $1000 or less. In the first six months of 1999 he raised $36.3 million, and by the autumn had so much money that several other potential candidates (such as Elizabeth Dole) were deterred from entering the race. Overall Bush's campaign raised more than $100 million, leaving Forbes and McCain in his wake in the fund-raising stakes.

McCain himself pushed campaign finance reform as a central focus of his bid for the nomination, giving the issue both publicity and credibility among a wider public. His reputation enhanced, McCain's resumption of efforts to pass legislation through the Senate following the 2000 elections had a new momentum. His passion and commitment to the cause won new supporters even while his sweeping claims about corruption continued to irritate and embarrass his colleagues in the Senate.

In the fight to control Congress, spending levels also rose to over a billion dollars, 36 per cent more than two years earlier (FEC, 2001). The year 2000 saw the most expensive House race ever, with over $10 million being spent in the California district where Republican James Rogan faced a challenge from Democrat Adam Schiff. Self-financed candidates also had a notable impact in Senate races: Maria Cantwell (D-Wash.) and Mark Dayton (D-Minn) defeated Republican incumbents, while Jon Corzine (D-NJ) spent over $60 million of his own fortune in winning an open seat. Together these wealthy Democrats helped reduce the Republicans' majority and the new Senate was evenly split, 50–50. This new balance of power was to be a key factor in providing valuable extra votes for the McCain–Feingold bill when it was re-introduced in the 107th Congress.

Senate passage of the McCain–Feingold bill

The Senate debated the McCain–Feingold bill for two weeks at the end of March 2001, culminating in its passage by 59–41 on April 2. All but three Democrats voted for the bill and they were joined by 12 Republicans. Converts among the Republicans included conservatives such as Thad Cochran (Miss.) and Pete Domenici (N-Mex.).

The procedure used allowed members to submit numerous amendments (Taylor, Willis and Cochran, 2001). A number of significant changes were made during the debate. These included a provision that would allow candidates facing a self-financed challenger to raise money with higher limits on individual contributions depending upon the size of the state's voting age population. The most controversial amendment passed was one that extended the ban on issue commercials naming a candidate in the run-up to an election from unions and corporations to other pressure groups. The sponsors of the bill opposed the change because of fears about its constitutionality but, with the support of some Republican opponents of the bill who voted tactically to expose the conflict with First Amendment rights, it was approved by 51–46. Significantly an amendment was also passed which would allow state and local parties to raise limited amounts of soft money to mobilize voters in federal elections as long as they did not mention individual candidates by name, thus preventing the bill from being accurately described as a total ban on soft money. However, McCain and Feingold were successful in defeating an amendment which would have meant the whole bill would be nullified if the Supreme Court had declared any particular provision unconstitutional.

A significant amendment in terms of gaining more Republican support for the bill was the increase to $2,000 in the amount which individuals could give in hard money contributions, as well as a commitment to index the amount in future to rise with inflation. Initially Republicans had proposed an increase to $3,000, but even the $2,000 compromise was opposed by many Democrats. They argued that allowing more money into the system was not real reform, but they were also concerned that the provision would help the Republicans who have more affluent supporters and are more successful in raising hard money.

Republicans opponents of the bill did not use the filibuster tactic as in the past, partly in recognition of the new party balance in the chamber and partly because of the new political dynamic of having a Republican president in the White House. Although Bush did issue a list of reform principles on March 15, some of which appear to conflict with the Senate bill, he also stated that he looked forward to signing "a good piece of legislation" and many observers doubted whether he would wish to veto what would be seen as a "reform" bill and further alienate McCain who could become a dangerous opponent within the party.

In the House, where some Democrats were getting cold feet at the prospect of reform legislation actually passing, members faced a choice between the Shays–Meehan proposal which closely followed the Senate bill, while maintaining the $1,000 limit on contributions for House elections, and an alternative drafted by the Republican-controlled House Administration Committee. By seeking to cap soft money donations to national parties at $75,000 rather than banning them altogether, and by maintaining the hard money limit for individuals at $1,000, the sponsors hoped to draw support from those Democrats, such as some members of the Congressional Black Caucus, who believed that soft money was essential for mobilizing voters in their mainly low-income districts.

In the event the House debate in July descended into chaos and farce as procedural wrangling over the rules to be adopted for considering amendments to the Shays–Meehan bill prevented any vote from being taken on either proposal. It appeared likely that, with the congressional agenda being dominated by the repercussions of the terrorist attacks in New York and Washington, once again reform proposals would not pass into law during the session. However, the financial collapse of the giant energy firm Enron and its pattern of widespread campaign donations to legislators and presidential candidates created a new momentum for reform. Many wavering members in both houses became convinced that public support for legislation would become overwhelming.

House supporters of the bill managed to force a new debate and in February 2002 they overcame the resistance of the Republican leadership. The House passed the Shays–Meehan proposal by 240 votes to 189, with 21 Republicans joining all but 12 Democrats in support. The bill incorporated an amendment, passed by only 218–211, to raise the limit for individual hard money donations to $2,000, bringing it into line with the Senate version. The following month the Senate again passed the McCain–Feingold bill, this time by 60 votes to 40, paving the way for President Bush to sign it into law. Despite reservations about "some legitimate constitutional questions" the president said he supported these "common-sense reforms."

Therefore, after a series of battles which had frustrated them since the mid-1980s, the reformers appeared to have eventually triumphed. The Enron scandal may have provided the final impetus for congressional passage of the legislation but other factors, such as the shift in focus by the reformers in 1997, McCain's presidential bid, Bush's neutrality on the issue, the changed political balance in the Senate after 2000, and the compromises and refinements made by the legislators' sponsors, were all highly significant. What is certain is that the new law's opponents will challenge its constitutionality in the courts. One chapter in the saga closes, a new one opens.

Chapter 19

The United States in Evolution: Majoritarian Reforms in a Madisonian System

BRUCE CAIN

Many foreign observers and some Americans were surprised to discover that the popular vote winner in the 2000 presidential election would not become the President of the United States. Instead, the Republican candidate, George W. Bush, won the office by virtue of a narrow margin in the Electoral College after a much disputed and very close victory in Florida, even though he received a half million fewer votes nationally than the Democratic candidate, Al Gore. Adding mechanical insult to institutional injury, Americans also were embarrassed by the revelation of antiquated voting technologies and lax poll worker supervision in Florida, and by the absence of a nationally uniform method for recounting disputed ballots (see Chapter 2). Eventually, given sufficient attention and resources, the technical voting problems may get fixed, but the same cannot be said of the Electoral College problem. Despite decades of discussion about getting rid of the Electoral College, no reform has been successful to date and none is likely to succeed in the near future.

The Electoral College dispute highlights the fact that the US federal government still retains important anti-majoritarian eighteenth-century constitutional features despite decades of democratic changes. Ironically, many "newer" Eastern European and Asian democracies, countries that followed more circuitous and uncertain paths to popular rule, now have constitutions that conform more closely on paper to modern democratic expectations. Consequently, the American system looks as if it is badly in need of a major overhaul to rid itself of old institutions and practices.

This is not to imply that the US political system has been static over the years. The least democratic features of the US system have been under constant attack throughout its history. Democratic reforms, usually initiated at the state level, have steadily eroded such original features as indirect US Senate elections, franchise restrictions, meaningful bicameralism in state government, and judicial independence. Nonetheless, important remnants of the original system (such as the Electoral College and the allocation of Senate seats by unequally populated states) persist, and attempts to bring state level populist reforms – such as term limits and direct democracy – have been successfully resisted by the federal government so far.

Why have some features of America's original constitutional system been abolished and others retained? What forces prevent the United States from getting rid of institutions such as the Electoral College even when a majority of Americans would prefer direct election of the President? More generally, does the original Madisonian design still serve a purpose in the USA, and has its erosion been a positive development? These are the questions the chapter will address.

Madisonian logic considered

Most introductory texts on American politics begin with a review of the Founding Fathers' logic as set out in the Federalist papers. They teach that the framers wanted to establish a government that was democratic, but not subjected to the twin tyrannies of the majority and the minority. The tyranny of the majority could result when a majority faction used state power to achieve its will without regard for the basic rights of those in the minority. The tyranny of the minority described situations in which powerful small groups had the ability to obstruct or veto the popular will. Since factionalism and passion were assumed to be inevitable, the purpose of governmental design was to contain abuse of either sort through such mechanisms as checks and balances, a bill of rights, judicial independence, an extended republic, dispersion of power through Federalism and various forms of indirect democracy.

Consider the Electoral College in this context. There were some delegates at the Constitutional Convention who favored the direct election of the Chief Executive, but the position that prevailed was one that was fearful of leaving a critical choice of this sort in the hands of general electorate. In the words of one delegate, George Mason: "It would be as unnatural to refer the choice of a proper magistrate to the people as it would the choice of colors to a blind man." The Founding Fathers certainly did not envision the current United States practice of using tracking polls of Presidential approval in order to make policy decisions. Deriving from the Founding Fathers' deep skepticism about the solidity and value of popular opinion, the motivation for the Electoral College was to place the important decision of choosing the chief executive in the hands of an enlightened group of citizens.

An important point to notice – since it sheds some insight upon how majoritarian or populist pressures have altered aspects of the original system over time – is that the exact method for selecting Electoral College delegates was left to the states. This is significant because the state structures themselves were less protected against popular pressures than the federal system. Hence, by 1836, all states except Maine chose their electors by a winner-take-all system that was tied to the popular Presidential vote in the state. And in Maine's case, they awarded delegates according to the Presidential vote outcome in its Congressional districts.

The expectation that electors should exercise independent judgement also changed in the nineteenth century. While there have been a handful of so-called "faithless electors" – that is, electors who did not vote the way they were supposed to – the vast majority have complied with the state electorate's mandate. In fact, about a third of the states have laws that make it illegal for electors to vote against the popular mandate. Typically, the two major political parties avoid this problem by nominating as electors a slate of party loyalists and political hacks. Moreover, cultural pressures work against efforts to woo the electors of opposing slates. When, in the interval between the 2000 Florida recount and the official meeting of the Electoral College, a Gore loyalist attempted to contact and persuade Bush delegates to shift their votes from Bush to Gore in order to uphold the majority principle, the effort met with no success and considerable criticism. For most Americans, the sense that it is unfair to change the rules after a contest is over is stronger than their allegiance to pure majority rule *per se*.

Hence, in these two ways (tying elector share to votes and depriving electors of independence) the Electoral College was partially subverted by more purely democratic principles from an early point in US history. To some degree, it exemplifies a successful institutional adaptation to modern democratic needs. But, as the 2000 election graphically demonstrated, the adaptation comes with a risk: namely, that the outcome of the Electoral College might not be the same as a national direct election. The 2000 election was not the first example of this. John Quincy Adams in 1824, Rutherford B. Hayes in 1876 and Benjamin Harrison in1888 all obtained Electoral College victories without winning popular vote majorities.

How is this possible? First, a state's Electoral College share is not exactly proportional to its population share since the former is determined by the combined sum of its House and Senate delegations, and thus gives a bonus to smaller states. Second, because most of the states use winner-take-all rules, the winner's delegate share does not reflect the margin of victory. Hence, a candidate that wins a state's electors with 51 percent of the vote is treated the same with respect to delegate allocation as one who wins with 73 percent. If one candidate has a disproportionate number of close victories and the other a disproportionate number of lopsided ones, it could be lead to a discrepancy between the elector share and popular vote.

And lastly, the geographic distribution of support can advantage one candidate over another. In the instance of the 2000 election, George Bush enjoyed greater support in the smaller Rocky Mountain and Plains states, while Gore's support was concentrated in larger coastal states and the North Central region.

In addition, the failure of any candidate to achieve a majority of Electoral College votes throws the determination of the final outcome into the Congress. At various times in the Florida recount dispute, it looked as though the President might be chosen by party line voting in the Congress rather than by popular election. It is likely that Americans' belief in obeying the rules they agreed to beforehand would have prevailed in this scenario as well, but it certainly would have strained the perception of the incoming administration's legitimacy to an even greater degree than it did in 2001. So it can be said that while the Electoral College has evolved in a more majoritarian direction, it is not a perfect proxy for an electoral majority.

Can it be abolished or reformed to yield more majoritarian outcomes? Most likely, the answer is no. In order to abolish the Electoral College, it would take a constitutional amendment passed by both Houses of Congress and the subsequent approval of three-quarters of the state legislatures. Several small states, in the wake of the 2000 election and as discussion about the need for Electoral College reform heated up, immediately passed legislative resolutions opposing any abolition of the Electoral College. This is understandable not only because these states receive a disproportionate elector share, but also because, as Virginia Sapiro suggests in Chapter 2 on electoral politics, candidates would be likely to ignore them in favor of large states if the President were elected by a nationwide popular vote. To put it another way, the anti-majoritarian nature of the constitutional amendment process protects the anti-majoritarian features of the Electoral College.

Even more modest changes at the state level, such as the allocation of electors in proportion to the popular vote, are likely to be stymied by self-interest. Assume for instance that the state of California, which voted for Al Gore overwhelmingly in the 2000 Presidential contest, wanted to reform the Electoral College process to make the outcome more proportional. If it adopted even the mildest form of proportionality, the allocation of electors by Congressional district, then the Republican candidate in 2004 would be virtually guaranteed to get at least some Electoral College votes from the highly Republican areas in Orange and San Diego counties. But if solidly Republican states like Texas do not follow suit, then the California Democrats will have put their party's Presidential candidate at a disadvantage without any compensating gains from Texas. This kind of cooperative dilemma can only be solved by a national agreement, but the

Constitution delegates this decision to the individual states. Again, an anti-majoritarian feature of the original US system, federalism, stands in the way of Electoral College reform.

State government and majoritarianism

The Electoral College controversy thus nicely illustrates the tension between the pressures for majoritarian reform (that is, reforms that give more power to electoral majorities) and the protective resistance that federal institutions offer to them. At the same time, the Electoral College issue is anomalous in the sense that US electoral institutions have actually been the most susceptible to majoritarian pressures. Almost all of the most significant political reforms in the USA have concerned voting. The transition from an indirectly elected to a popularly elected Senate, the extension of the franchise to women and racial minorities, the "one person, one vote" apportionment principle (guaranteeing that election districts are as close to equally populated as possible) and the introduction of direct democracy (the initiative, referendum and recall) are all examples of this trend. Why did these electoral reforms succeed when the Electoral College cannot?

There are several reasons. In some cases, reformers have managed to overcome the Constitutional hurdles because there was a sufficiently high level of national consensus to overcome them: for instance, woman's suffrage and voting rights for ethnic minorities. In the former case, the right of women to vote did not threaten small state interests in the way the Electoral College does. When the public's acceptance of women's equality became sufficiently widespread, there was support in enough states for the Nineteenth Amendment to pass in 1920. In the case of minority rights, the defeat of the South in the Civil War resulted in the passage of the civil rights amendments (the Thirteenth, Fourteenth and Fifteenth Amendments). Later, relying on the Fourteenth Amendment in particular, the Supreme Court overturned the Jim Crow laws that had been erected after Reconstruction. When the Court seemed to hit a limit of activism in this area, Congress passed in 1965 and then amended in 1982 the Voting Rights Act (VRA) to put more statutory resolve in the Court's protective role. (Grofman and Davidson, 1992). While some of the Court's decisions in the late 1980s and early 1990s extended beyond any majority consensus about racial justice, this was corrected in a series of decisions beginning with *Shaw* v. *Reno.* (1993) (see also Chapter 7). But the initial applications of the VRA were generally favored outside the South. In sum, both the women's and racial minorities examples illustrate reforms that either did not threaten small state interests or could be imposed as a form of victor's justice upon states that were on the losing side of the country's only internal military conflict.

In most other cases, however, electoral reforms emerged because the US Constitution gave the states considerable power over the time, place and manner of elections, and because the states themselves were highly permeable to majoritarian influences. A good illustration of the former is the expansion of the primary system for nominating presidential candidates. During most of the nineteenth century, American political parties met in caucuses to nominate the candidates who would represent them in general election. Gradually, a number of states (beginning with South Carolina in 1896 and Wisconsin in 1903) began to require the political parties to participate in state-sponsored primary elections. For a country that leans as heavily on its right to free speech and association as the USA does, this intrusion into party rights was quite notable. In essence, many states began to require the political parties to participate in their state-run primaries and to dictate the rules those primaries would follow.

When the parties attempted to free themselves from this requirement, the Supreme Court upheld the states' right to compel a primary election. The issue of whether states can also dictate the *form* of the primary to the parties is a more ambiguous question. Several recent Court decisions suggest that the Supreme Court would like to allow political parties some freedom to determine the primary contest rules in recognition that the rules do have an impact on the kind of candidates selected and the message they send forward to the voters (see *California Democratic Party* v. *Jones* [2000]). But the Court is also mindful that it had to intervene strongly when the Texas Democrats attempted to close their primaries to African-American voters: hence, the ambiguity of the Court's current position (see *Smith* v. *Allwright* [1944]). But the Court's position aside, these party primary reforms might not have occurred as soon as they did, or indeed at all, if the states had not been given responsibility over federal elections under the Constitution.

A second aspect of the state's role in electoral reform is the openness of the states to populist influences. While ostensibly state structures mimic the federal form with three branches of government and state constitutions, the reality is that they are constituted very differently. Most states have adopted several constitutions in their history: the national average is 2.94 (Cain, Ferejohn, Najar and Walther, 1995) As a consequence, only a few states have constitutions from the eighteenth century, and most are products of the nineteenth and twentieth centuries. The fundamental premises of state constitutions are very different from the federal one. The federal Constitution was intended as an enduring framework that would only be altered occasionally. State constitutions are frequently amended by popular initiative or their own legislatures.

California, for instance, amended its constitution 489 times between 1879 and 1994. By contrast, there have been only 27 amendments to the federal constitution.

The method for altering state constitutions varies widely. In all cases – whether the proposed changes were developed in a Constitutional Convention, Constitutional Revision Commission, state legislature or by popular initiative – the amendments are placed before the statewide electorate for approval. To put it another way, majority public opinion has the ultimate say in the states' laws and procedures. If the states had followed the national example, constitutional amendments would have been placed before each of the counties for their approval just as federal amendments are placed before the state legislatures. The difference is that counties are merely administrative units of the states, whereas states have constitutionally protected sovereignty over certain policy areas. Approval by a statewide electorate is easier to accomplish and harder to derail than getting approval from three-quarters of the state legislatures. Moreover, the outcome more closely conforms to the median voter outcome.

It is also important to see how state constitutions purposely blur the distinctions between policy, rights and process. Whereas the federal constitution has a limited set of ten basic rights, the states often include an expanded number such as the right to hunt, fish or receive a minimum wage. States cannot diminish federal rights, but they can add to them. Other provisions in state constitutions concern policy matters that would normally be found in statutes (Cain and Noll, 1995): for instance, state constitutions might contain provisions regulating insurance, setting the minimum level of school spending, limiting taxes and so forth. By placing policies into the constitution, the electoral majority limits the capacity of legislative majorities to alter or deter the public will. In states that have the popular initiative, it also removes policy-making from the normal legislative process complete with the problems of bicameralism, committee government, special interest influence, gubernatorial veto, and so on, and places it into a simple electoral mandate.

The combined effect of states having recognized jurisdiction in most electoral matters (that is, those not set out by the Federal Constitution) and the states being more susceptible to majoritarian influences is that the states have been an incubator of election reform. To take a good example, term limits for state legislatures have been passed in all states that have direct democracy, but in only one state that does not. The motivations for supporting limited legislative terms are varied, but mostly the impetus arises from the perception of legislatures that are too responsive to special interests, lobbyists, administrative agencies and party leaders to make laws that reflect the popular will (Southwell, 1995). Proponents argue that limiting the terms of office assures that there is regular turnover in representation and lessens the ability of nonmajoritarian interests to capture the legislative process.

Opponents predicted that legislative term limits would diminish the expertise and competence of the legislature. On the whole, opponents of term limits tend to favor a republican form of government in which the public defers to representatives to make choices and then judges them retrospectively on their actions in periodic elections. Many term limit proponents are more populist in orientation, preferring that the people's mandate be implemented with less filtering (Kurfirst, 1996). Both in the sense that the preferred policy outcomes are more voter-driven and that term limits have been very popular in the United States, it is fair to call them a majoritarian reform.

Term limitations for Congress have also been passed in several states, but the Supreme Court has ruled that this violates the US Constitution because it adds another qualification to Congressional office, and the only method by which qualifications can be changed is by amendment (*US Term Limits* v. *Thornton* [1995]). The familiar pattern appears once again. A majoritarian reform, Congressional term limitations, runs up against Constitutional hurdles and fails.

Direct democracy and the majoritarian frontier

Apart from the differences between state and federal constitutions, another important reason that political reforms have tended to bubble up from the states is the popularity of direct democracy in recent years. While the term direct democracy encompasses referendums and recall elections, it is the so-called popular initiative (measures that are placed on the ballot after a sufficient level of signatures have been gathered) that is most relevant to this subject. As outlined in Chapter 15 by Elisabeth Gerber, the frequency of popular initiatives has been on the rise since the late 1970s. As she explains, initiatives can be either statutory or constitutional, and can cover a wide variety of topics. The rules governing the procedures and substance of initiatives vary a great deal from state to state. There is some debate as to how these variations affect usage rates across states. Having a higher signature threshold in order for an initiative to qualify for the ballot, for instance, might not affect the number of initiatives placed on the ballot *per se*, but might simply favor well-financed and organized groups over more grassroots and disorganized groups.

However, in all states that have the popular initiative, they can be used to bring about political reform. The fact that term limits have been passed in every state that has the popular initiative, and in only one without, is graphic illustration of the role that reform initiatives have played. It is easy to see why the popular initiative is a tool of political reform in the USA. To begin with, as the term limits example demonstrates, popular initiatives bypass the vested legislative interests problem. Legislators are understandably reluctant to place limitations on their terms of office. Whether or not such limitations are a good idea (and there are many political scientists who think that they are not), the fact remains that it would be hard for legislators to think about this issue in a detached manner, since how long they can serve in a particular office affects their careers. Politics is an uncertain profession to begin with, and having to rotate out of office after a couple of terms only adds to the anxiety. Whether term limits are good or bad for the polity as a whole, they complicate the life of the career politician considerably. For personal reasons alone, it would be hard to get legislators voluntarily to limit their careers in this way.

The problem is not restricted to term limits. It also applies to other forms of legislative regulation such as open meeting laws, freedom of information statutes, conflict of interest regulation and campaign finance reform. The powerful logic of vested interests does not rule out all legislative passed reforms. A well-publicized scandal can turn up the popular pressure such that legislators feel that they have to vote for reform for fear of ballot box retribution. For instance, the most significant federal campaign finance measure of the postwar period, the 1974 amendments to the Federal Election Campaign Act, followed the fund-raising scandals of the Watergate era. But popular initiatives lower the threshold of resistance to reform by taking the matter outside the legislative process.

Popular initiatives are also a preferred reform mode because they can be insulated from subsequent change and amendment by the legislature. Clearly, reform gains could be easily undone if the legislature can amend them after they are passed, but there are two ways that reformers can guard against that eventuality. First, they can pass the reform as a constitutional amendment, requiring those who would change the reform to introduce another constitutional change as well. This ensures that the measure would have to come back before the people either as a legislative initiative or as a popular initiative. Or, alternatively, if the reform is statutory, it can specify in the measure the terms by which future amendments can be made. This latter feature causes many problems with respect to normal lawmaking in various policy areas (such as by introducing inflexibilities and constraints on budget making), but works well in the governmental reform area because it guards against attempts to undermine genuine reform.

Another important positive feature of initiative-based reform is that it usually reflects the interests of citizen groups. While there is a great debate as to whether the initiative process as a whole has been captured by the very special interests it was meant to counter (Gerber, 1999; Broder,

2000), the concern has not focused on government reform measures so much as substantive policy-making ones. More specifically, it is easier to make a case for special interest capture when looking at popular initiatives dealing with insurance or education policy than with governmental reform initiatives. Parties or specific candidates might choose to sponsor a particular governmental reform, but rarely if at all do big businesses or trade unions, although they have on occasion sponsored the worker's rights measures.

Finally, reforms passed by the popular initiative process tend to be stable, because they reflect a majority consensus. Unless opponents can convince the majority that they made a mistake or that conditions have changed, the odds are that voters will choose the same way if given a second chance. Hence, no state has repealed term limits, and even attempts to improve term limits by lengthening the terms have a hard time gathering support. Because they are passed by a majority of voters, they tend to reflect that majority's interest. This, as we shall see later, has raised some questions about minority rights for the Courts to deal with.

What types of government reform tend to be favored by the initiative process? Many of them have curbed the power and discretion of the legislature to make policy. Term limits, cuts in legislative pensions, and requirements for voter consent are direct examples of this. But sometimes the policy measures themselves have the impact of further contributing to changing the process. The measures may pass on substantive grounds, but their cumulative effect can be procedural. For instance, the property tax measures that were popular in the early 1980s limited the ability of the legislature to adjust property taxes to revenue needs. A number of other initiative-driven measures earmarked funds for particular programs, or required that specified amounts of money be spent on particular policy areas. Aside from affecting policies in those areas, these measures had the cumulative effect of limiting the legislature's discretion over taxing and spending. In these cases, the reform of the budget process was implied rather than explicit and, to some degree, an accidental byproduct rather than an intended reform.

At the same time, reforms that have democratized the policy-making process have affected the types of policiy the states tend to produce. The bias of the initiative process is majoritarian; because it favors the median voter of the statewide electorate. By comparison, the legislative process has multiple pressures. Each legislator has to be responsive to the demands of their particular district (which means to the district median voter) while the legislative outcome, *ceteris paribus*, favors the median of the medians (that is the median legislator among legislators who represent the district medians). There is no reason to assume that the median of the statewide electorate will be the same as the median of the medians. If, in addition, the pressures of parties, special interest money and lobbyists and even the legislator's own ideology are added to the mix, there is every reason to expect the legislative and statewide initiative outcomes to vary, sometimes in important ways.

Even when a policy is not introduced through the initiative process, the threat of the initiative process can force a legislature to pass measures that it otherwise might not for fear that its authority would be pre-empted by a statewide measure. This has happened with the passage of parental consent abortion laws. In this indirect sense, the majoritarian pressures of the initiative process can force the legislature itself to be more majoritarian than it would otherwise.

Parties and political reform

One of the distinctive characteristics of US political reform is that it frequently seeks to limit the influence of political parties. Political parties, it is widely believed, are sources of corruption and unnecessary contention. This suspicion of political parties has its roots in the anti-factionalism of the Founding Fathers. Democracies, they believed, fell apart when people sorted themselves into contending factions based on different interests and values. Since the sources of faction lie in human nature, there was no hope in eliminating them, but their bad effects on government could be contained in an extended republic in which interests and groups could be set against one another. Dominant factions were more problematic since they could not be counterbalanced and, hence, could become tyrannical.

Although modern political parties could not have been anticipated in an era of limited franchise, the Madisonian argument against dominance still lingers in contemporary American pluralist thought. Citizens may be sorted into groups, and some groups may prevail over others in a particular skirmish, but dominance in one contest or even in several contests in one issue area does not bother the pluralist as long as a different coalition can be dominant in another policy area or branch of government. So defined political parties might or might not fit the pluralist model, depending upon their structure. Arguably, the broad, loose coalitions of interests under the US party umbrellas are consistent with the pluralist vision, but others do not see them that way. What parties do by their very nature is link people and groups with both common and complementary interests into a consistent voting and support faction. Thus environmentalists can be linked with civil rights advocates in support of each other's cause where separately they might only take a position on their own issue.

Ideologies provide a justification for linking these positions together in an apparently logical manner.

However, the pluralist or Madisonian suspicion of permanent factions is not the only strain of anti-partyism in American political culture: another influential line of reform thought in the United States is the Progressive. Reacting against the political, ethnic urban machines of the northeast and midwest, middle-class Progressives at the turn of the century attempted to reform government by making it more efficient and less partisan. Governmental decisions could be founded on neutral expertise and decided by individuals chosen on the basis of merit, not patronage or political loyalty. Party labels could be eliminated, forcing voters to choose candidates based on their individual statements and achievements. Voters did not need to be herded like sheep to the polls to slavishly support the local political machine. To this end, the Progressives introduced the nonpartisan ballot for local elections, the city manager form of local government, civil service reforms, and commission decision-making.

As opposed to the more general pluralist/Madisonian suspicion of parties, the Progressives more explicitly identified political parties with inefficient and corrupt government management. As the literature on political parties teaches, political parties are held together by several types of incentives, including the so-called "solidaristic" (see, for example, Wilson, 1966). These can be material (patronage jobs) or sentimental (ties of friendship and loyalty). While those incentives are critical to holding the party as organization together, they threaten efficiency in the sense that jobs or decisions that the parties give out may not go to the most objectively meritorious person, but to the loyalist. The merit norm is undermined by the organizational imperative.

However, as if the pluralist suspicion and the Progressive antagonism toward political parties were not enough, the populists, the third important variety of American reform, also envision a world without parties. The populist sees the potential for inherent evil in the mediation of the popular will. When the people can speak directly to an issue (for example, in the form of popular initiative), the popular will is likely to be reflected accurately, but when representatives or political parties attempt to stand for the popular will, it gets distorted and manipulated. The pure unmediated public will is always preferable to decision-making by political actors in artificial alliances. The political parties, populists believe, tend to serve opposing special interests, leaving the common man undefended and unrepresented.

The convergence of these three reform positions has created a strong anti-party bias in contemporary American reform efforts. This has been manifested in several recent controversies. Consider, for instance, the discussion of political parties in the current debate over campaign finance reform. The rules governing the financing of federal campaigns were set out in the Federal Election Campaign Act of 1971. This law established contribution limits and disclosure in Congressional elections, and contribution limits, expenditure limits, disclosure and public financing in the Presidential elections. Parties were limited in the amount of money that they could directly contribute to their own candidates. Since the only rationale that the US Supreme Court allows for limiting the first amendment rights of those who would give money to candidates is the prevention of quid pro quo corruption (see *Buckley* v. *Valeo* [1976]), the implicit assumption of the law was that parties could serve as conduits for corrupt private interests who would give money to the party to support a particular candidate, and thereby gain access and influence on policy-making.

At the time that FECA was passed, US political parties played a relatively subordinate role in running and financing campaigns. The 1970s were years in which candidate-centered campaign organizations reigned supreme. Political parties were regulated as an afterthought: a potential loophole that needed to be plugged, but nothing more than that. However, as the demand for political money increased and the contribution limits remained fixed, candidates needed to find alternative ways to raise the large sums of money to run campaigns that increasingly relied on paid consultants, computer-generated mail and television advertising. They found two ways to use political parties to solve their supply problem.

The first, as discussed in chapters 3 and 18, was the soft money exception. Soft money refers to money that is raised in unlimited amounts for the sake of party-building activities. Based on a ruling of the Federal Election Commission, political parties were allowed to raise this unregulated money as long as it was not used to directly urge voters to vote for a particular candidate. What the FEC had in mind was get-out-the-vote and registration activities; but what the political parties discovered in the 1990s was that they could use this money to fund generic party advertising (so-called issue advocacy) which in effect attacked the other party's candidate, and built support for their candidates as long as the advertisements omitted any terms that expressly advocated a vote for a particular candidate. Funds for soft money issue advertisements rose exponentially in the 1990s, as Chapter 18 underlines, finally reaching parity with the sums of hard money (that is money raised and spent under the FECA limits) in 2000.

The second loophole, which will be much harder to close, is the independent spending provision. The Supreme Court ruled in *Buckley* v. *Valeo* (1976) that if a group or individual wanted to spend funds to advocate on behalf of a candidate and did not coordinate or communicate with that candidate (that is, they did so independently), the legislature could not constitutionally limit what the group or individual spent. Subsequently, the

Court ruled in a case involving the Colorado Republican Party that political parties could make independent expenditure even when the opponent they attacked was officially a nominee of the other party (*Colorado Republican Federal Campaign Committee* v. *FEC* [1996]).

The upshot of this was to move political parties from a peripheral role to the center of campaign finance activities by the late 1990s. The thrust of recent reform efforts has been to curb the parties' role by either prohibiting or limiting them as regards raising soft money and spending on federal election activity. The reformers' goals are to close the contribution loophole that soft money creates and to restore parties to a status more equivalent to other interest groups and PACs. The goal is at one level perfectly understandable: clearly, the concept of limiting individual and group influence is undercut if they can give unlimited amounts to support candidates through the party. The only problem with this logic is that even if the soft money loophole is closed, the parties have an even bigger loophole to fall back upon: namely, the independent expenditure option. Basically if unofficially affiliated party committees decide to make their expenditures independent, they will be able to accomplish the same goals within the framework of any proposed regulation. Moreover, any attempt to close that loophole will likely be ruled unconstitutional.

The second goal, reducing the role that parties play in US federal elections, derives from the general suspicion of political parties discussed earlier and some additional considerations. First, as Eric Schickler underlines in Chapter 6, partisanship in the Congress has been on the rise and the bitterness of the late Clinton years left many voters weary of aggressive partisanship. Second, as Dean McSweeney notes in Chapter 3, American parties increasingly became campaign service organizations for the candidates: that is, more efficient extensions of the candidate-centered organizations. Parties more effectively target funds into the most competitive areas than do other organizations.

However, the parties and their activists play no more of a role in the determination of policy than they did in previous decades. Indeed, the parties have become even more top-down as opposed to grassroots-oriented in recent years. Some have even suggested that an unintended consequence of the parties' new campaign finance role has been to nationalize party structure, making state parties instruments of national party organizations. The perception of national party interference in state races has rubbed some voters and observers the wrong way. The service orientation emphasis of parties also feeds the perception of conduit corruption: that parties merely act as pass-throughs for special interest influence rather than serving traditional party functions of linking the grassroots activists to the candidates.

Another example of reformist suspicion of parties is the recent controversy over presidential nomination rules. The question of nomination rules has persisted over several decades. In the early twentieth century, a handful of states began to require that parties select their delegates to the presidential nominating conventions with elected primaries. Then, beginning with the McGovern-Fraser reforms, the Democratic Party led the way to opening up the process and changing the rules by which delegates were allocated to reflect election results in order to get more proportionality. Some of these rules have gone back and forth over time, but the general trend has been to have more elections as opposed to caucuses, and to open the party elections to independents and others who would like to participate in the nomination process.

On the face of it, these rule disputes may seem a bit esoteric and not particularly important. In reality, the rules can greatly affect the process and help determine the eventual winners. Allowing a number of states to move to the front of the nomination calendar has in effect front-loaded the process, giving an advantage to the well-funded front-runners. Winner-take-all rules (giving all of the state's delegates to a winning candidate in the manner of the Electoral College) have the effect of hastening the final outcome because it deprives the second-place finisher of a chance to accumulate enough delegates to seem credible to voters and donors in the next states in the sequence. Campaign finance rules which require that candidates perform above a certain level in order to qualify for federal matching funding also have this effect, and dictating to the parties the rules by which the primary election will be held affects both the types of nominees that are chosen and the campaign messages that the parties will go forward with in the November election.

The latter was the key question in California's blanket primary controversy (Cain and Gerber, 2001). A blanket primary is one in which voters get a ballot with all the names of all the candidates from all the parties, and can freely vote in any party's primary for any office. Hence, a voter in a blanket primary can vote in the Democratic primary for President and the Republican primary for US Senator, and so on. Having such a ballot encourages larger numbers of cross-over voters: (that is, voters who are normally affiliated with one party or no party, but who decide to vote in another party's primary). To the blanket primary's proponents that is a good thing, because the types of voter who cross over into another party's primary tend on average to be moderate independent and other party identifiers. Hence, the cross-over activity tends to help moderate candidates and to weaken the influence of the hard left and right.

Is it right for the state to dictate the rules by which parties select their nominees? Does it potentially open the door to manipulation? In Connecticut, a Democratically controlled state legislature had tried to prevent the minority Republican Party from adopting rules that would have allowed independents to vote in Republican state primaries. The Supreme Court overruled this effort, finding that this was an unwarranted intrusion into the associational rights of the parties (*Tashjian* v. *Republican Party of Connecticut* [1986]). But, in other cases, the courts have allowed state intrusions of as great or greater magnitude. For instance, the Court has upheld the right of a state to require primaries instead of caucuses, and prevented the Texas Democratic Party from closing its primaries to black voters (*Smith* v. *Allwright* [1944]).

In the minds of many reformers, political parties should be treated as regulated utilities. The two-party system produces an unnatural duopoly, discouraging the prospects of minor parties. Therefore the role of government, as in the case of the economic market place, is to limit the parties' anti-competitive behavior through regulation. On the other hand, the government that regulates the parties is also clearly political, and hence there is no protection for the rights of party members if a majority government abuses its powers. In California, the voters had approved of the blanket primary in a statewide initiative despite the objections of the parties themselves. In fact, the blanket rules violated the national party rules governing presidential nominations. Could the voters in a given state, some of whom were not members of a given party, impose nomination rules upon that party in the interests of opening up the process and encouraging more participation?

In the end, the Supreme Court struck down California's blanket primary rules, maintaining that parties have to have the freedom to make these decisions themselves. To most voters in California, this was an unpopular ruling. Most of them would have preferred to keep the blanket system and would have enjoyed the freedom of dabbling in the different primaries. To blanket primary proponents, closed systems only promote aggressive partisanship and ideological differences. To blanket primary opponents, the precedent of allowing the state (as a legislature or an initiative) to impose rules on the parties was a dangerous one, and to do this in the name of making the parties more moderate went against the First Amendment tradition.

Both of these cases – campaign finance reform and the open primary battle – illustrate the opposition that modern US reform has towards political parties. Progressives and populists prefer a world in which individuals are more influential. Pluralists prefer one in which there are no dominant groups and permanent alliances. In the end, the only protections political parties receive are from the courts, which are anti-majoritarian institutions.

Conclusion

The thrust of most reform in America today is majoritarian. Populist suspicion of authority is rampant, and the evolution of the Internet and cable television (as described in Chapter 17 on the media) has strengthened the idea that individuals do not need traditional organizations to mediate their political decisions for them. This has also reinvigorated the passion for direct democracy. The vision of a citizenry that can make choices directly via the Internet has captured the imagination of a younger generation who believe that new forms of technology can transform traditional ways of governance. They discount the possibility that the old problems merely resurface in new forms. Progressives are more sympathetic to the need for expert mediation, but are skeptical about whether traditional institutions, such as political parties, can handle this responsibility. Even the pluralists seek to break the duopoly of the two-party structure in the name of enhanced competition.

At the federal level in particular, the new reforms get slowed down and stopped by the anti-majoritarian features of the national government. The amendment process and the appointed judiciary have gutted many of the boldest reforms: term limits, campaign finance reform, party nomination changes, Electoral College reform and the like. To those who fear the consequences of the unchecked popular will, this is a good thing; but to those who do not, the anti-majoritarian features lead to frustration and even more convoluted reform strategies.

Guide to Further Reading

Note: Readers should bear in mind that websites may change. Additional links and general updates for the book may be found at www.gillianpeele.com/dap4.

Chapter 1   Introduction

Bok (2001) offers an analysis of the problem of government. Barone (2001) is a provocative examination of the new American population which might usefully be read alongside King (2000). Dissatisfaction with the workings of American democracy is discussed in Shafer (1997) and Sandel (1996). Putnam (2000) examines the problem of declining civic involvement. Eck (2001) looks at the impact of religions outside the Judaeo Christian tradition on American society. Among websites, <www.census.gov> (the official website of the US Census Bureau) gives a wealth of detail on the American population. For a recent survey of American attitudes to religion see The Pew Center for People and Press, "Religion and Politics: The Ambivalent Center," September 2000. See also on faith-based initiatives Dennis Hoover, "Charitable Choice and the New Religious Center" in *Religion in the News*, Spring 2000, 4–7.

Chapter 2   Electoral Politics

Ceaser and Bush (2000), Dionne and Kristol (2001) and Rakove, Kaysaar and Brady (2001) are useful books on the 2000 election. The *New York Times* (2001) chronicles the election crisis. Flanigan and Kingale (1989) provide an overview of voting behaviour. Useful websites include The National Election Studies site <http://www.umich.edu/~nes> which includes data on all presidential and congressional elections up to the present plus a massive bibliography and many reports. History Central: US Presidential elections <http://www.multied.com/elections/> includes information on all presidential elections up to the present. The *Washington Post* On Politics site <http://www.washingtonpost.com/wp-dyn/politics/elections/2000/> includes its full archive on the 2000 elections website as well as connections to its archive on 1998 and 2002. Project Vote Smart <http://www.vote-smart.org/index.phtml> is a website devoted to informing American votes in a nonpartisan and judicious manner. It contains lots of useful information on the electoral system and contemporary elections.

Chapter 3   Political Parties

A broad overview of parties is provided in Epstein (1986). Aldrich (1995) traces the existence of parties to the performance of functions in elections and government. Hrebnar *et al.* (1999) concentrate on parties in elections. Herrnson and

Green (1997) survey the minor parties. Green and Shea (1999) cover a range of party functions.

Chapter 4   Participation

On expanded agendas and social movements see Freeman and Johnson (1999) for case studies, and McAdam, McCarthy and Zald (1996) for theories. On intensified pressure see Cigler and Loomis (1998b) and Goldstein (1999), which is a case study. On declining social capital see Putnam (2001), and for an alternative view see Schudson (1998).

Chapter 5   The Presidency

Jones (1994) remains an unparalleled introduction to the presidency. Jones (1998) is a major, and useful, work on presidential transitions that can be treated as a companion to Pfiffner's excellent 1996 work on the same subject. More recently, the Clinton years have seen a great deal of scholarly attention focused on the relationship between politics and policy. J. E. Cohen (1997) and Jacobs and Shapiro (2000) both address this question.

Web resources are plentiful, but particularly useful are the Weekly Compilation of Presidential Documents <http://www.access.gpo.gov.nara/nara003.html> which can be a revelation. For a more general route into resources on the executive branch see the invaluable Library of Congress site <http://lcweb.loc.gov/global/executive/fed.html>

Chapter 6   Congress

Dodd and Oppenheimer (2001) provide a collection of articles summarizing recent research on Congress. Evans and Oleszek (1997) trace many of the reforms brought about by congressional Republicans after their 1995 takeover. Sinclair (2000) offers a detailed account of recent innovations in the legsislative process. Fenno (2000) compares two members of Congress representing the same Georgia district: a Democrat in the 1970s and a Republican from the 1990s. Mayhew (2000) examines the impact of members of Congress on the American political system as a whole.

<http://www.congresslink.org/> provides information about how the Congress works, its members and leaders, and the public policies it produces. It also includes reference   and   historical   materials   related   to   congressional   topics. <http://lcweb.loc.gov/global/legislative/mega.html> is a guide to websites about Congress, put together by the Library of Congress. <http://thomas.loc.gov/> is a guide to current legislation, members, and committees.

Chapter 7 The Supreme Court and the Constitution

General studies of the Rehnquist Court, its justices, and record include Belskey (2001), Gottlieb (2000), Savage (1993), Sunstein (1999), and Yarbrough (2000). Among works focusing on specific issues are Graber (1996) and Smith (1995). Accounts of *Bush* v. *Gore* include Dershowitz (2001), Dionne and Kristol (2001), and Posner (2001). Abraham (1999) profiles individual justices, their appointments, and records. Goldman (1997) focuses on aspects of federal judicial selection. The legal information Institute (www.law.cornell.edu) and Emory Law School's links <www.law.emory.edu> are useful sites.

Chapter 8 Federal Bureaucracy

Aberbach and Rockman (2000) deal with the federal bureaucracy in the broadest sense. Kettl(2000) addresses the issues of management in a global context. Krause (1999) examines the modern administrative state and its distinctive features while Light (2000a) presents an up-to-date look at the new public service.

Chapter 9 Federalism and Intergovernmental Relations

Walker (2000) provides a thorough overview of trends in federalism. Sabato (1983) is a spirited analysis of the role of the governor. Nathan (1987) offers an interesting insight into Reagan's relationship with the states. DiIulio and Kettl (1995) analyses the reality of American federalism while DiIulio and Thompson(1998) looks at the relationship between federalism and health care, as does Hackey and Rochefort (2001). Wright (1988) is a careful account of intergovernmental relations. Thorough study of the subject of federalism can be found at Temple's Center for the Study of Federalism, <http://www.temple.edu/federalism/> The National Governor's Association can be accessed at <http://www.nga.org/>.

Chapter 10 Economic Policy

The US Government websites contain a wealth of data about the performance of the American economy. The following websites provide gateways to most of the best sites: <http://www.whitehouse.gov/fsbr/esbr.html>, <http://www.fedstats.gov/imf/>, <http://usinfo.state.gov/usa/infousa/trade/govdocsi.htm>. The annual reports of the Congressional Budget Office and the Council of Economic Advisors also provide useful summaries of current developments. A good overview of the role of government in managing the economy is Gosling (2000).

Chapter 11   Law and Order

Spitzer (1995) is a good introduction to the politics of gun control. Dizard, Muth and Andrews (1999) and Bruce and Wilcox (1998) both offer excellent detailed analyses of all aspects of the firearms conflict. Henigan, Nicholson and Hemenway (1996) argue that the Second Amendment does not confer an individual right to gun ownership. On opposite sides of the conflict, Diaz (1999) argues for strengthening gun laws while Lott (1998) provides a strong endorsement of concealed carry laws. The National Rifle Association can be accessed at <www.nra.org> and the Coalition to Stop Gun Violence at <www.csgv.org>. Bedau (1997) and Sarat (2001a, 2001b) provide good discussions of capital punishment, sympathetic to the abolitionist case. Haines (1996) offers the best analysis of the evolving strategies and successes of the abolitionist movement in America. Bertram, Blachman, Sharpe and Andreas (1996) provide a comprehensive analysis of the politics of drugs in America; For arguments strongly against drug legalization see <http://www.mfiles.org/mariweb/user_impact/b3_source17.htm>. For further analysis on drug politics and policy see National Families in Action, <www.nationalfamilies.org>.

Chapter 12   Social Policy

Cloward and Piven (1993) provides an overview of public welfare as does Dinitto (1999).

Gans (1996) and Gilens (2000) provide robust analyses of the politics of welfare policy. Katz (1989) charts the evolution of poverty policy in recent years and Skocpol (1995) and Trattner (1999) provide historically informed analyses. Mink (1998) provides a stimulating perspective on recent policies. Quadagno (1996) explores the relationship between race and welfare. Schram (2000) and Schmidtz and Goodin (1998) are excellent studies which highlight the role of values in welfare policy. Two websites are particularly relevant for welfare and poverty: <www.acf.dhhs.gov/news/welfare> (Department of Health and Human Services, Administration for Children and Families) has much on TANF, Medicaid, Child Poverty, state welfare and social services, and <www.childstates.gov> is the official website of the Federal Interagency Forum on Child and Family Statistics. Among other useful websites, <www.urban.org/welfare/overview.htm> is the Urban Institute website with much detail on the effect of welfare overhaul; <www.iwpr.org> is the site of the Institute for Women's Policy Research which investigates the impact of policy on women and their children. <www.clasp.org> provides access to the work of the Center for Law and Social Policy which researches the effects of law and policy on the poor. Finally <www.childrensdefense.org> is an advocacy organization which makes available material on child poverty and rights.

Chapter 13   Health Care Policy

Rodgers (1998a) gives an excellent introduction to the historical background of American ideas about social policy generally, paying more attention than most commentators to the trans-Atlantic flow of policy ideas. The same author's essay (1998b) in Molho and Wood provides a useful discussion of how American scholarship tends to ignore the European origins of US policy, assuming that the American experience is distinctive and exceptional. Anderson, Rice and Kominski (2001) provides a thorough analysis of contemporary proposals for health care reform. Weissert and Weissert (1996) offer an overview of the politics of health care policy. Hackey and Rochefort (2001) offer a timely collection focusing on the state level of health care. Cleverly (1992) is still a useful guide to the details of health care finance. Bodenheimer and Grumback (1998) approach the subject of health care policy from a clinical perspective. Congressional Quarterly's (2000) review of health policy surveys current issues in a plain and fair-minded way.

One of the best gateway sites offering links to a wide variety of health policy organizations, agencies and issues is at Duke University's Center for Health Policy, Law and Management <www.hpolicy.duke.ed/cyberexchange/>.

Chapter 14   Foreign and Security Policy

A good introductory text is Jentleson (2000). Brown (1997) and Kapstein and Mastanduno (1999) are both excellent collections of essays on various aspects of America's foreign relations. Lieber (1997) and Neuchterlein (2001) both provide comprehensive interpretations of America's role in the world and the choices facing American policy-makers. The Foreign Policy Association <http://www.fpa.org> and the American Foreign Policy Council <http://www.afpc.org> have good websites with plenty of information and useful links.

Chapter 15   Direct Democracy

Cronin (1989) provides a useful overview of the role of direct democracy in American history. Gerber (1999) is a comprehensive review of the subject. Bowler, Donovan and Tolbert (1998) is a stimulating and contemporary collection covering aspects of citizen lawmaking and referendums. Sears and Citrin (1982) provides an in-depth analysis of the California tax revolt. The website of the Initiative and Referendum Institute <http://iandrinstitute.org> contains a wealth of information about direct democracy in the United States and other countries.

Chapter 16   Religion and Morality

Corbett and Corbett (1999) provide an overview of religion and politics in the United States, as does Wald (1996). Kintz and Lesage (1998) is a useful collection which focuses on the related roles of media and culture, with special attention to the new right. Kohut, Green, Keeter and Toth (2000) provide a contemporary account of the changing role of religion, and Witte (2000) explores the relationship between religion and American constitutionalism.

Chapter 17   The Media

Norris (2000) provides an overview of the role of political communications in democracy. Lupia and McCubbins (1998) raise important questions about the relationship between the media and democracy. Jamieson, (2001) is an excellent overview of media influence. Kurtz (1998) looks at the way the Clinton administration handled propaganda. The Pew Center for Civic Journalism provides a useful site: www.pewcenter.org.

Chapter 18   Campaign Finance

Sorauf (1992) provides an excellent history and analysis of different models of campaign finance reform. Grant (2000) surveys the criticisms of the system as it developed in the 1990s and examines recent proposals for reform. Gierzynski (2000) is a concise and stimulating overview of the issues involved in the debate about reform. <www.fec.gov>. The Federal Election Commission is the official agency regulating elections and its site provides information on aspects of campaign spending by candidates, political parties and political action committees (PACs). <www.opensecrets.org> is the website of the Center for Responsible Politics and investigates and publishes details of financial contributions to candidates and analyses the impact of money on elections.

Chapter 19   The United States in Evolution

Gerber (1999) is a useful overview of recent tensions in American understandings of democracy. Broder (2000) is a highly readable account of the role of initiatives and direct democracy. Kazin (1998) offers a historical account of American history that focuses on the populist strand of US culture. Cain and Noll (1995) examine the process of constitutional reform in one state (California).

Bibliography

Aberbach, J. D. and B. A. Rockman (2000) *In the Web of Politics*, Washington, DC: The Brookings Institution.

Abraham, Henry J., (1999) *Justices, Presidents and Senators*, Lanham MD.: Rowman & Littlefield.

Abramson, Jill (2000) "The Religious Right vs. McCain." *New York Times*, March 5.

Adams, Rebecca (2000) "Many States Failing to Insure Children", *CQWR*, August 12.

Aho, James (1996) "Popular Christianity and Political Extremism in the United States" in Christian Smith (ed.) *Disruptive Religion: The Force of Faith in Social Movement Activism*, New York: Routledge.

Albright, Madeleine (1998) "The Testing of American Foreign Policy", *Foreign Affairs* 77.

Aldrich, John R. (1995) *Why Parties? The Origin and Transformation of Parties in America*, Chicago, Il: University of Chicago Press.

Aldrich, John H. and David W. Rohde (1999) "The Consequences of Party Organization in the House: Theory and Evidence on Conditional Party Government," Paper presented at the Annual Meeting of the American Political Science Association, Atlanta, GA.

Alexander, Garth (2001) "Darkness Looms for Sunshine State," *The Sunday Times*, January 14.

Allred, Victoria (2001) 'Versatility with the Veto', *CQWR*, January 20.

Almond, Gabriel A. and Sidney Verba (1989) *The Civic Culture*, Newbury Park, CA: Sage.

Alvarez, Lizette (2000) "House Republicans Fret About 'Do-Nothing' Tag," *New York Times*, June 26.

Alvarez, R. Michael (1997) *Information and Elections*, Ann Arbor, MI: University of Michigan Press.

Anderson, Ronald, Thomas Rice and Gerald Kominski (eds) (2001) *Changing the U.S. Health Care System*, San Francisco, CA: Jossey-Bass.

Appleby, Joyce (1992) *Liberalism and Republicanism in the Historical Imagination*, Cambridge, MA: Harvard University Press.

Arnold, P. E. (1986) *Making the Managerial Presidency*, Princeton, NJ: Princeton University Press.

Aronowitz, Stanley (1995) "Against the Liberal State: ACT-UP and the Emergence of Postmodern Politics" in Linda Nicholson and Steven Seidman (eds), *Social Postmodernism: Beyond Identity Politics*, Cambridge: Cambridge University Press

Bailey, Christopher J. (1999) "Clintonomics," in Dilys Hill and Paul Herrnson (eds) *The Clinton Presidency*, London: Macmillan – now Palgrave.

Balz, Dan (2001) "Despite Wins, Bush Faces Battles Ahead," *Washington Post*, August 3.

Banfield, Edward C. (1970) *The Unheavenly City: the Nature of our Urban Crisis*, Boston: Little, Brown.

Barnes, James A. (2001) "Bush's Insiders," *National Journal*, June 23.

Barone, Michael (2001a) "The 49% Nation" in Michael A. Barone with Richard E. Cohen and Grant Ujifusa, *The Almanac of American Politics 2002*, Washington, DC: National Journal Group.

Barone, Michael (2001b) *The New Americans* Lanham, MD: Regnery Publishing.

Barr, S. (2001) "The New Management Insists that Better Need Not Be Costlier," *The Washington Post*, 22 June

Barstow, David and Dexter Filkins (2000) "For the Gore Team, a Moment of High Drama," *The New York Times*, December 4.

Bartels, Larry M. (2000) "Patisanship and Voting Behavior 1952–1996", *American Jounal of Political Science*, 44.

Bartels, Larry and John Zaller (2001) "Presidential vote models: A recount," *PS:* 2001.

Bedau, Hugo Adam (ed.) (1997) *The Death Penalty in America: Current Controversies*, Oxford: Oxford University Press.

Behr, Edward (1998) *Prohibition: The Thirteen Years That Changed America*, (Harmondsworth: Penguin.

Bellesiles, Michael A. (2000) *Arming America: The Origins of a National Gun Culture*, New York: Knopf.

Belskey, Martin H. (ed.) (2001) *The Rehquist Court: A Retrospective*, New York: Oxford University Press.

Bertram, Eva, Morris Blachman, Kenneth Sharpe and Peter Andreas (1996) *Drug War Politics: The Price of Denial*, Berkeley, CA: University of California Press

Bettelheim, Adriel (2001) "State of the Presidency: What Bush Inherits," *CQWR*, January 20.

Bibby, John F. (1999) "Party Networks: National-State Integration, Allied Groups, and Issue Activists," in John C. Green and Daniel M. Shea (eds.), *The State of the Parties*, 3rd ed, Lanham, MD: Rowman & Littlefield.

Bickers, Kenneth N. and Robert M. Stein (2000) "The Congressional Pork Barrel in the Republican Era," *Journal of Politics*, 62.

Blumberg, Melanie J., William C. Binning and John C. Green (1999) "Do the Grassroots Matter? The Coordinated Campaign in a Battleground State," in John C. Green and Daniel M. Shea (eds), *The State of the Parties*, 3rd ed, Lanham, MD: Rowman & Littlefield.

Bodenheimer, Thomas and Grumbach, K. (1998) *Understanding Health Policy, A Clinical Approach*. Stanford, CA: Appleton & Lange.

Bok, Derek Curtis (1996) *The State of the Nation: Government and the Quest for a Better Society*, Cambridge, Mass.: Harvard University Press.

Bok, Derek Curtis (2001) *The Trouble with Government*, Cambridge, Mass.: Harvard University Press.

Bolton, Alexander (2001) "GOP Finds Skirting Seniority Pays," *The Hill*, April 25.

Bond, Jon R. and Richard Fleisher (1990) *The President in the Legislative Arena* Chicago, Il: University of Chicago Press.

Borenstein, Seth (2001) "States are too lax in punishing water polluters, EPA says," *The Miami Herald*, August 23.

Bowler, Shaun, Todd Donovan and Caroline Talbert (1998). *Demanding Choices: Opinion, Voting, and Direct Democracy*, Ann Arbor, MI: University of Michigan Press.

Broder, David S. (2000) "Bush's Desire to Unite Will Be Tested," *Washington Post*, December 14.

Brown, Michael (ed.) (1997) *America's Strategic Choices*, Cambridge, MA: MIT Press.

Brown, E. Richard (2001) "Public Policies to Extend Health Care Coverage," in Ronald Anderson, Thomas Rice and Gerald Kominski (eds), *Changing the U.S. Health Care System*, San Francisco, CA: Jossey-Bass.

Bruce, John M. and Clyde Wilcox (1998) *The Changing Politics of Gun Control*, Lanham, MD: Rowman & Littlefield.

Burstein, Paul (1998) "Interest Organizations, Political Parties, and the Study of Democratic Politics," in Anne L. Costain and Andrew S. McFarland (eds), *Social Movements and American Political Institutions*, Lanham, MD: Rowman & Littlefield.

Bush, George W. (2001) "Address to a Joint Session of Congress and the American People," Washington, DC, September 20.

Cain, Bruce E., John Ferejohn, Margarita Najar and Mary Walther (1995) "Constitutional Change: Is it Too Easy to Change Our Constitution?" in Bruce E. Cain and Roger Noll, (eds) *Constitutional Change in California*, Berkeley: Institute of Governmental Studies Press.

Cain, Bruce E., and Roger Noll (1995) "Introduction" to Bruce E. Cain and Roger Noll, (eds) *Constitutional Change in California*, Berkeley: Institute of Governmental Studies Press.

Cain, Bruce E., Gillian Peele and Meg Mullin (2001) "City Caesars? The Role of Mayoral

Leadership in California" paper delivered to the Annual Meeting of the American Political Science Association, San Francisco.

Cain, Bruce E. and Elizabeth Gerber (2001) *Voting at the Political Fault Line: California's Experiment with the Blanket Primary*, Berkeley: University of California Press.

California Internet Voting Task Force (2000) "A Report on the Feasibility of Internet Voting," <www.ss.ca.gov/executive/ivote/final_report.htm>.

Campbell, Duncan (2001) "Party's over, but the band is still playing," *Guardian*, January 9.

Carey, Mary Agnes (1997) "Voters Urge Change in Managed Care," *CQWR* December 13.

Carey, Mary Agnes (2000) "Uninsured Americans Linger on Congress's Waiting List," *CQWR* September 9.

Carney, Dan (1997) "Immigrant Vote Swings Democratic as issues Moves Front and Centre," *CQWR* May 10.

Carney, Dan, Karen Foerstel and Andrew Taylor (1998) "A New Start for the House," *CQWR*, December 19.

Carney, Eliza Newlin (1999) "No Cop on the Beat," *National Journal*, 23 January.

CBO (2000) "The Budget and Economic Outlook: Fiscal Years 2001–2010," US Congress, CBO, January.

CBO (2001) "The Budget and Economic Outlook: Fiscal Years 2002–2011," US Congress, CBO, January.

CDF (1998) "Welfare to What: Early Findings on Family Hardship and well-Being," December:

CEA (2001) "Annual Report," Council of Economic Advisors, Washington, DC, January.

Ceaser, James W. and Andrew E. Bush (2001) *The Perfect Tie*, Lanham MD: Rowman & Littlefield.

Center for Voting and Democracy (2000) "Voter Turnout," <www.igc.apc.org/cvd/turnout/index.html>.

Chavez, Mark (2001) "Faith-based fallacies; Bush's initiative overlooks the realities of church charity in America," *Pittsburgh Post-Gazette,* February 22.

Chernay, André M. (2000) "Analysis of Internet Voting Proposals," Research Report, University of the Pacific, McGeorge School of Law.

Cigler, Allan J. and Burdett A. Loomis (1998) "From Big Bird to Bill Gates: Organized Interests and the Emergence of Hyperpolitics," in Allan J. Cigler and Burdett A. Loomis (eds), *Interest Group Politics*, 5th edn, Washington, DC: Congressional Quarterly Press.

Clarke, Ian (1997) *Globalization and Fragmentation: International Relations in the Twentieth Century*, Oxford, Oxford University Press.

Clark, Terry Nichols and Vincent Hoffman-Martinot (eds) (1998) *The New Political Culture*, Boulder, CO: Westview.

Cleverly, William (1992) *Essentials of Health Care Finance*, 3rd edn, Gaithersburg, MD: Aspen.

Cloward, Richard A. and Francis F. Piven *Regulating the Poor: The Functions of Public Welfare*, 2nd edn, New York: Vintage Press.

Clymer, Adam and Marjorie Connelly (2000) "Poll Finds Delegates to the Left of Both Party and the Public," *New York Times*, August 14.

Cochran, John (2001) "Campaign Finance Decision Could Come Down to the Wire,"*CQWR*, July 7, p. 1642.

Cohen, Jeffrey E. (1997) *Presidential Responsiveness and Public Policy-Making: The Public and the Policies that Presidents Choose*, Ann Arbor, MI: University of Michigan Press.

Cohen, Richard (2001) "Hastert's Hidden Hand," *National Journal*, 33.

Committee on Governmental Affairs (2001) *Government at the Brink: Urgent Federal Management Problems Facing the Bush Administration*, Washington, DC: Senate Committee on Governmental Affairs.

Committee on Political Parties (1950) "Towards a More Responsible Two-Party System," *American Political Science Review*, 44, supplement.

Congressional Quarterly (2000) *Issues in Health Policy*, Washington, DC: Congressional Quarterly Press.

Conn, Joseph L. (2001) "The bishops' biased blessing: politics in the Roman Catholic Church," *Church and State*, 53: 10.

Cope, Megan (1997). "Responsibilities, Regulation, and Retrenchment: The End of Welfare?" in Lynn A. Staeheli, Janet E. Kodras and Colin Flint (eds) *State Devolution in America: Implications for a Diverse Society*, London: Sage.

Cook, John (2001) "CNN's Free Fall" *Brills Content*, April.

Cooper, Joseph and David Brady (1981) "Institutional Context and Leadership Style: The House from Cannon to Rayburn," *American Political Science Review*, 75.

Corbett Michael and Julia M. Corbett (1999) *Politics and Religion in the United States*, New York: Garland Publishers.

Cornfield, Michael (2001) "The Week of the New," *Campaigns and Elections*, Dec/January.

Cox, Gary and Mathew D. McCubbins (1993) *Legislative Leviathan: Party Government in the House*, Berkeley, CA: University of California Press.

CQWR "2000 Legislative Summary: Appropriations Summary," December 16.

Cronin, Thomas E. (1989) *Direct Democracy: The Politics of Initiative, Referendum, and Recall*, Cambridge, MA: Harvard University Press.

Crozier, Michel, Samuel Huntington and Joji Watanuki (1975) *The Crisis of Democracy: Report on the Governability of Democracies to the Trilateral Commision*, New York, New York University Press.

D'Agnostino, Joseph A. (2000) " Bishop bars Ridge from Catholic functions," *Human Events*, 56: 3.

Dahl, Robert A. (1967) *Pluralist Democracy in the United States*, Chicago, IL: Rand McNally.

Dalton, Russell J. (1996) *Citizen Politics: Public Opinion and Political Parties in Advanced Industrial Democracies*, 2nd edn, Chatham, NJ: Chatham House.

Daniels, Norman (1985) *Just Health Care*, New York: Cambridge University Press.

Dao, James (2000) "Platform Is Centrist, Like G.O.P.'s, but Differs in Details," *New York Times*, August 14.

Dershowitz, Alan M. (2001) *Supreme Injustice: How the High Court Hijacked Election 2000*, Oxford: Oxford University Press.

Diaz, Tom (1999) *Making A Killing: The Business of Guns in America*, New York: The New Press.

Di Iulio, John and D. Kettl (1995) *Inside the Reinvention Machine: Appraising Governmental Performance*, Washington, DC: Brookings.

Di Iulio, John and Frank J. Thompson (1998) *Medicaid and Devolution: A View from the States*, Washington, DC: Brookings.

Dinitto, Diana M. (1999) *Social Welfare: Politics and Public Policy*. Boston: Allyn & Bacon.

Dionne, E. J., G. M. Pomper and W. G. Mayer (2001) *The Election of 2000: Reports and Interpretations*, Chatham, NJ: Chatham House.

Dionne, E. J. and William Kristol (eds) (2001) *Bush v. Gore. The Court Cases and Commentary*, Washington, DC: Brookings.

Dizard, Jan E., Robert Merrill Muth and Stepehn P. Andrews, Jr. (1999) *Guns in America: A Reader*, New York: New York University Press.

Dodd, Lawrence C. and Bruce I. Oppenheimer (2001) "A House Divided: The Struggle for Partisan Control, 1994–2000," In Lawrence C. Dodd and Bruce I. Oppenheimer (eds), *Congress Reconsidered* 7th edn, Washington, DC: Congressional Quarterly Press.

Doherty, Carroll J. and Jeffrey L. Katz (1998) "Firebrand Class of '94 Warms to Life on the Inside," *CQWR*, January 24.

Donovan, Todd, and Shaun Bowler (1998) "Direct Democracy and Minority Rights: An Extension," *American Journal of Political Science*, 42 (July).

Downes, David (2001) "The Macho Penal Economy: Mass Incarceration in the US – A European Perspective," in Anthony Giddens (ed.), *The Global Third Way Debate*, Cambridge: Polity Press.

Doyle, Michael (1995) "On the Democratic peace" *International Security* 19.

Dubois, Phillip L. and Floyd F. Feeney (1992) *Improving the California Initiative Process: Options for Change.* Berkeley, CA: California Policy Seminar, University of California.

Dukakis, Michael S. (2001) "The Governors and Health Policymaking," in Robert B. Hackey and David A Rochefort (eds), *The New Politics of State Health Policy*, Lawrence, Kansas: University Press of Kansas.

The Economist (2001) "Lexington: A Leader is Born," September 22.

Eck, Diana (2001) *A New Religious America,* San Francisco: Harper.

Eckstein, Harry (1988) "A Culturalist Theory of Political Change," *American Political Science Review*, 82.

Edsall, Thomas B. (1998) "Christian network to pay IRS fine," Washington Post, March 21.

Edsall, Thomas Byrne and Mary D. Edsall, (1991) *Chain Reaction: The Impact of Race, Rights and Taxes on American Politics*, New York: Norton.

Edwards, Catherine (2000) "Democrats play the religion card," <www.find articles.com> September 11.

Eisner, Robert (1994) *The Misunderstood Economy: What Counts and How to Count It,* Boston, MA: Harvard Business School Press.

Ellison, Michael (2000) "Signs of recession turn up the heat on Bush," *The Guardian,* December 27.

Epstein, Leon (1986) *Political Parties in the American Mold,* Madison, Wisc.: University of Wisconsin Press.

Evans, Lawrence C. and Walter J Oleszek (1997) *Congress Under Fire: Reform Politics and the Republican Majority,* New York: Houghton Mifflin.

Evans, C. Lawrence. (2001). "Committees, Leaders, and Message Politics," in Lawrence C. Dodd and Bruce I. Oppenheimer (eds), *Congress Reconsidered* 7th edn, Washington, DC: Congressional Quarterly Press.

Federal Election Commission (2001) "FEC Reports on Congressional Financial Activity for 2000," 15 May.

Felzenberg, A S. (2001) "Fixing the Appointment Process: What the Reform Commission Saw," *Brookings Review*, 18 (2).

Fenno, Richard F. (2000) *Congress at the Grassroots: Representational Change in the South 1970–98,* Chapel Hill: University of North Carolina Press.

Fiorina, Morris (1999) "Whatever Happened to the Median Voter?" unpublished manuscript, Stanford University, California.

Flanigan, William H. and Nancy H. Kingale (1998) *Political Behaviour of the American Electorate,* 9th edn, Washington, DC: Congressional Quarterly Press.

Foerstel, Karen (2000) "Choosing GOP Chairmen," *CQWR,* June 17.

Foerstel, Karen (2001a) "A Defining Role for DeLay?," *CQWR,* February 3.

Foerstal, Karen (2001b) "'527' Law Gratifies Political Watchdogs: Affected Groups See Mixed Results," *CQWR,* 17 March.

Freeman, Jo and Victoria Johnson (eds) (1999) *Waves of Protest: Social Movements since the Sixites,* Lanham, MD: Rowman & Littlefield.

Frendreis, John and Alan R. Gitelson (1999) "Local Parties in the 1990s: Spokes in a Candidate-Centred Wheel," in John C. Green and Daniel M. Shea (eds), *The State of the Parties*, 3rd edn, Lanham, MD: Rowman & Littlefield.

Frey, Bruno S. and Lorenz Goette (1998) "Does the Popular Vote Destroy Civil Rights?" *American Journal of Political Science*, 42 (October).

From, Al (2001) "Remarks by Al From at the DLC Forum Why Gore Lost and How Democrats Can Come Back", <http://www.NDOL.org>.

Gallup, George Jr (2001) "Americans More religious Now than ten years ago," <www.gallup.com.

Gallup, George, Jr and Jim Castelli (1989) *The People's Religion: American Faith in the 90's,* New York: Macmillan – now Palgrave.

Gallup Organization (1999) *Gallup Poll Monthly*, December.

Gallup Organization (2000) *Gallup Poll Monthly*, March.

Gallup Organization (2001) "Education Reform: The Public's Opinion," <www.gallup.com, January 24.

Gallup Organization (2001) "Presidential Ratings – Job Approval," <www.gallup.compoll/trends/ptjobapp.asp>.

Gallup Organization (2001) "Confidence in Institutions", <www.gallup.com, January 22.

Gamble, Barbara (1997) "Putting Civil Rights to a Popular Vote," *American Journal of Political Science*, 41 (January).

Gans, Herbert J. (1996) *The War Against the Poor: The Underclass and Antipoverty Policy*, New York: Basic Books.

GAO (2001) *Combating Terrorism: Selected Challenges and Related Recommendations*, Washington, DC: USGA, September, GAO-01-822.

Garrett, Elizabeth (1995) "Perspective on Direct Democracy: Who Directs Direct Democracy?" *University of Chicago Law School Roundtable*, 17.

Garrett, Elizabeth (1999) "Money, Agenda Setting, and Direct Democracy," *Texas Law Review*, 77.

Garrett, Elizabeth, and Elisabeth R. Gerber (2001) "Money in the Initiative and Referendum Process: Evidence of its Effects and Prospects for Reform," in M. D. Waters (ed.), *The Battle over Citizen Lawmaking*, Durham, NC: Carolina Academic Press.

Gerber, Elisabeth R. (1996). "Legislative Response to the Threat of Popular Initiatives," *American Journal of Political Science*, 40.

Gerber, Elisabeth R. (1998). "Pressuring Legislatures through the Use of Initiatives," in S. Bowler, T. Donovan and C. Tolbert (eds), *Citizens as Legislators*, Columbus: Ohio State University Press.

Gerber, Elisabeth R. (1999) *The Populist Paradox: Interest Group Influence and the Promise of Direct Legislation*, Princeton: Princeton University Press.

Gerber, Elisabeth R. and Simon Hug (2001) "Legislative Responses to Referendum," in M. Mendelsohn and A. Parkin (eds), *Referendum Democracy: Citizens, Elites, and Deliberation in Referendum Campaigns*, Toronto: Macmillan/St. Martin's Press, 191–210.

Gerber, Elisabeth R., Arthur Lupia, Mathew D. McCubbins, and D. Roderick Kiewiet (2000) *Stealing the Initiative: How State Government Responds to Direct Democracy*, New York: Prentice-Hall.

Gerber, Eve (2001) "Divided We Watch," *Brills Content*, February.

Gergen, David (2000) *Eyewitness to Power: The Essence of Leadership, Nixon to Clinton*, New York: Simon & Schuster.

Gerson, Michael (1998) "Who Will Vote?", *US News and World Report*, October 12.

Gierzynski, Anthony (2000) *Money Rules:Financing Elections in America*, Boulder, CO: Westview Press.

Gilens, Martin (2000) *Why Americans Hate Welfare: Race, Media and the Politics of Antipoverty Policy*, Chicago: University of Chicago Press.

Gill, Stephen (2000) "Toward a Postmodern Prince? The Battle in Seattle as a Moment in the New Politics of Globalization," *Millennium*, 29.

Gilmour, R. S. and A. A. Halley (1994) *Who Makes Public Policy?*, Chatham, NJ: Chatham House.

Glassman, James K. (1999) "Republicans in a Bind over the Economy," *Intellectual Capital.com*, September 16.

Glazer, Nathan and Daniel Patrick Moynihan (1970) *Beyond the Melting Pot*, 2nd edn, Cambridge, MA: MIT Press.

Glendon, Mary Ann (1991) *Rights Talk: The Impoverishment of Political Discourse*, New York: The Free Press.

Golden, M. M. (2000) *Bureaucratic Behavior in a Bureaucratic Setting*, New York: Columbia University Press.

Goldman, Sheldon (1997) *Picking Federal Judges: Lower Court selection from Roosevelt through Reagan*, New Haven: Yale University Press.

Goldsmith, Stephen (1997) *The Twenty First Century City: Resurrecting Urban America*, New York: Rockefeller Foundation.

Goldstein, Kenneth M. (1999) *Interest Groups, Lobbying, and Participation in America*, Cambridge: Cambridge University Press.

Goodstein, Laurie (2001) "A clerical and racial gap over federal help," *New York Times*, March 24.

Gosling, James J. (2000) *Politics and the American Economy*, New York, Longman

Gottlieb, Stephen E. (2000) *Morality Imposed: The Rehnquist Court and Liberty in America*, New York University Press.

Graber, Mark (1996) *Rethinking Abortion: Equal Choice, the Constitution and the Courts*, Princeton: Princeton University Press.

Grant, Alan (1995) "Political Action Committees in American Politics," in Alan Grant (ed.), *Contemporary American Politics*, Aldershot: Dartmouth.

Grant, Alan (2000) "The Reform of Campaign Finance," in Alan Grant (ed.), *American Politics: 2000 and Beyond*, Aldershot: Ashgate.

Gray, Virginia, and David M. Lowery (1996) *The Population Ecology of Interest Representation: Lobbying Communities in the American States*, Ann Arbor, MI: University of Michigan Press.

Green, John C., John S. Jackson and Nancy L. Clayton (1999) "Issue Networks and Party Elites in 1996," in John C. Green and Daniel M. Shea (eds), *The State of the Parties*, 3rd edn, Lanham, MD: Rowman & Littlefield.

Green, John C. and Daniel M. Shea (eds) (1999) *The State of the Parties*, 3rd edn, Lanham, MD: Rowman & Littlefield.

Greenhouse, Linda (2000) "Justices approve U.S. financing of religious schools' equipment," *New York Times*, June 29.

Greenspan, Alan (1997) "Testimony," US House of Representatives, Committee on Banking and Financial Services, Subcommittee on Domestic and International Monetary Policy, July 22.

Grofman, Bernard and Chandler Davidson (1992) *Controversies in Minority Voting: The Voting Rights Act in Perspective*, Washington, DC: Brookings.

Guth, James L. *et al.* (1995) "Onward Christian Soldiers: Religious Activist Groups in American Politics," in Allan J. Cigler and Burdett A. Loomis (eds), *Interest Group Politics*, 4th edn, Washington, DC: Congressional Quarterly Press.

Hackey, Robert B. (2000) "The Politics of Reform," *Journal of Health Politics Policy and Law*, 25 (1).

Hackey, Robert B. and David A. Rochefort (eds) (2001) *The New Politics of State Health Care Policy*, Lawrence, Kansas: University Press of Kansas.

Haines, Herbert H. (1996) *Against Capital Punishment: The Anti-Death Penalty Movement in America, 1972–1994*, Oxford: Oxford University Press.

Hajnal, Zoltan L., Elisabeth R. Gerber and Hugh Louch (2001) "Minorities and Direct Legislation: Evidence from California Ballot Proposition Elections," Forthcoming, *Journal of Politics*.

Hall, Jane (2001) "Cable Flying High," *Columbia Journalism Review*, Jan/February.

Halliday, Fred (2000) "Getting Real about Seattle," *Millennium*, 29.

Handler, Joel (2000) "'Ending Welfare as We Know It': The Win/Win Spin or the Stench of Victory," UCLA School of Public Policy and Social Research Typescript.

Handler, Joel (2001) "Welfare Reform: Something Old, Something New," UCLA School of Public Policy and Social Research Typescript.

Hardt, Michael, and Antonio Negri (2000) *Empire*, Cambridge, MA: Harvard University Press.

Harris, Daniel (1995) "AIDS, the Politically Correct and Social Theory," in Stanford M. Lyman (ed.), *Social Movements: Critiques, Concepts, Case-Studies*, London: Macmillan – now Palgrave.

Harris, John F. and Dan Balz, (2001) "Conflicting Image of Bush Appears," *Washington Post*, April 29.

Hart, J. (1995) *The Presidential Branch From Washington to Clinton* (Chatham, NJ: Chatham House).

Hartz, Louis (1955) *The Liberal Tradition in America*, New York: Harcourt, Brace.

Heclo, H. (1978) "Issue Networks and the Executive Establishment," in A. King, (ed.), *The New American Political System*, Washington, DC: American Enterprise Institute.

Heclo, Hugh and Lester M. Salamon (eds) (1981) *The Illusion of Presidential Government*, Boulder, CO: Westview.

Helms, Jesse (2000) "American sovereignty and the United Nations," *The National Interest*, 62.

Henigan, Dennis A., E. Bruce Nicholson and David Hemenway (1996) *Guns and the Constitution: The Myth of Second Amendment Protection for Firearms in America*, Amherst, MA: Aletheia Press

Hennessy, Rosemary (1995) "Queer Visibility in Commodity Culture", in Linda Nicholson and Steven Seidman (eds), *Social Postmodernism: Beyond Identity Politics*. Cambridge: Cambridge University Press.

Herrnson, Paul S. and Diana Dwyre (1999) "Party Issue Advocacy in Congressional Election Campaigns," in John C. Green and Daniel M. Shea (eds), *The State of the Parties*, 3rd edn, Lanham, MD: Rowman & Littlefield.

Herrnson, Paul S. and John C. Green (1997) *Multiparty Politics in America*, Lanham, MD: Rowman & Littlefield.

Hill, Kevin A. and John E. Hughes (1998) *Cyberpolitics: Citizen Activism in the Age of the Internet*, Lanham, MD: Rowman & Littlefield.

Hodgson, Godfrey (2000) "The Call of a Second Reagan," *The Independent on Sunday*, November 5.

Hoover, Dennis R. (2001) "Faith-based Update: Bipartisan Breakdown," *Religion in the News*, 4.2 Summer.

Hrebnar, Ronald J., Matthew J. Burbank and Robert C. Benedict (1999) *Political Parties, Interest Groups and Campaigns*, Boulder, CO: Westview Press.

Hunter, James Davison (1991) *Culture Wars: The Struggle to Define America*, New York: Basic Books.

Huntington, Samuel (1996) *The Clash of Civilisations and the Remaking of World Order*, New York: Simon and Schuster.

Hutcheson, Ron (2001) "Bush to push faith-based aid," *Philadelphia Inquirer*, January 26.

Inglehart, Ronald (1977) *The Silent Revolution: Changing Values and Political Styles Among Western Publics*, Princeton, NJ: Princeton University Press.

Inglehart, Ronald (1997) *Modernization and Postmodernization: Cultural, Economic, and Political Change in 43 Societies*, Princeton, NJ: Princeton University Press.

Ingraham, P. W. and D. P. Moynihan (2001) "Beyond Measurement: Managing for Results in State Government," in D. Forsythe (ed.), *Quicker, Better, Cheaper?: Managing Performance in American Government*, Albany, NY: Rockefeller Institute.

Initiative and Referendum Institute (2001a) "Historical Database," <http://iandrinstitute.org>, October.

Initiative and Referendum Institute (2001b) "Swiss Government Federal Ballots List," <http://www.admin.ch/ch/d/pore/va/liste.html>, October.

Ivins, Molly and Lou Dubose (2000) *Shrub: The Short but Happy Life of George W. Bush*, New York: Vintage.

Jacobs, Lawrence R. and Robert Y. Shapiro (2000) *Politicians Don't Pander: Political Manipulation and the Loss of Democratic Responsiveness*, Chicago, IL: University of Chicago Press.

Jacobson, Gary C. (2000) "Party Polarization in National Politics: The Electoral Connection," in Jon R. Bond and Richard Fleisher (eds), *Polarized Politics: Congress and the President in a Partisan Era*, Washington, DC: Congressional Quarterly Press.

Jacobson, Gary C. (2001) *The 2000 Elections and Beyond*, Washington, DC: Congressional Quarterly Press.

Jamieson, Katharine Hall (1996) *The Media and Politics*, Thousand Oaks: Sage.

Jamieson, Katharine Hall (2001) *The Interplay of Influence: News, Advertising, Politics and the Mass Media*, Belmont CA: Wadsworth.

Jentlesen, Bruce (2000) *American Foreign Policy: the Dynamics of Choice in the 21st Century*, New York, Norton.

Johnson, Paul E. (1998) "Interest Group Recruiting: Finding Members and Keeping Them," in Allan J. Cigler and Burdett A. Loomis (eds),. *Interest Group Politics* 5th edn, Washington, DC: Congressional Quarterly Press.

Johnson, Paul and Richard Neuhaus (ed.) (1986) *Unsecular America*, Grand Rapids, MI: Eerdmans.

Johnson, Victoria (1999) "The Strategic Determinants of a Countermovement: The Emergence and Impact of Operation Rescue Blockades," in Jo Freeman and Victoria Johnson (eds), *Waves of Protest: Social Movements Since the Sixties*, Lanham, MD and Oxford: Rowman & Littlefield.

Jones, Charles O. (1994) *The Presidency in a Separated System*, Washington, DC: The Brookings Institution.

Jones, Charles O. (1996) "Campaigning to Govern: The Clinton Style," in C. Campbell and B. A. Rockman, *The Clinton Presidency: First Appraisals*, Chatham, NJ: Chatham House.

Jones, Charles O. (1998) *Passages to the Presidency: From Campaigning to Governing*, Washington, DC: The Brookings Institution.

Jordan, Grant and William A. Maloney (1997) *The Protest Business? Mobilizing Campaign Groups*, Manchester: Manchester University Press.

Jorgenson, Dale W. and Kevin J. Stiroh (2000) "Raising the Speed Limit: US Economic Growth in the Information Age," *Brookings Papers on Economic Activity, 2000,* 1: 125–235.

Kagan, Robert 91999) "History Repeats Itself: Liberalism and Foreign Policy," *The New Criterion*, April.

Kapstein, Ethan and Michael Mastanduno (eds), (1999) *Unipolar Politics*, New York: Columbia University Press.

Karp, Jeffrey A. (1998). "The Influence of Elite Endorsements in Initiative Campaigns," in Shaun Bowler, Todd Donovan and Caroline J. Tolbert (eds), *Citizens as Legislators: Direct Democracy in the United States*, Columbus: Ohio State University Press.

Katz, Jeffrey L. and David S. Cloud (1996) "Welfare Overload Leaves Dole Campaign Dilemma," April 20.

Katz, Jeffrey L. (1997a) "Fierce Debate looms as Congress Turns to Social Security Rescue," *CQWR*, January 11.

Katz, Jeffrey L. (1997b) "Worker Protections Remain for Welfare Recipients," *CQWR*, August 2.

Katz, Jeffrey L. (1997c) "Longterm Challenges Temper Cheers for Welfare Successes," *CQWR*, October 25.

Katz, Michael (2001) *The Price of Citizenship: Redefining the American Welfare State*, New York: Metroplitan Books.

Katz, Michael B. (1989) *The Undeserving Poor: From the War on Poverty to the War on Welfare*, New York: Pantheon.

Kazin, Michael (1998) *The Populist Persuasion: An American History*, rev. edn, Ithaca, NY, and London: Cornell University Press.

Kellstedt, Lyman A. and John C. Green (1992) " Knowing God's many people: denominational preferences and political behaviour," in David C. Leege and Lyman A. Kellstedt (eds), *Rediscovering the Religious Factor in American Politics*, Amornk, NY: M.E. Sharpe, pp. 53–69.

Kellstedt, Paul M. and Lyman A. Kellstedt (1999) "Communication," in Richard Wuthnow (ed..), *Encyclopedia of Politics and Religion*, Washington, DC: Congressional Quarterly Press.

Kernell, Samuel (1997) *Going Public: New Strategies of Presidential Leadership,* 3rd edn, Washington, DC: Congressional Quarterly Press.

Kerwin, C. (2000) *Rulemaking*, 2nd edn, Washington, DC: Congressional Quarterly Press.

Kettl, D. (2000) *The Global Public Management Revolution*, Washington, DC: The Brookings Institution.

Khan, Muqtedar (2000) "A growing synergy: American Muslims and American Politics," *Washington Report on Middle Eastern Affairs*, October/November.

King, Desmond (1999) *In the Name of Liberalism*, Oxford: Oxford University Press.

King, Desmond (2000) *Making Americans*, Oxford: Oxford University Press.

Kintz, Linda and Julia Lesage (eds) (1998) *Media, Culture and the Religious Right*, Minneapolis, MI: University of Minnesota Press.

Kitfield, James (1999) "The Folks Who Live on the Hill," *National Interest*, Winter.

Knowlton, Brian (2001) "Treasury Chief Upgrades His Assessment of U.S. Economy," *International Herald Tribune*, March 26.

Kohut, Andrew, John C. Green, Scott Keeter and Robert C. Toth (2000) *The Diminishing Divide: Religion's Changing Role in American Politics*, Washington, DC: Brookings Institution.

Kolodny, Robin (1999) "Moderate Success: Majority Status and the Changing Nature of Factionalism in the House Republican Party," in Nicol C. Rae and Colton C. Campbell (eds), *New Majority or Old Minority: The Impact of Republicans on Congress*, Lanham, MD: Rowman & Littlefield.

Kraft, Michael E. and Denise Scheberle (1998) "Environmental Federalism at Decade's End: approaches and strategies," *Publius*, 28.1.

Krause, G. (1999) *A Two Way Street: The Modern Administrative State*, Pittsburgh, PA: University of Pittsburgh Press.

Krugman, Paul (1994) *The Age of Diminished Expectations*, Cambridge, MA: MIT Press.

Krugman, Paul (2001) "The New Reality Is Old Economy Shortages," *International Herald Tribune*, January 3.

Kuklinski, James H., Paul J. Quirk, Jennifer Jerit, David Schwieder and Robert F. Rich (2000) "Misinformation and the Currency of Democratic Citizenship," *Journal of Politics*, 62.

Kull, Steven (1999) *Misreading the Public: The Myth of a New Isolationism*, Washington, DC: Brookings.

Kurfist, Robert (1996) "Term Limit Logic: Paradigms and Paradoxes," *Polity* 29, 119–41.

Kurtz, Howard (1998) *Spin Cycle: Inside the Clinton Propaganda Machine*, New York: Free Press.

Ladd, Everett and Bowman (1998) *What's Wrong: A Survey of American Satisfaction and Complaint*, Washington, DC: AEI Press.

Lane, Charles (2001) "Court Backs Limits on Campaign Spending," *Washington Post*, 26 June, p. A01.

Langdon, Steve (1997) "With Campaign Dust Settling Medicare Chances Brighter," *CQWR*, January 18.

Levine, C. and P. Benda (1988) "Reagan and the Bureaucracy: The Bequest, the Promise and the Legacy," in C. O. Jones (ed.), *The Reagan Legacy*, Chatham, NJ: Chatham House.

Lieber, Robert (ed) (1997) *Eagle Adrift: American Foreign Policy at the End of the Century*, New York: Longman.

Light, P. C. (1991) *The President's Agenda: Domestic Policy Choice from Kennedy to Reagan*, rev. edn, Baltimore, MD: Johns Hopkins University Press.

Light, P. C. (1997) *The Tides of Reform*, New Haven, CT: Yale University Press.

Light, P. C. (2000a) *New Public Service*, Washington, DC: The Brookings Institution.

Light, P. C. (2000b) "The Empty Government Talent Pool: The New Public Service Arrives," *Brookings Review*, 18 (1).

Lipset, Seymour Martin (1996) *American Exceptionalism: A Double-Edged Sword*, New York: W. W. Norton.

Lizza, Ryan (2001) "White House Watch: Salvation," *New Republic*, April 23.

Longley, Lawrence D. and Neal R. Peirce (1999) *The Electoral College Primer 2000*, New Haven, CT: Yale University Press.

Loomis, Burdis A. and Allan J. Cigler (1998) "Introduction; The Changing Nature of Interest Group Politics," in Allan J. Cigler and Burdett A. Loomis (eds), *Interest Group Politics*, 5th edn, Washington, DC: Congressional Quarterly Press.

Lott, John R. Jr (1998) *More Guns, Less Crime: Understanding Crime and Gun Control Laws,* Chicago, IL: University of Chicago Press.

Lowenstein, Daniel Hayes (1982) "Campaign Spending and Ballot Propositions: Recent Experience, Public Choice Theory and the First Amendment," *UCLA Law Review,* 29.

Lupia, Arthur (1994) "Shortcuts Versus Encyclopedias: Information and Voting Behavior in California Insurance Reform Elections," *American Political Science Review,* 88.

Lupia, Arthur and Mathew D. McCubbins (1998) *The Democratic Dilemma: Can Citizens Learn What They Need To Know?,* Cambridge; Cambridge University Press.

Lynch, Cecilia (1998) "Social Movements and the Problem of Globalization," Alternatives, 23.

McAdam, Doug (1999) *Political Process and the Development of Black Insurgency, 1930–1970,* 2nd edn, Chicago, IL: University of Chicago Press.

McAdam, Doug, John D. McCarthy and Mayer Zald (eds) (1996) *Comparative Perspectives on Social Movements; Political Opportunities, Mobilizing Structures and Cultural framings,* Cambridge; Cambridge University Press.

McAdam, Doug, Sidney Tarrow and Charles Tilly (1996) "To Map Contentious Politics," *Mobilization,* 1.

McCarthy, Eugene J. and Keith C. Burris (2000) "The singular piety of politics," *New York Times,* September 30.

McCarthy, John D. and Clark McPhail (1998) "The Institutionalization of Protest in the United States," in David S. Meyer and Sidney Tarrow (eds), *The Social Movement Society: Contentious Politics for a New Century,* Lanham, MD: Rowman & Littlefield.

McEnery, Tom (1994) *The New City State,* Ninot, CO.

McFeely, William S. (2000) *Proximity To Death,* New York: W. W. Norton.

Mackenzie, G. C. (2001) "'Nasty and Brutish Without Being Short': The State of the Presidential Appointment Process," *Brookings Review,* 18 (2).

Madison, James, Alexander Hamilton and John Jay (1987) *The Federalist Papers.* Harmondsworth: Penguin.

Magleby, David (2001) "Election Advocacy: Soft Money and Issue Advocacy in the 2000 Congressional Elections," <ww.byu.edu/outsidemoney/2000general>.

Mahtesian, Charles (2000) "Veto Happy", *Governing Magazine,* September.

Mandelbaum, Michael (1996) "Foreign Policy as Social Work," *Foreign Affairs,* 75.

Marcus, Ruth (2000) "Costliest Race in US History Nears End," *Washington Post,* November 6.

Marcus, Ruth and Sarah Cohen (2001) "The Loophole Lesson in Soft Money," *Washington Post,* March 18.

Marmor, Theodore (1970) *The Politics of Medicare,* Chicago, IL: Aldine.

Martin, Marty E. (1999) "United States," in Richard Wuthnow (ed.), *Encyclopedia of Politics and Religion,* Washington, DC: Congressional Quarterly Press.

Martin, Mitchell (2001a) "Fed Chairman Warns Growth 'Is Close to Zero,'" *International Herald Tribune,* January 26.

Martin, Mitchell (2001b) "Consumers in U.S. Lose Confidence," *International Herald Tribune,* January 31.

Martin, Mitchell (2001c) "Fed Chief Offers Brighter Outlook," *International Herald Tribune,* February 14.

Mayer, William G. (1992) *The Changing American Mind,* Ann Arbor, MI: University of Michigan Press.

Mayhew, David R. (1996) "Innovative Midterm Elections," in Philip A. Klinkner (ed.), *Midterm: The Elections of 1994 in Context,* Boulder, CO: Westview Press.

Mayhew, David (2000) *America's Congress: Actions in the Public Sphere, James Madison Through Newt Gingrich,* New Haven: Yale University Press.

Mead, Lawrence (1996) "Welfare Policy: The Administrative Frontier," *Journal of Policy Analysis and Management,* 15.

Melkers, J. and K. Willoughby (1998) "The State of the States: Performance-Based Budgeting Requirements in 47 out of 50," *Public Administration Review* 58.

Milbank, Dana and Richard Morin (2001) "Public Is Unyielding in War Against Terror," *Washington Post*, September 29.

Miller, Alan C. and Nick Anderson (2000) "Cost of ballot reforms nationwide put at $9 billion; Some officials say expense will deter them from improving process," *Milwaukee Journal Sentinel*, December 22.

Miller, Kenneth P. (1999) "The Role of the Courts in the Initiative Process: A Search for Standards," paper presented at the 1999 Annual Meeting of the American Political Science Association, Atlanta, GA.

Mink, Gwendolyn (1998) *Welfare's End*, Ithaca, New York: Cornell University Press.

Mintz, Elana (1997) "Means Testing Around Since the Beginning," *CQWR*, July 26.

Mintz, John and Dan Keating (2000) "A Racial Gap in Voided Votes: Precinct Analysis Finds Stark Inequity in Polling Problems," *Washington Post*, December 21.

Mitchell, Alison (2001) "Blacks and Hispanics in House balk on campaign finance bill," *New York Times*, May 8.

Mookas, Ioannis (1998) "Faultiness: homophobic innovation in gay rights/special rights." Pp. 345-362 in Linda Kintz and Julia Lesage (eds), *Media, Culture, and the Religious Right*, Minneapolis: University of Minnesota Press.

Moore, David W. (1993) "Catholics at odds with church teachings," *Gallup Poll Monthly*, August 21–31.

Morone, James (1990) "American Political Culture and the Search for Lessons from Abroad," *Journal of Health Politics Policy and Law*, 15 (1).

Morone, James A. (1998) *The Democratic Wish: Popular Participation and the Limits of American Government*, rev. edn, New Haven, CT: Yale University Press.

Morris, Aldon C. (1984) *The Origins of the Civil Rights Movement: Black Communities Organizing for Change*, New York: Free Press.

Morris, Aldon C. (1999) "A Retrospective on the Civil Rights Movement: Political and Intellectual Landmarks," *Annual Review of Sociology*, 25.

Morris, Dick, (1999) *Behind the Oval Office: Getting Reelected Against All The Odds*, Los Angeles, CA: Renaissance Books.

Morton, Rebecca (1996) "Legislative Response to the Threat of Popular Initiatives," *American Journal of Political Science*, 40.

Mueller, John E. (1973) *War, Presidents and Public Opinion*, New York: John Wiley.

Nagourney, Adam and Janet Elder (2000) "Poll of Delegates Shows Convention Solidly on the Right," *New York Times*, July 31.

Nathan, Richard P. (1987) *Reagan and the States*, Princeton: Princeton University Press.

Nather, David (2000a) "The Medicaid – Welfare Trap," *CQWR*, September 9.

Nather, David (2000b) "Health Care Costs Poised to Surge Again," *CQWR*, October 14.

Nather, David and Adriel Bettelheim (2001) "2000 Vote Studies: Moderates and Mavericks Hold Key to 107th Congress," *CQWR*, January 6.

Navarro, Vincente (1996) "Why Some Countries Have National Health Insurance, Others Have National Health Services, and the U.S. Has Neither," *Social Science and Medicine*, 28 (3).

Nelson, Michael (ed.) (2001) *The Elections of 2000*, Washington, DC: Congessional Quarterly Press.

Neuchterlein, Donald (2001) *America Recommitted: A Superpower Assesses its Role in a Turbulent World*, Lexington Kentucky: University of Kentucky Press.

Nelson, Zed (2000) *Gun Nation*, London: Westzone.

Neustadt, Richard (2001) "The Weakening White House," *British Journal of Political Science*, 31, p. 1–11.

Newport, Frank (1999) "Americans remain very religious but not necessarily in conventional ways," *Gallup Poll Monthly*, December.

New York Times, (Correspondents) (2001) *How Race is Lived in America: Pulling Together, Pulling Apart*, New York: Henry Holt.

New York Times (2001) *The Complete Chronicle of the 2000 Presidential Election Crisis*, New York: Times Books.

Niemi, Richard G. and Herbert F. Weisberg (eds) (2001) *Controversies in Voting Behavior*, 4th edn, Washington, DC: Congressional Quarterly Press.

Norquist, John O. (1998) *The Wealth of Cities: Revitalizing the Centers of American Life*, Reading, MA: Addison-Wesley.

Norris, Pippa (1999) *Critical Citizens: Global Support for Democratic Government*, Oxford: Oxford University Press.

Norris, Pippa (2000) *A Virtuous Circle; Political Communications in Post-Industrial Societies*, Cambridge: Cambridge University Press.

Offe, Claus (1985) "New Social Movements: Challenging the Boundaries of Institutional Politics," *Social Research*, 52.

Olasky, Marvin (2000) "What is Compassionate Conservatism and Can it Transform America?" <http://www.heritage.orglibrary/lecture>.

Oliver, Thomas (1999) "The Dilemmas of Incrementalism: Logical and Political Constraints in the Design of Health Insurance," *Journal of Health Politics Policy and Law*, 18 (4).

Olson, Mancur (1965) *The Logic of Collective Action*, Cambridge, MA: Harvard University Press.

OMB (2001) Catalogue of Domestic Federal Assistance, Washington, DC.

Owens, John R. and Larry L. Wade (1986) "Campaign Spending on California Ballot Propositions (1924–1984): Trends and Voting Effects," *Western Political Quarterly* 39.

Pearlstein, Steven (2001) "Memo From Wall Street: Even Harder Path Ahead," *International Herald Tribune*, September 10.

Peele, Gillian (1984) *Revival and Reaction: The Right in Contemporary America*, Oxford: Oxford University Press.

Peters, B. G. (1993) *American Public Policy: Promise and Performance*, 3rd edn, Chatham, NJ: Chatham House.

Peters, B. G. (2001) *The Politics of Bureaucracy*, 5th edn, London: Routledge

Peters, B. G. (2002) "The Anglo-American Administrative Tradition," in J. A. Halligan (ed.), *Anglo-American Administrative Systems*, Cheltenham: Edward Elgar.

Peters, B. G., R. A. W. Rhodes and V. Wright (1999) *Administering the Summit*, Oxford: Oxford University Press.

Peters, Ronald (1997) *The American Speakership: The Office in Historical Perspective*, 2nd edn, Baltimore, MD, and London: Johns Hopkins University Press.

Pfiffner, James P. (1996) *The Strategic Presidency: Hitting the Ground Running*, 2nd edn, Lawrence, KS: University Press of Kansas.

Pianin, Eric and Juliet Eilperin (2000) "No Love Lost for Hastert, Gephardt," *Washington Post*, March 20.

Pitney, John J. (2001). "Extension of Remarks: War on the Floor," *APSA Legislative Studies Section Newsletter*, 24 (January).

Piven, Frances Fox and Richard A. Cloward (1979) *Poor People's Movements: Why They Succeed, How They Fail*, New York: Vintage Books.

Plotke, David (1992) "The Political Mobilization of Business," in Mark P. Petracca (ed.), *The Politics of Interests: Interest Groups Transformed*, Boulder, CO: Westview.

Plotke, David (1995) "What's so New about New Social Movements?", in Stanford M. Lyman (ed.), *Social Movements; Critiques, Concepts, Case-Studies*, London: Macmillan – now Palgrave.

Polsby, Nelson W. (1997) "A Revolution in Congress?" Inaugural Lecture, John M. Olin Chair in American Government.

Pollitt, C. and G. Bouckaert (2000). *Public Management Reform*. Oxford: Oxford University Press.

Posner, Richard A. (2001) *Breaking Deadlock: The 2000 Election*, Princeton, NJ: Princeton University Press.

Powell, Colin (1992) "US Forces: Challenges Ahead," *Foreign Policy*, 71.

Powell, Lynda W. and Richard G. Niemi (2000) "Constituency Representation: The Role of Liberalism-Conservatism in House Primary and General Elections," unpublished paper.

Putnam, Robert D. (2000) *Bowling Alone: The Collapse and Revival of American Community*, New York: Simon & Schuster

Putnam, Robert D. (2001) "A Better Society in a Time of War," *New York Times*, October 19, <http://www.nytimes.com.2001/10/19opinion/19PUTN.html>.

Quadagno, Jill (1996) *The Colour of Welfare: How Racism Undermined the War on Poverty*, Oxford: Oxford University Press.

Quirk, P. J. and Joseph Hinchliffe (1996) "Domestic Policy: The Trials of a Centrist Democrat," in Campbell, C. and B. A. Rockman, *The Clinton Presidency: First Appraisals*, Chatham, NJ: Chatham House.

Radin, B. A. (1998) "The Government Performance and Results Act (GPRA): Hydra-Headed Monster or Flexible Management Tool?," *Public Administration Review*, 58.

Raichur, Arvind and Richard W. Waterman (1993) "The Presidency, The Public and the Expectations Gap," in Richard W. Waterman (ed.), *The Presidency Reconsidered*, Itasca, IL: F. E. Peacock.

Rakove, Jack N., Alex Kaysaar and Henry Brady (2001) *The Unfinished Election of 2000*, New York: Basic Books.

Rasmussen Research (2001) "Government Operations," conducted April 29–May 1.

Rast Joel (1999) *Remaking Chicago:The Politics of Urban Industrial Change*, De Kalb, IL. University of Northern Illinois Press.

Rich, Andrew and R. Kent Weaver (1998) "Advocates and Analysts: Think Tanks and the Politicization of Expertise," in Allan J. Cigler and Burdett A. Loomis (eds) *Interest Group Politics* 5th edn, Washington, DC: Congressional Quarterly Press.

Rochon, Thomas R. (1998) *Culture Moves: Ideas, Activism, and Changing Values*, Princeton, NJ: Princeton University Press.

Rockman, Bert A., (2000) "Cutting with the Grain: Is there a Clinton leadership legacy?" in Campbell, C. and B. A. Rockman, *The Clinton Presidency: First Appraisals*, Chatham, NJ: Chatham House.

Rodgers, Daniel (1998a) *Atlantic Crossings: Social Politics in a Progressive Age*, Cambridge, MA: Harvard University Press.

Rodgers, Daniel (1998b) "Exceptionalism," in Anthony Molho and Gordon Wood (eds), *Imagined Histories: American Historians and the Past*. Princeton, NJ: Princeton University Press.

Rohde, David W. (1991) *Parties and Leaders in the Postreform House*, Chicago, IL, and London: University of Chicago Press.

Rom, Mark Carl, Paul E. Peterson and Kenneth F. Scheve (1998) "Interstate Competition and welfare Policy," *Publius*, 28, 3.

Rose, Gideon (1999) "Present Laughter or Utopian Bliss," *National Interest*, Winter 41–7.

Rosenau, Pauline V. (2001) "Market Structure and Performance: Evaluating the U.S. Health System reform," *Journal of Health and Social Policy*, 13 (1).

Rosenbaum, David E. (2001a) "Congress Adopts Plan to Cut Taxes Over Next Decade," *The New York Times*, May 11.

Rosenbaum, David E. (2001b) "News Analysis: Tax Cut Become Law, for Now," *The New York Times*, June 8.

Rosenstiel, Tom, Carl Gottlieb and Lee Ann Brady (2000) "Time of peril for Local TV News," *Columbia Jouirnalism Review*, November/December.

Rosenthal, Donald B. (ed.), (1980) *Urban Revitalization*, Beverly Hills, CA: Sage.

Rothman, D. J. (1993) "A Century of Failure: Health Care Reform in America," *Journal of Health Politics Policy and Law*, 18 (2).

Rozell, Mark J. and Clyde Wilcox (1995) *God at the Grassroots: The Christian Right in the 1994 Elections*, Lanham, MD: Rowman & Littlefield.

Sabato, Larry J. (1983) *Goodbye to Good-time Charlie: The American governorship transformed*, 2nd edn, Washington DC: Congressional Quarterly Press.

Sandel, Michael J. (1996) *Democracy's Discontent; America in Search of a Public Philosophy*, Cambridge, Mass.: The Belknap Press.

Sanger, D.E. and Marc Lacey (2001) "Survey Says Bush Gets Fewer Stories," *New York Times*, April 30.

Sanger, D. E. (2001) "Trying to Run a Country Like a Corporation," *New York Times*, July 8.

Sanger, David E. and Elisabeth Bumiller (2001) "In One Month a Presidency is Transformed," *New York Times*, October 11.

Sarasohn, Judy (2001) "Fortune: NRA is No. 1 on Capitol Hill, *Washington Post*, May 17.

Sarat, Austin (ed.), (2001a) *The Killing State: Capital Punishment in Law, Politics and Culture*, Oxford: Oxford University Press

Sarat, Austin (2001b) *When The State Kills: Capital Punishment and the American Condition*, Princeton, NJ: Princeton University Press.

Savage, David G. (1993) *Turning Right: The Making of the Rehnquist Supreme Court*, New York: Wiley.

Schickler, Eric (2001) *Disjointed Pluralism: Institutional Innovation and the Development of the U.S. Congress*, Princeton, NJ: Princeton University Press.

Schlesinger, Arthur M. Jr (1974) *The Imperial Presidency*, New York: Popular Library.

Scholte, Jan Aart (2000) *Globalization: A Critical Introduction*, Basingstoke: Palgrave.

Schlozman, Kay Lehman and John T. Tierney (1983) "More of the Same: Washington Pressure Group Activity in a Decade of Change," *Journal of Politics*, 45.

Schmidt, Susan (2000) "Last-minute donations a boon for both parties," *The Washington Post*, December 19.

Schmidtz, David and Robert E. Goodin (1998) *Social Welfare and Individual Responsibility (For and Against)*, Cambridge: Cambridge University Press.

Schram, Sanford F. (2000) *After Welfare: The Culture of Post-Industrial Society*, New York: New York University Press.

Schudson, Michael (1998) *The Good Citizen: A History of American Civic Life*, New York: Free Press.

Scott, Alan and John Street (2000) "From Media Politics to E-Protest: The Use of Popular Culture and New Media in Parties and Social Movements," *Information, Communication and Society*, 3.

Sears, David O. and Jack Citrin (1982) *Tax Revolt: Something for Nothing in California*, Cambridge, MA: Harvard University Press.

Seeley, Katharine Q. and Frank Bruni (2001) "A long process that led Bush to his decision," *New York Times*, August 11.

Seidman, H. (1998) *Politics, Position and Power: The Dynamics of Federal Organization*, New York: Oxford University Press.

Shafer, Byron E. (1997) *Present Discontents: American Politics in the very late Twentieth Century*, Chatham, NJ: Chatham House.

Shafer, Byron E. (1998) "Partisan Elites, 1946–1996," in Byron E. Shafer, (ed.), *Partisan Approaches to Postwar American Politics*, New York: Chatham House.

Shefter, Martin (1986) "Trade Unions and Political Machines: The Organization and Disorganization of the American Working Class in the Late Nineteenth Century," in Ira Katznelson and Aristide R. Zolberg (eds), *Working-Class Formation: Nineteenth-Century Patterns in Western Europe and the United States*, Princeton, NJ: Princeton University Press.

Shenon, Philip (2001) "Showdown Looms as Democrats Move to Burst GOP Budget," *The New York Times*, June 19.

Shepard, Alicia (2000) "How They Blew It: A Behind-the-scenes Look at the Television Networks' Dismal Performance on Election Night," *American Journalism Review*, January/February.

Simmons, Wendy W. (2001a) "Gallup Poll release: Public Has Mixed Feelings About Tax Cuts," <www.gallup.com>, January 24.

Simmons, Wendy W. (2001b) "Gallup Poll Release: Though Very Religious, Americans Most Likely to Say Government is Responsible for the Poor," <www.gallup.com>, January 30.

Simon, Stephanie (2001) "Kansas restores evolution in schools," *Pittsburgh Post-Gazette,* February 15.

Sinclair, Barbara (2000) *Unorthodox Lawmaking; New Legislative Processes in the US Congress,* 2nd edn, Washington, DC: Congressional Quarterly Press.

Sinclair, Barbara (2001) "The New World of U.S. Senators." in Lawrence C. Dodd and Bruce I. Oppenheimer (eds), *Congress Reconsidered,* 7th edn, Washington, DC: Congressional Quarterly Press.

Singh, Robert (1999) "Gun Politics in America," *Parliamentary Affairs,* 52 (1).

Skocpol, Theda (1995) *Social Policy in the United States: Future Possibilities in Historical Perspective,* Princeton, NJ: Princeton University Press.

Skowronek, Stephen (1993) *The Politics Presidents Make: Leadership from John Adams to George Bush,* Cambridge, MA: Belknap Press.

Smith, Daniel A. (2001) "Campaign Financing of Ballot Initiatives in the American States," in Larry J. Sabato, Howard R. Ernst and Bruce A. Larson (eds), *Dangerous Democracy? The Battle Over Ballot Initiatives in America,* Lanham, MD: Rowman & Littlefield.

Smith, David and Garth Alexander (2001) "Can He Fix It?," *The Sunday Times,* January 7.

Smith, Steven D. (1995) *Foreordained Failure: The Quest for a Constitutional Principle of Religious Freedom,* New York; Oxford University Press.

Smith, Steven S. and Gerald Gamm, (2001) "The Dynamics of Party Government in Congress," in Lawrence C. Dodd and Bruce I. Oppenheimer (eds), *Congress Reconsidered,* 7th edn, Washington, DC: Congressional Quarterly Press.

Sneyd, Ross (2000) "Election results mean law won't be repealed." Associated Press wire report, November 8. <web.lexis-nexis.com/universe/doc> (January 19 2001).

Sombart, Werner (1906) *Why is There No Socialism in the United States?,* republished 1976, New York, White Plains; International Arts and Sciences.

Sorauf, Frank (1992) *Inside Campaign Finance: Myths and Reality,* New Haven, CT: Yale University Press.

Southwell, Patricia (1995) "'Throwing the Rascals Out' versus 'Throwing in the Towel': Alienation, Support for Term Limits and Congressional Voting Behaviour," *Social Science Quarterly,* 76.

Spitzer, Robert J. (1995) *The Politics of Gun Control,* Chatham, NJ: Chatham House.

Stelzer, Irwin (2001) "Recession fear has made us all tax cutters," *The Sunday Times,* January 14.

Stevenson, Richard W. (2001) "The Check is in the Mail. Almost," *The New York Times,* April 29.

Stewart, Heather and Larry Elliot (2001) "US Confidence Slumps," *The Guardian,* September 26.

Stone, Peter H. (2000) "Going for Gold," *National Journal,* October 14.

Stone Walter J. and Ronald B. Rapoport (2001) "Its Perot Stupid; The Legacy of the 1992 Perot Movement in the Major-Party System 1992–2000," *PS,* 49.

Sunstein, Cass R. (1999) *One Case at a Time: Judicial Minimalism and the Supreme Court,* Cambridge, Mass: Harvard University Press.

Sunstein, Cass R. and Richard A. Epstein (eds) (2001) *The Vote: Bush, Gore and the Supreme Court,* Chicago, IL: University of Chicago Press

Tarjani, Judy (2001) "Muslims worked religiously to get out vote," *Pittsburgh Post-Gazette,* March 20.

Taylor, Andrew (2000) "Issues Held Hostage in War Between Action, Gridlock," *CQWR,* February 26.

Taylor, Andrew (2001a) "Senate GOP to Share Power," *CQWR,* January 6.

Taylor, Andrew (2001b) "A Senate of Singular Personalities and Possibilities," *CQWR,* January 27.

Taylor, Andrew with Derek Willis and John Cochran (2001) "McCain – Feingold Survives Hard Fight over Soft Money," *CQWR,* March 31.

Thompson, J. R. (1999) "Devising Administrative Reforms that Work: The Example of the Reinvention Lab Program," *Public Administration Review,* 59.

Thompson, J. R. (forthcoming) "The Clinton Reforms and the Administrative Ascendancy of Congress," *American Review of Public Administration*.

Tocqueville, Alexis de (1966) *Democracy in America*, New York: Harper & Row.

Tolbert, Caroline J. (1998) "Changing Rules for State Legislatures: Direct Democracy and Governance Policies," in Shaun Bowler, Todd Donovan and Caroline J. Tolbert (eds), *Citizens as Legislators: Direct Democracy in the United States*, Columbus: Ohio State University Press.

Tolbert, Caroline J. (2001) "Public Policy and Direct Democracy in the Twentieth Century: The More Things Change, the More They Stay the Same," in M. Dane Waters (ed.), *The Battle Over Citizen Lawmaking*, Durham, NC: Carolina Academic Press.

Trattner, Walter (1999) *From Poor Law to Welfare State: A History of Social Welfare in America*, 6th edn, New York: Free Press.

Trend, David (1997) *Cultural Democracy: Politics, Media, New Technology*, Albany, NY: State University of New York Press.

Uchitelle, Louis (2001) "U.S. Jobless Rate Rose to 4.5% in April," *The New York Times*, May 5.

US Census Bureau (2000) *Statistical Abstract of the United States*, Washington, DC: GPO.

Uslaner, Eric M. (1999) "Democracy and Social Capital," in Mark E. Warren (ed.), *Democracy and Trust*, Cambridge: Cambridge University Press.

Utter, Glenn H. and John W. Storey (1995) *The Religious Right: A Reference Handbook*, Santa Barbara, CA: ABC-Clio.

Wald, Kenneth (1996) *Religion and Politics in the United States*, 3rd edn, Washington, DC: Congressional Quarterly Press.

Waldo, D. (1984) *The Administrative State: A Study of the Political Theory of American Public Administration*, 2nd edn, New York: Holmes & Meier.

Walker, David (2000) *The Rebirth of Federalism*, 2nd edn, Chatham, NJ: Chatham House

Walker, Jack L. Jr (1991) *Mobilizing Interest Groups in America: Patrons, Professions, and Social Movements*, Ann Arbor, MI: University of Michigan Press.

Washington Post National Weekly Edition (1995) "A Fetid System," August 21–27.

Wayne, Leslie (2000) "Popularity is Increasing for Balloting Outside the Box," *The New York Times*, November 4.

Wayne, Stephen J. (1999) "Clinton's Legacy: The Clinton Persona," *PS*, 23:3.

Weisert, Carol S. and Sanford F. Schram (2000) "The State of US Federalism," *Publius*, 30.

Weissert, W. and Carol Weissert (1996) *Governing Health: The Politics of Health Policy*, Baltimore, MD: Johns Hopkins University Press.

Wildavsky, Aaron (1975) "The Two Presidencies," in A. Wildavsky (ed.), *Perspectives on the Presidency*, Boston, MA: Little, Brown.

Willis, Derek (2001) "Debating McCain-Feingold" *CQWR*, March 10.

Wills, Garry (1999) *A Necessary Evil: A History of American Distrust of Government*, New York: Simon & Schuster.

Wilson, James Q. (1966) *The Amateur Democrat*, Chicago, IL: University of Chicago Press.

Wirls, Daniel (2001) " Voting behavior: the balance of power in American politics," in Michael Nelson (ed.), *The Elections of 2000*, Washington, DC: Congressional Quarterly Press.

Witte, John Jr (2000) *Religion and the American Constitutional Experiment*, Coulder, CO: Westview Press.

Wolpert, Julian (1997) "How Federal Cutbacks Affect the Charitable Sector" in Staeheli, Lynn A., Janet E. Kodras and Colin Flint (eds), *State Devolution in America: Implications for a Diverse Society*, London: Sage.

Woodward, Kenneth L. (2000) "Does God belong on the stump?" *Newsweek*, September 11.

Wright, Deil (1988) *Understanding Intergovernmental Relations: Public Policy and Participants Perspectives in Local, State and National Governments*, Belmont, CA: Wadsworth.

Wright, Kendra E. and Paul M. Lewin (1998) *Drug War Facts*, Washington, DC: Common Sense for Drug Policy Foundation.

Yarbrough, Tinsley E. (2001) *The Rehnquist Court and the Constitution*, Oxford: Oxford University Press.

Zinni, Frank P., Laurie A. Rhodebeck and Franco Mattei (1997) "The structure and dynamics of group politics, 1964–1992," *Political Behavior*, 19.

Zoellick, Robert (2000) "A Republican Foreign Policy," *Foreign Affairs*, 79.

Zuckerman, Mortimer (1998) "A Second American Century," *Foreign Affairs*, 77.

Zwerman, Gilda, Patricia G. Steinhoff and Donatella della Porta (2000) "Disappearing Social Movements: Clandestinity in the Cycle of New Left Protest in the U.S., Japan, Germany, and Italy," *Mobilization*, 5.

Index